Time Pressure and Stress in Human Judgment and Decision Making

Time Pressure and Stress in Human Judgment and Decision Making

Edited by

Ola Svenson
Stockhom University
Stockholm, Sweden

and

A. John Maule
University of Leeds
Leeds, England

PLENUM PRESS • NEW YORK AND LONDON

Library of Congress Cataloging-in-Publication Data

Time pressure and stress in human judgment and decison making / edited
  by Ola Svenson and A. John Maule.
      p.   cm.
    Includes bibliographical references and index.
    ISBN 0-306-44426-7
    1. Decision-making. 2. Judgment. 3. Time pressure. 4. Stress
(Psychology) 5. Job stress.   I. Svenson, Ola.   II. Maule, A. John.
BF448.T56 1993
153.8'3--dc20   93-11985
                                                              CIP

ISBN 0-306-44426-7 ✓

© 1993 Plenum Press, New York
A Division of Plenum Publishing Corporation
233 Spring Street, New York, N.Y. 10013

Printed in the United States of America

Contributors

Barbara Barnett, McDonnell-Douglas Aircraft Co., P.O. Box 516, St. Louis, Missouri 63166-0516

Lehman Benson, III, Department of Psychology, Lund University, S-22350 Lund, Sweden

James R. Bettman, The Fuqua School of Business, Duke University, Durham, North Carolina 27706

Jerome R. Busemeyer, Department of Psychological Sciences, Purdue University, West Lafayette, Indiana 47807

Ulf Böckenholt, Department of Psychology, University of Illinois at Urbana–Champaign, Champaign, Illinois 61820

Peter J. Carnevale, Department of Psychology, University of Illinois at Urbana–Champaign, Champaign Illinois 61820

Geri Anne Dino, Department of Psychology, Frostburg State University, Frostburg, Maryland 21532

Anne Edland, Department of Psychology, Stockholm University, S-10691 Stockholm, Sweden

Fred Hyman, National Transportation Safety Board, Washington, DC 20008

G. Robert J. Hockey, Department of Psychology, University of Hull, Hull HU6 7RX, England

Eric J. Johnson, Department of Marketing, The Wharton School, University of Pennsylvania, Philadelphia, Pennsylvania 19104-6371

Martin F. Kaplan, Department of Psychology, Northern Illinois University, De Kalb, Illinois 60115

Keith Kroeger, Department of Psychology, University of Illinois at Urbana–Champaign, Champaign, Illinois 61820

Frank J. Landy, Center for Applied Behavioral Sciences, Pennsylvania State University, University Park, Pennsylvania 16802

Ulf Lundberg, Department of Psychology, Stockholm University, S-10691 Stockholm, Sweden

Cynthia M. Lusk, Center for Research on Judgment and Policy, University of Colorado, Boulder, Colorado 80309-0344

Donald MacGregor, Decision Research, 1201 Oak Street, Eugene, Oregon 97401

A. John Maule, School of Business and Economic Studies, University of Leeds, Leeds LS2 9JT, England

Christopher McCusker, Department of Psychology, University of Illinois at Urbana–Champaign, Champaign, Illinois 61820

Kathleen M. O'Connor, Department of Psychology, University of Illinois at Urbana–Champaign, Champaign, Illinois 61820

John W. Payne, The Fuqua School of Business, Duke University, Durham, North Carolina 27706

Haleh Rastegary, Center for Applied Behavioral Sciences, Pennsylvania State University, University Park, Pennsylvania 16802

James Shanteau, Department of Psychology, Kansas State University, Manhattan, Kansas 66506

Martin Schürmann, Universität Bielefeld, Abteilung für Psychologie, Postfach D-4800, Bielefeld, Germany

Joachim Stiensmeier-Pelster, Universität Bielefeld, Abteilung für Psychologie, Postfach D-4800, Bielefeld, Germany

Alan Stokes, Aviation Research Laboratory, Universtiy of Illinois at Urbana–Champaign, Willard Airport, Savoy, Illinois 61874

Ola Svenson, Department of Psychology, Stockholm University, S-10691 Stockholm, Sweden

Thomas S. Wallsten, Department of Psychology, University of North Carolina, Chapel Hill, North Carolina 27599-3270

L. Tatiana Wanshula, Department of Psychology, Northern Illinois University, De Kalb, Illinois 60115

Christopher D. Wickens, Aviation Research Laboratory, University of Illinois at Urbana–Champaign, Willard Airport, Savoy, Illinois 61874

Dan Zakay, Department of Psychology, Tel-Aviv University, Ramat Aviv, Israel

Mark P. Zanna, Department of Psychology, University of Waterloo, Waterloo, Ontario, N2L 3G1, Canada

Preface

Some years ago we, the editors of this volume, found out about each other's deeply rooted interest in the concept of time, the usage of time, and the effects of shortage of time on human thought and behavior. Since then we have fostered the idea of bringing together different perspectives in this area. We are now, therefore, very content that our idea has materialized in the present volume.

There is both anecdotal and empirical evidence to suggest that time constraints may affect behavior. Managers and other professional decision makers frequently identify time pressure as a major constraint on their behavior (Isenberg, 1984). Chamberlain and Zika (1990) provide empirical support for this view, showing that complaints of insufficient time are the most frequently reported everyday minor stressors or hassles for all groups of people except the elderly. Similarly, studies in occupational settings have identified time pressure as one of the central components of workload (Derrich, 1988; O'Donnel & Eggemeier, 1986).

Given that many human actions are taken under time limits and deadlines, it is perhaps surprising that there are so few studies investigating the ways in which these constraints change either behavior in general or judgment and decision making in particular. The primary aim of the present volume is to bring together a number of contributions that consider how time constraints, and the time pressure and time stress associated with these constraints, can affect the nature of human judgment and decision making. The contributions focus, almost exclusively, on the behavior of individuals. Time constraints are also known to affect the processes underlying decision making in groups (e.g., Janis, 1982, 1989), in organizations (e.g., Bronner, 1972), and in complex political situations (e.g., Holsti & George, 1975). Although these areas have important contributions to make, we believe that there is, at present, an urgent need to bring together studies of individual judgments and decisions. This more focused approach will lay the foundations for further considerations of time pressure in these more complex situations.

As indicated above, there have been comparatively few studies in the area of judgment and decision making under time pressure. Those that have been published often manipulate time as an independent variable to investigate some other aspect of the decision-making process from a specific theoretical standpoint (e.g., its effects on the costbenefit calculations determining decision strategies; see Bettman, Johnson, & Payne, 1990). Also, these studies have been developed from many different standpoints, reflecting the diversity of approaches in the area of decision research as a whole (cf. Maule & Svenson, this volume). Given the way research has developed and the relatively small number of studies in this area, we believe that the field, as yet, is not mature enough for the development of a strong, unifying theory. This belief is reflected in the aims of the present volume that are (1) to review the major approaches developed to consider the effects of time constraints, time pressure, and stress on individual decision making; (2) to explore the relevance of a number of theoretical issues and approaches drawn from other areas of psychology and not previously considered in the context of time pressure research; (3) to present examples of contemporary empirical research in the area; (4) to look critically at relevant methodological issues and consider their implications for the development of future research; and (5) to provide a volume that summarizes our current state of understanding of the area and one that suggests priorities for future research.

To meet these aims the volume is structured in the following way. Part I sets the scene by presenting three review chapters covering issues of general importance. It includes broad reviews of decision research, of the effects of time pressure on decision making, and of the psychobiology of stress and health. This part of the volume provides relevant background material, and a context in which to set the other contributions to this volume. The chapters in Part II take a more detailed look at a number of different perspectives, exploring each in terms of the theoretical and methodological issues it raises for our understanding of time pressure effects. In some instances, the perspective has already been applied to the area, in other instances it has not, and the chapter explores the contribution that the approach can make to our understanding of the area. Taken together, the contributions in this section discuss many important theoretical and methodological issues and suggest a number of different ways in which we may understand present findings and develop future research. The six empirical studies in Part III investigate how individuals adapt to time pressure in a variety of different judgment and decision tasks. Together, the studies provide a sample of contemporary research in the area. The ways in which individuals adapt to time pressure is further developed in Part IV, by considering the importance of individual differences in the ways in which people adapt to time constraints. Finally, in Part V, three studies are presented that consider the effects of time pressure and stress in complex and everyday work settings. Not only do they provide a different context in which to consider time pressure effects, but they also remind us that these constraints are an important feature of the work environment. Each part of the volume is preceded by a brief introduction that provides both a description of the common themes to emerge from that part of the book and a summary of the contents of individual chapters. We close by presenting some concluding remarks, which bring together some of the major issues and problems raised by the contributions to this volume.

We would like to acknowledge the support and assistance of many colleagues during all stages of this project. First of all, the authors of the chapters making up this volume are acknowledged for their contributions.

Many of the authors and other colleagues reviewed the chapters, and their assistance is also greatly appreciated. The Swedish Council for Research in the Humanities and Social Sciences, the Swedish Work Environment Fund, and the Nuclear Power Inspectorate, in Sweden, and Leeds University, in England, awarded us the necessary research grants and resources for carrying through the project. We would also like to thank Anne Edland, Alison Lynn, and Wivianne Runske for their most valuable support and assistance. Finally, a word of thanks to our families for their persistent support and for their patience with the over-committed editors. Our thanks to Anita, in Sweden, and Beth, Simon, and Martin, in England.

References

Bettman, J. R., Johnson, E. J., & Payne, J. W. (1990). A componential analysis of cognitive effort in choice. *Organisational Behavior and Human Decision Processes, 45,* 111–139.

Bronner, R. (1972). *Decision making under time pressure.* Lexington MA: Lexington Books.

Chamberlain, K., & Zika, S. (1990). The minor events approach to stress: Support for the use of daily hassles. *British Journal of Psychology, 81,* 469–481.

Derrick, W. L. (1988). Dimensions of operator workload. *Human Factors, 30,* 95–110.

Holsti, O. R., & George, A. L. (1975). The effects of stress on the performance of foreign policy makers. *Political Science Annual, 6,* 255–319.

Isenberg, D. J. (1984). How senior managers think. *Harvard Business Review,* November–December, 81–90.

Janis, I. L. (1982). *Groupthink: Psychological studies of policy decisions and fiascoes.* Boston: Houghton Mifflin.

Janis, I. L. (1989). *Crucial decisions; Leadership in policymaking and crisis management.* New York: Free Press.

O'Donnel, R., & Eggemeier, F. T. (1986). *Workload assessment and methodology.* In K. Boff, L. Kaufman, & J. Thomas (Eds.), *Handbook of perception and human performance* (Vol. 2, pp. 673–738). New York: Wiley.

Contents

PART II. PERSPECTIVES ON TIME PRESSURE AND STRESS: THEORY AND METHOD

7. Adapting to Time Constraints 103

Eric J. Johnson, John W. Payne, and James R. Bettman

8. Time Pressure in Negotiation and Mediation 117

Peter J. Carnevale, Kathleen M. O'Connor, and Christopher McCusker

PART III. EXPERIMENTAL STUDIES OF TIME PRESSURE

14. **The Effect of Time Pressure in Multiattribute Binary**
    Choice Tasks **195**

Ulf Böckenholt and Keith Kroeger

PART IV. INDIVIDUAL DIFFERENCES

15. **The Interactions Among Time Urgency, Uncertainty,**
    and Time Pressure **217**

Helen Rastegary and Frank J. Landy

16. Information Processing in Decision Making Under Time Pressure: The Influence of Action Versus State Orientation 241

Joachim Stiensmeier-Pelster and Martin Schürmann

17. Time Pressure and Information Integration in Social Judgment: The Effect of Need for Structure 255

Martin F. Kaplan, L. Tatiana Wanshula, and Mark P. Zanna

PART V. TIME PRESSURE AND STRESS IN APPLIED SETTINGS

20. Assessing Components of Judgment in an Operational Setting: The Effects of Time Pressure on Aviation Weather Forecasting . 309

Cynthia M. Lusk

Concluding Remarks 323

A. John Maule and Ola Svenson

I

Decision, Time Pressure, and Stress— Setting the Scene

In line with the general purpose of this volume, Part I sets the scene with contributions from the decision, time pressure, and psychobiological stress research perspectives.

The first chapter by Maule and Svenson presents different theories and paradigms for the study of human judgment and decision making. They differentiate between structural approaches, in which final judgments and decisions are analyzed, and process approaches, in which information is collected about different stages of judgment and decision processes. Different theories and paradigms within these two approaches are explored with respect to their inclusion of time and time pressure and their potential for elaborations to include these variables if not already part of the theory and paradigm.

Although process approaches, also called componential approaches, seem to have a great potential for studies of time pressure effects, most research has been performed within structural approaches. In conclusion, both approaches are well suited for the study of time pressure, given that the underlying model includes adequate inclusion of the time parameter. Presently, this is rarely the case.

The chapter by Maule and Svenson points out the width and diversity of judgment and decision research. Because time pressure research has been spread across this wide field, there is no single tradition of time pressure research based on a common theory and body of empirical research, which is clearly demonstrated in the chapter by Edland and Svenson. This chapter reviews previous research on the effects of time pressure on individual judgment and decision making.

Most research on time pressure has concerned decision-making processes and much less effort has been spent on judgment. Although the research has been quite scattered, some generic results emerge from the literature and are summarized in the chapter by Edland and Svenson. To exemplify, increased selectivity, including giving more weight to already important information and the transition to noncompensatory decision rules under pressure, is among those generic findings. Most of these studies use a "cold" rather than a "hot cognition" framework. In the latter, emotional and psychobiological aspects are included in the understanding of reactions to time pressure, as exemplified by Janis and Mann, cited by Edland and Svenson. The next and last chapter of this part, by Lundberg, is derived from this perspective and links time pressure, arousal, and stress in a psychobiological approach. In this review chapter, time pressure is analyzed as one of several stressors with which man has to cope through social, cognitive, and biological strategies. One crucial aspect of successful coping, pointed out by Lundberg, is to allow each individual enough influence and control over the planning of his or her own life. Successful coping involves appraisal and reappraisal of goals and strategies for completing a task, as well as contingent appraisal of the energetic resources needed and available at any time in the process. This process, going on in parallel with the decision process, will be one of the themes of Part II.

1

Theoretical and Empirical Approaches to Behavioral Decision Making and Their Relation to Time Constraints

A. John Maule and Ola Svenson

Introduction

This chapter provides a general background to the studies of decision making addressed by the other contributors to the book. These contributions draw on a number of approaches, differentiated in terms of the aspects of the decision-making process that are the focus of attention and the theoretical and methodological approaches taken when conceptualizing and investigating the process. For instance, some contributions have investigated judgment, others choice, each adopting an approach that focuses primarily on the outcome of these activities or the nature of the cognitive processes that underlie them. In additon to identifying different approaches to the study of decision making, the potential of each approach for developing our understanding of the effects of time constraints on judgment and decision making are elaborated. This provides a broad coverage of issues, putting into perspective the different studies of judgment and decision making included in this volume.

A. John Maule • School of Business and Economic Studies, University of Leeds, Leeds LS2 9JT, England.   **Ola Svenson** • Department of Psychology, Stockholm University, S-10691 Stockholm, Sweden.
Time Pressure and Stress in Human Judgment and Decision Making, edited by Ola Svenson and A. John Maule, Plenum Press, New York, 1993.

On the Psychology of Decision Making

In recent years there have been several extensive reviews of the psychology of judgment and decision making (Abelson & Levi, 1985; Baron, 1988; Bettman, Johnson, & Payne, in press; Dawes, 1988; Einhorn & Hogarth, 1981; Payne, Bettman, & Johnson, 1992; Pitz & Sachs, 1984; Slovic, Lichtenstein, & Fischhoff, 1988; Yates, 1990). The present chapter is not designed to be as comprehensive as these, but rather a selective review to aid the reader's understanding of the other contributions to the present book.

In trying to impose some structure on an otherwise disparate and wide-ranging field, Abelson and Levi (1985) identified a number of key distinctions within the area of decision research. The present chapter also uses some of these as an organizing principle. The first distinction is between *structural* and *process* approaches (cf. Svenson, 1979). Structural approaches are concerned with the relation between input, defined in terms of the information provided about each alternative, and output as represented by judgments of or choice between the alternatives. In contrast to this, process approaches are concerned with how decisions are made in terms of the underlying cognitive processes. The second distinction drawn is between *riskless* and *risky* decision situations. In the former, the individual knows with certainty the outcomes that follow the choice of a particular alternative, whereas in the latter there is uncertainty about which among a number of outcomes will occur. In reality, it may be impossible to find a situation in which there is not at least some minimum level of uncertainty associated with all outcomes, making the distinction between these two approaches relative rather than absolute. Finally, it is possible to distinguish between *normative, prescriptive,* and *descriptive* approaches. The first two consider how rational people should choose and the latter how people actually do choose. The difference between normative and prescriptive theories is that the latter takes into account how people evaluate and integrate information and prescribe decisions on these grounds. Normative theories are formalizations that do not consider these human characteristics. However, descriptive theories provide the primary focus for this review.

There are other ways of classifying decision making that provide important insights into the nature of this activity. For example, Svenson (1990) described an approach based on classifying different decision problems at different *levels,* according to the psychological processing they invoke (e.g., habitual decisions associated with automatic processing as compared with decisions demanding the creation of decision alternatives associated with more deliberate forms of processing). The distinction between *static, sequential,* and *dynamic* situations is another approach that is relevant in the context of this volume. In static situations, the focus is on one decision made on the basis of the information about acts, outcomes, and contingencies available at the moment of choice. In sequential situations, there is a series of decisions, each changing the situation for future decisions. In dynamic situations, each decision represents an input to a system that is continuously changing according to its own dynamics even when the decision maker does nothing. Different aspects of static, sequential, and dynamic decision making can be studied using both structural and process approaches.

The distinctions outlined above provide useful ways of organising the field of decision-making research and provide the basis for the present review.

Structural Approaches

As mentioned above, structural approaches are primarily concerned with the relationship between the inputs and outcomes showing how the subjects' judgments and choices can be explained in terms of the information provided about each alternative. In the past, judgments of the overall value of individual alternatives were assumed to predict the choice between them; that is, that subjects always choose the alternative judged highest in overall attractiveness. However, this has repeatedly been shown not to be the case, suggesting that each activity should be considered in its own right.

Judgments

Most studies have investigated judgment in terms of ratings of the overall attractiveness of alternatives. For instance, people may be asked to judge the attractiveness of cars, each described in terms of cue dimensions or attributes like comfort, acceleration, and efficiency. Subjects are required to combine this information into a global evaluation of the worth of each car. The major research effort in this area has focused on developing mathematical models that describe and predict these global judgments from the attribute information provided.

The many studies using this approach have demonstrated a remarkable consistency in showing that judgments can be captured very successfully by a simple linear model based on a weighted combination of cue values (Slovic & Lichtenstein, 1971). Though people often claim that their judgments are more complex and involve interactions between cues, mathematical models that take account of such interactions are no better at capturing the outcomes of their judgments.

Though there is a large body of research demonstrating that human judgment can be successfully captured by linear models, there is doubt about whether these models accurately reflect the underlying judgment process. As early as 1960, Hoffman argued that structural theories are paramorphic; that is, that the processes underlying judgment do not necessarily follow a similar linear additive mode of functioning. More systematic studies of the underlying processes indicate that judgments are made in a different way (e.g., Svenson, 1984, 1985). Think-aloud protocols generated during the judgment process indicate nonadditive treatment of information, a finding that may indicate either the inability of linear models to describe the judgment process or that think-aloud protocols are an inappropriate way of investigating judgment processes, or both (Fischhoff, 1988). In addition, current views of the nature of human information processing assume a sequence of mental operations across time (e.g., Payne, 1976, 1982; Maule, 1985; Svenson, 1979). Given this is also true for judgment processes, there is a need to link process explanations defined in these terms to explanations based on importance weights derived from linear regression.

A number of areas of judgment research have extended beyond description in terms of simple linear models, and two of these, Social Judgment Theory and Information Integration Theory are important in the context of the present book.

Social Judgement Theory (SJT), developed from Brunswik's ecological approach to psychology (Hammond, 1966), assumes that an object being judged is perceived in terms of cues, each of which reflects, in a probabilistic way, the true state of the object. In this respect, the theory is concerned with judgments under uncertainty. This uncertainty is represented by different degrees of covariance between cues and the criterion or "correct judgment." Research has investigated the extent to which human judges can develop a judgment policy in which their combination of cues accurately reflects the true covariance values, and whether this policy can be applied consistently (Brehmer & Joyce, 1988). A key feature of this approach is the imperative that investigations of human judgment should use experimental situations in which the relations between different cues are probabilistic and representative of those found in the everyday world, rather than including a set of atypical examples for the purpose of completing a balanced experimental design. Hammond, Stewart, Brehmer, and Steinmann (1975) argued that SJT can be distinguished from other approaches in terms of its concerns with being life-relevant, its essentially descriptive rather than "law-seeking" approach, and its emphasis on aiding human judgment in social decision-making situations.

Information Integration Theory (IIT) (Anderson, 1981) represents an approach to judgment based on the use of full factorial designs to investigate how cue information is evaluated and combined when making global judgments. In contrast to SJT, the theory does not a priori postulate what is a correct or incorrect judgment. The goal of this approach is to identify how people scale the individual stimulus items when determining their subjective value, and the rules governing how this scaled information is combined to form the global judgment. IIT research has used a diverse set of situations, including judgments of objects, people, and social situations. People have often been found to use an averaging rule for combining cue information in which cue dimensions are weighted for importance and the overall judgment is the sum of the products of weight and value for all cues, divided by the number of cues. However, people's judgments are not simply based on the information provided within the experiment, but also on the knowledge and initial impressions that subjects bring to the situation (Kaplan, 1976). This highlights aspects neglected by other areas of judgment research, and this may become particularly important in judgments under time constraints (Kaplan, Wanshula, & Zanna, this volume).

Another important issue for research in human judgment and decision making mentioned briefly above has been the relation between judgment and choice. Early researchers assumed that these two activities were equivalent and that people would always choose the alternative judged highest in value (cf. Slovic & Lichtenstein, 1971). However, more recent evidence has suggested that this is not the case. For instance, people may give a higher value to one of a pair of alternatives, yet when asked to choose between them, choose the other (Lichtenstein & Slovic, 1973; Slovic, 1975; Tversky, Sattah, & Slovic, 1988). This inconsistency has been attributed to such factors as differences in the cognitive strategies underlying choice and judgment (Billings & Scheerer, 1988) and the compatibility hypothesis, stating that the weightings of stimulus attributes are related to their compatibility with the mode of response (Slovic, Griffin, & Tversky, 1990). Because judgment and choice require different responses, they will be associated with different weightings of the stimulus attributes. Such findings highlight the need to trace psychological processes rather than simply relying on structural approaches.

Potential of Judgment Research to Capture Time Pressure Effects

In principle the approaches considered in the previous section appear to provide some scope for determining the effects of time constraints. To exemplify this, assume that a linear model describes judgments given in a no-time-pressure condition. Then, there are three ways in which this model can be used as a reference for changes under time pressure.

First, the same linear model may be the best fit for a time pressure condition, but the degree of fit is reduced. For example, Rothstein (1986) found increased variability in judgments under time pressure and a corresponding decrease in fit to a linear model. Second, the weights in a linear model may change under time pressure. To exemplify, one attribute may be given more weight under time pressure, or the relative weights between two attributes may change. Third, a linear model may no longer be the best-fit model under time pressure. For example, a log linear or another model may be a better description under time pressure. In each case, these changes may reflect changes in the nature of judgment under time pressure. Also, theories extending beyond simple linear models, like IIT or SJT can raise a number of relevant issues, for example, the importance of the knowledge and initial impressions that individuals bring to a judgment situation and how this may change under time pressure (see Kaplan, Wanshula, & Zanna, this volume).

Although the general approaches described above would seem to have some scope for determining changes in judgment under time constraints, there are limitations associated with them. As indicated earlier, it is not clear whether statistical models, derived through regression can be used to describe changes in underlying psychological processes under time pressure. For instance, regression weights derived statistically may not necessarily reflect the judge's own balance of priorities between attributes. These limitations make it necessary to be cautious when interpreting these findings in terms of changes in underlying psychological processes.

Decision

In the introduction we indicated that decision problems are usually classified as riskless or risky, depending on whether following the choice of an alternative, the outcome was certain or uncertain. This distinction provides the basis for organizing the review of research on decisions.

Riskless Decision Situations

One approach to the study of riskless decisions has centered on the use of decision rules, each of which specifies the type and order that information is processed to determine a choice (cf. Svenson, 1979). These structural approaches require that particular decision rules can be specified mathematically so that the use of the rule can be tested by determining the extent to which the mathematical model satisfactorily predicts choice behavior (e.g., Einhorn, 1971; Tversky, 1972). For instance, Tversky (1972) used this approach to test the validity of the Elimination-by-Aspects rule (EBA). This rule assumes that subjects choose between alternatives by selecting the most important attribute and rejecting all alternatives that fail to meet the cutoff value or level of acceptability on this attribute. Then subjects choose the second most important attribute and so on until just one alternative is left. Tversky (1972) showed that the EBA rule predicts choice behavior and argued that this provides a good model of human decision making. However, mathematical modeling of this type uses, as most structural approaches, averages of choice behavior often based on performance across several problems and subjects. This contrasts with more recent views suggesting that human decision processes involve dynamic elements of behavior likely to be used interchangeably from problem to problem and with different frequencies by different subjects (cf. Payne, 1976; Maule, 1985). Thus, modeling based on averages can be misleading, and this has led experimenters to turn increasingly to methodologies that focus on the underlying processes, to be presented later.

Another line of riskless decision research is concerned with binary choice (i.e., choosing between just two alternatives) and has led to a set of Criteria Dependent Choice models (Albert, Aschenbrenner, & Schmalhofer, 1989). These models assume a sequential evaluation of information about alternatives that terminates once one alternative is sufficiently better than the other. There are a number of assumptions concerning the nature of information evaluation, the most important of which is that it is sequential and biased in favor of evaluating important dimensions first. The criteria determining when attractiveness differences are sufficient also varies according to individual and task characteristics. By varying features of information evaluation and the criterion needed for choice, many of the well-known choice rules summarized by Svenson (1979) can be incorporated into the model.

Potential of Riskless Decision-Making Research to Capture Time Pressure Effects

Studies of riskless decision making have used mathematical modeling to identify decision strategies, and this could be utilized to reveal changes in strategy following the imposition of time constraints. However, we have already indicated that there may be problems with modeling that would make it a less sensitive method of determining changes in strategy. The second approach involving CDC models of binary choice appears to have more potential. A critical feature of these models is the fixing of an attractiveness-difference criterion needed to determine choice. The imposition of a time constraint may alter this criterion leading to changes in underlying information processing. This possibility and the implications of it for our understanding of the effects of time constraints on judgment and decision making are discussed by Bockenholt (this volume), Busemeyer (this volume), and Wallsten (this volume).

Risky Decisions

Risky decision problems are characterized by couplings between alternatives and outcomes that are probabilistic and thereby cannot be predicted with certainty. For example, the outcome of a choice between two alternative investment plans is not certain and depends on a set of factors in the future, each of which could be modeled probabilistically. Much of the research has tested the extent to which formal decision models, often derived from normative approaches, fit individuals' judged preferences and decisions. Because these formal models assume that risky decisions can be represented in terms of choices between gambles (Shafer 1986), the most common experimental setting for basic research has been gambling, with subjects required to choose one from a number of gambles described in terms of probabilities of winning and losing amounts of money.

Expectancy/Value Approaches

The most important of the models investigated in risky decision making is the family of expected value/utility models. These models can be illustrated by considering the following situation requiring a choice between two gambles:

Gamble A
Probability of winning is .8 and amount to win is $2
Probability of losing is .2, amount $1

Gamble B
Probability of winning .2, amount $80
Probability of losing .8, amount $18

One version of the expected value approaches is the expected value (EV) principle in which the value of each alternative is calculated by summing the products of the values and probabilities associated with each outcome. This may be expressed mathematically in the following terms

$$EV = \Sigma p_i v_i \tag{1}$$

The expected value of Gamble A is $(.8 \times \$2) + (.2 \times -\$1) = \$1.4$, and the expected value of gamble B is $(.2 \times \$80) + (.8 \times -\$18) = \$1.6$

Because Gamble B has a higher expected value, it is predicted that subjects should choose it, rather than Gamble A. The EV principle has long since been challenged, following recognition that decision-makers' choices are based on their own representations of these entities, with subjective probability and utility replacing probability and monetary worth. This has led to an alternative expectancy value approach called the Subjective Expected Utility (SEU) principle (Edwards 1954, 1961) in which the subjective variables replace their objective counterparts in Eq. (1)

Although the SEU model has been developed primarily as a normative theory founded on certain axioms or assumptions (Wright, 1984), it has also been considered as a descriptive theory by looking at the extent to which it predicts how people make decisions. The descriptive validity has been tested by evaluating the extent to which peoples' choices in simple decision-making situations can be predicted by SEU and by evaluating whether people accept the axioms that underlie the theory and behave consistently with them. Both approaches have found only limited support for the theory (for reviews of research, see Wright, 1984; Fischhoff, Goiten, & Shapira, 1982; Machina, 1987; Slovic, Fischhoff, & Lichtenstein, 1977). In a series of studies, Tversky and Kahneman (1981, 1986) have provided a number of examples in which people's choice behavior violates the axioms of SEU. An example is the invariance axiom that states that preference for one alternative over another should not depend on the manner in which they are described. To illustrate, consider the following classical choice situation, the Asian disease problem (percentages in parentheses indicate proportions of the subjects who preferred an alternative in the original study):

> Imagine that the United States is preparing for the outbreak of an unusual Asian disease, which is expected to kill 600 people. Two alternative programs to combat the disease have been proposed. Assume that the exact scientific estimates of the consequences of the programs are as follows:
> If Program A is adopted, 200 people will be saved (72%).
> If Program B is adopted, there is a one-third probability that 600 people will be saved and a two-thirds probability that no one will be saved (28%).
> Which program do you favor?

Imagine the same cover story followed by a choice between two further alternatives:

> If Program C is adopted, 400 people will die (22%).
> If Program D is adopted, there is a one-third probability that nobody will die and a two-thirds probability that 600 people will die (78%).

Although both choice situations are formally identical, the percentage of subjects choosing each option shows a reversal of preference that is a violation of the invariance axiom.

This is one of several examples of violations of the axioms that led Kahneman and Tversky to develop an alternative theory of risky decision making called Prospect Theory.

Prospect Theory

Prospect theory assumes that decision making is divided into two phases— editing and evaluation. Editing is the initial phase in which the decision maker builds an internal representation of the decision problem, incorporating the acts, outcomes, and contingencies associated with the decision situation. This internal representation is called a decision frame. Tversky and Kahneman (1981) identify a number of editing operations that are responsible for organizing and reformulating the alternatives, often resulting in a simplified representation of the choice situation. Further, they suggest that the frame adopted by a decision maker depends partly on the way the problem is formulated and also on "the norms, habits and personal characteristics of the decision maker" (Tversky & Kahneman, 1981, p. 453). As such, the theory assumes that identical problems may be framed in different ways depending on these factors. Following the framing phase, the second or evaluation phase occurs in which the framed alternatives are evaluated. Similar to the expectancy value models, the theory assumes that evaluation is based on the product of two fundamental variables related to value and probability, though these are more complex in a number of ways.

First, during the editing phase the values of outcomes associated with the alternatives are not represented as final states of wealth as suggested by the EV models, but rather as positive or negative deviations (i.e., gains or losses) from a neutral reference point, which is assigned a value of zero. It is argued that the shape of the function describing the relation between gains/losses and subjective value is concave (as seen from the X-axis) when outcomes are conceptualized as gains and convex when outcomes are conceptualized as losses in relation to the current reference point. As a consequence of the shape of the value function, people tend to be risk averse in positive or gain situations and risk seeking in negative or loss situations. This explains the apparent inconsistency in the choice behavior in the Asian disease problem presented above. In version one, the expected value of alternatives A and B are equal. But because the description of the alternatives emphasizes lives saved, people frame the alternatives as gains and therefore are risk averse, choosing alternative A associated with the certain outcome. In the second version, which emphasizes death and loss, people frame the alternatives as losses and are therefore risk seeking, choosing alternative D associated with risk. Thus the apparent inconsistency in choice behavior found across the two versions of the problem may be explained in terms of the ways in which people frame and evaluate each version of the problem.

Second, the probability term in Prospect Theory is described as a decision weight $(*p)$ that is related to but not the same as the objective probability. The relation between probability and $*p$ has a number of properties, including a general overweighting of very low probabilities, underweighting of moderate and high probabilities, and important differences between the objective probability and $*p$ near the endpoints (i.e., when the objective probability is close to one or zero). Tversky and Kahneman show that this has important implications when evaluating alternatives and can also lead to inconsistencies in choice behavior.

Though Prospect Theory is predominantly structural in approach, it does include process elements, and therefore can be seen as bridging the gap between structural and process theories. This approach has generated much research, including an evaluation of the assumptions underlying the proposed value function (Hershey & Schoemaker 1980), an analysis of verbal protocols to assess whether different versions of the problem do lead to different decision frames (Maule, 1989), and various attempts to extend these ideas by looking at the gain/loss framing effect in different situations, for example, bargaining and negotiation (Bazerman & Neal, 1983), framing effects based on aspects other than gain/loss differences (Samuelson & Zeckhauser, 1989; Thaler, 1980), and the extent to which these effects generalize to more realistic, everyday situations (van Schie & van der Plight, 1990).

Potential of Risky Decision-Making Research to Capture Time Pressure Effects

Interpreted literally, SEU theory assumes that decision making involves combining utilities and probabilities. Though time constraints could affect the way people assess and combine probabilities and utilities, the theory does not discuss how these are derived, and a consideration of factors like time constraints seems to fall outside its frame of reference.

In contrast to this, Prospect Theory does appear to have some potential. Framing, a key feature of this theory, is assumed to involve a number of information-processing routines, for example, editing, which extend over time. Therefore, imposition of a time constraint may change these routines affecting the frame adopted and thereby change the decision.

Finally, both SEU and Prospect Theory assume that decisions are determined by combining some aspects of utility and subjective probability and either or both of these could change in the context of time constraints. Studies show that utility judgments are different when the outcomes of choice are immediately available as compared with an availability sometime in the future (e.g., Christensen-Szalanski & Northcraft 1985; Wright & Weitz, 1977). Similarly, time perspective has been shown to affect subjective probability estimates (Bjorkman, 1984). The imposition of a time constraint brings the outcomes of choice closer in time and thereby may change the value of both the utility and probability terms. However, studies showing these effects have used time intervals differing by days and months, whereas most current research on time constraints has used intervals differing by seconds. With such short intervals, corresponding systematic changes in utility and subjective probability are yet to be demonstrated.

Process Approaches

Process approaches are concerned with how decisions are made, described in terms of the underlying psychological processes and how they evolve over time. An important distinction for process research has been the difference between well-defined and ill-defined problems. Well-defined decision problems are characterized by a clear definition of the following three elements: goals or objectives of the choice situation, the available choice alternatives, and information about each alternative in terms of the values and uncertainties associated with outcomes. As a situation provides less information about one or more of these elements, so it may be thought of as increasingly ill-defined. Given that most research in decision making in general, and on time pressure/stress in particular has focused on well-defined situations, the present review considers only these studies and not those based on ill-defined situations.

In his 1979 review, Svenson cited only a handful of studies from the 1960s and about 20 studies in the 1970s investigating decision making from a process standpoint. Since then, the field has expanded considerably, with Ford, Schmitt, Scheitman, Hults, and Doherty (1989) able to cite over 50 such studies. As Maule (1985) points out, these have increasingly drawn on methods and theories from cognitive psychology.

Methodological Issues

Typically, process studies have asked subjects to make a decision among a set of alternatives each described in terms of a number of attributes (for reviews, see Svenson, 1979; Abelson & Levi, 1985; Ford et al., 1989; Payne et al., 1992). The principal aims of this research have been to identify the underlying information-processing strategies, described in terms of the decision rules used by subjects and to identify the factors determining which rules are adopted. The strategy adopted by any particular individual may involve a number of different types of decision rules, differentiated in terms of the order, type, and amount of attribute information processing. The primary methodological problem has been to develop a procedure for identifying which rules a subject is using, and this has involved finding ways of determining the order in which the aspects (the value of an alternative on a particular attribute) are accessed (cf. Svenson, 1979). It is assumed that this pattern of information acquisition is indicative of the underlying decision rules. There have been three principle methodologies developed for indentifying information acquisition patterns.

The first, based on eye fixations, makes all the information permanently available to subjects and uses fixation patterns to determine the information-acquisition strategy (e.g., Russo & Rosen, 1975). The second method, the information board, involves putting the value of each aspect on a card, with all the cards presented face down in a matrix. Though the information is hidden, subjects know the location of any particular aspect for any alternative, and the order in which the cards are turned over provides a measure of information acquisition.

Johnson, Payne, Schkade, and Bettman (1989) have developed a computer version of this situation. The third method, based on verbal protocols, requires subjects to think aloud as they undertake a decision task. The protocols are analyzed to identify the information acquisition patterns and other indications of what decision rules are being used. Verbal protocols often provide additional information about the attractiveness values and relative importance of attributes, as well as about the underlying decision rules being used by subjects. Some researchers have argued that verbal protocols are invalid, unreliable, and place demands on subjects that are likely to change the nature of the underlying cognitive activity (e.g., Nisbett & Wilson, 1977). In response to this criticism, Ericcson & Simon (1984) suggested that protocols may be an appropriate method for identifying processes that are in focal attention. Information acquisition would seem to involve focal attention and thereby an appropriate methodology for studying decision strategies. Svenson (1989) provides some useful guidelines on how to collect and analyze protocols, and Russo et al. (1989) have further validated the think-aloud method and reported limited reactivity to think-aloud instructions for prolonged cognitive processes.

Some Findings from Process-Tracing Studies

In their review of process-tracing studies, Ford et al. (1989) identified two key research issues: (a) describing the range of decision rules used by people and (b) explaining why, at any one time, a particular decision rule is adopted. The review indicated that people use a variety of different rules. One way of classifying these is in terms of a compensatory/noncompensatory distinction. Compensatory rules involve all the information about each alternative being combined together into one rating, such that a poor aspect on one attribute can be compensated for by a good aspect on another. Alternatives are chosen on the basis of these combined ratings. The SEU rule mentioned earlier belongs to this category. In contrast, noncompensatory rules are based on only a subset of the information, with each aspect often processed in a simpler way. An example is the conjunctive rule in which the decision maker has a minimum acceptable level for each attribute and immediately rejects an alternative if it falls below this level. Once rejected, the alternative is omitted from all further consideration. There are many different compensatory and noncompensatory rules (Svenson, 1979). In general, compensatory rules are considered to be more complex and requiring greater mental effort but likely to lead to better or more optimal decisions (Einhorn & Hogarth, 1981).

A second important distinction between decision rules is the relative proportions of interattribute and intraattribute search associated with each (Payne, 1976). In the former, search is organized around alternatives, with successive stages of information search directed toward different attributes of the same alternative. In the latter, search is organized around attributes, with successive stages of search directed toward different alternatives along the same attribute. Payne (1976) has developed a formula that expresses the proportion of interattribute versus intraattribute search across the decision process.

In binary choice situations, intraattribute rules predominate (cf. Albert et al., 1989), but where the number of alternatives increases, either rule may occur, depending on other characteristics of the choice situation. In general, as the complexity of the decision task increases, subjects tend to switch from compensatory to noncompensatory rules. Complexity is varied by changing the number of alternatives and/or the number of attributes. When the total number of aspects is constant, an increase in number of attributes decreases the total amount of information searched more than if the set of alternatives is increased (Svenson, 1979). As complexity increases, subjects tend to use noncompensatory rules early in the process until the number of alternatives is reduced to two or three (cf. Svenson, 1979; Ford et al., 1989; Montgomery & Svenson, 1989). The final choice between the remaining alternatives is then often determined by a compensatory rule. Similarly, there are information search differences depending on whether the task requires subjects to make a judgment or a decision. For instance, Billings and Scheerer (1988) found that judgment led to a greater depth of search, whereas choice led to more intraattribute search.

Although most research has been concerned with decision rules and task characteristics, a few studies have looked at environmental factors. For instance, the imposition of time constraints leads to fewer pieces of information being processed, a greater selectivity in favor of more important information, a general speeding up in processing, and in some cases more attribute-based processing, (Edland & Svenson, this volume; Johnson et al., this volume).

Finally characteristics of the decision maker have been investigated in a few studies. Bettman and Park (1980) found a greater amount of information search prior to choice for individuals with moderate levels of expertise as compared with those with high or low levels of expertise. Furthermore, more knowledgeable individuals also tended to engage in more alternative-based processing, whereas the less knowledgeable made greater use of attribute-based processing. In consonance with these findings, people who are more skilled decision makers are found to adopt different decision rules in comparison to those who are less skilled (Klayman 1985).

Process Theories

The predominant type of theory used in conjunction with process tracing studies has been based on a cost/benefit approach (Beach & Mitchell, 1978;

Bettman, Johnson, & Payne, 1990; Payne, 1982; Payne, Bettman, & Johnson, 1988; Payne et al., 1990). This approach assumes that a decision rule is adopted on the basis of a cost/benefit appraisal, with cost derived in terms of such factors as time, effort, and resources needed to implement the rule or set of rules and the benefit derived from the outcome accruing from making a decision according to these rules. All other things being equal, the more important the decision, the greater the amount of resources mobilized, enabling the use of a more complex decision strategy.

A major difficulty with this approach has been to specify cost and benefits with sufficient precision to provide an adequate test of the theory. Payne and his associates have addressed these issues in a series of studies using both experiments and simulations. They have developed and tested a number of ways of measuring cost and benefits, showing how these could account for the way subjects adopt decision rules (Bettman et al., 1990; Johnson et al., this volume; Payne, et al., 1992).

Janis and Mann (1977) presented a rather different process theory founded on an analysis of important everyday decision situations rather than laboratory tasks. Their theory assumes a number of key stages in the decision process involving the recognition of the need for a decision, the evaluation of the personal risks involved, and the opportunities for developing and evaluating a reasonable set of alternatives. Heavy emphasis is placed on conflict and affective elements associated with decision making and the ways in which these may lead to suboptimal information-processing strategies (e.g., bolstering, avoidance) and thereby a defective decision. The theory provides some important insights and takes account of conflict and emotion, key psychological factors normally omitted from process theories. However, the empirical support for the theory is not strong, and there is a need for a more systematic investigation of its predictions.

The process approaches considered so far have primarily been concerned with identifying the range of rules used by decision makers and the basis on which one rather than another is adopted. Though these reflect the major issues addressed by process research, there are other approaches looking at different aspects of the decision process. Montgomery (1983, 1989) presented Dominance Structuring Theory, which assumes that decisions are governed by the desire to meet the criteria of one decision rule, dominance; that is, to choose an alternative that is better on one attribute and at least as good on all the others. Because states of dominance rarely occur naturally, people are assumed to restructure their internal representation of the decision problem with the intention of producing this state. Montgomery identified a number of restructuring activities used by decision makers in the pursuit of dominance, for example, bolstering, where an initial evaluation of an attribute is increased to make it look at least as good or better than evaluations of the attributes for other alternatives.

Beach (1990) provides a different approach, Image Theory, which draws heavily on mainstream cognitive psychology. The theory emphasizes the importance of a wider set of issues like the need to take account of the knowledge that decision makers bring to a situation and that decisions are embedded in the broader context of a stream of behavior. Beach argues that there are three different categories of knowledge, or what he calls the *value image,* the *trajectory image,* and the *strategic image.* The value image reflects the values, ethics, and morals that a person has; the trajectory image the set of goals that the person is currently trying to attain; and the strategic image the ways in which the goals identified within the trajectory image are to be attained. Beach argues that there are two types of decisions—adoption and progress.

First, adoption decisions are responsible for adding new goals or plans to the trajectory and strategic images, respectively. This consists of either one or two steps. In all cases the first step is a compatibility test to determine whether the new candidate or alternative is compatible with existing information about values and plans contained within the value and trajectory images. This may be executed by a conjunctive rule. If there are several alternatives and more than one passes the compatibility test, then a second or profitability test is applied. This test is assumed to involve the kinds of decision rules that have been the major focus of process research, that is, those rules considered in the first part of this section.

Second, progress decisions are responsible for determining whether current information and feedback about actions and plans are sufficiently compatible with the trajectory image goals to warrant continuation. Progress decisions are based solely on a compatibility test as described previously. Though Beach's approach represents a significant and potentially interesting departure from previous theorizing in decision research, many aspects of the approach are, as yet, insufficiently worked out in detail.

Svenson (1991) recently introduced Differentiation and Consolidation Theory of decision making that considers both predecision differentiation processes and postdecision consolidation processes. Only the predecision processes as modeled in the theory are discussed here. Decision making is regarded as an active process in which one alternative is gradually differentiated from the others until finally chosen. Thus, the goal of a decision process is to differentiate one alternative from its competitors. Because there are different potential threats to a decision in the postdecision phase (e.g., new facts about alternatives, unfortunate outcomes, changes in the decision maker's value system), it is not sufficient to select the best alternative. According to the theory, the preferred alternative has to be sufficiently differentiated from its closest competitor before a decision can be made. If the chosen alternative is sufficiently better than its competitors, then it is more likely to withstand any adverse consequences after the decision has been made.

Differentiation processes are either of a *process* or a *structural* character. In process-related differentiation, one or several decision rules are applied to a decision problem in order to differentiate one alternative from the rest. In structurally related differentiation, the decision maker's representation of the decision problem undergoes changes to differentiate the finally chosen alternative from its closest competitor.

Potential of Process-Tracing Research to Capture Time Pressure Effects

Process approaches conceptualize decision making in terms of the underlying psychological processes extending over time. The type, order, and form of these processes varies as a function of task, environmental, and personal characteristics (e.g., Payne, 1982). Because time constraints can be conceptualized both as an environmental and task characteristic, process methodologies and theories provide an obvious way of considering the effects of these constraints on decision making. In terms of methodology, most of the procedures outlined earlier have been used to investigate time constraints (see Edland & Svenson, this volume). The one exception is the verbal protocol. The demands associated with the generation of a protocol are assumed to reduce the speed of task-related information processing (cf. Ericsson & Simon, 1984; Russo et al., 1989), and this is likely to disrupt task-related processing if the situation is time constrained. Therefore, think-aloud protocols may be unsuited for time pressure research when deadlines are in terms of seconds or minutes. For longer periods of time they may be used.

In general, process theories have considerable potential for explaining the effects of time constraints. As mentioned above, the dominant theoretical approach has been in terms of cost/benefit theory. Johnson et al. (this volume) have discussed time constraints in terms of its effects on effort/value considerations underlying strategy selection, and Beach (1990) has developed a very similar argument in the context of effects on the profitability test phase of Image Theory. Together these accounts have provided useful ways of developing our understanding of the effects of time constraints on decision making.

Janis and Mann's theory is distinctive in that it emphasizes the importance of affect and stress on decision strategies. Time constraints are one among a number of variables identified as inducing stress states. The theory predicts that these states induce a range of strategy changes that reduce the efficiency of decision making. From this standpoint, the effects of time constraints on decision strategy are mediated by stress levels rather than the "cold" cost/benefit calculations assumed by other process approaches. Maule and Hockey (this volume) discuss these different interpretations and provide a theoretical framework that combines these different accounts.

Time is also a critical variable for Differentiation and Consolidation Theory (Svenson, 1991). The imposition of a time constraint provides less opportunity for differentiation between the chosen alternative and its most serious competitor. If subjects are forced to choose before differentiation is complete, the decision may not be affected, but there is likely to be an effect in terms of attained differentiation that may be reflected in attractiveness differences and later post-decision consolidation processes.

Finally, it is worth commenting on the relevance of the levels of decision making (Svenson, 1990). This is a conceptual framework for thinking about processes rather than a process theory in its own right. Nevertheless it does have some important implications for research on time because it assumes that there are different kinds of psychological processes underlying each type or level of problem. For instance, Level 1 decisions occur in familiar or repeated situations and are assumed to involve largely automatic processes. As such, the sequence and form of the underlying processes are fixed, and there appears to be little scope for adapting to time constraints, unless the level at which the problem is conceptualized is changed. In contrast to this, Level 4 decisions involve such activities as generating alternatives and thereby more complex and time-consuming processing involving conscious control. These decisions provide a much greater opportunity to adapt to time constraints. Given Level 4 decisions are generally associated with a longer and potentially more adaptive decision process, they have more potential for studies of time pressure.

Sequential and Dynamic Approaches and Their Potential for Time Pressure Research

So far this review has considered approaches to decision making where only one decision at a time or a sequence of nonrelated decisions have been made. These approaches assume that the ever-changing world can be projected on the present, using, for example, uncertainty as a means of taking account of the stream of future events and outcomes. However, there are other approaches that emphasize the dynamic aspects of decision making, focusing on the factors that are important when people must make a sequence of interrelated choices in the context of either a static or dynamic external environment.

Sequential decision making represents situations in which the decision maker's next decision problem depends on his/her earlier decision in a sequence. In this way the decision problem offers opportunities of learning through feed-back. However, it is only the decision maker him or herself who creates the new situation in conjunction with static properties of the situation. For example, all one-person card games belong to this type of decision problem. However, many real-world complex decision situations are dynamic rather than static, and the major research effort has been directed toward dynamic situations.

Edwards (1962) described the key characteristics of dynamic situations in the following way: The goal can only be achieved through a series of decisions; each decision is not independent of the others; the decision problem state changes both autonomously and as a consequence of the decision maker's actions. Brehmer (1991) added a fourth characteristic arguing that dynamic situations require decisions to be made in real time. According to Holtgrave (1990), most dynamic decision-making research in the past has used fluid physical systems that the decision maker must control (e.g., MacKinnon & Wearing, 1985; Kleinmuntz & Thomas, 1987). This usually involves laboratory simulations of such activities as controlling disease processes, forest fires, and activities within a small town.

Brehmer (1991) views research in this area as having developed in two broad areas. The first, concerned with individual differences, has tried to identify what distinguishes good and poor performers. This has often involved relating performance on the dynamic decision task to scores from various psychological tests. In general these studies have been disappointing, showing few reliable differences. The second, or experimental approach, has investigated the effects on performance of system characteristics like task complexity and feedback delay. A number of general effects have been reported showing that these variables can affect decision-making behavior. However, there are some difficult methodological issues raised by this research. The major problem has been control because the dynamic nature of the task makes it impossible to ensure that all subjects in a particular experimental group receive the same distinctive set of conditions. Thus controlled manipulation of independent variables is almost impossible. Related to this, task characteristics like complexity have been difficult to define in a way that allows them to be manipulated in a consistent way across different situations. At present the body of research in this area is still quite small, making it difficult to draw reliable conclusions.

Given the paucity of research on sequential decision making, there is little to evaluate in the context of research on time constraints. However, dynamic approaches appear to have much more relevance, particularly because a key characteristic of these situations is that decisions are made in real time. The rate of change is a key characteristic of a dynamic system and one that has been shown to affect performance efficiency (Brehmer & Allard, 1991, reported in Brehmer, 1991). The contributions by Wickens et al. (this volume) and Lusk (this volume) illustrate both the great relevance of time pressure studies of dynamic decision situations, their great applied potential, and the methodological difficulties that have to be addressed.

Concluding Remarks

The present overview has demonstrated the breadth and diversity of judgment and decision research. Because studies of time pressure have been spread across this wide research area, there is no single tradition of time pressure research in which one finds a set of studies interlinked through theory and empirical findings. This is clearly reflected in Edland and Svenson's review of the literature presented in the next chapter.

Current theories of judgment and decision making are not explicit about the role played by the time parameter, even less about the effects of time pressure. Some models have a potential for addressing time usage and time pressure. However, to reach this goal, further developments of the theories are needed as exemplified in Part III of this volume.

With the exception of think-aloud protocols, most methods used for studying decision making could be applied to investigate time pressure effects. Finally, there is a need to bring together studies of time pressure to enable the creation of a common research area and a framework for future research. The present volume intends to provide a contribution toward reaching this goal.

References

Abelson, R. P., & Levi, A. (1985). Decision making and decision theory. In G. Lindzey & E. Aronson (Eds.), *The handbook of social psychology* (3rd ed. Vol. 1, pp. 231–309). New York: Random House.

Albert, D., Aschenbrenner, K. M., & Schmalhofer, F. (1989). Cognitive choice processes and the attitude-behavior relation. In A. Upmeyer (Ed.), *Attitudes and behavioral decisions* (pp. 61–99). New York: Springer Verlag.

Anderson, N. H. (1981). *Foundations of information integration theory.* New York: Academic.

Ashenbrenner, K. M., Albert, D., & Schmalhofer, F. (1984). Stochastic choice heuristics. *Acta Psychologica, 56,* 153–166.

Baron, J. (1988). *Thinking and deciding.* New York: Cambridge University Press.

Bazerman, M. H., & Neale, M. A. (1983). Heuristics in negotiation: Limitations to dispute resolution effectiveness. In M. H. Bazerman & R. J. Lewicki (Eds.), *Negotiation in organizations* (pp. 51–67). Beverly Hills: Sage.

Beach, L. R. (1990). *Image theory: Decision making in personal and organisational contexts.* Chichester; Wiley.

Beach, L. R., & Mitchell, T. R. (1978). A contingency model for the selection of decision strategies. *Academy of Management Review, 3,* 439–449.

Bettman, J. R., & Park, C. W. (1980). Effects of prior knowledge and experience and phase of choice process on consumer decision processes: A protocol analysis. *Journal of Consumer Research, 7,* 234–248.

Bettman, J. R., Johnson, E. J., & Payne, J. W. (1990). A componential analysis of cognitive effort in choice. *Organizational behavior and human decision processes, 45,* 111–139.

Bettman, J. R., Johnson, E. J., & Payne, J. W. (in press). Consumer decision making. In H. H. Kassarjian & T. S. Robertson (Eds.), *Handbook of consumer theory and research.*

Billings, R. S., & Scheerer, L. M. (1988). The effects of response mode and importance on decision making strategies: Judgment versus choice. *Organizational Behavior & Human Decision Making, 41*, 1–19.

Bjorkman, M. (1984). Decision making, risk taking and psychological time: A review of empirical findings and psychological theory. *Scandinavian Journal of Psychology, 44*, 31–49.

Brehmer, B. (1991). *Dynamic decision making: Human control of complex systems.* Paper presented to SPUDM 13, Fribourg, Switzerland.

Brehmer, B., & Joyce, C. R. B. (1988). *Human judgement: The SJT view.* Amsterdam: North Holland.

Christensen-Szalanski, J. J. J., & Northcraft, G. B. (1985). Patient compliance behavior: The effects of time on patients' values of treatment regimems. *Social Science and Medicine, 21*, 263–273.

Dawes, R. M. (1988). *Rational choice in an uncertain world.* San Diego: Harcourt Brace Jovanovitch.

Edwards, W. (1954). The theory of decison making. *Psychological Bulletin, 51*, 380–417.

Edwards, W. (1961). Behavioral decision theory. *Annual Review of Psychology, 12*, 473–498.

Edwards, W. (1962). Dynamic decision theory and probabilistic information processing. *Human Factors, 4*, 59–73.

Einhorn, H. J. (1971). Use of nonlinear, compensatory models as a function of task and amount information. *Organizational Behavior & Human Performance, 6*, 1–27.

Einhorn, H. J., & Hogarth, R. M. (1981). Behavioral decison theory: Processes of judgment and choice. *Annual Review of Psychology, 32*, 53–88.

Ericsson, K. A., & Simon, H. A. (1984). *Verbal protocol analysis.* Cambridge MA: MIT Press.

Fischhoff, B. (1988). Judgment and decision making. In R. J. Sternberg & E. E. Smith (Eds.), *The psychology of human thought* (pp. 153–187). New York: Cambridge University Press.

Fischhoff, B., Goiten, B., & Shapira, Z. (1982). The experienced utility of expected utility approaches. In N. T. Feather (Ed.), *Expectations and actions: Expectancy-value models in psychology* (pp. 315–339). Hillsdale, NJ: Erlbaum.

Ford, J. K., Schmitt, N., Scheitman, S. L., Hults, B. M., & Doherty, M. L. (1989). Process tracing methods: Contributions, problems and neglected research questions. *Organizational Behavior & Human Decision Processes, 43*, 75–117.

Hammond, K. R. (1966). Probabilistic functionalism: Egon Brunswik's integration of the history, theory and method of psychology. In K. R. Hammond (Ed.), *The psychology of Egon Brunswik* (pp. 15–80). New York: Holt, Rinehart & Winston.

Hammond, K. R., Stewart, T. R., Brehmer, B., & Steinmann, D. O. (1975). Social judgment theory. In M. F. Kaplan & S. Schwartz (Eds.), *Human judgment and decision processes* (pp. 271–312). New York: Academic Press

Hershey, J. C., & Shoemaker, P. J. H. (1980). Prospect theory's reflection hypothesis: A critical examination. *Organizational Behavior & Human Performance, 25*, 395–418.

Hoffman, P. J. (1960). The paramorphic representation of clinical judgement. *Psychological Bulletin, 57*, 116–131.

Holtgrave, D. R. (1990). Constructing models of dynamic choice behaviour. In K. Borcherding, O. I. Larichev, & D. M. Messick (Eds), *Contemporary issues in decision making* (pp. 409–428). Amsterdam: North Holland.

Janis, I. L., & Mann, L. (1977). *Decision making: A psychological analysis of conflict, choice and commitment.* New York: The Free Press.

Johnson, E. J., Payne, J. W., Schkade, D. A., & Bettman, J. R. (1989). *Monitoring information processing and decisions: The Mouselab system.* Unpublished manuscript, Fuqua School of Business, Duke University, Durham NC.

Kaplan, M. F. (1976). Measurement and generality of response dispositions in person perception. *Journal of Personality, 44,* 179–194.

Klayman, J. (1985). Children's decison strategies and their adaption to task characteristics. *Organization Behavior & Human Decision Processes, 35,* 179–201.

Kleinmuntz, D. N., & Thomas, J. B. (1987). The value of action and inference in dynamic decision making. *Organisational Behaviour and Human Decision Processes, 39,* 341–364.

Lichtenstein, S., & Slovic, P. (1973). Response induced reversals of preferences in gambling: An extended replication in Las Vegas. *Journal of Experimental Psychology, 101,* 16–20.

Machina, M. J. (1987). Decision-making in the presence of risk. *Science, 236,* 537–543.

MacKinnon, A. J., & Wearing, A. J. (1985). Systems analysis and dynamic decision making. *Acta Psychologica, 58,* 159–172.

Maule, A. J. (1985). Cognitive approaches to decision making. In G. N. Wright (Ed.), *Behavioral decision making* (pp. 61–84). New York: Plenum Press.

Maule, A. J. (1989). Positive and negative decision frames: A verbal protocol analysis of the Asian disease problem of Kahneman and Tversky (1981). In H. Montgomery & O. Svenson (Eds.), *Process tracing approaches to decision making* (pp. 164–180). Chichester: Wiley.

Montgomery, H. (1983). Decision rules and the search for a dominance structure: Towards a process model of decision making. In P. C. Humphreys, O. Svenson, & A. Veri (Eds.), *Analysing and Aiding Decision Processes* (pp. 343–369). Amsterdam: North Holland.

Montgomery, H. (1989). From cognition to action: The search for dominance in decision making. In H. Montgomery & O. Svenson (Eds.), *Process tracing approaches to decision making* (pp. 23–49). Chichester: Wiley.

Montgomery, H., & Svenson, O. (1989). (Eds.). *Process and structure in human decision making.* Chichester: Wiley.

Nisbett, R. E., & Wilson, T. D. (1977). Telling more than we can know: Verbal reports on mental processes. *Psychological Review, 84,* 231–259.

Payne, J. W. (1976). Task complexity and contingent processing in decision making: An information search and protocol analysis. *Organisational Behaviour and Human Performance, 16,* 366–387.

Payne, J. W. (1982). Contingent decision behaviour. *Psychological Bulletin, 92,* 382–402.

Payne, J. W., & Braunstein, M. L. (1977). *Contingent processing in risky choice: A process tracing investigation.* Carnegie Mellon University, unpublished manuscript.

Payne, J. W., Bettman, J. R., & Johnson, E. J. (1988). Adaptive strategy selection in decision making. *Journal of Experimental Psychology: Learning, Memory and Cognition, 14,* 534–552.

Payne, J. W., Johnson, E. J., Bettman, J. R., & Caipey, E. (1990). Understanding contingent choice: A computer simulation approach. *IEEE Transactions on Systems, Man and Cybernetics, 20,* 296–309.

Pa ne, J. W., Bettman, J. R., & Johnson, E. J. (1992). Behavioral decision research: A constructive processing perspective. *Annual Review of Psychology, 43,* 87–131.

Pitz, G. F., & Sachs, N. J. (1984). Judgement and decision: Theory and application. *Annual Review of Psychology, 35,* 139–163.

Rothstein, H. G. (1986). The effects of time pressure on judgment in multiple cue probability learning. *Organizational Behavior & Human Decision Processes, 37,* 83–92.

Russo, J. E., & Rosen, L. D. (1975). An eye fixation analysis of multialternative choice. *Memory & Cognition, 3,* 267–276.

Russo, J. E., Johnson, E. J., & Stephens, D. L. (1989). The validity of verbal protocols. *Memory and Cognition, 17,* 759–769.

Samuelson, W., & Zeckhauser, R. (1989). Status quo bias in decision making. *Journal of Risk and Uncertainty, 1,* 7–59.

Shafer, G. (1986). Savage revisited. *Statistical Science, 1,* 463–485.

Slovic, P. (1975). Choices between equally valued alternatives. *Journal of Experimental Psychology: Human Perception and Performance, 1,* 280–287.

Slovic, P., & Lichtenstein, S. (1971). Comparison of Bayesian and regression approaches to the study of information processing in judgement. *Organizational Behavior & Human Performance, 6,* 649–744.

Slovic, P., Fischhoff, B., & Lichtenstein, S. (1977). Behavioural decision theory. *Annual Review of Psychology, 28,* 1–39.

Slovic, P., Lichtenstein, S., & Fischhoff, B. (1988). Decision making. In R. D. Atkinson, R. J. Herrnstein, G. Lindzey, & R. D. Luce (Eds.), In *Steven's handbook of experimental psychology. 2; Learning and Cognition* (pp. 673–738). New York: Wiley.

Slovic, P., Griffin, D., & Tversky, A. (1990). Compatability effects in judgment and choice. In R. M. Hogarth (Ed.), *Insights in decision making: A tribute to Hillel J. Einhorn* (pp. 5–27). Chicago: The University of Chicago Press.

Svenson, O. (1979). Process description of decision making. *Organisational Behaviour & Human Performance, 23,* 86–112.

Svenson, O. (1984). Cognitive processes in judging cumulative risk over different periods of time. *Organizational Behavior & Human Performance, 33,* 22–41.

Svenson, O. (1985). Cognitive strategies in a complex judgement task: Analyses of concurrent verbal reports and judgement of cumulated risk over different exposure times. *Organizational Behavior & Human Decision Processes, 36,* 1–15.

Svenson, O. (1989). Eliciting and analysing verbal protocols in process studies of judgment and decision making in H. Montgomery & O. Svenson (Eds.), *Process and structure in human decision making* (pp. 65–81). Chichester: Wiley.

Svenson, O. (1990). Some propositions for the classification of decision situations. In K. Borcherding, O. Larichev, & D. Messick (Eds.), *Contemporary issues in decision making* (pp. 17–31). Amsterdam: North Holland.

Svenson, O. (1991). *Differentiation and consolidation theory of human decision making.* Paper presented at the 13th SPUDM Conference, August 18–23, 1991, in Fribourg, Switzerland.

Svenson, O., & Montgomery, H. (1974). *A frame of reference for the study of decision processes.* Reports from the Psychological Laboratories, University of Stockholm, No. 409.

Svenson, O., Edland, A., & Slovic, P. (1990). Choices between incompletely described alternatives under time stress. *Acta Psychologica, 75,* 153–169.

Thaler, R. (1980). Toward a positive theory of consumer choice. *Journal of Economic Behavior and Organization, 1,* 39–60.

Tverksy, A. (1972). Elimination by aspects: A theory of choice. *Psychological Review, 79,* 281–299.

Tversky, A., & Kahneman, D. (1981). The framing of decisions and the psychology of choice. *Science, 211,* 453–458.

Tversky, A., & Kahneman, D. (1986). Rational choice and the framing of decisions. *Journal of Business, 59,* 251–278.

Tversky, A., Sattah, S., & Slovic, P. (1988). Contingent weighting in judgment and choice. *Psychological Review, 95,* 371–384.

van Schie, E. C. M., & van der Plight, J. (1990). Problem representation, frame preference, and risky choice. *Acta Psychologica, 75,* 243–259.

Wright, G. (1984). *Behavioural decision theory.* Harmondsworth: Penguin.

Wright, P., & Weitz, B. (1977). Time horizon effects on product evaluation strategies. *Journal of Marketing Research, 14,* 429–443.

Yates, J. F. (1990). *Judgment and decision making.* Englewood Cliffs, NJ: Prentice Hall.

2

Judgment and Decision Making Under Time Pressure
Studies and Findings

Anne Edland and Ola Svenson

Introduction

The aim of the present chapter is to provide a review of empirical studies involving time pressure, judgment, and decision making, which have been published during the past three decades. The chapter will not cover theoretical approaches to decision making and judgment or biological aspects related to time pressure because these issues are well covered elsewhere in this volume (the chapters by Maule & Svenson; Lundberg; Maule & Hockey). Svenson (1990, 1991) suggests that higher level decision processes involve problem-solving processes, and therefore a few references including time pressure from that research area will also be cited as examples of relevant research.

In general, the research on judgment, decision making, and time stress has not been motivated primarily by one or more theories related to the effects of time pressure on cognitive processes. Instead, the rather disparate literature mostly reflects the introduction of a deadline variable generating time pressure and studied in relation to a judgment or decision problem, which was relevant to

Anne Edland and Ola Svenson • Department of Psychology, Stockholm University, S-10691 Stockholm, Sweden.
Time Pressure and Stress in Human Judgment and Decision Making, edited by Ola Svenson and A. John Maule, Plenum Press, New York, 1993.

explore in itself even without the deadline variable. When the effects of varying deadlines have been related to a more generic framework for time pressure, "the minimization of cognitive effort" principle has been a leading theme (Beach & Mitchell, 1978; Payne, Bettman, & Johnson, 1988). Another important often cited theoretical contribution is that of Miller (1960) who listed a number of strategies of coping with time pressure and information overload. The most frequently cited strategies are filtering (processing some parts of the information more, and others less), acceleration, and omission (ignore particular parts of the information). Another often cited study is that of Easterbrook (1959) in which the effects of emotional arousal on cue utilization were summarized. Because time pressure has been assumed to lead to arousal (cf. Maule & Hockey, this volume), Easterbrook's results have been found relevant also in the time pressure context.

Studies of Time Pressure Effects on Judgments

The by-far most influential early study of the effects of time pressure was published in 1974 by Wright, who studied judgments under time pressure and noise distraction (Wright, 1974). The subjects were given descriptions of 30 hypothetical car models described on five attributes and judged each car according to the likelihood that they would purchase it. Three groups operated under varying time pressure conditions, and the levels of time pressure were manipulated by the instructions to the subjects. The results indicated that under high time pressure subjects changed their strategies and used more negative evidence when making their judgments as reflected in regression equations linking judgments to available information. In doing so, they gave relatively less weight to the positive and more to the negative information. In addition, subjects also seemed to use fewer attributes under time pressure than when there was no deadline. These results were considered a generally valid finding. That is, under time pressure, people weigh negative information more heavily, which was also interpreted as more risk-avoidant behavior.

Svenson, Edland, and Karlsson (1985) and Edland (1985) studied the effects of time pressure on judgments of preference. The experience of time pressure and stress was measured in a questionnaire. A subject's task was to judge the attractiveness of a set of student apartments with and without time pressure. The apartments were characterized by their size, standard, and traveling time to the university. The results showed that the negative aspect of the most important attribute, in this case traveling time, became much more important for the judgments under time pressure. Thus, the alternatives with poor values on this important attribute became relatively much poorer than under no time pressure. Time pressure seemed to have the effect of both giving one attribute more weight in relation to the others, as well as making the alternatives generally less attractive (on all attributes) as compared to judgments under no time pressure. This may parallel the results of Wright (1974) in that decision makers weigh negative consequences more heavily under time pressure. The results may also be related to the Easterbrook (1959) finding of a tendency to focus more on central information and not paying as much attention to less central cues under stress.

Rothstein (1986) studied the effects of time pressure on judgment within the Multiple Cue Probability Learning paradigm. Subjects were trained to use cues, with linear or curvilinear function forms to a criterion variable, which they were asked to predict. The time pressure condition required subjects to respond to each problem within 6 seconds. In the no-time-pressure condition there was unrestricted time for responding. The experimental session was divided into a training stage and a test stage. The lens model approach was used, in which cognitive matching and cognitive control were measured. *Cognitive matching* is defined as the correlation between predicted scores obtained from the environment with those from the judgment policy. Cognitive control is a measure of the consistency with which a judgment policy is implemented. Another dependent variable is the differential cue utilization, which is defined as the difference in the proportions of variance in judgments accounted for by the two cues. The analyses were used to determine whether poor performance under time pressure was attributable to degraded control, altered policy, or both. The results indicated that cognitive control deteriorated under time pressure, whereas cognitive matching remained unchanged. The time pressure effect for differential cue utilization showed that time pressured individuals tended to rely rather more on one of the cues than on the two cues. This parallels the earlier findings and adds the information of increasing variability under time pressure.

Kruglanski and Freund (1983) studied the impact of time pressure on judgments. They found that primacy effects, the effects of ethnic categorization and of anchoring played a greater role under time pressure.

To summarize, studies of judgment under time pressure seem to indicate greater weight given to less positive and more important attributes, greater variability of judgments, and a tendency of using a smaller number of attributes. It should be noted, however, that there are quite a few studies in the area and that the wider generalizability of these results still remains to be proven.

The Effects of Time Pressure on Decision Making

General Remarks

In contrast to judgments, decision problems may be experienced as more stressful in themselves because of attractiveness conflicts between alternatives, the selection of only one winning candidate, and accompanying mobilization of more commitment. Time pressure may increase the level of arousal and psychological stress (cf. Holsti, 1971; Frankenhauser, 1979; Keinan, Friedland, & Ben-Porath, 1987; Maule & Hockey, this volume; Lundberg, this volume). Janis (1983) points out that when the level of stress is very high, a decision maker is likely to display premature closure—making a decision without generating all the available alternatives. Time pressure is also suggested to lead to a shallower search for information, that is, an increased search across all alternatives and less search in depth of the alternatives (cf. Janis & Mann, 1977). However, most existing empirical studies of time pressure and decision making have deemphasized the specific role of the arousal component and studied decision making from a primarily "cold" cognitive-process perspective. This will be illustrated in the following.

Decisions and Confidence Ratings

Wallsten and Barton (1982) and Wallsten (this volume) studied choices and confidence ratings for alternatives characterized by five attributes. The task for the subjects was to decide whether a sample of information, containing five binary attributes, was more likely to come from population A or B. Half of the subjects in the experiment were under time pressure, whereas the other half was not. Crossed with this time manipulation was a payoff manipulation. The results indicated that subjects under no time pressure attended equally to all five attributes, whereas subjects in the time pressure condition made decisions primarily based on the first few attributes. However, when there was time pressure and substantial payoff, the tendency toward attempting to process all attributes again was strengthened, but the decisions were still based mainly on the first three attributes. Wallsten (this volume) has developed this interesting study further, and the reader is referred to his chapter. In conclusion, Wallsten and coworkers have shown that independently controlled payoffs interact significantly with time pressure in affecting the decision maker's judgments of confidence in his or her decision.

Risky Decisions

The payoffs used in an experiment can also be part of the decisions as for example in a lottery. This was the case in Busemeyer's (1985) experiment in which he included different deadline conditions when testing different models for making decisions between a certain alternative and an uncertain risky alternative. The results indicated that the proportion of choices of the risky alternative was not affected by time pressure in a low-variance condition (of the uncertain alternatives). However, when the expected value was negative in the high-variance condition, time pressure tended to increase uncertain alternative choices. In contrast, when the expected value was positive, time pressure decreased uncertain alternative choices. In other words, time pressure increased risk taking when expected value was negative, and decreased risk taking when expected value was positive. Note, however, that the values at stake in these experiments were all relatively small. If the values are substantial or have ethical or moral aspects linked to them, other effects may occur.

Ben Zur and Breznitz (1981) also studied the effects of time pressure on risky choice. Their subjects made decisions between gambles under three different levels of time pressure. The results indicated that subjects made less risky choices under high time pressure. In other words, they preferred alternatives with high probabilities of small gains among alternatives with the same expected value. Furthermore, subjects tended to spend relatively more time observing negative information (amount and probability of losing) under conditions of high time pressure than when they were given more time.

In summary, in risky decision making with small risks at stake, subjects' decisions depend on expected value, variance, of the alternatives, and time pressure. The effects of time pressure seem to be stronger for high-variance situations and to lead to avoidance of risky altenatives, if the expected value was positive. If it is negative, more risk taking can be expected under time pressure. These results may be related to the subject's aspiration levels induced in the experiments.

Decision Making and Attribute Weight

Svenson and Edland (1987) studied students who made choices between apartments under time pressure and no time pressure. The apartments were characterized by three attributes (traveling time to the university, size, and standard) and were presented in pairs. It was found that in the no-time-pressure condition alternatives with the greater sizes and longer traveling times were preferred most often, whereas in the time pressure condition the alternatives with the shorter traveling time and smaller size were preferred most often. This result indicated subjects giving more weight to the most important attribute (traveling time) under time pressure. However, as the most important attribute also denoted an attribute that was inherently negative in character, the results may also indicate greater weight given to negative information under time pressure.

To summarize, these results correspond to those found in attractive judgment experiments indicating greater weight being given to already important attributes and less to those less important from the beginning.

Decision Strategies and Decision Rules

Decision rules are often characterized as either compensatory or noncompensatory. In compensatory rules, a poor evaluation on one attribute may be compensated by a positive evaluation on another attribute (e.g., high rent may be compensated by a nice location of a flat). In noncompensatory rules, this is not possible (e.g., a poor location of a flat makes it an impossible choice).

The use of noncompensatory or compensatory rules (Svenson, 1979) in association with different levels of information load (varied without manipulation of time pressure) has been studied in a few investigations (Billings & Marcus, 1983; Olshavsky, 1979; Payne, 1976), suggesting that subjects use more noncompensatory rules under high information load. This can be interpreted as indicating that noncompensatory strategies could be easier and quicker to use than compensatory strategies under time pressure. Zakay (1985) investigated the relationships between time pressure, type of decision process, and postdecisional confidence. Choice situations were created such that the choice of one alternative would suggest a compensatory decision process, whereas the choice of the other alternative would suggest a noncompensatory process. Subjects made choices, and after each choice they rated their postdecisional confidence. Zakay found that under time pressure, there was a more frequent use of noncompensatory strategies, and that postdecisional confidence was greater after noncompensatory decisions as compared to decisions with compensatory strategies. This latter finding is somewhat unexpected as one may ask why people should be more content with time pressured noncompensatory decisions. The answer may be derived from considerations of task appraisal, aspiration level, and resource mobilization (cf. contributions by Maule & Hockey, Svenson & Benson, this volume).

Time available plays a significant role in the contingency model presented by Beach and Mitchell (1978) for the selection of decision strategies. Following this model, Smith, Mitchell, and Beach (1982) investigated the effects of time constraints on the choice among five decisions strategies given by the experimenter. The results indicated that when under moderate time pressure, complex decision rules were preferred and that confidence in the decisions decreased with time pressure.

Christensen-Szalanski (1980) also studied the effects of deadlines on strategy selection. The subjects were required to analyze six four-page case studies of administrative problems and select a solution. For three of the problems there was a 5-minute deadline. After the task, subjects were asked to indicate if they would have preferred to use a different strategy from the one they used if there had been no deadline imposed. If they would have preferred another than the one used, they were asked whether the preferred strategy of analysis was more or less complex than the one they actually used. The results showed that subjects in a

5-minute-deadline condition reported a preference for using a different and more complex strategy than the one they actually used, whereas subjects in the more distant deadline condition reported no preference for using a different strategy from one they actually had used.

To summarize these studies, mild time pressure seems to increase the use of more complex compensatory decision rules, whereas more strict deadlines seem to induce noncompensatory rules. It is unclear how confident people are after having used noncompensatory rules, which may depend on the fact that no data on task appraisal or resource mobilization have been reported.

Svenson, Edland, and Slovic (1990) investigated the effects of time pressure on decisions between candidates to a university program presented pairwise. Each candidate was described by grades on only two of the three available attributes and on one common attribute in each pair. The subjects were divided into three groups: high time pressure, medium time pressure, and no time pressure. The results indicated that the *Min* rule (do not choose the candidate with the poorest grade) was generally most applicable and that time pressure resulted in a shift in the mix of decision strategies toward greater use of the *Max* rule, in which the alternative with the best grade is chosen. Thus, these results indicate that positive aspects gain in importance under time pressure (cf. Edland, this volume). This is contradictory to Wright's (1974) findings and is based on experimental manipulations in contrast to Wright's fits of data to regression equations.

In summary, under severe time pressure, noncompensatory rules become more popular, and a number of studies have challenged Wright's (1974) findings that the avoidance of a negative aspects tendency is increased under time pressure. Some studies indicate increased use of positive aspects and some no change in this respect as a function of time pressure. Most of these studies have investigated the decision process in static designs, but Maule and Mackie (1990) used a process approach in which different decision subprocesses were postulated and studied independently.

Thus, in an experimental judgment and choice task, Maule and Mackie (1990) let subjects judge the attractiveness of cars described with information on six dimensions. They found that decreasing deadlines had the effect of increasing the speed of processing and responding. Different subprocesses were accelerated to different degrees.

In contrast with other findings, their results did not show any systematic changes in final judgments or choices when imposing deadlines. Furthermore, their study did not replicate Wright's (1974) result in terms of increased importance given to negative information. This is, together with unpublished work (Maule personal communication), probably the most important of the experiments not supporting Wright's (1974) results.

Decisions and Normative Theory

Payne, Bettman, and Johnson (1988) presented a set of experiments investigating the impact of time pressure on decision strategies. The first study investigated the generality of the Johnson and Payne (1985) study, which was concerned with the use of different decision rules. Payne et al. (1988) added four more strategies to those investigated by Johnson and Payne (1985) and included time pressure. In concordance with earlier results reported above, it was found that strategies involving an initial processing of all alternatives across a limited set of attributes do well under time pressure. Under high time pressure, the processing of at least some information about all alternatives is important. It was predicted in follow-up experiments that under high time pressure accuracy should be lower and that information should be processed more rapidly. In this study, an optimal response was determined through a normative formula, which was not the case in other decision approaches cited in this chapter, except the Zakay and Wooler (1984) study reported below and the Rothstein study of judgments cited earlier. Payne et al. concluded from their experiments that people adapt to time pressure by first accelerating their speed of processing, and if that is not sufficient, by increasing the selectivity of processing, (cf. Miller's filtration) and finally by moving toward a more attributewise information search and processing, in line with the elimination by aspects and lexicographic rules (cf. Svenson, 1979). This is in line with prior research and also demonstrates more specific changes in information processing as a function of time pressure in a minimization of cognitive effort in a cost/benefit frame of reference.

Zakay and Wooler (1984) studied time pressure, training, and decision effectiveness in relation to normative theory. Their subjects made decisions with and without training in the process of compensatory MAU decision making. The tasks were (1) choosing the best refrigerator from five offered and (2) choosing the best oven from five offered. The alternatives were characterized by cost, size, service quality, electricity consumption, and brand name. There were three different deadline conditions varying the time available for making a decision (2 minutes, 30 seconds and 15 seconds, respectively). They found that their training did not improve the quality of decision making when decisions had to be made under time pressure and that the effectiveness (measured by the utility of the alternatives actually chosen) of the decisions was significantly lower under time pressure than under no time pressure. It should be noted that these results could be related to the relatively short length of the learning period.

In conclusion, studies related to normative theory and to what may be called a learning tradition, because feedback about judgment or decision quality is provided, show that subjects adapt attempting to keep the quality (closeness to criterion) of their decisions stable, but sometimes they are unable to do so.

Unfolding a Decision Problem Over Time

Schwartz and Howell (1985) studied variation in performance as a function of the manner in which a progressively unfolding decision problem was displayed over time. The results indicated that the inclusion of time pressure on individual decision making and the consequential reduction in opportunity for processing the available information appeared to have caused subjects to oversample information, that is, seek more information and postpone terminal decisions longer. On the other hand, there was a systematic decrease in accuracy, so the increase in oversampling does not seem to be very helpful. This was predicted by Janis and Mann (1977).

Decision Making and Problem Solving

As mentioned above, some decision problems involve problem solving for creation of alternatives (cf. Svenson, 1990), and therefore two important studies of problem solving and time pressure are included in this review. Problem-solving as well as judgment and decision-making processes involve subprocesses that are successfully managed, but also incorrect subprocesses that go wrong at least at first. However, incorrect subprocesses are often corrected and changed to be correct. Thus, even quite successful problem solving involves errors (which are eliminated before the final solution is produced). Rizzo, Bagnara, and Visciola (1988) used the task of using a database system to explore error detections without any time limit. In all, 780 of 924 errors were detected, and slip (unintentional) errors (when one knows better) (cf. Rasmussen, Duncan, & Leplat, 1987) increased, whereas knowledge- (insufficient knowledge) based errors decreased with the more problems one had solved of the whole set of problems. As expected, slips had a much greater probability of detection than knowledge-based mistakes.

Norman (1981) stresses that successful cognitive processes may include temporary cognitive errors that are corrected without external feedback. Allwood (1984) found that it was the ability to correct one own's errors that seemed to differentiate between good and poor problem solvers. Therefore, it is hypothesized that time pressure can affect the use of corrective subprocesses in problem solving, leading to more errors.

In his classical study, Luchins (1942) investigated problem solving and the tendency to lock into a specific problem-solving strategy, and not realizing that another strategy is needed when new but similar problems appear. Luchins (1942) also explicitly manipulated the time pressure parameter in his studies (cf. Svenson, 1988, or the original source for an introduction to the problems used). When time pressure was increased through "decreasing the time allotted per problem and making subjects work against time, this did increase the E-effect / = locking into old strategy/ and minimize the efficacy of the recovery factor/instruction" Luchins (1942, p. 56). When more time than normally used by the subjects was provided, along with the instruction to use the extra time to "seek a more sensible and *more direct* solution," good recovery was obtained.

In conclusion, time pressure typically increased the tendency of locking into one problem-solving strategy and decreased the openness to alternatives. It also seemed as if the disturbance of the cognitive processes was exaggerated in some people by the fact that when they found out that one problem could not be solved by the old strategy, they were so disturbed that they did not proceed to other (solvable) problems (Luchin, 1942, p. 56). This observation fits in with, for example, Maule and Hockey's (this volume) view.

The well-known work by Bruner, Goodnow, and Austin (1956) on problem solving showed that time pressure had a relatively small effect on the focusing process, but a major effect on the success of the scanning process. In their study, *focusing* refers to a process in which the subject chooses the order of the instances that he/she will consider in order to test a hypothesis. *Scanning* is a process in which one hypothesis at a time is formulated and tested. Typically, subjects hold on to a hypothesis as long as confirming instances are encountered, changing only to another hypothesis when a contradictory instance is encountered.

Relating these results to the generation of decision alternatives under time pressure would predict difficulties in finding new alternatives and locking into the existing decision problem formulation under time pressure. Also, time pressure might affect scanning of information, in particular in breath to find new alternatives and to discard members of the set of decision alternatives under consideration.

Conclusions

Time pressure does not always lead to measurable changes in cognitive processes. This is probably because time pressure triggers coping processes to balance the effects of time pressure and retain the same output. When time pressure does have an effect, the following changes have been found: (1) Under time pressure, most studies report an increased selectivity of input of information. Some researchers have suggested increased use of many pieces of information but in a more shallow way under time pressure. (2) More important attributes are given more importance or weight during time pressure than in situations with no time pressure. (3) The accuracy of human judgments decreases under time pressure. (4) Under severe time pressure, the use of noncompensatory decision rules becomes more frequent than compensatory rules requiring value tradeoffs. (5) Time pressure leads to a tendency of locking in on a strategy and to decrease competence of finding alternative strategies in problem solving. (6) Some evidence indicates that decision makers increasingly tend to avoid negative consequences under time pressure. However, other evidence indicates no such tendency or increased use of positive evidence. These seemingly conflicting results should be integrated in a common framework in which the importance of attributes, the goals of the decision maker, the importance of the decision problem, and other task characteristics are used to predict changes under time pressure. (7) There are conflicting results as to whether time pressure leads to more or less risk taking. (8) Payoff and motivation can attenuate the effects of time pressure.

The research on time pressure, judgment, and decision making published before the present volume has produced important results. Yet, the generalizability of the results across the paradigms in which they were found may be hampered by lack of some knowledge. For example, the effects of short deadlines on feelings of time pressure depends on subjects' assessments of available resources and resources needed (Svenson & Benson, this volume). These assessments are made continuously and seem to be fundamental for coping with different deadline conditions. Such coping may involve mobilization of energetic resources on the supply side and revisions of strategies and goals on the demand side. The present volume sheds more light on these and other important issues.

Decision making under time pressure and stress are parts of many peoples' daily life and appear to be a chronic state in many professional activities. Therefore, there is a great applied need for increased research efforts in this research area for improved understanding and more knowledge about how to counteract the negative aspects of time pressure. In addition and not least important, time pressure elicits many theoretical issues of relevance for understanding the basic principles behind judgment and decision processes, such as the role played by goal hierarchies and the influence of situational characteristics and emotional states on decision behavior.

In general, decision makers seem to cope with time pressure in ways that attempt to keep judgments and decisions as close as possible to those made under no time pressure. This may require energetic resources, speeding up and changing the process so as to lose as little as possible in information input and processing quality.

To summarize so far, the literature shows that there are systematic changes of cognitive process when decisions have to be made under time restrictions. To elaborate, coping with increasingly more severe time restrictions may go step by step as hinted above (Miller, 1960; Payne et al., 1988). First, there may be an attempt to accelerate or speed up the processing. Second, as time pressure increases and there is no possibility to process the information faster, increased input selectivity is likely to follow. When time becomes extremely short, the third step of coping with the situation is to change strategies. Avoidance of the problem may occur only when the time pressure is intolerable and there is no possibility of changing the strategy and solve the decision problem.

ACKNOWLEDGMENT. The authors are very grateful for comments and assistance from John Maule and Wivianne Runske. Funds to Ola Svenson from the Swedish Work Environment Fund and the Swedish Council for Research in the Humanities and Social Sciences supported this study.

References

Allwood, C. M. (1984). Error detection processes in statistical problem solving. *Cognitive Science, 8*, 413–437.
Beach, L. R., & Mitchell, T. R. (1978). A contingency model for the selection of decision strategies. *Academy of Management Review, 3*, 439–449.
BenZur, H., & Breznitz, S. J. (1981). The effect of time pressure on risky choice behavior. *Acta Psychologica, 47*, 89–104.
Billings, R. S., & Marcus, S. A. (1983). Measures of compensatory and non-compensatory models of decision behavior: Process tracing versus policy capturing. *Organizational Behavior and Human Performance, 31*, 331–352.
Bruner, J. S., Goodnow, J. J., & Austin, G. A. (1956). *A study of thinking.* New York: Wiley.
Busemeyer, J. R. (1985). Decision making under uncertainty: A comparison of simple scalability, fixed sample and sequential sampling model. *Journal of Experimental Psychology: Learning, Memory and Cognition, 11*, 538–564.
Christensen-Szalanski, J. J. (1980). A further examination of the selection of problem solving strategies: The effects of deadlines and analytic aptitudes. *Organizational Behavior and Human Performance, 25*, 107–122.
Easterbrook, J. A. (1959). The effects of emotions on cue utilization and the organization of behavior. *Psychological Review, 66*, 183–201.
Edland, A. (1985). Attractiveness judgments of decision alternatives under time stress. *Cognition and Decision Research Unit*, University of Stockholm, Report No. 21.
Frankenhauser, M. (1979). Psychoneuroendocrine approaches to the study of emotions as related to stress and coping. In H. E. Howe & R. A. Dienstbier (Eds.), *Nebraska Symposium on Motivation 1978* (pp. 123–161). Lincoln: University of Nebraska Press.
Holsti, O. R. (1971). Crisis, stress, and decision making. *International Social Science Journal, 23*, 53–67.
Janis, I. L. (1983). Decision making under stress. In L. Goldberger & S. Breznitz (Eds.), *Handbook of stress* (pp. 69–87). New York: The Free Press.
Janis, I. L., & Mann, L. (1977). *Decision making: A psychological analysis of conflict, choice and commitment.* New York: The Free Press.
Johnson, E. J., & Payne, J. W. (1985). Effort and accuracy in choice. *Management Science, 31*, 395–414.
Keinan, G., Friedland, N., & Ben-Porath, Y. (1987). Decision making under stress: Scanning of alternatives under physical threat. *Acta Psychologica, 64*, 219–228.

Kruglanski, A. W., & Freund, T. (1983). The freezing and unfreezing of lay inferences: Effects on impression primacy, ethnic stereotyping and numerical anchoring. *Journal of Experimental Social Psychology, 19,* 448–468.

Luchins, A. S. (1942). Mechanizations in problem solving: The effect of Einstellung. *Psychological Monographs, 54,* (Whole No. 248).

Maule, J., & Mackie, P. (1990). A componential investigation of the effects of deadlines on individual decision making. In K. Borchering, O. I. Larichev, & D. M Messick (Eds.), *Contemporary issues in decision making* (pp. 449–461). Amsterdam: North-Holland.

Miller, J. G. (1960). Information input overload and psychopathology. *American Journal of Psychiatry, 116,* 695–704.

Norman, D. A. (1981). Categorization of action slips. *Psychological Review, 88,* 1–15.

Olshavsky, R. W. (1979). Task complexity and contingent processing in decision making: A replication and extension. *Organizational Behavior and Human Performance, 24,* 300–316.

Payne, J. W. (1976). Task complexity and contingent processing in decision making: An information search and protocol analysis. *Organizational Behavior and Human Performance, 16,* 366–387.

Payne, J. W., Bettman, J. R., & Johnson, E. J. (1988). Adaptive strategy selection in decision making. *Journal of Experimental Psychology: Learning, Memory & Cognition, 14,* 534–552.

Rasmussen, J., Duncan, K., & Leplat, J. (1987). *New technology and human error.* Chichester: Wiley.

Rizzo, A., Bagnara, S., & Visciola, M. (1988). Human error detection processes. In E. Hollnagel, G. Mancini, & D. Woods (Eds.), *Cognitive engineering in complex dynamic worlds* (pp. 99–114). London: Academic Press.

Rothstein, H. G. (1986). The effects of time pressure on judgment in multiple cue probability learning. *Organizational Behavior and Human Decision Processes, 37,* 83–92.

Schwartz, D. R., & Howell, W. C. (1985). Optional stopping performance under graphic and numeric CRT formatting. *Human Factors, 27*(4), 433–444.

Smith, J. F., Mitchell, T. R., & Beach, L. R. (1982). A cost benefit mechanism for selecting problem-solving strategies: Some extensions and empirical tests. *Organizational Behavior and Human Performance, 29,* 370–396.

Svenson, O. (1979). Process descriptions of decision making. *Organizational Behavior and Human Performance, 23,* 86–112.

Svenson, O. (1988). Cognitive psychology, operator behavior and safety in the processing industries with emphasis on nuclear power plant applications. Stockholm University, Department of Psychology, *Cognition and Decision Research Unit,* Report No 29.

Svenson, O. (1990). Some propositions for the classification of decision situations. In K. Borchering, O. I., Larichev, & D. M. Messick (Eds.), *Contemporary Issues in Decision Making* (pp. 17–31). Amsterdam: North Holland.

Svenson, O. (1991). *Differentiation and consolidation theory of human decision making.* Paper presented at the SPUDM conference, Fribourg, Switzerland, 1991.

Svenson, O., & Edland, A. (1987). Change of preferences under time pressure: Choices and judgments. *Scandinavian Journal of Psychology, 29*(4), 322–330.

Svenson, O., Edland, A., & Karlsson, G. (1985). The effect of numerical and verbal information and time stress on judgments of the attractiveness of decision alternatives. In L. B. Methlie & R. Sprague (Eds.), *Knowledge representation for decision support systems* (pp. 133–144). Amsterdam: North-Holland.

Svenson, O., Edland, A., & Slovic, P. (1990). Choices between incompletely described alternatives under time stress, *Acta Psychologica, 75*(2), 153–169.

Wallsten, T. S., & Barton, C. N. (1982). Processing probabilistic multidimensional information for decisions. *Journal of Experimental Psychology; Learning and Memory and Cognition, 8,* 361–384.

Wright, P. (1974). The harassed decision maker: Time pressure, distraction and the use of evidence. *Journal of Applied Psychology, 59,* 555–561.

Zakay, D. (1985). Post-decision confidence and conflict experienced in a choice process. *Acta Psychologica, 58,* 75–80.

Zakay, D., & Wooler, S. (1984). Time pressure, training and decision effectiveness. *Ergonomics, 27,* 273–284.

3

On the Psychobiology of Stress and Health

Ulf Lundberg

Introduction

According to the theoretical formulations by Lazarus (1966), as further developed by Frankenhaeuser (1986), Levi (1972), Kagan and Levi (1974), McGrath (1970), Magnusson and Öhman (1987), and several others, psychological stress is considered as an interactional process, where situational demands are weighed against each individual's resources to meet these demands. The cognitive evaluation of this balance is the major determinant of the stress response, as reflected in the activation of specific biological systems. As a consequence of this cognitive evaluation, considerable interindividual differences exist in response to a specific stressful situation. The individual's ability, personality characteristics, earlier experiences, and genetic dispositions may further contribute to the idiosyncrasy of the stress responses.

Intense time pressure, work overload, too much responsibility, threat, competition, role strain, role conflicts, and the like are well-known factors contributing to overstimulation and stress in the individual. It is also assumed that long-term exposure to such conditions of pressure and overload contributes to the development of a specific behavior pattern, known as "Type A behavior" (Friedman & Rosenman, 1974). This behavior pattern is characterized by an extreme

Ulf Lundberg • Department of Psychology, Stockholm University, S-10691 Stockholm, Sweden.
Time Pressure and Stress in Human Judgment and Decision Making, edited by Ola Svenson and A. John Maule, Plenum Press, New York, 1993.

sense of time urgency, impatience, restlessness, competitiveness, and aggression/hostility.

The theoretical models (e.g., Frankenhaeuser, 1986) also predict that stress is induced when the balance between the demands and the resources is upset because the demands are too low; for example, when the individual lacks stimulation from meaningful activities, when work pace is too low, tasks too simple, or he/she is unable to communicate with other individuals. Specific stress is induced in individuals exposed to conditions with long periods of passive understimulation interrupted by short periods of active overstimulation. This kind of stress is associated with nonoptimal functioning in, for example, decision processes (Frankenhaeuser, 1985).

Successive coping with various life requirements, such as increased demands on efficiency, work reorganizations, applications of new methods and technology, and so forth is assumed to tax the individual's adaptation resources. Holmes and Rahe (1967) constructed the "social readjustment scale" in order to measure the perceived time and energy necessary to adjust to various kinds of everyday life stress, such as illness and death in the family, a divorce, moving to a new home or a new job. Even positive events, such as having a new baby, getting married, were assumed to exact a toll on the individual that, in addition to other life events, accumulates over time and increases the risk of negative health outcomes (Dohrenwend, 1973; Dohrenwend & Dohrenwend, 1974; Rahe, 1972, 1975, 1979).

Stress induced by role strain and role conflicts has increased considerably in recent years (Frankenhaeuser, Lundberg, & Chesney, 1991). Men and, in particular women, are stressed by the combined demands on their available time from job/career and from responsibility for child care, home, and marriage. This problem has become increasingly important as most women in the Western world now are part of the labor force. In 1989 about 70% of the women in the United States and 85% in Sweden were employed outside the home.

Psychobiological Stress Responses

The work by Cannon (1914) on the "emergency function" of the adrenal medulla and later, the work by Selye (1956) on the "general adaptation syndrome" and the stress mechanisms, form the basis for modern stress research. Selye was mainly concerned with the pituitary–adrenal cortical system, that is, the secretion of the corticosteroids (e.g., cortisol), whereas the "fight–flight" response described by Cannon is closely connected to sympathetic arousal and the secretion of the catecholamines adrenaline and noradrenaline.

Following a period of extensive experimental and methodological research on the neuroendocrine responses to stress in animals and humans (cf. reviews by

Mason, 1968a,b; Levi, 1972; Frankenhaeuser, 1971, 1979), psychoneuroendocrine research has been spread to various naturalistic situations. Successive recordings of psychological and biological functions in humans have been made during daily stress at work, at home, at school, at day-care centers, at hospitals, on commuter trains, on buses, and the like. Scandinavian researchers have made significant contributions to this field (cf. review by Lundberg, 1984).

Psychological stress activates cardiovascular and neuroendocrine functions aimed at mobilizing energy to the muscles and the heart and, at the same time, reducing the blood flow to the internal organs and the gastrointestinal system. In ancient times, when physical threat was the most common form of stress, this was an efficient means for survival by increasing the organism's capacity to fight the enemy or escape from the situation. Today, however, threats are more often of a social or mental rather than a physical nature. The possible health consequences of intense, repeated, and/or long-lasting activation of this psychobiological program in response to mental stress is a major objective for stress research.

Two neuroendocrine systems—the sympathetic adrenal–medullary system, with the secretion of the catecholamines adrenaline and noradrenaline and the pituitary adrenal–cortical system with the secretion of corticosteroids, for example, cortisol—are of central interest in stress–health research (Cannon, 1914; Selye, 1974). Numerous studies have demonstrated the sensitivity of these systems to various environmental demands (see reviews by Levi, 1972; Frankenhaeuser 1979, 1983; Henry & Stephens, 1977; Lundberg, 1984; Usdin et al., 1980; Ursin et al., 1978, Axelrode & Reisine, 1984). The results (including data from clinical and animal research) form a relatively consistent pattern. The sympathetic adrenal–medullary system is activated by mental and physical effort and by unpleasant as well as pleasant emotional stimulation, whereas the pituitary adrenal–cortical system responds more selectively and is activated mainly in conditions characterized by distress, anxiety, depression, and lack of control (Henry & Stephens, 1977; Frankenhaeuser & Lundberg, 1985; Frankenhaeuser, 1991; Levine, Coe, & Wiener, 1989).

These two different psychoneuroendocrine coping patterns have been described by Henry (1976) as (1) the defence or fight–flight response pattern ("threat to control") and (2) the conservation–withdrawal or depression response ("loss of control"), respectively. The sympathetic adrenal–medullary system is activated when the individual is challenged in its control of the environment, whereas the pituitary adrenal–cortical system becomes involved when there is a loss of control. Long-lasting, elevated catecholamine and cortisol levels are considered to contribute to the development of atherosclerosis and predispose to myocardial ischemia (Karasek et al., 1982; Krantz & Manuck, 1984; Rozanski et al., 1988).

Type A Behavior, Competitive Drive, Time Urgency, and Stress Responses Inducing Cardiovascular Disease

Since the first indications of the Type A or coronary-prone behavior as a major cause of death in heart attack (Friedman, 1969; Friedman & Rosenman, 1974), a large amount of research has been devoted to the study of this behavior pattern (review by Rosenman & Chesney, 1980). The proposed relationship with coronary heart disease (CHD) was first demonstrated in the Western Collaborative Group Study (Rosenman et al., 1976), where 3,000 middle-aged men were classified as Type A or Type B on the basis of an interview (the Structured Interview). At the $8^{1}/_{2}$ year follow-up, the incidence of CHD was found to be about twice as high among Type A's as among Type B's, after controlling for traditional CHD risk factors, such as age, smoking, high blood pressure, high serum cholesterol levels, and so on. Similar findings were obtained in a couple of subsequent longitudinal studies (e.g., Haynes et al., 1978). A review panel of the American Heart Association (1981) concluded that Type A behavior

> is associated with an increased risk of clinically apparent CHD in employed, middle aged U.S. citizens. This risk is greater than that imposed by age, elevated values of systolic blood pressure and serum cholesterol, and smoking and appears to be of the same order of magnitude as the relative risk associated with the latter three of these other factors (Review Panel, 1981, p. 1200)

However, results from more recent studies have been less convincing (see below).

The most significant trait of the Type A individual is the habitual sense of time urgency or "hurry sickness" (Friedman & Rosenman, 1974). The Type A person feels that he/she doesn't have enough time to do all the things he/she believes should be done or wishes to do, that is, the Type A individual is involved in an everlasting struggle with time. The Type A person eats fast, walks quickly, and will hurry to a meeting, even when there is plenty of time. He/she resents being stopped in his/her striving to accomplish too much or participate in too many events in the amount of time available.

In line with this, Type A individuals are also characterized by an excessive drive, competitiveness, and signs of aggression and hostility (Matthews, 1982), and they tend to perform close to their maximum capacity in every task (Contrada & Krantz, 1988). Specific voice and speech characteristics are also associated with Type A behavior, such as a loud and explosive voice, abruptness of speech, and short response latencies (Musante et al., 1983). Type A individuals, who are trying to "achieve as much as possible in the shortest possible time," respond to "challenges" with a greater increase in systolic blood pressure, heart rate, and catecholamine secretion than do their more relaxed "Type B" counterparts (Krantz et al., 1987).

The sympathetic stress responses are assumed to link Type A behavior to CHD. Repeated blood pressure responses may induce thickening of the arteries and narrowing of the blood vessels, thus increasing the load on the heart. The catecholamines, which are involved in blood pressure homeostasis, facilitate blood clotting and release lipids into the blood that may be taken up by the artery walls. High catecholamine levels may also predispose to cardiac arrhythmias.

In accordance with current models of the relationship between psychological stress, physiological reactivity, and illness susceptibility (cf. Levi, 1972; Kagan & Levi, 1974; Venables & Christie, 1975; Levine & Ursine, 1980; Frankenheauser, 1979, 1986; Lazarus, 1976), it is assumed that environmental factors, such as time pressure, heavy workload, achievement orientation, competition, and burdensome responsibility contribute to the development of Type A behavior and its pathophysiological correlates. Data from numerous studies support this assumption and show that Type A individuals are more reactive in response to "Type A-relevant" demands but do not differ from others in terms of either their physiological baseline levels or their general responses to stress (Krantz et al., 1987).

Interventions to change the behavior of Type A individuals have not been particularly successful (Roskies et al., 1978), except in the treatment of postinfarction patients (Friedman et al., 1984). A possible reason for this is the fact that the economic and social values of the Western world encourage people to maintain their Type A characteristics, that is, to keep a high pace and be competitive, productive, and efficient.

Glass (1977) has suggested that Type A individuals are motivated by a constant striving for control; in keeping with this, it has been found that the threat of uncontrollability produces more pronounced behavioral and physiological responses in Type A's than in Type B's (Chesney et al., 1981; Glass & Carver, 1980; Glass & Contrada, 1983).

Type A behavior also seems to interact with the pace of the environment, that is, Type A's are physiologically more aroused than Type B's during understimulation, but the pattern may be reversed during overstimulation (Frankenheauser, Lundberg, & Forsman, 1980a; Lundberg & Forsman, 1979; Snow & Glass, 1981). It is interesting to note that in a self-paced reaction time task with high controllability (Frankenhaeuser et al., 1980b), Type A's selected a faster pace and responded more rapidly but did not have higher catecholamine levels or higher heart rate than Type B's.

In summary, the frequent exposure of Type A individuals to challenges, such as time pressure, work overoad, etc. is assumed to enhance both their particular personality characteristics and their cardiovascular and neuroendocrine responses to stress. However, a certain biological underpinning of Type A behavior has also been indicated (Krantz et al., 1987).

More recent studies lend little support to the association between Type A behavior and CHD risk (Ragland & Brand, 1988; Shekelle et al., 1986). However, it is still to early to conclude that Type A behavior is no longer a risk factor for CHD. Alternative explanations for the negative findings may be related to the fact that (1) very different assessment techniques have been used (some of unknown reliability and validity), (2) several studies have been restricted to the study of special groups, for example, postmyocardial patients and other individuals already at risk, (3) very few prospective studies have been performed with representative samples, and (4) an increasing proportion of the population (70%–75%) in the West is now being classified as Type A, which makes the evaluation of this classification difficult. However, the possibility that global Type A behavior over the years has become a less important factor in the etiology of CHD cannot be excluded (Contrada & Krantz, 1988). Recent findings (Barefoot et al., 1983; Dembroski et al., 1985; Diamond, 1982; Shekelle, Gale, Ostfeld, & Paul, 1983; Williams et al., 1985) suggest that "hostility" is likely to be the most "toxic" component of the Type A behavior pattern with regard to CHD risk.

The Use of Time in Men and Women: Work Overload

"Total workload" (Mårdberg et al., 1991; Frankenhaeuser et al., 1990) or "productive activity" (Kahn, 1991) refers to the combined load from paid and unpaid duties, that is, paid employment, household chores, child care, care of elderly relatives, etc. Frankenhaeuser et al. (1990) found that Swedish women employed full time have a total workload of 78 hours per week compared with 68 hours for men, which corresponds closely with representative American data (Kahn, 1991; women = 80 hours; men = 68 hours). Women also report more role conflicts than men.

The chronic struggle with work overload and role strain is assumed to affect women's mental and physical health (Wortman et al., 1991). Even though women live longer than men and are less prone to develop CHD, women consistently show more symptoms of bad health than men, that is, more psychosomatic symptoms, seek medical care more frequently, use more drugs, and are on sick leave more often (cf. Statistics, Sweden, 1990).

In a study of psychobiological stress responses in male and female white-collar workers (Frankenhaeuser et al., 1989), female managers were found to carry the heaviest load and to reveal a number of behavioral and physiological stress markers: high Type A scores, high serum cholesterol levels, and elevated blood pressure and catecholamine levels after work ("slow unwinding").

In this context, it is interesting to note that overtime at work has been found significantly correlated with catecholamine levels at home in women, but not in men (Dunne & Mullins, 1989; Lundberg & Palm, 1989) and with increased risk of CHD in women, but not in men (Alfredsson, Spetz, & Theorell, 1985).

As to possible negative health consequences of women's work overload, recent data (Hall, 1990) from women in blue-collar work show that exposure to adverse job and home characteristics are significantly associated with an increased risk of psychosomatic strain and physical illness. However, women's employment per se does not seem to have negative health effects (e.g., Repetti, Matthews, & Waldron, 1989; Waldron, 1991), although mortality rates of men and women have started to shift and resulted in a decreasing advantage for women (Rodin & Ickovics, 1990). Particular work characteristics (high job strain, low personal control) have similar negative health consequences in women as in men (Haynes, 1991). However, the relationship between stress, work, and health seems to be more complex in women than in men, probably because the stress associated with paid and unpaid work interact, and several job related factors act as powerful "stress buffers," for example, social support from co-workers, high self-esteem, and economic independence (Frankenhaeuser, Lundberg, & Chesney, 1991).

Mental Stress, Time Pressure, and Musculoskeletal Problems

Recent studies (e.g., Bigos et al., 1991) indicate that stress and time pressure play an important role in the development of musculoskeletal problems. In spite of considerable ergonomic improvements at the workplace, the number of musculoskeletal problems, such as pain from the shoulders, neck, arms, lower back, etc., has increased progressively in recent years. These problems are particularly pronounced in repetitive assembly-line work under time pressure, and women are generally more exposed than men.

In a prospective study of manufacturing employees (age = 21–67 years, 78% men) at an aircraft industry in the United States (Bigos et al., 1991), it was found that absenteeism from work due to back pain was more closely correlated with low job satisfaction than with physical factors at work (Battié, 1989). This is in agreement with several earlier epidemiological studies, showing that back problems are almost as frequent in sedentary work as in physically heavy jobs (Gyntelberg, 1974; Hult, 1954; Magora, 1974; Porter, 1987). The importance of psychosocial factors for neck and shoulder pain in video display terminal workers has also been demonstrated (Aronsson et al., 1988; Schnorr et al., 1987). A recent laboratory experiment showed that physiological deactivation was slower after a monotonous data-entry task than after a stimulating and interesting learning task (Lundberg et al., 1993).

Studies at a car engine factory confirm that repetitive assembly-line work is associated with low job satisfaction, time pressure, irritation, tiredness, and elevated physiological arousal as assessed by self-reports and measurements of blood pressure, heart rate, and catecholamine excretion (Lundberg et al., 1989).

Catecholamine and blood pressure responses were found to be significantly correlated with self-reports of time pressure and demands at work. Measurements of the physical loads on the lumbar spine suggest that the back-problem complaints among these young workers cannot be attributed to high loads on the spine (Magnusson et al., 1990). Stress from monotony, time pressure, and low job satisfaction are more likely causal factors. Results also show that perceived back load was correlated with perceived stress at work but not with physical load, and that physiological stress responses during work were associated with decreased physical performance after work (Lundberg, 1990).

Concluding Remarks

An impressive amount of research during the last decades has been devoted to the study of stress, human well-being, health, and efficiency. Dramatic changes in the pace of life, social roles, and illness patterns during this century have stimulated this interest. The biopsychosocial approach (Frankenhaeuser, 1986), combining theories and techniques from social psychology, psychophysiology, and biomedicine in various laboratory and natural settings, has increased our understanding of the mechanisms linking stress and behavior to ill health and has provided guidelines for intervention and prevention. Coping with a stressful environment involves social, cognitive as well as biological aspects and strategies (see, e.g., Lazarus, 1976). Several other chapters of this volume deal with such strategies as a way of coping with time stress.

The health issue has usually been the major focus of these studies, based on the awareness that stress and human behavior are strongly linked to the dominating causes of morbidity and mortality in modern society. However, stress and time urgency also affect human efficiency, performance, work satisfaction, and quality of life. Frankenhaeuser (1981, 1986) suggests that a moderately intense and varied input from the environment is a prerequisite for the optimal functioning of the human brain and for the individual's well-being and efficiency. A major objective is thus to provide possibilities for both men and women to combine their different roles in life—career, marriage, parenting, etc.—in a productive and stimulating way without exposing themselves to mental or physical health risks. An important tool to reach this goal is to provide each individual enough influence and control over the planning and pace of his/her work, in order to adjust the load according to their ambition, ability, skill, and education and to give feedback about his/her amount of success in their efforts.

ACKNOWLEDGMENT. Research reported in this chapter was supported by grants from the Swedish Medical Research Council, The Swedish Council for Research in the Humanities and Social Sciences, and the John D. and Catherine T. MacArthur Foundation Network on Health and Behavior, Chicago.

References

Alfredsson, L., Spetz C-L., & Theorell, T. (1985). Type of occupation and near-future hospitalization for myocardial infarction and some other diagnoses. *International Journal of Epidemiology, 14*, 378–388.

Aronsson, G., Örelius, M., & Åborg, C. (1988). *Datoriseringens vinnare och förlorare* [The winners and losers of computerization]. Statshälsan.

Axelrod, J., & Reisine, T. D. (1984). Stress hormones: Their interaction and regulation *Science, 224*, 452–459.

Barefoot, J. C., Dahlstrom, W. G., & Williams, Jr., R. B. (1983). Hostility, CHD incidence, and total mortality: A 24-year follow-up study of 255 physicians. *Psychomatic Medicine, 45*, 59–64.

Battié, M. C. (1989). *The reliability of physical factors as predictors of the occurrence of back pain reports.* A prospective study within industry. Doctoral Dissertation, Gothenburg University, Gothenburg.

Bigos, S., Battié, M., Spengler, D., Fisher, L., Fordyce, W., Hansson, T., Nachemson, A., & Wortley, M. (1991). Perspective studies of work perception and psychosocial factors affect. The report of back injury. *Spine, 16:1*, 1–6.

Cannon, W. B. (1914). The emergency function of the adrenal medulla in pain and the major emotions. *American Journal of Physiology, 33*, 356–372.

Chesney, M. A., Sevelius, G., Black, G. W., Ward, M., Swan, G. E., & Rosenman, R. H. (1981). Work environment, Type A behavior, and coronary heart disease risk factors. *Journal of Occupational Medicine, 23*, 551–555.

Contrada, R. J., & Krantz, D. S. (1988). Stress, reactivity, and Type A behavior: Current status and future directions. *Annals of Behavioral Medicine, 10*, 64–70.

Dembroski, T. M., MacDougall, J. M., Williams, R. B., Haney, T. L., & Blumenthal, J. A. (1985). Components of Type A behavior, hostility and anger in relationship to angiographic findings. *Psychosomatic Medicine, 47*, 219–233.

Diamond, E. L. (1982). The role of anger and hostility in essential hypertension and coronary heart disease. *Psychological Bulletin, 91*, 410–433.

Dohrenwend, B. S. (1973). Life events as stressors: A methodological inquiry. *Journal of Health & Social Behavior, 14*, 167–175.

Dohrenwend, B. S., & Dohrenwend, B. P. (Eds.). (1974). *Stressful life events: Their nature and effects.* New York, London, Sydney, Toronto: Wiley.

Dunne, E. Q., & Mullins, P. A. (1989). Sex differences in psychological and psychophysiological arousal patterns: A study of 'working couples.' *Work and Stress, 3*, 261–268.

Frankenhaeuser, M. (1971). Behavior and circulating catecholamines. *Brain Research, 31*, 241–262.

Frankenhaeuser, M. (1979). Psychoneuroendocrine approaches to the study of emotion as related to stress and coping. In H. E. Howe & R. A. Dienstbier (Eds.), *Nebraska Symposium on Motivation* (pp. 123–161). Lincoln: University of Nebraska Press.

Frankenhaeuser, M. (1981). Coping with job stress—a psychobiological approach. In B. Gardell & G. Johansson (Eds.), *Working life. A Social Science Contribution to Work Reform* (pp. 213–233). London: Wiley.

Frankenhaeuser, M. (1983). The sympathetic-adrenal and pituitary-adrenal response to challenge: Comparison between the sexes. In T. M. Dembroski, T. H. Schmidt, & G. Blumchen (Eds.), *Biobehavioral Bases of Coronary Heart Disease* (pp. 91–105). Basel, New York: Karger.

Frankenhaeuser, M. (1985). To err is human: Psychological and biological aspects of human functioning. In *Nuclear war by mistake. Inevitable or preventable?* Distributed by physicians for Prevention of Nuclear War, Stockholm.

Frankenhaeuser, M. (1986). A psychobiological framework for research on human stress and coping.

In M. H. Appley & R. Trumbull (Eds.), *Dynamics of stress* (pp. 101–116). New York: Plenum Press.

Frankenhaeuser, M. (1991). The psychophysiology of sex differences as related to occupational status. In M. Frankenhaeuser, U. Lundberg, & M. Chesney (Eds.), *Women, Work and Health. Stress and Opportunities* (pp. 39–64). New York and London: Plenum Press.

Frankenhaeuser, M., & Lundberg, U. (1985). Sympathetic-adrenal and pituitary-adrenal response to challenge. In P. Pichot, P. Berner, R. Wolf, & K. Thau (Eds.), *Psychiatry* (Vol. 2; pp. 699–704). London: Plenum Press.

Frankenhaeuser, M., Lundberg, U., & Forsman, L. (1980a). Note on arousing Type-A persons by depriving them of work. *Journal of Psychosomatic Research, 24,* 45–47.

Frankenhaeuser, M., Lundberg, U., & Forsman, L. (1980b). Dissociation between sympathetic-adrenal and pituitary-adrenal responses to an achievement situation characterized by high controllability: Comparison between Type A and Type B males and females. *Biological Psychology, 10,* 79–91.

Frankenhaeuser, M., Lundberg, U., Fredrikson, M., Melin, B., Tuomisto, M., Myrsten, A-L., Hedman, M., Bergman-Losman, B., & Wallin, L. (1989). Stress on and off the job as related to sex and occupational status in white-collar workers. *Journal of Organizational Behavior, 10,* 321–346.

Frankenhaeuser, M., Lundberg, U., & Chesney, M. (Eds.). (1991). *Women, work and health. Stress and opportunities.* New York and London: Plenum Press.

Frankenhaeuser, M., Lundberg, U., & Mårdberg, B. (1990). The total workload of men and women as related to occupational level and number and age of children. (Report No. 726). Stockholm University: Department of Psychology.

Friedman, M. (1969). *Pathogenesis of coronary artery disease.* London: McGraw-Hill.

Friedman, M., & Rosenman, R. H. (1974). *Type A Behavior and Your Heart.* New York: Alfred A. Knopf.

Friedman, M., Thoresen, C. E., Gill, J. J., Powell, L. H., Ulmer, D., Thompson, L., Price, V. A., Rabin, D. D., Breall, W. S., Dixon, T., Levy, R., & Bourg, E. (1984). Alteration of Type A behavior and reduction in cardiac recurrences in postmyocardial infarction patients. *American Heart Journal, 108,* 237–248.

Glass, D. C. (1977). *Behavior patterns, stress, and coronary disease.* Hillsdale, NJ: Lawrence Erlbaum.

Glass, D. C., & Carver, C. S. (1980). Helplessness and the coronary-prone personality. In J. Garber & M. E. P. Seligman (Eds.), *Human Helplessness: Theory and Applications* (pp. 223–243). New York: Academic Press.

Glass, D. C., & Contrada, R. J. (1983). Type A behavior and catecholamines: A critical review. In C. R. Lake & M. Ziegler (Eds.), *Norepinephrine: Clinical Aspects* (pp. 346–367). Baltimore: Williams & Wilkins.

Gyntelberg, F. (1974). One year incidence of low back pain among male residents of Copenhagen aged 40–59. *Danish Medical Bulletin, 21,* 30–36.

Hall, E. M. (1990). *Women's work: An inquiry into the health effects of invisible and visible labor.* Doctoral dissertation, Karolinska Institute, Stockholm. Akademitryck.

Haynes, S. G. (1991). The effect of job demands, job control, and new technologies on the health of employed women: A review. In M. Frankenhaeuser, U. Lundberg, & M. Chesney (Eds.), *Women, work and health. Stress and opportunities* (pp. 157–169). New York: Plenum Press.

Haynes, S. G., Feinleib, M., Levine, S., Scotch, N., & Kannel, W. B. (1978). The relationship of psychosocial factors to coronary heart disease in the Framingham study: II. Prevalence of coronary heart disease. *American Journal of Epidemiology, 107,* 384–492.

Henry, J. P. (1976). Understanding the early pathophysiology of essential hypertention. *Geriatrics, 31,* 59–72.

Henry, J. P., & Stephens, P. M. (1977). *Stress, health, and the social environment. A sociobiologic approach to medicine.* New York, Heidelberg, and Berlin: Springer-Verlag.

Holmes, T. H., & Rahe, R. H. (1967). The social readjustment rating scale. *Journal of Psychosomatic Research, 11,* 213–218.

Hult, L. (1954). The Munkfors investigation. *Acta Orthopedica Scandinavica* (Suppl.), *16,* 1–76.

Kagan, A. R., & Levi, L. (1974). Health and environment—psychosocial stimuli: A review. *Social Science and Medicine, 8,* 225–241.

Kahn, R. L. (1991). The forms of women's work. In M. Frankenhaeuser, U. Lundberg, & M. Chesney (Eds.), *Women, work and health. Stress and opportunities.* (pp. 65–84). New York and London, Plenum Press.

Karasek, R. A., Russell, R. S., & Theorell, T. (1982). Physiology of stress and regeneration in job related cardiovascular illness. *Journal of Human Stress, 8,* 29–42.

Krantz, D. S., & Manuck, S. B. (1984). Acute psychophysiologic reactivity and risk of cardiovascular disease: A review and methodologic critique. *Psychological Bulletin, 96,* 435–464.

Krantz, D. S., Lundberg, U., & Frankenhaeuser, M. (1987). Stress and Type A behavior. Interactions between environmental and biological factors. In A. Baum and J. E. Singer (Eds.), *Handbook of pyschology and health (Vol. 5). Stress.* (pp. 203–228). Hillsdale, NJ, L. Erlbaum.

Lazarus, R. S. (1966). *Psychological stress and the coping process.* New York: McGraw-Hill.

Lazarus, R. S. (1976). *Patterns of adjustment.* New York: McGraw-Hill.

Levi, L. (1972). Stress and distress in response to psychosocial stimuli. *Acta Medica Scandinavica* (Suppl.) 528.

Levine, S., Coe, C., & Wiener, S. G. (1989). Psychoneuroendocrinology of stress: A psychobiological perspective. In *Psychoendocrinology* (pp. 341–377). Orlando: Academic Press.

Levine, S., & Ursin, H. (Eds.). (1980). *Coping and health.* New York and London: Plenum Press.

Lundberg, U. (1984). Human psychobiology in Scandinavia: II. Psychoneuroendocrinology—human stress and coping processes. *Scandinavian Journal of Psychology, 25,* 214–226.

Lundberg, U. (1990). *Psychobiological stress responses during and after work.* Abstracts. 22nd International Congress of Applied Psychology, Kyoto, Japan, July 22–27, 1990.

Lundberg, U., & Forsman, L. (1979). Adrenal-medullary and adrenal-cortical responses to understimulation and overstimulation: Comparison between Type A and Type B persons. *Biological Psychology, 9,* 79–89.

Lundberg, U., Granqvist, M., Hansson, T., Magnusson, M., & Wallin, L. (1989). Psychological and physiological stress responses during repetitive work at an assembly line. *Work & Stress, 3,* 143–153.

Lundberg, U., Melin, B., Evans, G. W., & Holmberg, L. (1993). Physiological deactivation after two contrasting tasks at a video display terminal: Learning versus repetitive data entry. *Ergonomics, 36,* 601–611.

Lundberg, U., & Palm, K. (1989). Workload and catecholamine excretion in parents of preschool children. *Work & Stress, 3,* 255–260.

Magnusson, D., & Öhman, A. (1987). *Psychopathology. An interactional perspective.* Orlando: Academic Press.

Magnusson, M., Granqvist, M., Jonson, R., Lindell, V., Lundberg, U., Wallin, L., & Hansson, T. (1990). The loads on the lumbar spine during work at an assembly line. The risks for fatigue injuries of vertebral bodies. *Spine, 15,* 774–779.

Magora, A. (1974). Investigation of the relation between low back pain and occupation. VI. Medical histories and symptoms. *Scandinavian Journal of Rehabilitation, 6,* 81–88.

Mårdberg, B., Lundberg, U., & Frankenhaeuser, M. (1991). The total workload of parents employed in white-collar jobs: Construction of a questionnaire and a scoring system. *Scandinavian Journal of Psychology, 32,* 233–239.

Mason, J. W. (1968a). A review of psychoendocrine research on the pituitary-adrenal cortical system. *Psychosomatic Medicine, 30,* 576–597.

Mason, J. W. (1968b). A review of psychoendocrine research on the sympathetic-adrenal medullary system. *Psychosomatic Medicine, 30,* 631–653.

Matthews, K. A. (1982). Psychological perspectives on the Type A behavior pattern. *Psychological Bulletin, 91,* 293–323.

McGrath, J. E. (1970). Settings, measures and themes: An integrative review of some research on social-psychological factors in stress. In J. E. McGrath (Ed.), *Social and psychological factors in stress* (pp. 58–96). New York: Holt, Rinehart & Winston.

Musante, L., MacDougall, J. M., Dembroski, T. M., & Van Horn, A. E. (1983). Component analysis of the Type A coronary-prone behavior pattern in male and female college students. *Journal of Personality and Social Psychology, 45,* 1104–1117.

Porter, R. W. (1987). Does hard work prevent disc protrusion? *Clinical Biomechanics, 2,* 196–198.

Ragland, D. R., & Brand, R. J. (1988). Type A behavior and mortality from coronary heart disease. *The New England Journal of Medicine, 318,* 65–69.

Rahe, R. (1972). Subjects' recent life changes and their near-future illness reports: A review. *Annals of Clinical Research, 4,* 250–265.

Rahe, R. H. (1975). Epidemiological studies of life change and illness. *International Journal of Psychiatry in Medicine, 6,* 133–146.

Rahe, R. H. (1979). Life change events and mental illness: an overview *Journal of Human Stress, 5,* 2–10.

Repetti, R., Matthews, K. A., and Waldron, I. (1989). Employment and women's health: Effects of paid employment on women's mental and physical health. *American Psychologist, 44,* 1394–1401.

Review Panel. Weiss, D. M. (Ed.). (1981). Coronary-prone behavior and coronary heart disease: A critical review. *Circulation, 63,* 1199–1215.

Rodin, J., & Ickovics, J. R. (1990). Women's health. Review and research agenda as we approach the 21st century. *American Psychologist, 45,* 1018–1034.

Rosenman, R. H., & Chesney, M. A. (1980). The relationship of Type A behavior to coronary heart-disease. *Activitas Nervosa Superior, 22,* 1–45.

Rosenman, R. H., Brand, R. J., Sholtz, R. I., & Friedman, M. (1976). Multivariate prediction of coronary heart disease during 8.5 year follow-up in the western collaborative group study. *American Journal of Cardiology, 37,* 903–910.

Roskies, E., Spevack, M., Surkis, A., Cohen, C., & Gilman, S. (1978). Changing the coronary-prone (Type A) behavior pattern in a nonclinical population. *Journal of Behavioral Medicine, 1,* 201–216.

Rozanski, A., Bairey, C. N., Krantz, D. S., Friedman, J., Resser, K. J., Morell, M., Hilton-Chalfen, S., Hestrin, L., Bietendorf, J., & Berman, D. S. (1988). Mental stress and the induction of silent myocardial ischemia in patients with coronary artery disease. *The New England Journal of Medicine, 318,* 1005–1011.

Selye, H. (1956). *The stress of life.* New York: McGraw-Hill.

Selye, H. (1974). *Stress without distress.* Philadelphia and New York: Lippincott.

Schnorr, T. M., Thun, M. J., & Halperin, W. E. (1987). Chest pain in users of video display terminals. *Journal of American Medical Association, 257,* 627.

Shekelle, R. B., Hulley, S. B., Neaton, J. D., Billings, J., Borhani, N. O., Gerace, T. A., Jacobs, D., Lasser, N., Mittlemark, M., & Stamler, J. (1986). Type A behavior and risk of coronary heart disease in the multiple risk factor intervention trial. In T. H. Schmidt, T. M. Dembroski, & G. Blümchen (Eds.), *Biological and psychological factors in cardiovascular disease* (pp. 41–55). Heidelberg: Springer-Verlag.

Shekelle, R. B., Gale, M., Ostfeld, A. M., & Paul, O. (1983). Hostility, risk of coronary heart disease, and mortality. *Psychosomatic Medicine, 45,* 109–114.

Snow, B. R., & Glass, D. C. (1981). *Differential reactivity of Type A and B individuals to congruent and incongruent environments.* Paper presented at the 52nd Annual Meeting of the Eastern Psychological Association, New York.

Statistics, Sweden. (1990). *Women and men in Sweden. Equality of the sexes 1990.*

Ursin, H., Baade, E., & Levine, S. (1978). *Psychobiology of stress.* A *study of coping men.* New York, San Francisco, and London: Academic Press.

Usdin, E., Kvetnansky, R., & Kopin, I. J. (Eds.). (1980). *Catecholamines and stress: Recent advances.* New York: Elsevier North-Holland.

Venables, P. H., & Christie, M. J. (Eds.). (1975). *Research in psychophysiology.* New York, London, and Sydney: Wiley.

Waldron, I. (1991). Effects of labor force participation on sex differences in mortality and morbidity. In M. Frankenhaeuser, U. Lundberg, & M. Chesney (Eds.). *Women, work and health. Stress and opportunities* (pp. 17–38). New York and London, Plenum Press.

Williams, R. B., Barefoot, J. C., & Shekelle, R. B. (1985). The health consequences of hostility. In M. A. Chesney & R. H. Rosenman (Eds.), *Anger and hostility in cardiovascular and behavioral disorders.* (pp. 173–185). New York: McGraw-Hill. pp. 173–185.

Wortman, C., Biernat, M., & Lang, E. (1991). Coping with role overload. In M. Frankenhaeuser, U. Lundberg, & M. Chesney (Eds.), *Women, work and health. Stress and opportunities.* (pp. 85–110). New York and London: Plenum Press.

II

Perspectives on Time Pressure
and Stress: Theory and Method

Part II contains chapters that take a more detailed look at a number of different
approaches, exploring each in terms of the theoretical and methodological issues
it raises for our understanding of the effects of time constraints. Though each
chapter draws on a different perspective, a number of general themes emerge.
For instance, MacGregor (Chapter 5) and Maule and Hockey (Chapter 6) are
critical of the way researchers have, in the past, imposed time constraints by
reducing base time to complete the task by some fraction. They discuss the
shortcomings of this method and make some suggestions about how procedures
for imposing time constraints can be improved. A second theme that emerges
concerns the need for a clearer understanding of the general role of time in
decision making. MacGregor argues that it is unlikely that any decision maker
has unlimited time, so even when no external deadline is imposed, an internally
derived deadline may nevertheless be in operation. However, we have virtually
no idea about how time is managed in the context of a decision process. Zakay
(Chapter 4) develops this theme further by arguing that deadlines require individuals to monitor time, with this activity disrupting the decision-making process
because it diverts limited resources to time perception processes. A third theme
concerns the kinds of processes that are assumed to mediate the changes in
judgment and decision making. Johnson, Payne, and Bettman (Chapter 7) discuss changes in terms of cost/benefit calculations, which are essentially "cold"
calculative processes. Maule and Hockey (Chapter 6) argue that there may also
be "hot" affective processes involved, and in their chapter they combine these
two rather different aspects within one theoretical framework. Finally, several
chapters argue that the effects of time constraints depend crucially on aspects of
the situation that have little or nothing to do with time. For instance, Carnevale,

O'Connor, and McCusker (Chapter 8), Maule and Hockey (Chapter 6), and Johnson et al. (Chapter 7) point out that task goals are important and that as these vary so the ways in which individuals adapt to a particular constraint can change.

In addition to these common themes, each contribution to this part of the book discusses a number of more specific issues. Zakay (Chapter 4) considers time pressure from a perspective based on time perception processes. He reviews a number of time perception models and uses these to develop an explanatory model in which time pressure is assumed to enhance the need to monitor the passage of time. As a consequence, attentional resources are invested in this activity at the expense of those required by the focal decision process. In this way he predicts changes in behavior under time pressure which are consistent with an explanation based on a shortage of resources. He also considers the implications of this model for training people to cope with time pressure.

MacGregor (Chapter 5) also focuses on the key role of time, arguing that previous research has assumed that time pressure acts as a stressor. As a result of this, explanations of time pressure effects have focused on how people manage this type of stress in judgment and decison-making situations. MacGregor suggests that if we wish to develop a better understanding of these effects we must first have a clearer idea of the general role of time in decision making. The chapter presents one view of this relationship, focusing on the transitions in the tempo or rate at which repeated decisions or choices must be made. A time constraint can lead to a sudden increase in task tempo making existing strategies inappropriate. As performance fails, so new strategies are adopted to cope with this new tempo. From this standpoint, time pressure acts as a cue for response strategy selection.

Maule and Hockey (Chapter 6) argue that previous research has been developed from one of two rather different approaches. One approach is essentially "hot," conceptualizing time pressure as a stressor, with changes in affective state assumed to mediate the changes in information-processing strategy. The other is essentially "cold," assuming that time constraints are one among a number of task/enviromnental characteristics that are incorporated into the cost-benefit calculations assumed in the context of a contemporary approach to stress and cognition and Variable State Activation Theory (VSAT). VSAT is a control theory of behavioral adaptation to stress and workload that allows both hot and cold processes to be discussed within a single theoretical framework. A key element in the theory is an appraisal process that evaluates both the demands of the situation (including time pressure) and the extent to which an individual has the cognitive and energetic resources to meet these demands. The authors show how the theory can explain some of the findings reported by previous time pressure research and, in addition, suggest other ways in which people may adapt that, so far, have not been investigated.

Johnson et al. provide, in Chapter 7, a detailed account of the cost-benefit approach described in the previous chapter. These authors have been involved in an extensive program of research concerned with the adaptivity of decision makers, investigating how characteristics of a decision task and the immediate task environment determine the strategies adopted by individuals. Time pressure is one such characteristic, and the authors summarize and interpret their findings founded on two different research procedures. One procedure uses computer simulation, based on production systems, to identify how particular strategies perform in terms of their efficiency and costs. The other uses a process-tracing methodology to determine the strategies that people actually use. Having examined findings based on these two procedures, the authors integrate them by considering such issues as the extent to which individuals respond to time pressure by changes in strategy and, if they do change, whether the new strategies are better under time pressure than those they have abandoned.

In Chapter 8, Carnevale et al. consider time pressure in the context of an aspect of group decision making concerned with negotiation and mediation. Their review indicates that in negotiation situations involving a single issue, time pressure changes the aspirations of negotiators, producing lower demands, faster concessions, and faster agreement. However, in situations involving multiple issues, the effects of time pressure depend on the goals of the negotiatiors. When negotiators have individualistic goals, then time pressure interferes with information exchanges, produces poor negotiations outcome, and heightens competitive behavior. If negotiators have cooperative goals, then time pressure has minimal effects. In the context of mediation, time pressure enhances forceful, pressing behavior, which is interpreted as indicating an attempt to lower negotiators' aspirations. The review emphasizes the importance of goals in determining the way individuals adapt to time pressure.

4

The Impact of Time Perception Processes on Decision Making under Time Stress

Dan Zakay

Introduction

The purpose of the present chapter is to introduce a model for explaining the noxious effects of time stress on decision-making optimality. Although the impact of time stress on decision making is well documented, there is no clear explanation for that phenomenon. So far, no specific theoretical model of decision making under time stress has been developed. The model presented here is based on time perception processes, a cognitive domain that is usually neglected in the decision-making literature.

The outline of the chapter is as follows: (1) a brief summary of the effects of time stress on decision making; (2) a review of time perception models; and (3) the presentation of a model connecting time perception and decision making under time stress.

Decision Making Under Time Stress

Decision making is a complex cognitive activity, sensitive to situational and environmental conditions (Payne, 1982). Man is not an optimal decision maker,

Dan Zakay • Department of Psychology, Tel-Aviv University, Ramat Aviv, Israel.
Time Pressure and Stress in Human Judgment and Decision Making, edited by Ola Svenson and A. John Maule, Plenum Press, New York, 1993.

especially while making intuitive decisions (Kahaneman, Slovic, & Tversky, 1982). One of the factors that decreases the optimality of intuitive decision making is psychological stress. It is argued that cognitive functioning in general, including decision-making processes, deteriorate under stress (e.g., Holsti, 1971; Smock, 1955). Psychological stress enhances the utilization of suboptimal cognitive processes and the appearance of cognitive errors and biases. Keinan (1987) found that under stress the range of alternatives and dimensions that are considered during a decision-making process is significantly restricted, as compared with normal conditions.

An important environmental factor that increases the feeling of psychological stress is time. Time stress is common in many settings, particularly in situations in which important and complex decisions must be reached (e.g., aviation, medicine, public administration, control rooms of chemical and nuclear plants in cases of crises, etc.). The negative effect of time stress on decision-making effectiveness has been reported by many investigators, and the pattern of the results obtained is quite homogeneous and consistent (Ben-Zur & Breznitz, 1981; Janis, 1982; Rothstein, 1988; Ben-Zur, 1983; Svenson & Edland, 1987, 1989; Svenson & Karlsson, 1989; Wright, 1974; Zakay, 1985; Zakay & Wooler, 1984). In brief, the effects of time stress on decision making are:

1. A reduction in information search and processing.
2. An increased importance of negative information.
3. Defensive reactions, such as neglect or denial of important information.
4. Bolstering of the chosen alternative.
5. A tendency to use a strategy of information filtration, that is, information that is perceived as most important is processed first, and then processing is continued until time is up.
6. Increased probability of using noncompensatory choice strategies instead of compensatory ones.
7. Forgetting important data.
8. Wrong judgment and evaluation.

In general, decision making under time stress may lead to the utilization of simple, nonlinear decision strategies resulting in suboptimal decisions.

These effects of time stress seem to be robust. Zakay and Wooler (1984) found that though training improved decision-making effectiveness when decision time was not limited, under time pressure it did not improve the quality of decision making at all.

This pattern of decision-making behavior under time stress calls for an explanatory mechanism. Such a mechanism, based on time perception processes, is presented in the following sections.

Review of Time-Perception Models

Subjective Time and Cognitive Processes

So far, no sense or sense organ for perceiving time directly has been identified, nor do we know what information humans utilize to make time estimates. It seems that subjective time is a product of cognitive functioning, and the experience of duration can be understood as a manifestation of temporal information processing (Michon, 1965). However, the realization that psychological time is a product of cognitive processes only occurred after it was recognized that the experience of time cannot be explained in terms of biological pacemakers. As things stand now, it looks as if the experience of duration of short intervals is a product of cognitive processes (Aschoff, 1984; Block, 1990).

Durations of seconds and minutes are the most important in terms of understanding human performance. Tasks, stimuli, and events of such durations are the building blocks of any human activity. In the range of seconds, especially, human beings rely on their subjective estimation of time, whereas for longer durations most people usually use watches and clocks. The implications of this is that the perception of short intervals of seconds and minutes is the most important in analyzing influences of time stress.

Cognitive Models of Short-Duration Estimation

The major focus for the study of estimating short durations has been the relationship between information-processing load during an interval and its estimated duration. A well-known phenomenon is the filled duration illusion. It is generally reported in the literature (e.g., Coren, Porac, & Ward, 1984) that "filled" durations are estimated as longer in comparison with equal "empty" durations. In some cases, however (e.g., Zakay, Nitzan, & Glicksohn, 1983), opposite findings were obtained. Assuming that empty intervals are less complex in terms of information-processing load than filled intervals, such opposing findings present researchers with a dilemma. Three main approaches—the storage size, the contextual change, and the attentional—have been suggested in the literature for explaining the relationship in question. The storage-size model is based on the notion that information stored in memory serves as the basis for time estimation. Ornstein's (1969) storage-size metaphor posits that time estimation of an interval is dependent on the amount of information stored in memory during that interval. Subjective duration is positively related to two general factors: (1) the number of events stored in and retrieved from memory and (2) the complexity of the events at the time of retrieval.

Ornstein's first inference, namely, that presenting more stimulus events during an interval lengthens the remembered duration was supported empirically (e.g., Buffardi, 1971; Goldfarb & Goldstone, 1963; Gray, 1982; Mo, 1971; Underwood, 1975).

Ornstein's second inference, that duration estimates increase with increases in the complexity of information processing, has been supported by some studies (e.g. Underwood, 1975; Underwood & Swain, 1973), but refuted by others (e.g., Curton & Lordahl, 1974; Hicks & Brandige, 1974; Zakay, 1989; Zakay, Nitzan, & Glicksohn, 1983; Zakay & Fallach, 1984). These later studies report a decrease in duration estimates with increases in the complexity of information processing. The storage-size model cannot account for these contradictory findings. It was also criticized by Block (1990) because it uses vague and unmeasurable terms like *storage size* or *stimulus complexity*.

The contextual change model claims that estimates of duration are based on the number of changes observed during an interval, or in Fraisse's (1963) words: "Psychological duration is composed of psychological changes" (p. 219). This model assumes that alternating cognitive operations increase the sense of subjectively experienced change, and in consequence increase the subjective experience of duration. Similarly, Block (1978, 1989, 1980) suggested that estimated duration is related to the amount of change in cognitive context, an hypothesis that was supported by Block and Reed (1978). An elaboration of the change model is the segmentation model (Poynter, 1983, 1989; Poynter & Homma, 1983). Poynter suggested that retrospective judgment of a filled interval might produce longer estimates than a relatively empty one, not because of the amount of processing or storage space the intervening events require but because filler events might serve as significant markers that segment experience. Processing these events might generate temporal referents in memory with which to reconstruct the duration of the time period. According to Poynter's view, what Fraisse referred to as changes and Block and Reed as contextual changes are events that segment the experience and provide subjective referents for the estimation of the passage of time. Poynter (1983) and Poynter and Homma (1983) found that even when task-complexity level and required level of information processing were kept constant, the more an interval was segmented by meaningful stimuli, so estimates of subjective duration increased. The findings suggest that segmentation and mental load are two different factors that influence separately the cognitive processes responsible for the subjective experience of duration (Zakay & Feldman, 1991).

The attentional model was presented by Frankenhaeuser (1959) and Priestly (1988), and later on elaborated by Hicks et al. (1977) and Zakay (1989). According to this model, subjective duration is related to the degree of attention that one is devoting to the passage of time itself. A cognitive timer is posited that requires mental energy for its "operation." This energy is obtained whenever one is paying attention to the passage of time itself. Any time such a mental event is taking place, subjective "time units" are recorded in the cognitive timer. When one is asked to estimate an interval, the number of subjective "time units" accumulated in the cognitive timer are translated into a duration estimate. The more attention is devoted to the passage of time itself, the more subjective "time units" are recorded in the cognitive timer and the longer the estimated subjective duration. Because attentional resources are limited, the more resources are demanded for performing a task the less attention is left for energizing the cognitive timer. Thus, a negative relationship between information-processing load required during a target interval and its subjective duration is predicted. This prediction was supported empirically by those studies (mentioned earlier) refuting the storage-size model, as well as by many more (e.g., Thomas & Cantor, 1978).

The concepts "cognitive timer" and "attention to the passage of time" were criticized as being unclear by Block (1990) and hence in need of further clarification. One way of extending this idea is by assuming that somewhere in working memory a counter[1] registers the number of times within a given interval that awareness to the passage of time takes place, like when one is asking one's self, "what time is it?" or "how long have I been doing this?" or "how much time should I wait until . . . ?" or "when will I finish this?", and so forth (Zakay, 1990). Any time such an event takes place, a registration is made in the cognitive counter. Attention to the passage of time is evoked whenever the time dimension becomes relevant and important, like when a time pressure exists. An increased sensitivity to time's cues and a "time-seeking" behavior are the behavioral manifestation of attention to time.

In Search of the Correct Model

The change model predicts a positive linear relationship between the number of contextual changes occurring during an interval and its estimated duration. The mechanism that is responsible here is the recording of changes in memory. An opposing prediction is derived from the attentional model, namely, a negative linear relationship between task complexity and information-processing load and the length of subjective duration. This prediction is based on the assumed characteristics of the cognitive timer. Because both predictions were empirically supported, it seems as if there is no escape from the conclusion that none of the approaches alone is sufficient.

A model in which elements of the two opposing approaches were integrated

---

[1]The idea of the counter is similar to the French philosopher Bergson's (1950) idea, about a register in which time is being inscribed. A similar idea was suggested as well by Berlyne (1966).

was proposed by Thomas and Weaver (1975). They assumed that a stimulus is analyzed by two processors: a timer P(T), which processes temporal information, and an information processor, P(I), which processes nontemporal information. Attention is divided between P(T) and P(I), according to the nature of the task and the information-processing load that is required for its performance. Subjective time is a function of both P(I) and P(T), where the weights assigned to each processor are a function of the amount of attentional resources allocated to it. The problem with this model is that unless the conditions that determine the division of attention between P(T) and P(I) are clearly defined, it cannot help in resolving the conflict between the contradicting findings.

The Contextual Approach

The solution to this puzzling situation lies in viewing time estimation as a context-dependent process. Many investigators have noted that subjective time can be understood only by taking into account the factors that determine the context within which it is measured (e.g., Allan, 1979; Clausen, 1950; Fraisse, 1984; Wallace & Rabin, 1960; Zakay, 1990). Block (1989) argued that a complete understanding of any kind of temporal experience is possible only by considering complex interactions among all the relevant contextual factors. Hicks, Miller, and Kinsbourne (1976) listed the following factors as influencing subjective estimates: (1) method of time estimation, (2) duration of estimated interval, (3) the nature of processing required during the estimated interval, and (4) the nature of the measurement paradigm—for example, a prospective paradigm in which the subject knows in advance that he or she will be required to estimate the elapsed time, or a retrospective paradigm in which the subject is told to do so only after the target interval is over. Block (1985, 1989) added to the list the following contextual factors: (1) the kind of temporal behavior involved, (2) the characteristics of the time period that a person experiences, and (3) the characteristics of the person and his/her activity during the target interval. It appears likely that the factors that determine the selection of either P(T) or P(I) as the relevant processor on which to base subjective time might be found among these two lists of factors. The most appropriate one seems to be the measurement paradigm.

Prospective versus Retrospective Time Estimations

Block (1974) referred to prospective duration as an experienced duration in contrast with retrospective duration that he called *remembered duration*. Hicks et al. (1976) suggested that time judgments in a retrospective paradigm are proportional to the amount of content retrieved from an interval rather than to the amount of processing performed during it. The attentional model was supported empirically only for prospective time estimates (Hicks et al., 1977; Zakay et al., 1983). Zakay (1990) argued that retrospective estimations must rely heavily on data stored in long-term memory because the estimator is not aware during the target interval itself of the need to pay attention to the passage of time. As a result, there is a need to look post factum for traces of relevant information that can enable time estimations. Under a prospective paradigm, on the other hand, an ongoing awareness to the passage of time exists, and relevant temporal information can be accumulated in the cognitive timer P(T). This information can be directly retrieved and used for making the time estimation. Hence it seems that prospective and retrospective times should be treated as products of different cognitive processes.

Resource Allocation Model of Time Estimation

Zakay (1989) proposed a resource allocation model of time estimation. This is an elaboration of the Thomas and Weaver (1975) model on the one hand and the contextual approach on the other. A basic assumption of the model is that attentional resources are divided among all tasks that the organism must perform, with more resources allocated to tasks of higher internal priority (Kahaneman, 1973). Time estimation is another cognitive task that consumes attentional resources and, as such, is in competition for resources with other tasks. In the context of prospective time judgment, high priority is assigned to the time estimation task, and as a result more resources are allocated to P(T). Because of this, temporal information that accumulates in P(T) in real time is available and is meaningful for making time estimations, and hence, P(T) becomes the sole source of prospective time estimation. In the context of retrospective time judgment, priority is given to P(I). Temporal information might also be registered in P(T), but this information is casual and not available for making the time estimation. Hence information produced by P(I) and stored in memory (including information about contextual changes) is available and used as the sole source of retrospective time estimation. The model can be summarized by equation (1):

$$SD = \alpha[P(T)] + \beta[P(I)] \qquad (1)$$

where: SD = subjective duration. β and α are weights assigned to the information existing in $P(T)$ and $P(I)$, respectively, at the moment of estimation ($\alpha + \beta = 1$)

$\alpha = 1$ under prospective conditions.

$\beta = 1$ under retrospective conditions.

The conclusions that are derived from this model are that (1) prospective time estimations are explained by the attentional model and (2) the relationship between it and level of information processing during a target interval should be negative and linear. On the other hand, retrospective time estimations are explained by the storage-size and the contextual change models. The relationship between retrospective estimations and level of information-processing load during a target interval should be positive and linear. Empirical evidence in support of the resource allocation model was provided by Zakay (1989), Zakay, Meran, and Ben-Shalom (1989), and Zakay and Tsal (1989). Another prediction of this model is that, contrary to the filled time illusion, prospective estimations of empty time should be longer than of filled time. The reason for this is that, during an empty interval, the level of information-processing load is minimal and hence most of the available resources should be allocated to P(T). This prediction was supported empirically by Zakay et al. (1983).

It can be concluded that the resource allocation model resolves the puzzling situation created by what seemed to be contradictory results supporting either one or the other of the two opposing models.

Decision Making Under Time Stress and Time Perception

Zakay (1990) made the distinction between perceived and declared estimation paradigms. It was argued that what really counts is not what is the declared paradigm according to experimenter's instructions but what is the subjective paradigm as perceived by subjects. What counts is the existence of any contextual elements that can create, from the subject's standpoint, expectations or an hypothesis related to the passage of time. Zakay (1990) listed some of these contextual elements. One element is the inducement of time stress, which might attract subject's attention to the passage of time. Another contextual element is an occupation with the passage of time, caused by the very nature of the task subjects are asked to cope with. The existence of either of these two related elements in a situation induces a situation comparable to the subjective prospective paradigm. Decision making is actually taking place under time stress only when decision makers are aware of and occupied with the passage of time. This is true not only in cases of laboratory experiments but in cases of real-life situations as well. Thus studies, manipulating deadlines to induce time stress, create a situation in which subjects are engaged in prospective time estimation. For example, Zakay and Wooler (1984) asked subjects in a time stress group to make decisions within 15 seconds. There is no doubt that, given such instructions, subjects keep asking themselves, "How much time is left," or "How am I doing with time," etc., suggesting that attention is divided between the passage of time and the decision process. Hence, we may suggest that when decision makers are aware of the time limit within which they must reach a decision, they automatically shift to the performance of two simultaneous cognitive tasks: decision making and time estimation under a perceived prospective paradigm. The result is a typical condition of divided attention; the more resources are allocated for the time estimation process, the less resources are left for the decision process. This analysis is reasonable both under the assumptions of limited resources models of attention (e.g., Kahanemen, 1973) and multiple resources models (e.g., Navon & Gopher, 1979), because both time estimation and decision processes are competing for common resources like working memory. It is not surprising, then, that time estimation was suggested as a potential method for measuring workload (Wickens, 1984). It can be concluded that decision making under time stress is actually decision making with limited resources.

The noxious impact of limited resources on cognitive performance in various domains is well documented (Wickens, 1984). Dichotic listening experiments (e.g., Broadbent, 1982; Cherry, 1953) showed that the ability of people to process two simultaneous messages is impaired as compared with the processing of only one message. However, even if parallel processing is assumed to be possible, it "either stops or is greatly attenuated at the point in the processing sequence at which selection of a discrete action is called for" (Wickens, 1984, p. 286). This conclusion, which is based on several empirical findings (e.g., Duncan, 1980; Moray & O'Brien, 1967; Moray et al., 1976), suggests that a breakdown in parallel processing occurs at the moment of decision making.

A model incorporating some of the previously mentioned ideas is presented in Figure 1.

According to the model, time stress is a product of either real-time constraints or because of a subjective perception of time stress due to personality traits or managerial style. The outcomes are similar because in both cases a problem of resource limitation arises. The model illustrates why simple and complex tasks are affected differentially by time stress.

An examination of the symptoms of decision making under time stress can easily lead to the conclusion that they reflect either errors caused by limited resources (i.e., forgetting important data or negligent information search and processing) or specific strategies (like filtration) adapted by the cognitive system to cope with the shortage of resources. The preference given by decision makers under time stress to the utilization of nonlinear, noncompensatory strategies can be explained by such strategies being cognitively simpler than linear compensatory ones (Einhorn, 1970).

If indeed, the model suggested here has the capability for explaining at least some of the characteristics of decision making under time stress, then some considerations regarding research methodologies in this area are in place. Zakay (1990) suggested that time perception is contingent upon contextual factors, such as the time estimation paradigm, external cues of time, and demand characteris-

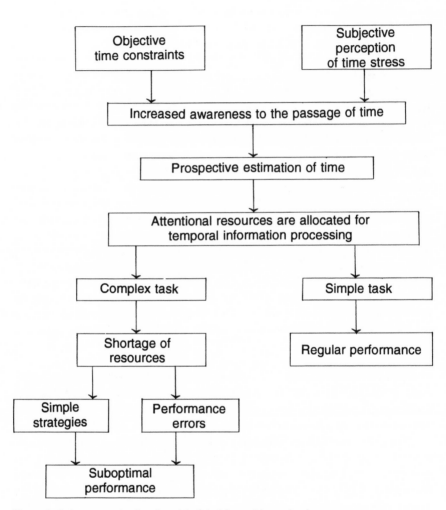

Figure 1. A time perception based model of decision making under time stress.

tics related to time. It follows that all these variables should be well controlled in time stress experiments because the subjective perception of time stress has similar outcomes to those of external time constraints.

The proposed model, also has interesting implications for training decision makers to cope with time stress. As mentioned earlier, Zakay and Wooler (1984) found that traditional training was not useful. It can be argued that such training is irrelevant or even counterproductive because the core of the problem is not an optimal utilization of rational strategies, but rather the decision maker's inability to allocate enough attentional resources to the decision process while overcoming the automatic occupation with the passage of time. Zakay and Tsal (1989) obtained some empirical findings supporting the feasibility of a training, aimed at a better resource allocation policy. Specific training methods, based on this idea, should be developed for decision making. Some words of caution are, however, needed. Although time estimation processes are assumed to operate whenever decisions are made under time limitation, time estimation is only one of the factors influencing decisions' optimalities. Hence, by dealing with time estimation, decisions' optimalities should be improved, but not all the effects of time stress are expected to be eliminated. Furthermore, individual differences are probably playing a significant role in transforming time limitations into time stress. Some people might even benefit and do better when a deadline is imposed (e.g., Christensen-Szalanski, 1980). Nevertheless, people showing a behavioral pattern known as "Type A behavior pattern" (Friedman and Rosenman, 1974) are prone to the harassed effects of time limits and might benefit from "resource allocation" training.

Further research should be conducted in order to validate the model presented above. This could be achieved by holding the objective time available to complete a decision constant, but at the same time manipulating factors that are known to either influence directly time perception processes or to increase awareness of the passage of time. If such manipulations produce a change in decision-making behavior consistent with those reported under time stress, then the changes could be attributed to the variations in time perception processes.

The model proposed in the present chapter has the potential to supply a consistent explanation for the impact of time stress on decision making and to contribute for the development of appropriate research methodologies and training methods in this domain.

References

Allan, L. G. (1979). The perception of time. *Perception and Psychophysics, 26,* 340–354.

Aschoff, J. (1984). Circadian timing. In J. Gibbon & L. Allan (Eds.), *Timing and time perception* (pp. 442–468). New York: New York Academy of Science.

Ben-Zur, H., & Breznitz, S. I. (1981). The effect of time pressure on risky choice behavior. *Acta Psychologica, 47,* 89–104.

Bergson, H. (1950). *Time and free will* (F. L. Pogson, trans.). London: George Allen & Unwin.

Berlyne, D. E. (1966). Effects of spatial order and inter item interval complexity. *Memory & Cognition, 6,* 320–326.

Block, R. A. (1974). Memory and the experience of duration in retrospect. *Memory & Cognition, 2,* 153–160.

Block, R. A. (1978). Remembered duration: Effects of event and sequence complexity. *Memory & Cognition, 6,* 320–326.

Block, R. A. (1985). Contextual coding in memory: Studies of remembered duration. In J. A. Michon & J. L. Jackson (Eds.), *Time, mind and behavior* (pp. 169–178). Berlin: Springer-Verlag.

Block, R. A. (1989). Experiencing and remembering time: Affordance, context and cognition. In I. Levin & D. Zakay (Eds.), *Time and human cognition: A life span perspective* (pp. 333–364). Amsterdam: North Holland.

Block, R. A. (1990). Models of psychological time. In R. A. Block (Ed.), *Cognitive models of psychological time* (pp. 1–36). Hillsdale, NJ: Erlbaum.

Block, R. A., & Reed, M. A. (1978). Remembered duration: Evidence for a contextual change hypothesis. *Journal of Experimental Psychology: Human Learning and Memory, 4,* 656–665.

Broadbent, D. E. (1982). Task combination and selective intake of information, *Acta Psychologica, 50,* 253–290.

Buffardi, L. (1971). Factors affecting the filled-duration illusion in the auditory, tactual and visual modalities. *Perception & Psychophysics, 10,* 292–294.

Cherry, C. (1953). Some experiments on the reception of speech with one and with two ears. *Journal of the Accoustical Society of America, 25,* 975–979.

Christensen-Szalanski, J. (1980). A further examination of the selection of problem solving strategies: The effects of deadlines and analytic aptitudes. *Organizational Behavior and Human Performance, 25,* 107–122.

Clausen, J. (1950). An evaluation of experimental methods of time judgment. *Journal of Experimental Psychology, 40,* 756–761.

Coren, S., Porac, C., & Ward, L. M. (1984). *Sensation and perception* (2nd ed.). New York: Academic Press.

Curton, E. D., & Lordahl, D. S. (1974). Attentional focus and arousal in time estimation. *Journal of Experimental Psychology, 103,* 861–867.

Duncan, J. (1980). The locus of interference in the perception of simultaneous stimuli. *Psychological Review, 87,* 272–300.

Einhorn, H. J. (1970). The use of nonlinear noncompensatory models in decision making. *Psychological Bulletin, 73,* 221–230.

Fraisse, P. (1963). *The psychology of time* (J. Leith, trans.). New York: Harper & Row.

Fraisse, P. (1984). Perception and estimation of time. *Annual Review of Psychology, 35,* 1–36.

Frankenhaeuser, M. (1959). *Estimation of time: An experimental study.* Stockholm: Almqvist & Wiksell.

Friedman, M., & Rosenman, R. H. (1974). *Type A behavior and your heart.* New York: Knopf.

Goldfard, J. L., & Goldstone, S. (1963). Time judgment: A comparison of filled and unfilled durations. *Perceptual and Motor Skills, 16,* 376.

Gray, C. (1982). Duration differences: Attentional demand or time error? *Perception, 11,* 97–102.

Hicks, R. E., & Bradige, R. (1974). Judgment of temporal duration while processing verbal and physiognomic stimuli. *Acta Psychologica, 38,* 447–453.

Hicks, R. E., Miller, G. W., & Kinsbourne, M. (1976). Prospective and retrospective judgments of time as a function of amount of information processed. *American Journal of Psychology, 89,* 719–730.

Hicks, R. E., Miller, G. W., Gaes, G., & Bierman, K. (1977). Concurrent processing demands and the experience of time-in-passing. *American Journal of Psychology, 90,* 431–446.

Holsti, O. R. (1971). Crises, stress and decision-making. *International Social Science Journal, 23,* 53–67.

Janis, I. L. (1982). Decision making under stress. In L. Goldberger & S. Breznitz (Eds.), *Handbook of stress* (pp. 69–80). New York: The Free Press.

Kahaneman, D. (1973). *Attention and effort*. New York: Prentice Hall.

Kahaneman, D., Slovic, P., & Tversky, A. (Eds.). (1982). *Judgment under uncertainty: Heuristics and biases*. New York: Cambridge University Press.

Keinan, G. (1987). Decision making under stress: Scanning of alternatives under controllable and uncontrollable threats. *Journal of Personality and Social Psychology, 52*, 639–644.

Michon, J. A. (1985). Studies on subjective duration II: Subjective time measurement during tasks with different information content. *Acta Psychologica, 24*, 205–219.

Mo, S. S. (1971). Judgment of temporal duration as a function of numerosity. *Psychonomic Science, 24*(2), 67–68.

Moray, N., Fitter, M., Ostry, D., Favreau, D., & Nagy, V. (1976). Attention to pure tones. *Quarterly Journal of Experimental Psychology, 28*, 271–285.

Moray, N., & O'Brien, T. (1967). Signal detection theory applied to selective listening. *Journal of the Accoustical Society of America, 42*, 765–772.

Navon, D., & Gopher, D. (1979). On the economy of the human processing system. *Psychological Review, 86*, 214–255.

Ornstein, R. E. (1969). *On the experience of time*. Middlesex, England: Penguin.

Payne, J. W. (1982). Contingent decision behavior. *Psychological Bulletin, 93*, 382–402.

Poynter, D. G. (1983). Duration judgment and the segmentation of experience. *Memory & Cognition, 11*, 77–82.

Poynter, D. G. (1989). Inferring time's passage. In I. Levin & D. Zakay (Eds.), *Time and human cognition: A life span perspective* (pp. 305–332). Amsterdam: North Holland.

Poynter, D. G., & Homma, D. (1983). Duration judgment and the experience of change. *Perception and Psychophysics, 23*, 548–560.

Priestly, J. B. (1968). *Man and time*. New York: Dell.

Rothstein, H. G. (1986). The effects of time pressure on judgement in multiple cue probability learning. *Organizational Behavior and Human Decision Processes, 37*, 83–92.

Smock, C. D. (1955). The influence of psychological stress on the intolerance of ambiguity. *Journal of Abnormal Psychology, 50*, 177–188.

Svenson, O., & Edland, A. (1987). Change of preferences under time pressure: Choice and judgments. *Scandinavian Journal of Psychology, 29*, 322–330.

Svenson, O., & Edland, A. (1989). Change of preferences under time pressure: Choices and judgments. *Scandinavian Journal of Psychology, 29*(4), 322–330.

Svenson, O., & Karlsson, G. (1989). Decision making, time horizons and risks in the very long time perspective. *Risk Analysis, 9*, 385–399.

Thomas, E. A., & Cantor, N. (1978). Interdependence between the processing of temporal and nontemporal information. In J. Requin (Ed.), *Attention and performance VII* (pp. 82–98). Hillsdale, NJ: Erlbaum.

Thomas, E. A., & Weaver, W. B. (1975). Cognitive processing and time perception. *Perception and Psychophysics, 17*, 363–367.

Underwood, G. (1975). Attention and the perception of duration during encoding and retrieval. *Perception, 2*, 191–198.

Underwood, G. S., & Swain, R. A. (1973). Selectivity of attention and the perception of duration. *Perception, 2*, 101–105.

Wallace, M., & Rabin, A. (1960). Temporal experience. *Psychological Bulletin, 57*, 213–235.

Wickens, C. D. (1984). *Engineering psychology and human performance*. Columbus: Charles E. Merrill.

Wright, P. (1974). The harassed decision maker: Time pressures, distractions and the use of evidence. *Journal of Applied Psychology, 59*, 555–561.

Zakay, D. (1985). Post-decisional confidence and conflict experienced in a choice process. *Acta Psychologica, 58*, 75–80.

Zakay, D. (1989). Subjective time and attentional resource allocation: An integrated model of time estimation. In I. Levin & D. Zakay (Eds.), *Time and human cognition: A life span perspective* (pp. 365–398). Amsterdam: North Holland.

Zakay, D. (1990). The evasive art of subjective time measurement: Some methodological dilemmas. In R. A. Block (Ed.), *Cognitive models of psychological time* (pp. 59–84). Hillsdale, NJ: Lawrence Erlbaum.

Zakay, D., & Fallach, E. (1984). Immediate and remote time estimation—a comparison. *Acta Psychologica, 57,* 69–81.

Zakay, D., & Feldman, T. (1991). *The role of segmentation and storage size in retrospective estimation.* Unpublished manuscript. Tel Aviv University.

Zakay, D., Meran, N., & Ben-Sahlom, H. (1989). Cognitive processes of time estimation [in Hebrew]. *Psychologica, 1,* 104–112.

Zakay, D., Nitzan, D., & Glicksohn, J. (1983). The influence of task difficulty and external tempo on subjective time estimation. *Perception and Psychophysics, 34,* 451–456.

Zakay, D., & Tsal, Y. (1989). Awareness of attention allocation and time estimation accuracy. *The Bulletin of the Psychonomic Society, 27,* 209–210.

Zakay, D., & Wooler, S. (1984). Time pressure, training and decision effectiveness. *Ergonomics, 27*(3), 273–284.

5

Time Pressure and Task Adaptation
Alternative Perspectives on Laboratory Studies

Donald MacGregor

Introduction

Given the tremendous importance of time as an organizing principle for behavior, it is surprising how little attention it has been given as a factor in decision making and choice. Indeed, by definition, to decide means to arrive at a conclusion or make up one's mind. Thus, decision making is rooted in the concept of time, and time is one of the primary resources that decision making and choice draw upon.

Inherent in the relationship between time and choice is the notion that better choices require more time. "Considered judgment," "careful deliberation," and "a timely conclusion" imply that the quality of one's decisions and judgments are reflected in the time afforded the process, carry the image of incubation in which information and values are carefully evaluated, and appropriate tradeoffs are made.

In contrast with the notion of time as a resource that facilitates decision making and choice, is time as a scarce commodity to be used wisely. The decision maker, for example, who uses too much time in making up his/her mind is labeled *indecisive,* implying a deficiency in decision-making skills; a wasting of time that perhaps could be better used for other purposes.

Donald MacGregor • Decision Research, 1201 Oak Street, Eugene, Oregon 97401.
Time Pressure and Stress in Human Judgment and Decision Making, edited by Ola Svenson and A. John Maule. Plenum Press, New York, 1993.

Thus a conflict arises: A good and prudent individual consciously allocates time to making decisions and choices, but not too much time. The establishment of a clear frame of time is an important element of "good" decision making, and a good decision maker manages time as an allocatable resource.

Given this model, all decisions and choices occur under time pressure, within a time frame that has a deadline, either self-imposed by an individual, or established by the external context in which the behavior occurs. The time frame is initiated by internal events (e.g., a perceived need to make a decision), external events (e.g., task demands of an occupation), or by both.

Despite the importance of understanding the relationship between decision making and temporal context, relatively few empirical studies are available that have directly addressed the effects of time pressure on judgment and choice. As will be discussed below, these studies have largely demonstrated time pressure effects in the context of laboratory tasks, but have provided little basis for distinguishing between alternative models of decision making that embody chronometric elements. This chapter explores alternative theoretical perspectives that may be useful in accounting for the time pressure effects that have been observed and presents a preliminary model for how transitory time pressure effects may occur as part of an individual's adapting to changes in task demands brought on by constraining time availability.

Manipulations of Time Pressure

Experimental studies form the core of what we know about the effects of time pressure on judgment and choice. It is important, therefore, to examine what constitutes time pressure in the context of laboratory studies.

We do not have a theory that chronometrically decomposes decision or choice processes. Experimental studies that examine time pressure effects have difficulty establishing how much to constrain time for the observation of task degradation. Usually, the time constraints needed are established through trial and error. The procedures used for four such studies are reproduced here to give the reader a clearer sense of how time pressure conditions have been established.

> During the design of the experiment various time constraints on the problem were tested. It was determined that a subject could obtain the optimum solution within a five minute time limit. (This was determined to be true expost given that approximately half of the subjects within the five minute treatment attained a performance of 99% of the optimum solution or better). Less time, e.g. 2 to 3 minutes, appeared to induce excessive strain and seriously impair performance. (Benbasat & Dexter, 1986)

> Subjects took about 50 seconds, on average, when under no time pressure in the pilot studies. Those pilot studies revealed that 15 seconds represented substantial time pressure for the subjects. (Payne, Bettman, & Johnson, 1988)

> The first group made the 36 decisions without any time pressure, while the second group was allowed only 20 seconds for each decision (20 seconds having been found in a pilot study to constitute severe time pressure). (Zakay, 1985)

> The choice of these durations was based on a pilot study which showed that average time taken for completing the experimental task by means of the MAU model was 60 s. (Zakay & Wooler, 1984)

Other important studies documenting time pressure effects do not specify how the time intervals were chosen, but also do not provide a theoretical rationale. For example,

> For time pressure manipulation three time values were chosen: 8 sec (High), 16 sec (Medium), and 32 sec (Low). (Ben Zur & Breznitz, 1981)

> The time pressure treatment required the subject to respond to each problem within 6 s. (Rothstein, 1986)

Thus, "time pressure" is the time constraint placed on a task that makes people feel time pressured. Although the effects that have been observed using this experimental paradigm are important, the lack of a time-based theoretical rationale for decision and choices processes is discomforting.

An alternative is to justify a time pressure manipulation on the basis of theory, as well as previous research results. The following rationale from Wright and Weitz (1977) provides an excellent example.

> Insight on how the 10-seconds or 40-seconds per option compares with natural decision times consumers display is gained from introspection and from experiments on decision times. First try introspecting. The stimulus profiles in this study had three attributes, so consider a decision among four such products. At 10 seconds per product, a person has 40 seconds to evaluate each one and choose. The reader can sit quietly for 40 seconds to determine how much deliberation is possible in that period. At 40 seconds per product, he has two minutes, 40 seconds to decide. A reader who tries thinking about a four-option, three-attribute problem steadily for that period will appreciate how liberal it is. The timps subjects took in experiments on complex choices are also relevant. Kiesler's (1966) children togk from 3 to 11 seconds to choose between two or four branded candy bars. Hendrick et al.'s (1968) young men took from 5 to 15 seconds per necktie in choosing from sets of four neckties. Pollay (1970) had men choose between four R & D projects for a firm. Excluding reading times, they took from 60 to 85 seconds per project, depending on how many attributes were displayed. Jacoby et al. (1974) found that women average from 14 to 40 seconds per concept in deciding between four-attribute packaged food concepts, depending on how many were available. So the time conditions used in the current study seem to represent points within the range of times people invest on everyday decisions of many types. (Wright & Weitz, 1977, Footnote 4)

Taxonomic work is not generally considered one of the more attractive research areas in the behavioral and cognitive sciences. Unfortunately, however, without taxonomies we have no systematic means of knowing how to interpret a broad range of experimental studies. The same is true of research on time pressure: Without a taxonomy to serve as a map of the temporal framework underlying decision and choice processes, we are easily left with a collection of laboratory effects that are difficult to translate into specific predictions about the conditions under which time constraints will degrade decision processes and in what ways.

Constructed Decisions

One speculation is that time pressure effects are the result of accelerated information processing. Some years ago, Miller introduced the notion that information overload plays an important role in the quality of adaptation between an organism and its environment (Miller, 1960). He proposed that systems, including biological and social systems, respond to the demands of information overload by increasing their processing rate. At a point where further acceleration is not possible, the system employs several mechanisms to manage the overload. The mechanisms he identified included omission (temporary nonprocessing), error (processing information incorrectly), queing (delaying processing of some information), filtering, cutting categories (responding in more general ways), multichannel processing, and escape. It is important to recognize that Miller was attempting to account for decrements in information processing under overload across a broad range of system levels, from single cells to social systems.

His set of mechanisms were proposed as "adjustments" that a system makes to allow it to continue responding to incoming stimuli. In a sense, Miller proposed that a speed versus precision tradeoff occurs in which an organism accelerates its response rate at the cost of a higher error rate or, perhaps, incomplete information processing. This leads to the hypothesis that accelerating information processing, such as through time pressure, overloads one's capacity and introduces errors and omissions that result in systematic biases.

Although Miller's concepts are attractive explanations of the time pressure effects that have been observed in the laboratory, the acceleration hypothesis assumes that decision making is *constructive* and that people decompose decision problems into smaller, more manageable subtasks that are organized in time. Although some theories of judgment and choice have proposed staged models (e.g., Goldstein & Einhorn, 1987; Kahneman & Tversky, 1979), details of the temporal organization of the strategies people use to solve decision and choice problems remains unclear. People may simply work faster and do a poorer job, rather than work faster but complete only part of the task.

Events as Time Pressure Cues

Various theories of time perception have proposed that the passage of time is judged on the basis of the number of intervening events during an interval (e.g., Fraisse, 1963; Ornstein, 1969). The larger the number of events that occur within a given time period, the longer the period is judged to be. By implication, anything that increases the perception that a number of events have transpired will also increase one's perception of the length of the time period of those events. More simply put, when many events take place, a large amount of time must have passed.

Events, then, can serve as a cue for how rapidly time is passing. This could be extended to include cognitive events, such as the processing of information relevant to a decision or choice. If cognitive events are used as a basis for judging the passage of time, then increasing cognitive activity should increase the amount of time that an individual will perceive as passing (e.g., Block, 1978; Block & Reed, 1978). Under conditions where a fixed amount of time is allowed for decision making, increased cognitive activity may exacerbate a perception that time is being consumed. Thus, the time-pressured individual experiences an increase in the perception of time pressure due to the increase in the number of cognitive events taking place.

Time pressure, in this sense, is experienced as a disturbance in one's internal clock or ability to judge the passage of time. Urgency is exacerbated by mental activity; the more the processing of information is accelerated, the greater the sense of time pressure. This hypothesis predicts that the *perception* of time pressure is not linear with veridical time but increases exponentially as deadlines draw near.

An alternative viewpoint, directly derived from the study of cognitive workload, is that time pressure effects are the result of the overload people experience associated with having to keep track of time (see Zakay, this volume). The concept of workload has been used to account for decrements in task performance when individuals are given multiple tasks to perform (see Wickens, 1991, for a review). One way in which cognitive workload can be assessed is "primary task interference" (e.g., Moray, 1979). In this paradigm, performance on a primary task degrades in quality as the demands of a secondary task are imposed. If people are attempting to monitor time availability when the demand to do so is created, motivated either by themselves or the demands of a context, then keeping track of time is a secondary task that may compete for cognitive resources with the primary task. Unfortunately, we know relatively little about the chronology of most decision-making tasks, and so it is difficult to make predictions about how temporal demands would induce monitoring and effect decision task performance, though we can use a primary–secondary task model to explain time pressure effects after they are observed.

Time and Task Adaptation

Empirical studies to date on time-pressured decision making and choice have focused on the perturbations in these processes when time constraints are relatively severe (e.g., Ben Zur & Breznitz, 1981; Rothstein, 1986). Indeed, the analysis presented in this chapter has argued that time pressure as conceptualized in the majority of laboratory studies is a condition under which an individual will adopt a steady-state strategy for managing a decision task that is different from the strategy they would use if more time was available. These strategies include, for example, conservatism and preference for negative information (Ben Zur & Breznitz, 1981) and underutilization of cues in a multicue judgment context (Rothstein, 1986). A key element in producing time pressure effects is that they must be persistent and observed repeatedly. Thus, if an individual is able to reestablish a compensatory strategy, for example, after the imposition of a particular degree of time constraint, then a time pressure effect is taken not to be present.

An alternative conceptualization of time pressure is that degradation in decision and choice processes occurs under lesser degrees of time constraint, at transitions in task tempo. Tempo transitions occur when performance demands are changed in a very short time frame, much as occurs in a supervisory control context where an operator spends large amounts of time monitoring information but must shift rapidly into responding to sudden changes in the state of a system (e.g., Sheridan & Ferrell, 1981). Consider the model shown in Figure 1.

During an initial time period, decision task tempo is fairly low, and an individual responding to task requirements will have adapted to this tempo. Task demands will be met with strategies that are most effective, or for which the individual has received training. In Figure 1, this is characterized as "high task performance". This can be measured by one of several indices depending on the task, including error rate, precision or accuracy, departures from optimality, and choice of task strategy. With a sudden transition to a new task tempo, a period of performance degradation occurs during which the strategies and information-processing demands appropriate for the initial tempo are inappropriate and/or ineffective. As performance falls, new task strategies are adopted to cope with the change in task tempo. This is an adaptation period, during which task efficiency increases as a function of how well the individual is able to identify and implement new response strategies. Task efficiency will return to its previous level according to several factors, including (a) the amount of change in task tempo, (b) the amount of time over which the change in tempo occurs, and (c) the availability of alternative response strategies.

This model assumes that people are capable of adaptation to changes in the amount of time they have to perform decision and choice tasks. Miller's model of adaptation to information overload (1960), for example, is rooted in the notion that people recognize, though perhaps at an unconscious level, when temporal resources are scarce and alter their information processing. Other research, more directly related to decision making, has found that sensitivities of preferences to time availability are brought about by changes in information-processing strategies (e.g., Svenson & Edland, 1987).

The acceleration model of information processing under time constraints (Miller, 1960) suggests that, within some limited boundaries, people should be able to return to a prior strategy after initially adopting an alternative strategy in response to time pressure. Thus, it is possible that a compensatory strategy of

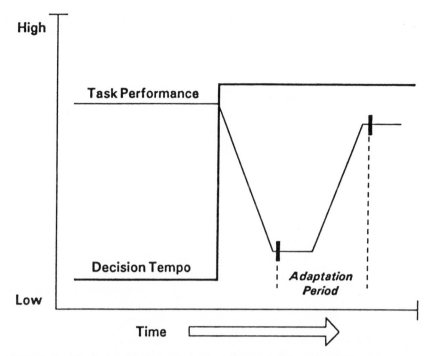

Figure 1. Hypothesized model of tempo transition effect on decision task performance.

decision making, for example, may be returned to under some time pressure conditions, after a noncompensatory strategy was selected for reasons of urgency.

Alternatively, once a strategy shift is made, the new strategy may be adhered to without reconsideration. For example, if an individual uses a compensatory strategy without time pressure, and a noncompensatory strategy is employed once time constraints are imposed, will they continue to use the noncompensatory strategy if time constraints are now relaxed? If the choice of a response strategy is a function of the time available for using it, then we would expect a return to the prior strategy. This assumes that people engage in some type of meta-analysis of the information-processing strategies they use for solving decision and choice problems. The overwhelming conclusion from research on human judgment and decision making is that people have a tendency to rely on relatively simple cognitive strategies (e.g., Kahneman, Slovic, & Tversky, 1982). This suggests that they would not return to a more complex strategy after adopting a more simple one in response to time pressure.

The potential for time pressure to act as a cue for response strategy selection is a critical issue in applied settings where time constraints vary widely. Ideally, an individual in such environments would adopt the *best* strategy he/she could given the time available and would return to a better strategy as time restraints were relaxed. However, anchoring on a response strategy that was adaptive for a relatively high-time-pressure situation may result in poor performance during subsequent time intervals that would permit the use of a different strategy. Whether people are reflexive when adopting decision and choice strategies in response to time pressures remains open to question.

Discussion

One way to determine the parameters or components of an unknown system is to expose it to increasing degrees of stress and observe how it degrades or changes its operation. Presumably, the more fragile elements of the system fail or change how they operate first, followed by the more resilient ones until the system ceases to function to any meaningful degree. The research to date on time pressure has been carried out much in this spirit; human decision makers have had imposed on them increasing time constraints such that their ability to act in the same way they would if they had more time for deliberation is so compromised as to be observable in their performance. What we have found so far is evidence that decision processes are perturbed by increasing degrees of time pressure. It is probably fair to say that this is not a surprising finding, though it does confirm our ideas that information processing associated with decision and choice is adaptive to task characteristics.

Ideally, our future research into the impact of time pressures on decision making would develop along at least two potential lines. The first is a better understanding of the chronology associated with decision processes. Though we have demonstrations that time pressure effects occur, we have no good theory that describes the temporal characteristics of decision processes. Such a theory would allow us to make better predictions of the components of decision making that are most likely to be effected by constraining the amount of time that decision makers have for information processing and strategy construction. Bettman, Johnson, and Payne (1990) have used componential analysis to identify the relative effort associated with subtasks that are a part of decision strategies. This paradigm could be used to study the chronometric properties of decision making as well, perhaps leading to a linkage between the effort required of decision task components and the effects of time pressure on component utilization in decision strategy selection.

A second line of research might lead to a better understanding of the links between time pressure effects and higher-order psychological processes. In an elegant speculative analysis of the psychological experience of time, Toda (1975) noted that an important role of a functioning cognitive system is the preservation or continuation of the individual in his/her environment. According to Toda, cognition is the means by which our identity is preserved over time. If this is so, then temporal resources are important not only for the information processing associated with decision task performance but also for psychodynamic functioning. Thus, the anxiety associated with time-pressured decision making may be in part due to the potential inability to achieve one's goals in a situation and to the (partial) loss of ability to maintain one's identity. This suggests that individual differences in psychodynamic functioning and tolerance for stress may play an important role in mediating the effects of time pressure on decision making.

ACKNOWLEDGMENT. This research was supported by the National Science Foundation under contract SES-9013069 to Decision Research. I would like to thank Ola Svenson and an anonymous reviewer for comments on an earlier draft that contributed significantly to the chapter.

References

Allan, L. G. (1979). The perception of time. *Perception and Psychophysics, 26,* 340–354.

Ben Zur, H., & Breznitz, S. J. (1981). The effect of time pressure on risky choice behavior. *Acta Psychologica, 47,* 89–104.

Benbasat, I., & Dexter, A. S. (1986). An experimental investigation of the effectiveness of color-enhanced and graphical information presentation under varying time constraints. *Management Information Systems Quarterly, March,* pp. 59–83.

Bettman, J. R., Johnson, E. J., & Payne, J. W. (1990). A componential analysis of cognitive effort in choice. *Organizational Behavior and Human Decision Processes, 45,* 111–139.

Block, R. A. (1978). Remembered duration: Effects of event and sequence complexity. *Memory and Cognition, 6,* 320–326.

Block, R. A., & Reed, M. A. (1978). Remembered duration: Evidence for a contextual change hypothesis. *Journal of Experimental Psychology: Human Learning and Memory, 4,* 656–665.

Fraisse, P. (1963). *The psychology of time.* New York: Harper & Row.

Goldstein, W. M., & Einhorn, H. J. (1987). Expression theory and the preference reversal phenomena. *Psychological Review, 94,* 236–254.

Hendrick, C., Mills, J., & Kiesler, C. A. (1968). Decision time as a function of the number and complexity of equally attractive alternatives. *Journal of Personality and Social Psychology, 8,* 315–318.

Jacoby, J., Speller, D., & Kohn, C. (1974). Brand choice as a function of information load: A replication and extension. *Journal of Consumer Research, 1,* 33–42.

Kahneman, D., & Tversky, A. (1979). Prospect theory: An analysis of decision under risk. *Econometrica, 47,* 263–291.

Kahneman, D., Slovic, P., & Tversky, A. (1982). *Judgment under uncertainty: Heuristics and biases.* New York: Cambridge University Press.

Kiesler, C. A. (1966). Conflict and the number of choice alternatives. *Psychological Reports, 18,* 603–610.

Miller, J. G. (1960). Information input overload and psychopathology. *American Journal of Psychiatry, 116,* 695–704.

Moray, N. (1979). *Mental workload: Its theory and measurement.* New York: Plenum Press.

Ornstein, R. E. (1969). *On the experience of time*. London: Penguin Books.

Payne, J. W., Bettman, J. R., & Johnson, E. J. (1988). Adaptive strategy selection in decision making. *Journal of Experimental Psychology: Learning, Memory, and Cognition, 14,* 534–552.

Pollay, R. W. (1970). The structure of executive decisions and decision times. *Administrative Science Quarterly, 15,* 459–471.

Rothstein, H. G. (1986). The effects of time pressure on judgment in multiple cue probability learning. *Organizational Behavior and Human Decision Processes, 37,* 83–92.

Schwartz, D. R., & Howell, W. C. (1985). Optional stopping performance under graphic and numeric CRT formatting. *Human Factors, 27,* 433–444.

Sheridan, T. B., & Ferrell, W. R. (1981). *Man-machine systems: Information, control, and decision models of human performance*. Cambridge, MA: The MIT Press.

Svenson, O., & Edland, A. (1987). Change of preferences under time pressure: Choice and judgments. *Scandinavian Journal of Psychology, 28,* 322–330.

Toda, M. (1975). Time and the structure of human cognition. In J. T. Fraser & N. Lawrence (Eds.), *The study of Time. II* (pp. 314–324). New York: Springer-Verlag.

Wickens, C. D. (1991). *Engineering psychology and human performance* (2nd ed.). Glenview, IL: Scott, Foresman and Co.

Wright, P. (1974). The harassed decision maker: Time pressures, distractions, and the use of evidence. *Journal of Applied Psychology, 59,* 555–561.

Wright, P. L., & Weitz, B. (1977). Time horizon effects on product evaluation strategies. *Journal of Marketing Research, 14,* 429–443.

Zakay, D. (1985). Post-decisional confidence and conflict experienced in a choice process. *Acta Psychologica, 58,* 75–80.

Zakay, D., & Woller, S. (1984). Time pressure, training and decision effectiveness. *Ergonomics, 27,* 273–284.

6

State, Stress, and Time Pressure

A. John Maule and G. Robert J. Hockey

Introduction

Research investigating the effects of time pressure on judgment and decision making has tended to conceptualize the effects of time constraints in one of two ways. One approach has considered the imposition of a deadline as a stressor, emphasizing the mediating role of changes in affective state in influencing cognition (Maule & Mackie, 1990; Svenson & Edland, 1989). The second approach has assumed that time constraints are one among a number of task and environmental factors that are included in a cost/benefit determination of cognitive strategy (Payne, Bettman & Johnson, 1988; Payne, Johnson, Bettman, & Coupey, 1990). The aim of the present chapter is to critically evaluate these approaches and to consider them in the light of recent research on the effects of stress on cognition. To meet these aims, the chapter is structured in the following way. First, there is a brief discussion of a number of key methodological issues. This is followed by a brief and selective review of major approaches investigating the effects of time constraints on judgment and decision making. Finally, there is a review of Variable State Activation Theory (VSAT) (Hockey, 1986; Hockey, Briner, Tattersall, & Wiethoff, 1989; Hockey & Hamilton, 1983) and an analysis of how it may provide a unifying approach to develop our understanding of the effects of time constraints on judgment and decision making.

A. John Maule • School of Business and Economic Studies, University of Leeds, Leeds L52 9JT, England. **G. Robert J. Hockey** • Department of Psychology, University of Hull, Hull HU6 7RX, England.
Time Pressure and Stress in Human Judgment and Decision Making, edited by Ola Svenson and A. John Maule. Plenum Press, New York, 1993.

Methodological Issues

In this chapter time pressure is identified with the imposition of a time horizon or deadline for completing a task. Other definitions, for example, in terms of pacing, are not considered here, except in passing. We consider deadlines primarily in terms of long-term constraints over time use, based on effects that build up over many minutes or more. Such an emphasis means that in experimental situations associated with many relatively short decisions our concerns are with aspects that are emergent from the whole session. In contrast to this, the effects of pacing are more generally thought of in terms of an increased workload and the reduction of control in the short term.

In general, time pressure has been investigated by comparing the behavior of subjects on a task with and without a time limit. This methodology raises a number of issues. Though the detailed procedure for imposing time constraints has differed from study to study, most have adopted the same general format by identifying the average time taken to complete a task and then imposing a deadline, which is some fraction of this average time. Some studies have used just one time-constrained condition, others two or three (see Svenson & Edland, this volume, for a review). The rationale underlying the manipulation of deadlines has also differed. One group of studies has emphasized the affective changes that occur with the imposition of a deadline, arguing that as the stringency of the deadline increases so there may be changes in affective state, loosely referred to as either time pressure or time stress (Svenson & Edland, 1989). Intuitively, this distinction seems reasonable. Most of us have experienced mild time pressure in terms of increased urgency and can distinguish this from more extreme forms of pressure, often called time stress, involving affective changes that are more intense and negative. The former can be facilitative and may act as the spur we need to get a task completed. In the case of the latter, the stronger negative affective feelings may have a disruptive effect on behavior. Studies have attempted to measure changes in affective state by asking subjects to use self-assessment rating scales to judge their current state in terms of anxiety, perceived pressure, etc. However, not only have different studies used different scales, but these scales have been developed without reference to current theories of affect (e.g., Watson & Tellegen, 1985) and without any check on validity (see Mano, 1992 for a more detailed discussion of these criticisms). Until these issues are resolved, it is unlikely that we will be able to establish whether there are different time-pressured states, how we can distinguish these states, how we can induce these states experimentally, and whether they change the nature of judgment and decision making.

A second group of studies have interpreted deadlines in a very different way, assuming that they represent one among a number of task characteristics that determine the costs and benefits of using particular strategies. From this standpoint time is treated as a continuous variable that is incorporated into a cost/benefit calculation to determine decision strategy. The precise form of the cost/benefit calculations are unknown, making it impossible to determine by how much the time normally taken needs to be reduced in order to induce a change in strategy.

Thus, time pressure has been considered in two rather different ways. Unfortunately, neither of these has been developed in sufficient detail to allow us to determine, in precise terms, how people take account of time in the decision-making process. This makes it very difficult for researchers to identify how to vary deadlines in order to provide a comprehensive account of the effects of time pressure on judgment and decision making. Most studies have operationalized time pressure by adopting a deadline that is some fraction of the usual time to complete the task, without any clear justifications why any particular fraction is adopted. Unless we can develop a more comprehensive account of how time is incorporated into the decision process, it will not be possible to determine whether this way of operationalizing time pressure is appropriate. These issues are reconsidered in the concluding section of this chapter, following a discussion of a new approach based on VSAT.

Empirical Findings and Theoretical Developments

This section provides a brief outline of research investigating how time constraints change cognitive strategy in judgment and decision-making situations (for a full review, see Edland & Svenson, this volume). Maule and Mackie (1990) suggested that there have been three broad approaches, one describing strategy changes at a macrolevel, a second describing changes at a microlevel, and a third combining these two. Each approach is briefly considered below.

Macrostrategy Research

One group of studies has considered strategy changes at a macrolevel in terms of the use of formal decision rules (Svenson, 1979). In their extensive review of research on decision strategies Ford, Schmitt, Scheitman, Hults, and Doherty (1989) showed that the imposition of time constraints is one of a number of task characteristics that can induce a change in strategy, involving a switch from compensatory to noncompensatory rules (compensatory rules involve a global rating of each alternative that allows a tradeoff between attributes. Noncompensatory rules, on the other hand, do not allow tradeoffs, with alternatives being rejected as soon as they fail to meet an acceptable level on any attribute; see Maule & Svenson, this volume, for a fuller explanation of this distinction.)

This finding has been interpreted in the context of contingency theories of strategy selection (e.g., Beach & Mitchell, 1978). Strategies are adopted on the basis of a cost/benefit analysis, with costs determined by the resource implications of implementing the strategy and benefits in terms of the value accruing to the decision maker from implementing the strategy in the particular situation under test. Time constraints are assumed to alter the choice of strategy because the preferred strategy for any particular choice/benefit combination may be unable to be implemented in the time allowed. Under these circumstances the subject adapts by adopting the best strategy given the time constraint (Christensen-Szalanski, 1980). This approach assumes that people adapt to time pressure as they would to other variations in task characteristics (e.g., number of alternatives or attributes). Though the term *time pressure* is often used to describe the deadline condition, there is no suggestion that the changes in behavior should be attributed to changes in affective state induced by this condition, and associated with pressure or stress. In addition, the cost/benefit calculations at the heart of contingency theories are not sufficiently described to allow specific predictions about the change in strategy that follows any particular reduction in the time allowed for the decision. This makes the theory difficult to test and ill-equipped to provide a full explanation of time-pressure-related strategy changes.

Microstrategy Research

A second group of studies has considered strategy change at a microlevel in terms of Miller's (1960) suggestions that people have characteristic ways of adjusting to information overload. He described seven mechanisms of adjustment, though research on time pressure has tended to focus on just three: *filtering, omission,* and *acceleration.* Evidence for each of these modes of adjustment is rather equivocal. Filtering occurs when individuals neglect certain low-priority categories of information while continuing to process others. Evidence for filtering under time constraints was first reported by Wright (1974) using a regression analysis of human judgment. He reported findings indicating that subjects filtered in favor of negative information. Though this negativity effect has been replicated several times (e.g., Ben Zur & Breznitz, 1981), other researchers have found contradictory findings. Svenson, Edland, and Slovic (1990) and Edland (this volume) found filtering in favor of positive information whereas Maule and Mackie (1988) reported several studies, including one that was direct replication of Wright's experiment, without providing any evidence for filtering at all. Omission occurs when individuals completely ignore aspects of task information, for example, when they stop processing all task-related processing temporarily. Maule and Mackie (1990) found evidence for omission in a simple judgment and decision-making task. Finally, acceleration involves a general speeding up of mental activity in order to keep up with increasing task demands. Several studies have indicated that individuals adapt to time constraints using acceleration, for example, by increasing the rate of information search during the decision process (Ben Zur & Breznitz, 1981; Maule & Mackie, 1990; Payne et al., 1988).

Although there is evidence to suggest that individuals do indeed use these strategies of cognitive adjustment under time constraints, there are some important limitations with this approach. First, such adjustments have been inferred on a post-hoc basis rather than by identifying and testing a set of predictions about why, when, and how they might occur in particular decision situations. Second, the findings described show that people use these modes of adapting to time pressure on some occasions but not on others and that they may implement them in different ways (e.g., filtering is sometimes in favor of positive information, at other times in favor of negative information). Some explanations of these differences is needed. Third, there have been few attempts to extend the discussion and consider findings in the broader context of research on changes in cognitive strategy. Two recent studies have tried to address some of these issues. Svenson and Edland (1989) linked filtering to the broader issues of information utilization under stress, initially discussed by Easterbrook (1959). However, as we shall see below, there is a good deal of controversy concerning Easterbrook's analysis of the effects of stress and emotion on cognition, and this mode of theorizing may only add further confusion to our understanding of the effects of time constraints. Maule and Mackie (1990) adopted a different approach, emphasizing the importance of stress on cognitive strategy in terms of the cognitive patterning of stress states (Hockey & Hamilton, 1983). This theory assumes that stressors induce characteristic changes in state that affect the operation of particular cognitive components. Maule and Mackie (1990) argued that time constraints should be treated as a stressor and considered in terms of how they affect the cognitive components that underlie decision making. They used a computer-controlled decision task divided into a number of separate components, such as information search and combination of information. These were assumed to be corollaries of independent cognitive components underlying human decision making. Results indicated that subjects adapted to the imposition of time constraints by using the modes of cognitive adjustment identified by Miller (1960). However, the predominant mode of adjustment was different from component to component. They argued that different decision tasks involve these cognitive components to different degrees. If one component predominated for a particular type of decision task, the mode of adjustment most frequently used for that component would generalize to the task as a whole. This approach has the potential for explaining why and how the different modes of adapting are used in particular situations. The research is, however, at an early stage of development.

Overall the research reported in this section appears to be at a pretheoretical stage in that it is possible to describe some of the effects of time pressure, but not to explain why and how they occur.

Combination of the Two Approaches

Recent research by Payne and his associates has tried to link micro- and macroapproaches (Bettman, Johnson & Payne, 1990, Johnson & Payne, 1985; Payne, Bettman & Johnson, 1988). Though the primary focus has been on macrostrategies, each strategy was defined at the microlevel in terms of a set of hypothetical elementary information processes (EIPs) needed to implement the strategy in a particular decision situation. Following the logic of contingency theory (Beach & Mitchell, 1978), it was assumed that each strategy had a cost and value when used in a particular situation.

Bettman, Johnson, and Payne (1990) argued that cost should be considered in terms of the cognitive workload associated with resourcing the EIPs involved. Value was assessed by calculating the expected value (EV) of each choice alternative and assuming that the alternative with the highest EV was the optimal or best choice. The value of a particular strategy was represented in terms of the proportion of occasions that the strategy led to the same choice as maximization of EV. As this proportion increases, so the value of adopting the strategy was assumed to be greater.

Payne and his associates used both experimental and computer-simulation approaches to investigate the factors determining strategy adoption in a gambling task. The simulation indicated that under time constraints there was a general decrease in the value associated with all decision rules, though this decrease was much greater for more complex compensatory rules than simpler noncompensatory rules. Under time-constrained conditions, the rule associated with the highest value was one of the simpler noncompensatory ones that ensured that at least some information about each alternative was evaluated prior to choice. The particular noncompensatory rule that was associated with the highest value changed as a function of other characteristics of the task.

The experimental findings indicated that people had a hierarchy of ways of adapting to deadlines, varying as a function of the deadline stringency. First, following Miller's ideas discussed earlier, individuals tried to accelerate processing, while maintaining the same strategy. Second, if the constraint was more severe and acceleration not sufficient to meet these demands, filtering was used in order to reduce the overall information-processing load. Third, if the stringency of the deadline meant that both acceleration and filtering were not effective, subjects changed strategy in the direction of an increased use of noncompensatory rules. The change under time constraints often involved an increased use of decision rules indicated by the simulation as having the highest value in that situation. This suggests that such changes were adaptive. Payne et al. suggested that acceleration involved greater effort, but this was assumed to be compensated for by the increased benefit of using a strategy with a high expected value outcome. However, as the stringency of the deadline became greater, even with acceleration there was insufficient time to complete such a strategy, thereby reducing the likelihood that it would lead to a valuable outcome. This altered the cost/benefit calculations and led to a change in strategy to one that provided at least some information about each alternative.

This approach has contributed most to our understanding of time pressure. However, it is essentially a "cold" theory, assuming that changes in strategy are due solely to the outcome of cost/benefit calculations. It fails to take account of "hot" affective factors and in doing so overlooks an important possible source of strategy change. In addition, it makes some oversimplifying assumptions concerning workload. For instance, the workload associated with particular mental operations can vary with such factors as the levels of fatigue and emotional stress experienced by individuals (Hockey et al., 1989). Thus cost/benefit approaches are incomplete in important ways and need to take account of factors relating to affect and workload. A possible way of bringing these different aspects of time pressure together is presented in the next section.

An Integrated Approach

In the previous section we identified what appear to be two different accounts of the effects of time constraints on decision making. Svenson and Edland (1989) and Maule and Mackie (1990) argued that time constraints should be conceptualized as a stressor and that a better understanding of them can be achieved by drawing on theories and research on the effects of stress on cognition. In contrast to this, Payne and his coworkers considered time constraints as a task variable, explaining how decision makers adapt to this and other task variables using a cost/benefit approach. In the present section we suggest a way in which these two approaches may be integrated within a control model of workload and stress. This model emphasizes both the central role of effort in decision making under stress, and the value of a cost/benefit analysis in determining the ways of adapting to time constraints. First, we should briefly summarize the current evidence on the nature of stress and effort.

Research on the Effects of Stress on Cognition

Until recently, theories of stress and cognition were dominated by the view that the effects of different stressors were mediated through a single dimension of arousal or activation (see Eysenck, 1982, for a review). It was argued that an external stressor changed the arousal level of the individual and that this in turn affected cognition. The classic statement of this position was the Yerkes–Dodson law (Yerkes & Dodson, 1908), suggesting an inverted U-relation between arousal and performance, with performance efficiency optimal at some moderate level of arousal. In addition, the strength of arousal was assumed to interact with task difficulty such that the optimal level of arousal was inversely related to task difficulty. Easterbrook (1959) suggested that the biphasic form of the arousal/ performance function was mediated by an attentional mechanism, with increases in arousal reducing the range of cues used. Initially this leads to a reduction in the processing of task-*irrelevant* cues, resulting in an *improvement* in performance. At high levels of arousal, further perceptual narrowing results in increasing neglect of task-*relevant* information and a consequent *impairment* in effectiveness. Easterbrook's ideas have been remarkably influential, though recent research has shown that the account is unsatisfactory (Eysenck, 1982; Hockey, 1979; Näätänen, 1973). Eysenck (1982, Chapter 4) provides a thorough review outlining some of the principal difficulties. Two of these criticisms are important for present considerations. First, there is increasing evidence that the effects of stressors do not operate in terms of a single dimension like arousal (Broadbent, 1971). Instead, the evidence suggests that changes in state induced by stressors should be considered in terms of several different indicators, with different stressors inducing a characteristic pattern of change along each (Hamilton, Hockey, & Rejman, 1977; Hockey, 1979; Hockey & Hamilton, 1983). Second, Eysenck (1982) reviewed a large number of studies indicating that changes in behavior consistent with the narrowing of attention hypothesis occur on some but not all occasions. He concluded that Easterbrook's original view that attentional narrowing under high arousal is a relatively passive and automatic process is probably wrong. Instead, he suggested that narrowing of attention is better thought of as an active response under voluntary control. It represents one among a number of ways in which individuals may adapt to stressors and therefore need not necessarily always occur following an increase in arousal.

This view of stress as something people can adapt to in an active and voluntary way, rather than a force acting on a passive organism, is consistent with other areas of stress research. Lazarus has developed a more general stress theory, based on the notion that people appraise both the situation they are in and the extent to which they have the resources to meet the demands of the situation (Lazarus & Folkman, 1984). A situation may be potentially damaging but will not be stressful if the individual has the resources to cope with the threat. What is important is the individual's interpretation of both the situation and the extent to which he/she can manage the demands it imposes on him/her. If the appraisal process leads individuals to conclude that they have access to coping resources, then the response to the situation is likely to be adaptive. If the threat is perceived as one for which coping resources are not available, the most likely outcome is one of reduced effectiveness, with the physiological, psychological, and behavioral symptoms of stress. Frankenhauser (1986) has distinguished these two modes of active and passive coping as states of *eu*stress and *di*stress, respectively. Eustress is a positive responsive state involving effort and challenge, activation of the sympathetic nervous system, high levels of effectiveness, but no negative affect. Distress, by contrast, is associated with anxiety and helplessness, as well as increased activity in biochemical indices of stress (cortisol).

This notion of appraising situations and coping with the demands of these situations when they are potentially stressful has become a unifying principle underlying contemporary theories of stress (Fisher, 1986). Individuals are assumed to have a range of different coping strategies and variable amounts of resources available to implement these strategies. Although this approach has emerged mainly within research on personality and general life stress, it has been developed most fully within the context of a more specific cognitive/energetic theory of the effects of stressors on human performance. The next section considers this theory in some detail as a basis for understanding the effects of time pressure on decision making.

Variable State Activation Theory (VSAT)

The ideas discussed in the previous section have recently been put forward by Hockey and his coworkers in the form of a general theory of behavioral adaptation to stress and workload (Hockey & Hamilton, 1983; Hockey, 1986; Hockey et al., 1989), and applied to both laboratory and field contexts. Analyses of patterns of performance under different stressors revealed qualitatively different changes in cognitive state, rather than simple decrements or increments in effectiveness. Thus, noise impaired tasks that relied more on working memory and high levels of accuracy, while being beneficial for those requiring speeded response or highly selective processing. Effects of sleep loss, drugs, or incentives produced cognitive states differing in their effect on these and other key indicator variables. The state produced by any stressor may or may not be appropriate for current processing demands. Decrements may be prevented, however, by compensatory shifts in the cognitive system through the operation of an executive control facility. This process is effortful, however, and attracts costs, both to biological and to affective components of the system. It may, for example, result in high levels of activation and subjective strain. This two-level control model has its origins in Broadbent's (1971) account of the effects of stress in laboratory tasks.

Recent versions of the theory have emphasized this regulatory function of the control model, aiming to determine the criteria for selection of alternative regulatory modes in response to perceived stress. Alternative modes of coping activity in this model are defined in terms of their implications for costs and benefits to overall system goals. Figure 1 illustrates the general form of the control model.

A disruption of equilibrium may be brought about either by unplanned surges in external environmental demands, or a fall in internal resources (e.g., through fatigue or sleepiness). Under normal circumstances, the system is self-regulating. Routine control, following minor disruptions, is handled by the usual negative feedback loop (not shown here in detail for the sense of simplicity). An "action monitor" (comparator) compares feedback from current cognitive activity with the target or goal state and activates familiar adjustments that modify behavior until it matches the target. It is assumed that the (frequent) discrepancies within the normal range are managed automatically through the use of low-cost, routine corrections. In simple terms, the system changes its speed, timing, memory use, and so on until its performance is satisfactory. When the discrepancy is high, this routine regulation may be inadequate to resolve the dysregulation, and a more active (high level) controlled response is needed. The regulatory activity here is characterized by high levels of cognitive effort and deliberate planning of actions, as well as by conscious choice of alternative goals. The involvement of this supervisory controller is postulated to be activated by a sensed increase in effort requirements of the low-level self-regulatory mechanism. The involvement of the high-level control is, however, associated with various options for regulatory activity: (1) "normal" effort levels may be overridden by the supervisory system, permitting control of cognitive resources to proceed with an increased "effort budget"; (2) the goal (or target state) may be modified (e.g., by reappraisal of demands, or by adopting different strategies demanding less effort), or disengaged completely (rare in work contexts); (3) environmental load may be controlled directly, through removal or moderation of stressors or objective demands; and (4) the system may also be left essentially unchanged, with the action discrepancy unresolved.

These control actions are similar to the description of coping strategies presented by Lazarus and Folkman (1984). The most effective actions in terms of preserving task priorities are the most costly in terms of resource deployment. Schönpflug and Battman's (1988) review of the costs and benefits of coping actions also emphasizes the central role of cost appraisal in the determination of coping actions. The nature and extent of costs varies both across different situations and for different personal goals. In the context of time constraints, they are likely to determine which kinds of adaptation to overload are adopted. Let us briefly examine the relevance of each of the above control modes for this question.

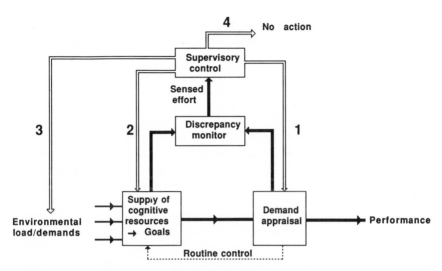

Figure 1. A control model of stress regulation. The diagram illustrates optional models of high-level control that may be used to resolve discrepancy between work demands and current cognitive resources (see text for explanation).

Changing the Cognitive State

Direct control involving changes to the cognitive state refers to the maintenance of performance goals at the expense of increased effort (in general terms a "trying-harder" reaction). In this case the sensed discrepancy is resolved through a recruitment of additional (effort-sensitive) resources, without changing the task goal. Such a strategy is effortful (Kahneman, 1973), because of its extended involvement of the high-level executive (or supervisory) function (Hamilton, Hockey, & Rejman, 1977; Hockey, 1986) and may be costly in terms of affective and physiological states. Maintaining effectiveness under continued stress or high workload is known to be associated with increased sympathetic activation (e.g., Lundberg, 1982; Wilkinson, 1962) or mental effort (Frankenhauser, 1986). Continued cognitive strain, through its effects on the depletion of central control resources, may in fact be regarded as the primary source of fatigue from mental work (Hockey et al., 1989).

Time constraints clearly demand an increase in the speed of work, which are likely to be outside the limits of normal routine control and therefore may only be achieved through direct executive control. However, increases in speed of work are only feasible up to a point. If the speed of work is already at a high level, then the costs associated with further increases in speed will be so great that they are likely to outweigh the advantages accruing from a small further gain in speed. In addition, there must be some upper limit on the speed of processing set by the operational limits of the system. As time constraints become more stringent, so the allocation of more central control resources becomes a less effective means of adapting. Norman and Bobrow (1975) describe this as a shift from a resource-limited to a data-limited situation. We might therefore expect direct control of this kind to become less appropriate as the imposed deadline becomes more stringent (i.e., situations demanding a considerable increase in the speed of work). This is consistent with Payne's findings reported earlier showing that, with increasingly stringent deadlines, people were less likely to adapt solely in terms of acceleration. VSAT makes a number of other predictions about the use of this mode of control. First, in relatively important situations, people should persevere longer with a control mode based solely on acceleration, because the ever-increasing costs of faster responding are more likely to be balanced by the benefits of using a more complex, high-accuracy strategy. Second, acceleration induces an aversive state associated with high levels of effort that is difficult to sustain, making direct control less likely to be successful when the decision process is extended over a prolonged period. These are readily testable predictions, though we know of no relevant data on them.

Changing the Target State

An alternate route to state resolution is through adoption of a form of "indirect" control. In this case, the discrepancy is resolved through a downward adjustment of central motivational priorities, in order to meet available resources. This amounts to a change in the goal for behavior (the target state). As implied above, the selection of this low-effort regulation strategy may take several forms. In general terms a shift to indirect control may be seen in terms of a reassessment of the costs and benefits of different goal-action plans, resulting, in the extreme case, in a shift away from high-cost performance-oriented goals in the direction of low-cost goals (e.g., emphasizing personal comfort or emotional stability). However, performance goals are rarely abandoned altogether. Rather, they are pursued with reduced priority (Schönpflug, 1983), or with modified specification requiring less use of high-cost processes such as working memory (Hamilton et al., 1977). Sperandio (1978) showed that air-traffic controllers shifted from highly intensive, individually based routing instructions to less cognitively demanding generalized instructions whenever the traffic load exceeded a critical amount, reducing the amount of time they had for each contact.

There is evidence from the decision-making literature to suggest that people may adapt to deadlines by means of indirect control, leading to a reconfiguration of task plans to minimize the use of high-effort operations. As described above, one way is a shift from high-cost performance goals to low-cost goals emphasizing personal comfort. A possible example is the tendency for subjects to refuse to complete a task that they judge to be too demanding. There is some anecdotal evidence suggesting that experimental subjects under deadline conditions absent themselves from test situations (e.g., Edland, this volume), and it is our impression that this occurs to a greater extent in time-pressured situations. However, this suggestion requires more systematic investigation. A second way of reconfiguring task plans is through a downward adjustment to the goal, thereby justifying the use of lower-effort operations. There is a good deal of evidence showing that deadlines induce a greater use of lower-effort strategies on both a small scale, involving filtering and on a large scale involving a switch from compensatory to noncompensatory rules. These findings are broadly consistent with the view being developed here.

However, this reconfiguration of the task plan to minimize the use of high-effort operations may only be feasible in certain situations. It is most likely to be adopted in contexts where the outcome of a decision process is less critical (e.g., where simpler strategies may be deemed appropriate). In these cases, the small marginal gains in decision accuracy from the adoption of a high level of involvement may be outweighed by the high level of cognitive and emotional costs incurred. This suggests the need for future research to consider more carefully such issues as the perceived importance of task goals and how these interact with other aspects of the decision process.

Changing the Environment

This mode of adapting is the most direct of all, involving the modification or elimination of the stressor at source. Again, such control is not always possible, particularly in the case of chronic or externally imposed stressors, though it represents the most effective procedure for restoring equilibrium. In the context of imposed time constraints, such a strategy would involve a renegotiation of the deadline, or a reduction in the workload (number or complexity of decisions to be made in the time). For deadlines that we fix for ourselves rather than being imposed externally, changes of this kind (e.g., extending the time allowed to complete a chapter for a book or reducing the scope of the chapter) would, in fact, be equivalent to a change in the goal set by the individual. We know of no studies that have investigated aspects of the negotiability of deadlines, though given the frequency with which many of us use this means of adapting, it should clearly be a priority for future research.

Doing Nothing

Last, individuals may do nothing in the face of the state of disequilibrium. This may reflect a lack of involvement in either the task or the environment. Equally, they may be unable either to change the environment or to implement a high-effort change in cognitive state (e.g., because of fatigue or unavailability of further cognitive resources). The lack of appropriate actions may be the result of a deadline being unreasonably strict for the work that must be done. Equally, individuals may be unwilling to relinquish strongly held task goals, because of inbuilt personal values. It is possible to conceive of situations where the deadline is not only very severe, but fixed and immutable, and the task too important to permit a reduction in aspiration level. The individual perceives threat without having access to normal coping resources. This situation may be associated with maladaptive states such as helplessness (Seligman, 1975) or panic (Janis & Mann, 1977). There has been very little analysis of the effects of time pressure in such situations (see Janis and Mann, 1977, for a limited discussion), though the implications for decision-making behavior are clearly important.

People would be expected to have a wide repertoire of these control activities, and one or more could follow a mismatch between the target and cognitive states. However, it is important to recognize that the action monitor continuously compares these two states (Cox, 1987) and may signal the need for a change in control activity at any time during the decision process. Decision researchers have tended to adopt a less dynamic view, assuming that following the imposition of a deadline, subjects adapt by identifying an appropriate strategy that is then implemented in its entirety until an alternative is chosen. In addition, it would be wrong to assume that all control activity is successful. Hockey (1986) considers a number of different modifications in these modes of control that vary in terms of their success and their costs, and he considers the possibility that people may show reliable and consistent differences not only in their use of different control activities but also in their base cognitive states. These ideas provide a number of interesting avenues for future research.

In conclusion, this approach assumes that subjects adapt to time constraints by comparing the demands of the situation to the current cognitive state and evaluating the costs and benefits of control activity to reduce any discrepancies identified by this comparison. Control activity involves expending effort, which is assumed to be limited in supply. If no appropriate control activity is available in a situation of some importance, then all the symptoms associated with panic and pressure would be expected.

Conclusion

We have identified two different approaches to explain the effects of time constraints on the cognitive strategies underlying judgment and decision making. One highlighted the adaptivity of decision makers to task demands through a cost/benefit determination of strategy. The other highlighted the role of pressure and stress induced by the constraints and the effects that these may have on the underlying cognitive processes. At the outset, these approaches seemed to attribute the effects of time constraints to very different mechanisms. However, we also outlined VSAT that included elements of both approaches.

VSAT assumes that people adapt to the imposition of a time constraint through an appraisal process comparing the demands of the task with the current cognitive state. This is similar to the mechanism assumed by cost/benefit decision theories. Indeed, the adoption of control or coping responses to redress discrepancies revealed by the appraisal process is assumed to involve weighing of costs and benefits (Schönpflug & Battman, 1988). Thus the principles underlying the explanation of time constraints included within the cost/benefit theories is present in VSAT.

VSAT also includes some discussion of affective states and how they are linked to changes in cognitive strategy. Previous theories assumed that stressors act on a passive organism and induce affective changes that in turn lead to automatic and involuntary changes in cognitive strategy. VSAT assumes a rather different relation between affect and cognition with variations in affective state occurring in a number of different ways. These can be illustrated in the context of time-constrained situations in the following ways. First, they may occur as a result of the need to change the cognitive state to match the increased priority for fast responding reflected in the new task target state. These control activities require a mobilization of effort, leading to a pattern of increased activation consistent with changes in affective state. People are likely to interpret these physiological changes by seeking appropriate environmental cues to determine the cause of the new physiological state (Weiner, 1982). Given that the significant environmental changes are related to time constraints, people are likely to interpret these physiological changes as feelings of time pressure. This is consistent with evidence from many studies indicating that the imposition of time constraints induces feelings of pressure (see Svenson & Edland, this volume).

Second, there may be no appropriate control activities to meet the demands of the situation, and given that the situation is important, this would be expected to lead to more extreme affective states associated with anxiety and panic. Lazarus has suggested that stress states occur when the appraisal process indicates a threat that cannot be reduced or eliminated by coping responses. This situation may be interpreted by people in a different way to time pressure and be better conceptualized as time stress. Time stress, like other stressors, is likely to be associated with a distinctive cognitive state that in turn may lead to further disequilibrium between the target task state and the current cognitive state. This pattern of an increasing disequilibrium under time constraints where no control activity is possible is illustrated by the increasing levels of panic exhibited by individuals in situations where threats to life are associated with time constraints, e.g., fires (Janis & Mann, 1977). Thus VSAT provides a way of thinking about the different states of time pressure and time stress identified in the second section.

The second section also raised the central methodological issue of how time pressure may be operationalized. Previous studies have reduced the usual time to complete the task by some fraction, assuming that this induces time pressure, with the additional possibility that a more extreme reduction might induce time stress. However, like other contemporary theories of stress, VSAT highlights the shortcomings of this view in that it overlooks the importance of an appraisal process in determining the effects of a stressor. Appraisal involves an evaluation of more than external factors like the available time. It includes such aspects as the relation between the perceived threat to individual goals as well as the availability and cost/benefits of control activities. By focusing only on the time allowed to complete the task, we are in danger of overlooking these other factors. For instance, VSAT suggests that the goals of the subjects are important because modifications to these provide one way of adapting to time pressure. This suggests that we need to pay more attention to individual goals both in terms of the specific instructions given to subjects, and the way these are translated in terms of subjects' own task goals. Similarly, the availability of appropriate coping responses is another important aspect of the appraisal process, and these are likely to vary from individual to individual. This view is supported by recent evidence indicating reliable individual differences in the way people adapt to time pressure (Kaplan, this volume; Steinsmeier-Pelster & Schurmann, this volume; Rastegary & Landy, this volume). Finally, there may be intraindividual differences in terms of changes in the base cognitive state (e.g., with the experience of effort limitations and cognitive fatigue). This will change the costs associated with particular control activities, thereby affecting their appropriateness even when the task itself remains constant. Thus, simply ensuring that all subjects receive a standard reduction in the time allowed to complete a decision task does not mean that they conceptualize these task conditions in the same way. Rather, we must consider the factors outlined above during the design stage of research and recognize that they may contribute to determining how a particular task situation will affect a particular decision maker. At present we do not have any clear way of undertaking this, though it does suggest a priority for future research in this area.

Discussion of VSAT also suggests that there is a wide range of control activities that people may use to adapt to the imposition of a time constraint. Though some of these have already been identified by research, others have not been considered at all. This suggests that we need to be investigating a broader range of modes of adapting to time constraints than has been the case up to now. Not only does VSAT indicate what these other modes may be, it also provides a theoretical framework suggesting some of the conditions that determine when each mode is used.

VSAT raises one other issue for decision researchers. The theory is based on research showing that the cost of implementing a particular strategy varies as a function of the current cognitive state. The amount of effort required will depend upon the match between the target and current cognitive states and the amount of control activity needed to bring these into equilibrium. As the current cognitive state varies (e.g., with experienced fatigue), so the effort involved in implementing a strategy changes, despite the fact that the mental processes involved remain the same. This highlights an important limitation in the measures of effort used by Payne and his coworkers, based simply on the number of elementary mental processes needed to implement the strategy in a particular situation. Such states need to be monitored on a within-individual basis independently of externally defined task conditions. In general, within-subject analyses of effort and costs are more appropriate than between subject or normative analyses.

Though VSAT is still in an early stage of development and many aspects of the model remain unspecified, it does appear to provide a way of linking the two apparently inconsistent approaches to time pressure research. By linking this area of decision research to the more fully developed area of stress and cognition we have not only extended the range of concepts and approaches in which to investigate the effects of time constraints but also ensured that we do not operate with models that stress researchers have already identified as inadequate.

References

Beach, L. R., & Mitchell, T. R. (1978). A contingency model for the selection of decision strategies. *Academy of Management Journal, 3*, 439–449.

Ben Zur, H., & Bresnitz, S. J. (1981). The effects of time pressure on risky choice behaviour. *Acta Psychologica, 47*, 89–104.

Bettman, J. R., Johnson, E. J., & Payne, J. W. (1990). A componential analysis of cognitive effort in choice. *Organisational Behaviour and Human Decision Processes, 45*, 111–139.

Broadbent, D. (1971). *Decision and stress*. London: Academic Press.

Christensen-Szalanski, J. J. J. (1980). A further examination of the selection of problem-solving strategies: The effects of deadlines and analytic aptitudes. *Organisational Behaviour and Human Performance, 25*, 107–122.

Cox, T. (1987). Stress, coping and problem solving. *Work & Stress, 1*, 5–14.

Easterbrook, J. A. (1959). The effect of emotion on cue utilization and the organization of behavior. *Psychological Review, 66*, 183–201.

Eysenck, M. W. (1982). *Attention and arousal*. Berlin: Springer-Verlag.

Fisher, S. (1986). *Stress and strategy*. Hillsdale, NJ: Erlbaum.

Ford, J. K., Schmitt, N., Scheitman, S. L., Hults, B. M., & Doherty, M. L. (1989). Process tracing methods: Contributions, problems, and neglected research questions. *Organisational Behaviour and Human Decision Processes, 43*, 75–117.

Frankenhauser, M. (1986). A psychobiological framework for research on human stress and coping. In M. H. Appley & R. Trumbell (Eds.), *Dynamics of stress* (pp. 101–116). New York: Plenum Press.

Hamilton, P., Hockey, G. R. J., & Rejman, M. (1977). The place of the concept of activation in human information processing theory: An integrative approach. In S. Dornic (Ed.), *Attention and performance VI* (pp. 463–486). Hillsdale, NJ: Lawrence Erlbaum.

Hockey, G. R. J. (1979). Stress and the cognitive components of skilled performance. In V. Hamilton & D. Warburton (Eds.), *Human stress and cognition. An information processing approach* (pp. 141–177). New York: Wiley.

Hockey, G. R. J. (1986). A state control theory of adaptation and individual differences in stress management. In G. R. J. Hockey, A. W. K. Gaillard, & M. G. H. Coles (Eds.), *Energetics and human information processing* (pp. 285–298). Martinus Nijhoff: Dordrecht.

Hockey, G. R. J., & Hamilton, P. (1983). The cognitive patterning of stress states. In G. R. J. Hockey (Ed.), *Stress and fatigue in human performance.* (pp. 331–362). Chichester: Wiley.

Hockey, G. R. J., Briner, R. B., Tattersall, A. J., & Wiethoff, M. (1989). Assessing the impact of computer workload on operator stress: The role of system controllability. *Ergonomics, 32,* 1401–1418.

Janis, I. L., & Mann, L. (1977). *Decision making: A psychological analysis of conflict, choice and commitment.* New York: Free Press.

Johnson, E. J., & Payne, J. W. (1985). Effort and accuracy in choice. *Management Science, 31,* 395–414.

Kahneman, D. (1973). *Attention and effort.* Englewood Cliffs, NJ: Prentice Hall.

Lazarus, R., & Folkman, S. (1984). *Stress, appraisal and coping.* New York: Springer.

Lundberg, U. (1982). Psychophysiological aspects of performance and adjustment to stress. In H. W. Krohne & L. Laux (Eds.), *Achievement, stress and anxiety* (pp. 75–91). Washington, DC: Hemisphere.

Mano, H. (1992). Judgments under distress: Assessing the role of unpleasantness and arousal in judgment formation. *Organisational Behavior and Human Decision Processes, 52,* 216–245.

Maule, A. J., & Mackie, P. M. (1988). *The harassed decision maker revisited.* Paper presented at the Third Symposium on Thinking. Aberdeen.

Maule, A. J., & Mackie, P. M. (1990). A componential investigation of the effects of deadlines on individual decision making. In K. Borcherding, O. I. Larichev, & D. M. Messick (Eds.), *Contemporary issues in decision making* (pp. 449–461). Amsterdam: North Holland.

Miller, J. G. (1960). Information input overload and psychopathology. *American Journal of Psychiatry, 116,* 695–704.

Näätänen, R. (1973). The inverted U-relationship between activation and performance—A critical review. In S. Kornblum (Ed.), *Attention and performance* (vol. IV, pp. 155–174). New York: Academic Press.

Norman, D. A., & Bobrow, D. J. (1975). On data limited and resource limited processes. *Cognitive Psychology, 5,* 44–64.

Payne, J. W., Johnson, E. J., Bettman, J. R., & Coupey, E. (1990). Understanding contingent choice: A computer simulation approach. *IEEE Transactions on systems, man and cybernetics, 20,* 296–309.

Payne, J. W., Bettman, J. R., & Johnson, E. J. (1988). Adaptive strategy selection in decision making. *Journal of Experimental Psychology: Learning, Memory & Cognition, 14,* 534–552.

Schönpflug, W. (1983). Coping efficiency and situational demands. In G. R. J. Hockey (Ed.), *Stress and fatigue in human performance* (pp. 299–330). Chichester: Wiley.

Schönpflug, W., & Battman, W. (1988). The costs and benefits of coping. In S. Fisher & J. Reason (Eds.), *Handbook of life stress, cognition and health* (pp. 699–713). Chichester: Wiley.

Seligman, M. E. P. (1975). *Helplessness.* New York: Freeman.

Sperandio, J. -C. (1978). The regulation of working methods as a function of work load among air-traffic controllers. *Ergonomics, 21,* 195–202.

Svenson, O. (1979). Process descriptions of decision making. *Organisational Behaviour and Human Performance, 23,* 86–112.

Svenson, O., & Edland, A. (1989). Changes of preference under time pressure: Choice and judgements. In H. Montgomery & O. Svenson (Eds.), *Process and structure in human decision making* (pp. 225–236). Chichester: Wiley.

Svenson, O., Edland, A., & Slovic, P. (1990). Choices between incompletely described alternatives under time stress. *Acta Psychologica, 75,* 153–169.

Watson, D., & Tellegen, A. (1985). Toward a consensual structure of mood. *Psychological Bulletin, 98,* 219–235.

Weiner, B. (1982). The emotional consequences of causal attributions. In M. Clark & S. T. Fiske (Eds.), *Affect and cognition: The 17th Annual Carnegie Symposium on Cognition* (pp. 185–209). Hillsdale, NJ: Erlbaum.

Wilkinson, R. T. (1962). Muscle tension during mental work under sleep deprivation. *Journal of Experimental Psychology, 64,* 565–571.

Wright, P. L. (1974). The harassed decision maker: Time pressures, distractions and the use of evidence. *Journal of Applied Psychology, 59,* 555–561.

Yerkes, R. M., & Dodson, J. D. (1908). The relation of strength of stimulus to rapidity of habit formation. *Journal of Comparative Neurological Psychology, 18,* 459–482.

7

Adapting to Time Constraints

Eric J. Johnson, John W. Payne, and James R. Bettman

Introduction

Consider the plight of an air-traffic controller choosing an altitude and course for an incoming flight, or a parent selecting a breakfast cereal during a hurried shopping trip accompanied by a cranky child. Although the consequences of these two decisions may vary, both decision makers face two potentially conflicting goals: (1) to make a good choice and (2) to reach a decision within a limited amount of time. Such choices illustrate the central topic of this chapter, the influence of time pressure upon decision making.

Under time pressure, decision makers often cannot simply employ a strategy that would select the best alternative because choices must be made within a reasonable amount of time. Normative analysis usually focuses on utility maximizations, but with time constraints, accuracy may have to be traded off for time savings. Thus, at a theoretical level, time constraints are of special interest because heuristics, under time constraints, may be even more accurate than a "normative strategy."

In this chapter we summarize some of the results of our program of research that examines how decision makers cope with this tradeoff. Our work has had two major components. First, we would like to characterize *how* decision makers *could* respond to time pressure. To do this, we analyze the performance of

Eric J. Johnson • Department of Marketing, The Wharton School, University of Pennsylvania, Philadelphia, Pennsylvania 19104-6371.   **John W. Payne and James R. Bettman** • The Fuqua School of Business, Duke University, Durham, North Carolina 27706.
Time Pressure and Stress in Human Judgment and Decision Making, edited by Ola Svenson and A. John Maule. Plenum Press, New York, 1993.

several strategies when faced with time constraints. Our primary tool in this portion of our work is the use of computer simulations using production system representations of the various decision strategies. Second, we examine how decision makers *do* respond to time pressure. Here our primary tool is using process-tracing methodology to examine how decision makers access information in a choice task with time pressure, allowing us to infer the strategy that was used to make a choice.

Our final aim is to integrate these two analyses. To what extent do decision makers respond to time pressure by changing strategies? If they do change strategies, are those strategies better under time pressure than those they have abandoned? The answer to this question provides evidence to answer a broader question: Do decision makers change strategies in ways that are adaptive? Elsewhere we have been concerned with this broader question, and we see responses to time pressure as an important source of evidence concerning the ability of decision makers to select heuristic strategies that are adaptive to responses to different choice environments (see Payne, Bettman, & Johnson, 1993, for a further review of research relevant to this question).

The structure of this chapter is as follows: We first examine the performance of a variety of decision strategies under time pressure and identify those strategies that produce good choices under deadlines. We then discuss our empirical work, which examines how decision makers actually react to similar time constraints. Finally, we discuss how these reactions correspond to the predictions of the simulation.

Decision Making and Time Pressure: A Computer Simulation Analysis

Researchers have described a sizable number of potential decision strategies (see Svenson, 1979). Many of these strategies simplify the problem space (Newell & Simon, 1972) by (1) ignoring some potentially relevant information about the alternatives, and/or (2) by simplifying how that information is combined. We have examined a large number of these heuristics, but for the purpose of this chapter we will limit our examination to a set of rules commonly discussed in other simulations and empirical research (see Table 1). These heuristics vary substantially in the amount of information used and in the way that information is combined in order to make a choice. In addition, we examined two combined or "phased" decision strategies, because there is substantial evidence supporting their use in decision making (Payne, 1976). Both of these employed elimination-by-aspects (EBA) as a screening rule, followed by either an Additive Weighting or a Majority of Confirming Dimensions rule (Russo & Dosher, 1983). Both rules changed from EBA to the other heuristic when three alternatives were left.

Table 1. Decision Strategies Examined by the Simulation

Weighted additive: A version of expected utility maximization that develops a weighted value for each attribute by multiplying the weight (probability) by the value and then sums these weighted values over all attributes to arrive at an overall evaluation of an alternative. The rule selects the alternative with the highest evaluation.

Equal weight: Like weighted additive, it examines all alternatives and attribute values but ignores the weights (probabilities). It sums the attribute values for an alternative to get an overall score for that alternative and then selects the alternative with the highest evaluation.

Elimination by aspects: (Tversky, 1972). This rule begins by determining the most important attribute and then retrieves a cutoff value for that attribute. All alternatives with values below that cutoff are eliminated. The process continues with the most important remaining attribute(s) until only one alternative remains.

Majority of confirming dimensions: (Russo & Dosher, 1983) This strategy processes pairs of alternatives, comparing them on each attribute, and selecting the alternative from the pair with the greater number of superior attribute values. The alternative that is selected from the pair is then compared to another remaining alternative, and this pairwise comparison process continues until all alternatives have been considered.

Satisficing: This strategy (Simon, 1955) considers one alternative at a time, in the order they are presented. Each attribute of the current alternative is compared to a cutoff. If an attribute fails to exceed the cutoff, then the alternative is rejected. The first alternative to pass all the cutoffs is selected.

Lexicographic: This strategy first identifies the most important attribute and then selects the alternative that is best on this attribute. In the case of ties, the tied alternatives are compared on the next most important attribute, and so on.

Random: This heuristic simply selects one alternative at random with no search of the available information; it provides a baseline for measuring both accuracy and effort.

Measuring Time Pressure

To understand the effects of time pressure, we assumed that each decision rule could be decomposed into a set of common mental operations, called Elementary Information Processes (EIPs) by Newell and Simon (1972) (see also Huber, 1980, 1986, & Johnson, 1979). The use of this metric of decision effort is very useful in the study of time pressure. The number of EIPs required to accomplish a mental task has been used in a number of domains as a predictor of cognitive load and the time to complete the task (Card, Moran, & Newell, 1980). More specifically, Bettman, Johnson, and Payne (1990) have shown that a count of the number of mental operations is a good predictor of decision latency, accounting for 80% to 90% of the variance in the time required to use a given decision strategy. The count of mental operations was also superior to other possible predictors of decision latency, such as the amount of information that was considered or the number of alternatives or attributes examined. Because we are interested in what decision makers can accomplish in a given time, it seems reasonable to use the best available predictor of latency as a metric for decision effort.

Each rule was encoded in a production system representation, using a common set of Elementary Information Processes. We examined a no-time-pressure condition, along with three conditions of time pressure: low time pressure, which stopped after 150 EIPs had been used; moderate time pressure, which stopped after 100 EIPs had been used; and a severe time pressure condition, which stopped decisions after only 50 EIPs had been employed. Using a simple count of all EIPs implicitly assumes that all operations require the same amount of time. We have explored weighting the EIPs using empirically estimated weights and find very similar results (see Payne, Johnson, Bettman, & Coupey, 1990).

If a decision strategy exceeded a predetermined cutoff level of operations corresponding to the particular level of time pressure, the rule then selected was an alternative based upon the information considered so far. Several of the rules we employed (e.g., weighted additive, equal weight, and majority of confirming dimensions) selected the best from the alternatives already considered when time ran out. Others (EBA, lexicographic, and satisficing) picked randomly among all the alternatives not yet rejected. The two combined rules selected randomly among the remaining alternatives if in the EBA phase and picked the best option processed to date if in the weighted-additive or majority-of-confirming-dimensions phase.

Measuring Accuracy

To examine how well each decision rule performs under time pressure, we need to define what we mean by decision accuracy. An accurate decision can be defined using many different concepts. For example, one can appeal to coherence principles such as avoiding dominated alternatives or intransitive patterns of preferences. In many cases, the expected utility model can serve as a normative baseline derived from axiomatic principles. In our work, we have examined many definitions, including the avoidance of dominated alternatives and the frequency of selection of the alternative with the best expected utility or expected value. For this chapter we will report a measure that provides an indication of the performance of a choice heuristic relative to two baseline strategies: an Expected Value (weighted additive) maximization rule and random choice. Note that the EV and random strategies span the spectrum of information use: EV uses all relevant information, random none. To construct this measure, for which a value of 1 indicates the best performance, we use the formula:

$$Relative\ Accuracy = \frac{EV_{Heuristic\ rule\ choice} - EV_{random\ rule\ choice}}{EV_{Expected\ Value\ choice} - EV_{random\ rule\ choice}}$$

Johnson and Payne (1986) discusses this and a number other measures of rule performance.

Task and Context Effects

A major finding of prior work examining the performance of heuristic choice rules is that the accuracy of a heuristic depends upon characteristics of the decision environment (Johnson & Payne, 1985; Thorngate, 1980). We examined two important factors that have been shown both to make an important difference in the accuracy and effort of simulated choice strategies and also to have an impact upon the choice rules adopted by actual decision makers (see Payne, Bettman, & Johnson, 1988). The first of these is *task complexity*. Our simulations used either two, five, or eight alternatives and two, five, or eight attributes. It seems simple to hypothesize that an increase in task complexity should increase the impact of time pressure: Although a time constraint might have no impact upon a simple choice with two alternatives and two attributes, it might have a sizable effect when much more information is potentially relevant to the choice, such as in an eight alternative by eight attribute choice.

We also manipulated one context variable, the degree of dispersion in the probabilities (weights) given each outcome. To illustrate, four outcomes might have probabilities of .3, .2, .22, and .28, which would represent a low level of dispersion. On the other hand probabilities of .68, .12, .05, and .15 would represent a high level of dispersion. Another factor, manipulated in the simulation but not discussed here, was the presence or absence of dominated alternatives.

The production system representations of the choice rules were then used to make 200 decisions in each cell of a factorial design described by three levels of the number of alternatives (two, five, and eight), three levels of the number of attributes (two, five, and eight), two levels of dispersion of probabilities (low and high), and most important, the four levels of time pressure (none, low, medium, and high).

Results

Time constraints might have an important effect upon the accuracy of these choice rules. In fact under time pressure, some rules might produce better decisions than the weighted additive rule as time pressure increases. Our logic is simple: When faced with severe time constraints, a quick but incomplete evaluation of all the alternatives may lead to a better choice, on average, than a complete evaluation of a small subset of the alternatives that must be truncated when time runs out.

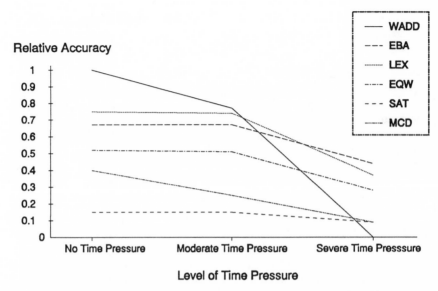

Figure 1. Performance of heuristics under time pressure. Moderate size (5 × 5) problem.

The simulation results largely supported this argument. Figure 1 plots the performance of various heuristics as time pressure increases, averaging over the two levels of dispersion. Although all heuristics do suffer from the effects of limited processing, certain heuristics are quite robust. Specifically, those heuristics that quickly evaluate many alternatives on a single dimension, particularly the lexicographic and elimination-by-aspects heuristics, seem to suffer the least under increased time pressure. In contrast, those rules that examine one alternative at a time, such as satisficing, majority of confirming dimensions, and the weighted additive rule, do not fare nearly as well.

An important caveat for this analysis is demonstrated by the performance of the equal weight rule under severe time pressure. The overall performance of this rule critically depends upon the context variable that we manipulated—the dispersion of probabilities. Table 2 displays these results. In the low dispersion environment, it is the best performing rule for severe time pressure, with a relative performance index of .72. However, when faced with a high level of dispersion, equal weight is inferior to both the lexicographic and elimination-by-aspects heuristics, achieving a relative performance index of .55. This comparison illustrates the more general point that although a given heuristic may do well in a single task environment, it may not provide good performance in every task environment. For a decision maker to do well when using heuristic choice rules, he or she needs to both (1) possess a repertoire of efficient heuristics and (2) know the conditions under which each heuristic will be efficient. We now turn to

Table 2. Results of Simulation by Time Pressure, Dispersion and Dominance

	Task Environment[a]											
	Dominance Possible						Dominance not possible					
	Low Dispersion			High Dispersion			Low Dispersion			High Dispersion		
Strategy[b]	LTP[c]	MTP	STP	LTP	MTP	STP	LTP	MTP	STP	LTP	MTP	STP
WADD	**.91**	.80	.28	**.91**	.80	.28	**.90**	**.77**	.12	**.92**	.82	.24
EQW	.88	**.82**	**.72**	.66	.65	.55	.41	.34	.26	.24	.25	.18
SAT	.38	.34	.30	.32	.34	.23	.03	.04	.06	.07	.05	.04
MCD	.58	.49	.23	.44	.35	.17	.03	-.01	-.02	.04	.03	.02
LEX	.70	.69	.47	.90	**.90**	.59	.69	.68	**.48**	.90	**.90**	.60
LEXSEMI	.71	.66	.40	.83	.83	.49	.63	.59	.43	.76	.75	.51
EBA	.70	.68	.49	.73	.73	**.65**	.63	.60	**.48**	.67	.67	**.61**
EBA + WADD	.86	.79	.43	.82	.82	.48	.73	.66	.27	.75	.74	.43
EBA + MCD	.74	.63	.44	.60	.60	.49	.35	.32	.27	.40	.41	.36

[a] The 95% confidence interval width is +/− .029. The most accurate rule in each task environment is printed in bold.

[b] WADD = weighted additive strategy. EQW = equal weight strategy. SAT = satisficing. MCD = majority of confirming dimensions. LEX = lexicographic. LEXSEMI = lexicographic semiorder. EBA = elimination by aspects. EBA + WADD = combined elimination-by-aspects followed by weighted additive. EBA + MCD = combined elimination by aspects followed by majority of confirming dimensions.

[c] LTP = low time pressure. MTP = moderate time pressure. STP = severe time pressure.

empirical studies that examine the descriptive validity of these processing patterns suggested by simulations.

Do Decision Makers Adapt to Time Constraints?

The results of the simulation provide a fairly clear outline of the efficacy of various decision strategies under time pressure. In this section, we examine two related questions: (1) Do people change strategies when faced with time pressure? and (2) If changes do occur, are they in the direction suggested by the simulation?

What does the simulation suggest? First, as time pressure increases, we may see decision makers abandoning attempts to executing a weighted additive rule. The complete processing implied by this rule is just not practical when time pressure increases. The simulation, however, suggests that *which* rules will be used will depend upon the dispersion in probabilities facing the decision maker. When dispersion is high, we might expect decision makers to adopt strategies that the simulation suggest will do well in this environment, such as the lexicographic and elimination-by-aspects heuristics. In contrast, when dispersion is low, the simulation suggests that an equal weight heuristic will be the most accurate.

Prior literature also suggests a range of adaptations to time pressure. Ben Zur and Breznitz (1981) adapted Miller's (1960) ideas about information overload, suggesting three different responses to increased time pressure. The first, which they term *acceleration,* consists of using the same strategy and information but attempting to process it at a faster rate. The second, which they call *filtration,* simply suggests that decision makers may look only at the most important subset of the information. Finally, one could shift to a different strategy when faced with time pressure. Both Ben Zur and Breznitz (1981) and Wright (1974) report evidence for filtration.

Together the simulation results and prior research suggest a broad set of possible responses to the imposition of time constraints. Some of these possible changes (e.g., acceleration, filtration) represent changes in the way a strategy is executed. Others suggest a change in the strategy itself. To examine this potentially broad range of reactions to time pressure, we examine the general characteristics of the decision process used by decision makers.

Our basic dependent measures involve the information acquisitions made by each subject while making a choice. To measure information acquisition, we employed MOUSELAB (Johnson, Payne, Schkade, & Bettman, 1991) a computer-based system that records the pattern and duration of search from an information display. To look at an item of information, the subject simply moves a cursor into a box, revealing its value. The box is closed again when the cursor leaves it.

MOUSELAB has been used in several studies of choice behavior (see Johnson et al., 1991 for a more complete description).[1] The display used in this study is shown in Figure 2.

We concentrate on a series of dependent measures derived from the trace of the acquisitions. Although our research has looked at a large set of possible measures, we will consider three that are particularly relevant to questions of strategy change. These are (1) the number of acquisitions, a measure of the amount of information search; (2) the proportion of time spent examining probabilities, a measure of the distribution of search, which also helps distinguish between those rules that attend to probability information (e.g., lexicographic and additive weighting) and those that do not (e.g., equal weight); and (3) the pattern of search. After Payne (1976), we calculated an index that has a value of 1 if search is entirely within alternatives and −1 if it is entirely within an attribute.[2] This helps distinguish between processes, like an additive weighting scheme, which are primarily within alternatives and those, like EBA and the lexicographic rule, which are primarily within attributes.

To see how decision makers respond to time pressure, we ran an experiment in which subjects made choices among sets of four gambles, each with four outcomes. Subjects received 10 choice sets characterized by low dispersion and/or by high dispersion in probabilities. One group of subjects received problems with either no time pressure or a time limit of 25 seconds; a second group had problems with either no time pressure or a more severe 15-second limit. The time pressure conditions were crossed with the dispersion conditions.

We can now examine how subjects responded to these choices. To illustrate how each of these measures discussed above changes in response to time pressure, we have plotted their means in Figure 3.[3] Along the X axis, moving from left to right, is the level of time pressure. Along the Y axis are the three process measures: number of acquisitions, proportion of time spent on probabilities, and the pattern index (these last two measures have been multiplied by 100 to fall on the same scale). The three-dimensional graph allows us to follow the simultaneous changes in each measure as time pressure increases.

To follow the various responses to time pressure, we can look from left to right. By imposing a 25-second limit, we provide strong evidence of filtration, because only half as much information is acquired as in the no-time-pressure case. However, the distribution of information search is largely unchanged: No

---

[1]Copies of the MOUSELAB can be obtained for a small distribution charge from the first author.
[2]The measured used was:

$$\frac{\text{Number of Alternative Transitions} - \text{Number of Attribute Transitions}}{\text{Number of Alternative Transitions} + \text{Number of Attribute Transitions}}$$

For a more extensive discussion of information search measures see Klayman (1983).
[3]The data is from the first of two sessions reported in Payne et al. (1989). Similar results were obtained in the second session, but only the first sessions data are shown here for simplicity.

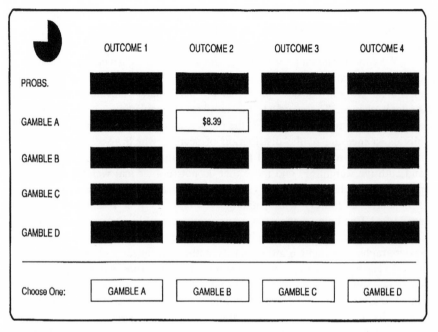

Figure 2. Example of a MouseLab Display with time pressure clock (from Payne, Bettman, & Johnson, 1988, p. 543).

more time is spent on probabilities than before. Finally, there is no shift toward attribute-based strategies, but instead a small increase in the number of alternative-based transitions. However, the imposition of a 15-second limit has a sizable impact. First, the amount of information searched, as measured by the number of acquisitions, continues to decrease. We also see a change in the distribution of search: More time is spent, relative to the rest of the information, looking at the probabilities. Finally, we see strong evidence of the predicted shift in the pattern of search: Specifically, there is a marked shift to attribute transitions, as would be expected from the simulation predictions.

Figures 4 and 5 show that these responses differ across the two dispersion conditions. Although the simulation, along with prior work, suggested that strategies may shift under time pressure, it also suggested that *which* strategy would be adopted could differ as a function of the dispersion of probabilities. Highly dispersed probabilities would be well handled by one of the attribute-based heuristics, such as the lexicographic or elimination-by-aspects. On the other hand, if there was little dispersion in weights, we would expect more alternative-based rules, such as the equal weight heuristic. By comparing Figures 4 and 5,

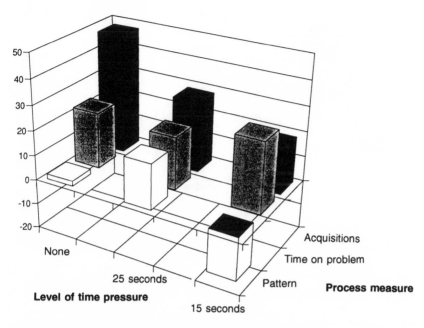

Figure 3. Responses to time pressure: high and low dispersion, combined.

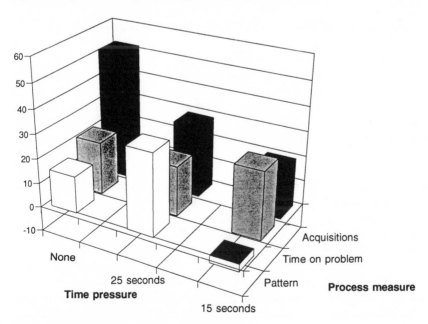

Figure 4. Responses to time pressure: low dispersion.

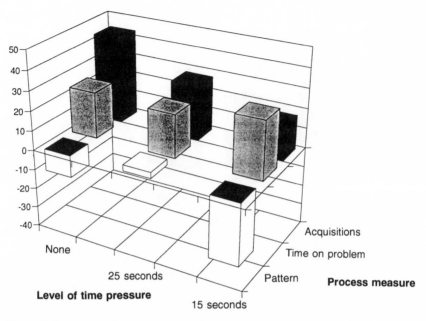

Figure 5. Responses to time pressure: high dispersion.

we can see whether actual behavior reflects the simulations predictions. Although the decreases in the amount of information searched and the changes in the distribution of search are similar in each case, the pattern of search differs: The low-dispersion decisions show a much more positive pattern for the pattern index overall, with only a small shift to a negative value under the most severe level of time pressure. In contrast, the high-dispersion case starts with a negative value, even in the absence of time pressure, and has a strong shift toward attribute-based search when time pressure increases. The dispersion of probabilities affects the use of choice strategies, even under fairly severe time pressure. Even when limited to 15 seconds to make a choice, subjects seem to adopt an appropriate choice strategy. To summarize, it appears that the decision makers in this task show a marked sensitivity to time constraints.

It is interesting to note that these changes in strategy occur without outcome feedback. Subjects are not told on a trial-by-trial basis how well they are performing. Despite this, they show marked adaptivity.

Finally, it is worth noting that we can compare, on an individual basis, those people who seem to change strategies when faced with time pressure to those who try to execute the same strategy. In fact, those who are more flexible perform better than those who do not (see Payne, Bettman, & Johnson, 1988, for details).

In sum, a somewhat optimistic view of human decision making emerges from this analysis of responses to time pressure. Our severe time pressure condition forces subjects to make decisions in less than a third of the time that they would desire to use without time constraints. However, because they adapt to the imposed time constraint, they manage to perform at levels that approach that of unconstrained subjects.

Conclusions

We close by discussing two points, one methodological, the other substantive. From a methodological perspective, one could argue that decision research has profited greatly from the use of a normative baseline. However, in many interesting applied areas, such as the analysis of time pressure or dynamic decision making (Kleinmuntz & Thomas, 1987), the appropriate normative analysis is not obvious or mathematically tractable. The advantage of simulation in these cases is twofold: First, it allows us to assess the performance of alternative decision policies in the task environment. Such an analysis allows us to better understand why decision makers shift strategies. Second, by using a simulation methodology that is guided by extant knowledge of human cognition, the assumptions that we make are both explicit and perhaps more plausible. As experimental environments become more complex, we believe that the use of simulation to assess the potential courses of action available to subjects may be a useful tool.

Substantively, the overriding theme of our research has been that decision makers adapt to time pressure in ways that appear to be sensitive to the accuracy of the decision process. Under moderate time pressure, decision makers appear to adapt by being more selective in the information they consider. Under severe time pressure, they shift to strategies that are qualitatively, and not just quantitatively different. There appear to be stages in how decision makers adapt to time pressure. At first adaptation seems to be a story about accelerating a specific process and operating on a subset of information. However, to truly adapt to severe time pressure, a very different set of strategies are used. The remarkable aspect of the current research is that those decision makers who do adapt do better than those who do not. The robustness of this finding seems worthy of further research.

ACKNOWLEDGMENT. This work is supported by ONR Grant N00014-BO-C-0114 and NSF Grants SES90-2351 and SES88-09299. We would like to thank Ola Svenson for his helpful comments on the chapter.

References

Ben Zur, H., & Breznitz, S. J. (1981). The effects of time pressure on risky choice behavior. *Acta Psychologica, 47,* 89–104.

Bettman, J. R., Johnson, E. J., & Payne, J. W. (1990). A componential analysis of cognitive effort in choice. *Organizational Behavior and Human Decision Processes, 45,* 111–139.

Card, S. K., Moran, T. P., & Newell, A. (1980). Computer test-editing: An information-processing analysis of a routine cognitive skill. *Cognitive Psychology, 12,* 32–74.

Huber, O. (1980). The influence of some task variables on cognitive operations in an information-processing decision model. *Acta Psychologica, 48,* 187–196.

Huber, O. (1986). Decision making as a problem solving process. *Directions in Research on Decision Making.* Amsterdam: Elsevier Science Publishers.

Johnson, E. J. (1979). *Deciding how to decide: The effort of making a decision.* Chicago: University of Chicago.

Johnson, E. J., & Payne, J. W. (1985). Effort and accuracy in choice. *Management Science, 31,* 395–414.

Johnson, E. J., Payne, J. W., Schkade, D. A., & Bettman, J. R. (1991). *Monitoring information processing and decisions: The MouseLab system version 5.0.* Department of Marketing, The Wharton School, University of Pennsylvania, Philadelphia.

Kleinmuntz, D. N., & Thomas, J. B. (1987). The value of action and inference in dynamic decision making. *Organizational Behavior and Human Decision Processes, 37,* 341–364.

Miller, J. G. (1960). Information input overload and psychopathology. *American Journal of Psychiatry, 116,* 695–704.

Newell, A., & Simon, H. A. (1972). *Human problem solving.* Englewood Cliffs, NJ: Prentice Hall.

Payne, J. W. (1976). Task complexity and contingent processing in decision making: An information search and protocol analysis. *Organizational Behavior and Human Performance, 16,* 366–387.

Payne, J. W., Bettman, J. R., & Johnson, E. J. (1988). Adaptive strategy selection in decision making. *Journal of Experimental Psychology: Learning Memory and Cognition, 14,* 534–552.

Payne, J. W., Bettman, J. R., & Johnson, E. J. (1990). The adaptive decision maker: Effort and accuracy in choice. In Robin M. Hogarth (Ed.), *Insights in decision making* (pp. 129–153). Chicago: University of Chicago Press.

Payne, J. W., Johnson, E. J., Bettman, J. R., & Coupey, E. (1990). Understanding contingent decision making: A computer simulation approach. *IEEE Transactions: Man, Systems and Cybernetics, 20,* 296–309.

Payne, J. W., Bettman, J. R., & Johnson, E. J. (1993). *The adaptive decision maker.* Cambridge: Cambridge University Press.

Russo, J. E., & Dosher, B. A. (1983). Strategies for multiattribute binary choice. *Journal of Experimental Psychology: Learning, Memory and Cognition, 9,* 676–696.

Simon, H. A. (1955). A behavioral model of rational choice. *Quarterly Journal of Economics, 69,* 99–118.

Svenson, O. (1979). Process descriptions of decision making. *Organizational Behavior and Human Performance, 23,* 86–112.

Thorngate, W. (1980). Efficient decision heuristics. *Behavioral Science, 25,* 219–225.

Wright, P. (1974). The harassed decision maker: Time pressures, distractions and the use of evidence. *Journal of Applied Psychology, 59,* 555–561.

8

Time Pressure in Negotiation and Mediation

Peter J. Carnevale, Kathleen M. O'Connor, and Christopher McCusker

Introduction

This chapter examines the role of time pressure in negotiation and mediation. Negotiation can be defined as discussion between two or more parties and joint decision making with the goal of reaching agreement. Mediation is a variation on negotiation in which one or more outsiders ("third parties") assist the parties in their efforts to reach agreement.

In negotiation, time pressure can be defined as the desire to reach agreement quickly. Time pressure can result from a small amount of time available to negotiate, or nearness to a deadline that, if reached, ends the negotiation without agreement. Some real-world examples of deadlines in negotiation that produce time pressure include a contract that will expire at midnight, another buyer who will soon make an offer, and a foreseeable point at which open hostilities will start. Time pressure can also arise from the perceived cost of continued negotiation, such as time lost from other pursuits, or when the goods being negotiated are deteriorating (e.g., the bananas that I want to sell will soon spoil).

Virtually all negotiation and mediation involve time pressure—all negotiation and mediation involve some time away from other pursuits. Time pressure

Peter J. Carnevale, Kathleen M. O'Connor, and Christopher McCusker • Department of Psychology, University of Illinois at Urbana–Champaign, Champaign, Illinois 68120.
Time Pressure and Stress in Human Judgment and Decision Making, edited by Ola Svenson and A. John Maule. Plenum Press, New York, 1993.

almost always increases as negotiation and mediation proceed, especially as the parties become fatigued or frustrated. Last-minute negotiations are common: In labor negotiations, Dunlop and Healy (1955) note that "the last-ditch all-night parlays are as familiar to newspaper readers as they are wearing on reporters. . . " (p. 57). In mediation, it is common to use deadlines as a tactic to facilitate compromises, as President Jimmy Carter did in the Camp David negotiations between Egypt and Israel in 1978 (Touval & Zartman, 1985). Labor mediators report that they sometimes schedule negotiation sessions late in the evening, believing that concessions are easier to extricate from negotiators at 3 A.M. than at 3 P.M.

Our purpose in the present chapter is to review the literature on time pressure in negotiation and mediation and to identify some common themes, interesting questions, and possible directions for future research. First, we focus on the impact of time pressure on the processes and outcomes of negotiation. Then we review the literature on time pressure in mediation, which is brief because the literature contains only few studies. We conclude with a sketch of the literature on time pressure in individual decision making that may be relevant to negotiation and mediation and that may stimulate additional research.

Components of Negotiation: Outcomes and Strategies

Much research on negotiation is based on the assumption that the outcome is determined by negotiator strategies and tactics (Carnevale & Pruitt, 1992). Time pressure has generally been regarded as a constraint of the situation or context and has been assumed to affect negotiation outcome by influencing negotiator strategies and tactics.

Negotiation Outcomes

The possible outcomes of a negotiation can be understood in terms of the joint utility space shown in Figure 1 (Carnevale & Pruitt, 1992). The points in this space correspond to the options available for settling an issue or set of issues, the solid points referring to options that are known at the beginning of negotiation and the hollow points to options that can be devised with some creative thinking. The axes give the utility (e.g., monetary value, level of happiness) to each party of the options shown. Imagine that at the start of negotiation, Party X is advocating Option 5 while Party Y is advocating Option 1. An example might be a negotiation over a pay increase with the employee (X) asking an increase of $12,000 and the employer (Y) offering $10,000. Options 2, 3, and 4 are various pay increases between these two figures. Options 6, 7, and 8 are possible mutu-

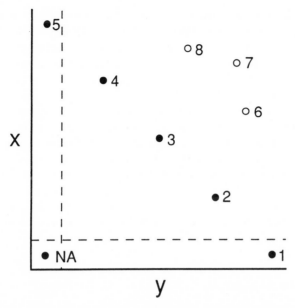

Figure 1. The joint utility space, showing known options (solid points) and possible alternatives (hollow points) available to two negotiators (x and y). The axes give the utility (e.g., monetary value, level of happiness) to each party of the options shown. The dashed lines stand for the two parties' limits (also called "reservation prices"), those levels of benefit below which they will not concede.

ally beneficial solutions in which the employer adds benefits (larger office, closer parking space, access to the executive restroom, etc.) that benefit the employee more than they cost the employer.

The negotiation can end in four possible ways: (1) No agreement, the utility of this to each party is shown by the point marked "NA"; (2) victory for one party, either Option 1 or Option 5.; (3) A simple compromise (options 2, 3 or 4), a compromise is defined as some middle ground on an obvious dimension connecting the two parties' initial offers (Pruitt, 1981), and (4) A win–win ("integrative") agreement (Options 6, 7, or 8) in which the parties achieve higher joint benefit than they could with a compromise agreement (Pruitt, 1981, Walton & McKersie, 1965), it is generally believed (e.g., Pruitt, 1981) that win–win agreements are longer lasting and more beneficial for the relationship between the parties than simple compromises, although the empirical evidence on this is scant.

The dashed lines in Figure 1 stand for the two parties' limits (also called "reservation prices"), those levels of benefit below which they will not concede (Raiffa, 1982). Options that are above and to the right of these lines are said to be "viable" in the sense of being mutually acceptable. Figure 1 shows a situation in which several known alternatives are viable. Agreement is likely to be reached in such a situation (Ben-Yoav & Pruitt, 1984; Carnevale & Lawler, 1986) but it is not inevitable because one or both parties may become locked into an unrealistic demand through a defect in strategy or understanding of the other party's constraints.

In some situations, the limits are so high that none of the obvious options are viable, but there are some viable win–win options just over the horizon if the parties will use their imagination. In our example, the employee may not be willing to accept the employer's minimal raise, but there are several possible packages of extras that are sufficiently attractive to the employee to warrant accepting a raise that will be acceptable to the employer. Such situations are said to have "integrative potential" (Walton & McKersie, 1965). In some situations, the parties' limits are so high that no viable alternative exists. In these cases, agreement is possible only if one or both parties lower their limits.

Negotiation Strategies

Early research on negotiation often used a "unidimensional" negotiation task, which involved a single issue (e.g., Options 1 to 5 in Figure 1), and with subjects instructed to adopt an individualistic orientation (to maximize individual profits). This work was largely concerned with the antecedents and consequences of various patterns of concession making. Underlying this research was a demand–concession model that viewed negotiators as starting at a particular level of demand and then conceding (reducing their demand) more or less rapidly until they reached one another's positions or negotiation was broken off. For example, the employee in Figure 1 might start at $12,000 (Option 5) and then concede after a considerable period of time to $11,500 (Option 4) and eventually to $11,000 (Option 3), stopping there. In the context of the options shown in Figure 1, this would be a "high" initial demand and a "slow" rate of concessions. There is a basic dilemma in these situations: Parties who make high demands and infrequent concessions are more likely to win but are more likely to fail to reach agreement (Pruitt, 1981).

Much of the recent laboratory research on negotiation uses a "multidimensional" negotiation task developed by Pruitt (1981). This task involves two or more issues that are of different priority to the disputants. Win–win solutions are achieved by means of logrolling, each party winning on the issues it finds important. This task also allows the parties to adopt a compromise on each issue, producing agreements like those at Points 2, 3, and 4 in Figure 1. But logrolling yields solutions like 6, 7, and 8 that are better for the parties collectively and often better for both parties individually.

In addition, recent research on negotiation has taken a broader view of negotiation process and has focused on three strategies, including concession making:

1. Concession making (also called *yielding*)–reducing one's demands or aspirations to accommodate the other party.
2. Contending—trying to persuade the other party to yield. Specific tactics that implement this strategy include threats and commitments not to concede.
3. Problem solving—trying to locate options that satisfy both parties' goals. There are a host of problem-solving tactics including active listening, providing information about own priorities, and brainstorming in search of solutions. Problem solving often involves information exchange, in which one or both parties provide information about their priorities (promoting the development of logrolling solutions) or the interests underlying their positions. There is both correlational (Pruitt, 1981) and experimental (Thompson & Hastie, 1990) evidence that information exchange promotes the development of win–win solutions.

The three strategies are alternative ways of moving toward agreement. Hence (assuming that agreement is sought) if conditions reduce the likelihood of using one strategy, the other two become more likely. If two of these strategies are ruled out, the use of the third becomes virtually certain. The research suggests that contending and problem solving are incompatible, although there is evidence that negotiations often proceed in stages from the former to the latter (Pruitt, 1981).

Time Pressure in Negotiation

Effects of Time Pressure on Concession Making (Yielding)

In negotiation research using a single-issue, unidimensional task, time pressure has been manipulated in several different ways. In some studies, it was the cost of continued negotiation, for example, a $2 charge for every offer made (Komorita & Barnes, 1969); in other studies, it was the time available to negotiate, for example, 45 versus 90 seconds (Smith et al., 1982). Other studies have combined these procedures; for example, Hamner (1974) gave subjects in the low-time-pressure conditions 30 trials (defined as an exchange of offers) without a penalty, and in the high-time-pressure conditions, allowed 20 trials of negotiations with no penalty followed by a 5% penalty for subsequent trials of negotiation. Some studies have examined time elapsed (Kelley, Beckman, & Fischer, 1967; Pruitt & Drews, 1969), under the assumption that time pressure increases over time.

The results of these diverse implementations of time pressure have been highly consistent: Time pressure produces lower demands, faster concessions, and faster agreement (Brookmire & Sistrunk, 1980; Hamner, 1974; Kelley et al., 1967; Komorita & Barnes, 1969; Pruitt & Drews, 1969; Pruitt & Johnson, 1970, Smith et al., 1982; Yukl, 1974). Evidence by Yukl (1974) suggests that these effects may be mediated by level of aspiration. Time pressure reduced the level of outcome that negotiators wanted to achieve (see Smith et al., 1982). In the study by Komorita and Barnes (1969), pressure to reach agreement was also implemented asymmetrically. When both parties had high pressure to reach agreement (high costs of continued negotiation), concession making was greater, and the number of trials to reach an agreement was less. When pressure was asymmetric, the party with the greater costs made more concessions and settled for a lower outcome than the party without the costs.

Effects of Time Pressure on Problem Solving and Contending

What influence does time pressure have on integrative bargaining? The research on time pressure in single-issue negotiation tasks, described above, suggests that time pressure increases the level of cooperativeness of negotiators because it facilitates concession making. However, this conclusion is inconsistent with Walton and McKersie's (1965) observation that high time pressure inhibits joint problem solving and the search for integrative agreements.

Yukl, Malone, Hayslip, and Pamin (1976) investigated the effects of time pressure on negotiation in a multidimensional task with integrative potential to test Walton and McKersie's (1965) hypothesis. Negotiators under high time pressure were given 30 extra points and told that a point would be deducted for every minute of negotiation; those under low time pressure did not receive this instruction. They reported that negotiators reached agreement sooner when there was high time pressure than when there was low time pressure (8.3 vs. 17.4 minutes), made fewer offers when there was high time pressure (11.6 vs. 17.9), and reached poorer joint outcomes when there was high time pressure (95.8 vs. 107.8, where 120 was the maximum possible and failure to reach agreement was 0). In addition, 65% of the dyads under low time pressure disclosed their true-issue priorities, whereas only 35% did so when there was high time pressure. These findings led Yukl et al. to conclude that time pressure interrupts integrative bargaining processes, and chiefly the processes of systematic concession making (e.g., proposing many offers) and problem solving (e.g., exchanging truthful information).

In an extension of the Yukl et al. (1976) study, Carnevale and Lawler (1986) argued that the effects of time pressure on integrative bargaining depend on whether negotiators have cooperative or competitive goals. All of the Yukl et al.

subjects were in a hostile, competitive context: They were instructed to attain the highest personal payoff and also were encouraged to mislead their opponent. Carnevale and Lawler argued that the subjects under high time pressure in the Yukl et al. study became more sensitive to the hostile context that they were in. This argument was based on the results of a study by Wright (1974), who found that people under high time pressure become more sensitive to negative information (see also Svenson & Edland, 1989). Thus the decrease in the disclosure of truthful information in the high-time-pressure condition of the Yukl et al. study may have reflected enhanced competitiveness. This reasoning led Carnevale and Lawler to hypothesize that time pressure would enhance competitiveness and produce poor negotiation outcomes only when negotiators were in a hostile, competitive context, but not when they were in a cooperative context.

Carnevale and Lawler (1986) operationalized time pressure in terms of the total amount of time available to negotiate (5 minutes vs. 25 minutes) and also manipulated negotiator goals, either to maximize individual profits or joint profits. As hypothesized, high time pressure produced poor negotiation outcomes and competitive behavior only when negotiators had individualistic goals; when negotiators had cooperative goals, they achieved high joint outcomes regardless of time pressure. In combination with an individualistic orientation, time pressure produced greater competitiveness, firm negotiator aspirations, and reduced information exchange; in combination with a cooperative orientation, time pressure led to enhanced cooperativeness and lower negotiator aspirations.

Time Pressure in Mediation

Mediation is a common form of dispute resolution in contexts as diverse as civil and criminal litigation, international relations, family disputes and divorce, environmental planning and siting, and decision making in organizations (Kressel & Pruitt, 1989). Unlike arbitrators, mediators cannot impose an outcome on the disputants but employ a variety of influence tactics in their effort to facilitate voluntary agreements. Recent research has focused on the decision processes of mediators and the impact of situational constraints, such as time pressure, on mediator's choice of tactics.

Mediators can do many things to affect negotiations, including dealing directly with the issues between the negotiators (Carnevale & Pruitt, 1992). This includes identifying the issues, uncovering underlying interests and concerns, setting an agenda, packaging, sequencing and prioritizing the issues, interpreting and shaping proposals, and making suggestions for possible settlement. Because they have greater access to the parties' underlying interests and aspirations, mediators can serve in an "analytic" capacity and help foster negotiator rationality by uncovering integrative, win–win agreements (Raiffa 1982, 1983).

Some mediator behaviors are more forceful and are designed to reduce a negotiator's reluctance to make concessions by, for example, applying forceful, pressing tactics such as negative sanctions, threats, and arguments (Kressel & Pruitt, 1989).

Mediators experience time pressure to the extent that they or the negotiators want to end the negotiation quickly. Although research on the effects of time pressure on mediator behavior is scant, evidence indicates that time pressure causes labor mediators to increase their use of forceful, pressing tactics (Kressel & Pruitt, 1989). These tactics apparently are designed to reduce the negotiators' aspirations and thus increase concession making and the likelihood of agreement.

One of the most consistent findings in mediation research is the observation that mediators become more forceful when they believe that the likelihood of agreement is low, such as when the disputants are intransigent (see Kressel & Pruitt, 1989). Carnevale and Conlon (1988) tested the hypothesis that time pressure reduces mediator's beliefs about the likelihood of agreement and thus leads them to be more forceful. This hypothesis was tested by examining changes in mediator behavior over time and also by manipulating the amount of time available to mediate. The data supported the hypothesis: Mediators were more forceful when there was high time pressure. In addition, mediators became increasingly forceful over time. The mediators reported that the likelihood of agreement was lower when there was high time pressure, supporting the proposition that this belief mediates the impact of time pressure on mediator behavior. Cooper and Carnevale (1990) replicated this effect and further showed that it was due to time pressure directly on the mediator and not to the mediator's beliefs about time pressure on the negotiators.

Conclusions and Future Research

In negotiation, one effect of time pressure is to speed up concession making and increase the likelihood of agreement, but this effect is found only in negotiations that are relatively simple and that involve a single issue or dimension of value. Another effect of time pressure is to create asymmetries in the outcome of negotiation, with the negotiator who is less susceptible to time pressure obtaining a more favorable outcome.

The effects of time pressure are more complex in complex negotiations that involve multiple issues. Time pressure can be a source of stress that creates blinders so that efficient, integrative alternatives get overlooked (see Walton & McKersie 1965; Janis & Mann, 1977). But this effect depends on the negotiators' cooperative or competitive orientation (Carnevale & Lawler, 1986). When negotiators have a competitive goal, time pressure enhances competitive behaviors and lessens the likelihood of agreement. But when negotiators have cooperative goals, time pressure has a lesser effect: It increases cooperative behaviors and the desire to reach agreement quickly. In mediation, the evidence is consistent in showing that time pressure leads mediators to adopt a forceful, pressing style in their effort to facilitate agreement.

One set of findings from research on time pressure in individual decision making that may be relevant to negotiation is the possible mediating role of risk attitudes and loss aversion. Several studies suggest that time pressure, for individuals, can produce more cautious, risk-avoiding behaviors, as well as greater motivation to avoid losses (Hansson, Keating, & Terry, 1974; Svenson & Edland, 1989; Wright & Weitz, 1977). A study by Carnevale, Gentile, and de Dreu (1993) speaks to these issues in negotiation. These authors manipulated time pressure, which was defined as closeness to a deadline. They also manipulated risk associated with impasse: in the no-risk, certain outcome condition, if there was an impasse, each negotiator would receive a predetermined outcome; in the risky, uncertain outcome condition, if there was an impasse, a coin toss would determine each negotiator's outcome. The impasse outcome for both conditions had equal expected value. Main effects for time pressure and risk at impasse were obtained—more concessions were made under high time pressure than low time pressure, and more when impasse was associated with uncertainty than certainty. But these two factors did not interact; the effects of time pressure on concession-making was as great when negotiators faced a certain impasse outcome than an uncertain impasse outcome. In other words, the data did not support the hypothesis that negotiators under high time pressure were more concerned about risk than negotiators under low time pressure.

Carnevale, Gentile, and de Dreu (1993) also manipulated the negotiators' decision frame—a "gain" frame, i.e., negotiation over profits, versus a "loss" frame, i.e., negotiation over expenses (cf. Tversky & Kahneman, 1981). Decision frame has been shown to be relevant to loss aversion as well as risk attitudes. In the Carnevale et al. (1993) study, the effects of time pressure interacted with frame—time pressure led to heightened concession-making only when negotiators had a gain frame. When negotiators had a loss frame, they made few concessions, and time pressures had no effect. This pattern was identical to the interaction pattern involving time pressure and limit obtained in prior research (Smith et al., 1982), suggesting that time pressure reduces loss aversion and resistance to making concessions.

A general conclusion that can be drawn from the research reviewed in this chapter is that time pressure can play an important role in negotiation and mediation. But our understanding of the scope and nature of these effects is limited—there simply have not been very many systematic investigations. Fortunately, however, there are numerous potentially interesting paths for future research, only one of which is the analysis of time pressure on loss aversion and risk attitudes in negotiation and mediation.

ACKNOWLEDGMENT. This material is based upon work supported by the National Science Foundation under Grant No. BNS-8809263 (Peter Carnevale, principal investigator). The authors are grateful to Andrea Hollingshead for her helpful comments on an earlier draft of this chapter.

References

Ben-Yoav, O., & Pruitt, D. G. (1984). Accountability to constituents: A two-edged sword. *Organizational Behavior and Human Performance, 34*, 283–295.

Brookmire, D., & Sistrunk, F. (1980). The effects of perceived ability and impartiality of mediators and time pressure on negotiation. *Journal of Conflict Resolution, 24*, 311–327.

Carnevale, P. J., & Conlon, D. E. (1988). Time pressure and strategic choice in mediation. *Organizational Behavior and Human Decision Processes, 42*, 111–133.

Carnevale, P. J., & Lawler, E. J. (1986). Time pressure and the development of integrative agreements in bilateral negotiation. *Journal of Conflict Resolution, 30*, 636–659.

Carnevale, P. J., & Pruitt, D. G. (1992). Negotiation and mediation. *Annual Review of Psychology, 43*, 531–582.

Carnevale, P. J., Gentile, S., & de Dreu, C. K. W. (1993). *Loss aversion versus risk attitude in bilateral negotiation.* Unpublished manuscript, Department of Psychology, University of Illinois at Urbana–Champaign.

Cooper, R., & Carnevale, P. J. (1990). *Effects of asymmetric time pressure on mediator perceptions and behavior.* Paper presented at the meeting of the Judgment and Decision Making Society, New Orleans, November 1990.

Dunlop, J. T., & Healy, J. J. (1955). *Collective bargaining: Principles and cases.* Homewood, IL: Richard D. Irwin.

Hamner, W. C. (1974). Effects of bargaining strategy and pressure to reach agreement in a stalemated negotiation. *Journal of Personality and Social Psychology, 30*, 458–467.

Hansson, R. O., Keating, J. P., & Terry, C. (1974). The effects of mandatory time limits in the voting booth on liberal-conservative voting patterns. *Journal of Applied Social Psychology, 4*, 336–342.

Janis, I. L., & Mann, L. (1977). *Decision making: A psychological analysis of conflict, choice, and commitment.* New York: The Free Press.

Kelley, H. H., Beckman, L. L., & Fischer, C. S. (1967). Negotiating the division of reward under incomplete information. *Journal of Experimental Social Psychology, 3*, 361–398.

Komorita, S. S., & Barnes, M. (1969). Effects of pressures to reach agreement in bargaining. *Journal of Personality and Social Psychology, 13*, 245–252.

Kressel, K., & Pruitt, D. G. (1989). *Mediation research.* San Francisco: Jossey-Bass.

Pruitt, D. G. (1981). *Negotiation behavior.* New York: Academic Press.

Pruitt, D. G., & Drews, J. L. (1969). The effect of time pressure, time elapsed, and the opponent's concession rate on behavior in negotiation. *Journal of Experimental Social Psychology, 5*, 43–60.

Pruitt, D. G., & Johnson, D. F. (1970). Mediation as an aid to face-saving in negotiation. *Journal of Personality and Social Psychology, 14*, 239–246.

Raiffa, H. (1982). *The art and science of negotiation.* Cambridge, MA: Harvard University Press.

Raiffa, H. (1983). Mediation of conflicts. *American Behavioral Scientist, 27*, 195–210.

Rubin, J. Z., & Brown, B. (1975). *The social psychology of bargaining and negotiations.* New York: Academic Press.

Smith, D. L., Pruitt, D. G., & Carnevale, P. J. (1982). Matching and mismatching: The effect of own limit, other's toughness, and time pressure on concession rate in negotiation. *Journal of Personality and Social Psychology, 42,* 876–883.

Svenson, O., & Edland, A. (1989). Changes of preferences under time pressure: Choices and judgments. In H. Montgomery & O. Svenson (Eds.), *Process and structure in human decision making* (pp. 225–236). New York: John Wiley & Sons.

Thompson, L. L., & Hastie, R. (1990). Social perception in negotiation. *Organizational Behavior and Human Decision Processes, 47,* 98–123.

Touval, S., & Zartman, I. W. (1985). *International mediation in theory and practice.* Boulder, CO: Westview Press.

Tversky, A., & Kahneman, D. (1981). The framing of decisions and the psychology of choice. *Science, 211,* 453–458.

Walton, R., & McKersie, R. (1965). *A behavioral theory of labor negotiations: An analysis of a social interaction system.* New York: McGraw-Hill.

Wright, P. (1974). The harassed decision maker: Time pressures, distractions, and the use of evidence. *Journal of Applied Psychology, 59,* 555–561.

Wright, P., & Weitz, B. (1977). Time horizon effects on product evaluation strategies. *Journal of Marketing Research, 16,* 555–561.

Yukl, G. A. (1974). Effects of situational variables and opponent concessions on a bargainer's perception, aspirations, and concessions. *Journal of Personality and Social Psychology, 29,* 227–236.

Yukl, G. A., Malone, M. P., Hayslip, B., & Pamin, T. A. (1976). The effects of time pressure and issue settlement order on integrative bargaining. *Sociometry, 39,* 277–281.

III

Experimental Studies of Time Pressure

Part III presents six empirical studies investigating the effects of time pressure on aspects of individual judgment and decision making. These studies draw on a number of different theoretical and methodological approaches and provide a sample of contemporary research in this area. The first three studies are similar in approach in that they consider time-pressure-related changes in terms of underlying cognitive processes. The major concern is to identify changes in cognitive strategy, considered in such terms as the type, order, and amount of information processing underlying judgment and choice. The chapters differ in terms of the particular aspect of underlying cognitive processing that is the focus for research.

In Chapter 9, Svenson and Benson report two studies considering the effects of time constraints on the framing of decisions. Subjects completed a number of problems under different deadline conditions, with each problem framed in one of two ways (e.g., one version emphasizing gains, the other losses). Choice and attractiveness difference judgments are reported, the latter providing the primary basis for the analysis. Results indicated that, for framing problems that include alternatives that are associated with relatively big losses, time pressure reduced the usually reported framing effect associated with risk aversion in the gain version and risk seeking in the loss version of the problem. The authors argue that this demonstrates that simply working for longer on a decision problem is not sufficient to overcoming the framing bias. They discuss their results in terms of Differentiation and Consolidation Theory, suggesting that deadlines truncate the differentiation process that, under normal conditions, is responsible for making one alternative clearly distinguishable and strongly preferred as compared with the other.

In Chapter 10, Edland also uses attractiveness difference judgments as a means of investigating time-pressure-related changes in the information-processing strategy. The strategy adopted by individuals was determined by considering which of four different rules best described their pattern of choice behavior. Results indicated that time pressure decreased the use of rules focusing on negative information in favor of rules giving increased importance to positive information. Because the former rules require an additional cognitive operation, this change is interpreted as being functional in coping with reduced time. This finding replicates an earlier study by Svenson, Edland, and Slovic (1990) using incomplete information but contradicts the previously dominant view that assumes an increased priority for negative information under time pressure (e.g., Wright, 1974).

Svenson and Benson, in Chapter 11, investigate the effects of variations in instructions concerning the adequacy of the time allowed to complete a task. The pattern of strategy change under time pressure reported by studies like Edland's (Chapter 10) is used as the basis for investigating these variations. Two groups completed a set of decision tasks under identical deadline conditions, with one group told that the deadline was "too short" to complete the task, the other told that it was "sufficient." In the "too-short" condition, subjects increased their use of the strategy that the earlier research had indicated was used most frequently when there was no time constraint. In the "sufficient" condition there was a decline in the use of this strategy, akin to the decline that previous studies like Edland's had demonstrated under "real" time pressure conditions. The authors argue that the instructions led subjects to appraise the task demands differently and thereby mobilized resources to complete the task to different degrees. This study emphasizes the importance of the way people appraise task demands and how these can lead to differences in judgment and decision making.

The final three studies in this part of the book focus on the effects of time pressure on binary choice, all drawing on Criteria-Dependent Choice (CDC) Models. These models assume that decision makers process information about alternatives one attribute at a time, accumulating the results of these comparisons until a critical value or criterion is reached favoring one of the alternatives. Also, the placing of the criteria or decision boundary is assumed to depend on the cost and payoff structure as well as the available time. Time pressure effects are explained in terms of a reduction in the critical value of the criteria. An important feature of these models is that they can be seen as including many of the classic compensatory and noncompensatory decision rules as special cases (cf. Svenson, 1979), thereby providing a different way of thinking about these rules.

In Chapter 12, Wallsten presents one version of this approach and applies it to a probabilistic inference task in which subjects choose which of two possible states of the world is responsible for some presented information. He presents a specific CDC model that predicts an interaction between time pressure and payoff structure. The experimental data support the theory in most respects except that there were sequential effects in processing the information dimensions.

The primary focus of Busemeyer's contribution (Chapter 13) is on the relation between speed and accuracy of decision making. He presents a sequential comparison model (SCM) of binary choice, similar to the CDC model. Predictions about the relation between the speed and accuracy of decision making made by SCM is compared with an alternative approach assuming that subjects adopt one from a number of strategies, based on a cost/benefit analysis (cf. Bettman, Johnson, & Payne, 1990). Busemeyer presents data supporting SCM and discusses these results in terms of Decision Field Theory, a theory recently applied to a number of other decision research phenomena.

Finally Böckenholt and Krueger, in Chapter 14, predict that changes in certain parameters within the CDC model can account for many of the reported effects of time pressure on decision making. The most important change predicted is a lowering of the critical value of the criterion under time pressure. They present data consistent with this prediction and the model, including faster information processing and a lowering of decision confidence.

Taken together, these three chapters demonstrate that CDC models provide a distinctive and potentially productive approach to our understanding of strategy change under time pressure and an interesting alternative to the more common cost/benefit approach.

References

Bettman, J. R., Johnson, E. J., & Payne, J. W. (1990). A componential analysis of cognitive effort in choice. *Organisational Behavior and Human Decision Processes, 45,* 111–139.

Svenson, O. (1979). Process descriptions of decision making. *Organisational Behavior and Human Performance, 23,* 86–112.

Svenson, O., Edland, A., & Slovic, P. (1990). Choices between incompletely described alternatives under time stress. *Acta Psychologica, 75,* 153–169.

Wright, P. L. (1974). The harassed decision maker: Time pressures, distractions and the use of evidence. *Journal of Applied Psychology, 59,* 555–561.

9

Framing and Time Pressure in Decision Making

Ola Svenson and Lehman Benson, III

Introduction

This study investigates the effect of time pressure on decision framing. Tversky and Kahneman (1981) introduced the term *decision frame* for a decision maker's representation of a decision problem including acts outcomes and contingencies associated with different alternatives (cf. Tversky & Kahneman, 1981). They showed that different decision frames can be induced from the same factual information. Two versions of a particular decision problem may be constructed that are formally identical, yet the wording of each is slightly different by emphasizing either the gains or the losses.

This apparently trivial difference may change the decision-maker's frame and lead to a reversal in preference for the alternatives. This is difficult to handle in formal decision theory (cf. Keeney & Raiffa, 1976), leading to alternative formulations like Prospect Theory (Kahneman & Tversky, 1979). This issue is

Ola Svenson • Department of Psychology, Stockholm University, S-10691 Stockholm, Sweden.   **Lehman Benson, III** • Department of Psychology, Lund University, S-22350 Lund, Sweden.
Time Pressure and Stress in Human Judgment and Decision Making, edited by Ola Svenson and A. John Maule. Plenum Press, New York, 1993.

illustrated by considering two versions of the following problem, the first emphasizing losses and the second gains:

> Imagine that Sweden is preparing to fight the AIDS disease, which is assumed to kill 600 people during a given time, if nothing is done. Two alternative programs have been developed to fight the disease. Assume that the exact scientific estimates of the effects of the two programs A and B are (a) if program A is chosen 400 people will die, and (b) if program B is chosen, there is a one-third probability that nobody will die and two-thirds probability that 600 people will die.

Which of the two programs do you prefer? In the positive framing condition the alternatives are instead: (a) If Program A is chosen, 200 people will be saved and (b) if B is chosen, there is a one-third probability that all will be saved and a two-third probability that nobody will be saved.

Typically, people choose the risky alternative (B) in the first version and the certain alternative (A) in the second version despite the fact that the two versions are formally identical (cf. Maule, 1989; Tversky & Kahneman, 1981). Though standard economic or decision theory cannot predict this finding, Prospect Theory can by assuming that the two versions of the problem are framed differently, as a choice between losses and a choice between gains, respectively. Risk taking is known to be different in losses as compared with gains. The act of framing, so critical to this explanation, is assumed to be the result of immediate automatic processes that are very quick and analogous to those underlying visual perception. As such, the imposition of a deadline should have little effect on the way that choice problems are framed, and therefore the usual reversal of preference identified above would be expected even under time pressure conditions.

In addition to Prospect Theory, there are other alternative theories, some of which model decision making as a process over time. One of these theories is Differentiation and Consolidation Theory (Svenson, 1992; Maule & Svenson, this volume) that models decision making as a process in which one alternative is gradually differentiated from other alternatives. This process requires time to allow the decision maker to reach a level of differentiation that is sufficient for a decision. If the deadline for a decision is too close, the resulting time pressure leads to a forced premature closure of the differentiation process. In other words, the decision is made but without sufficient deliberation. If framing effects are the result of more complex elaborative differentiation processes that are not speeded up to compensate for lack of time, then time pressure would weaken the framing effect. On the other hand, if framing effects are the result of immediate quick processes analogous to visual perception as suggested by Tversky and Kahneman (1981), time pressure would not weaken the framing effect significantly. The present study was designed to determine which of these two hypotheses is appropriate.

Experiment 1

Method

Subjects

Seventy six senior high-school students served as voluntary participants. They were each randomly assigned to one of four treatment groups, each containing 19 students.

Materials and Stimuli

The stimuli consisted of a series of pairs of decision problems. Each decision problem consisted of two options as exemplified in the introduction. The first four pairs were lotteries and included filler problems. They were followed by the AIDS problem, a rephrased version of the Asian disease problem (cf. Kahneman & Tversky, 1979).

A slide projector equipped with an automatic timer was used to regulate the time intervals. The problems were presented on slides projected on a screen in front of each group. In addition to marking their choices (Alternatives A or B) on the response sheets in front of them, the subjects were instructed to mark the size of the attractiveness difference between the two alternatives on the screen. This was done by circling a number (1 = no difference to 10 = great difference) on the response sheet. The layout of the response scale on the response sheet was counterbalanced with half of the answer sheets having the following layout from left to right: (1, 2, . . . 9, 10). The other half of the answer sheets had the opposite layout: (10, 9, 8 . . . 1). This control was performed to ensure that any effects of framing and/or time pressure could not be attributed to a response artifact.

This response scale gives a more sensitive measures of changes of preferences as compared with simple counts of A and B choices. This is because each choice is reflected not only on a binary scale but also on an interval rating scale. This rating scale was used successfully in earlier studies (cf. Svenson, Edland, & Slovic, 1990).

A measure of perceived stress was also developed, based on the scale described above. The only difference was that 0 on the scale = no stress and 10 = much stress. This scale was administered to all subjects before and after the experimental session. At the end of a session, the following additional statements were presented: (1) exposure time was too short, (2) had time to think, (3) experienced time pressure, and (4) satisfied with my decision. The subjects responded on a scale from zero = do not agree to 10 = agree a lot.

Design and Procedure

The four treatments involved: (1) Positive framing no time pressure, Pos-NoTp, (2) positive framing time pressure, PosTp, (3) negative framing no time pressure, NegNoTp, and (4) negative framing time pressure, NegTp.

The 38 subjects, who were in the no-time-pressure conditions, were allowed as much time as they needed to complete the task. Following each presentation of the stimuli, the experimenter asked if everybody was ready for the next stimuli to be presented. After the subjects had responded "yes" the experimenter displayed the next slide.

The 38 subjects, who were in the time pressure conditions were allowed only a certain amount of time to complete the task. The time limits were determined from data in an earlier pilot study and represented the average time taken to complete each task subtracted by one standard deviation. For the filler problems 1–4 the subjects had 12 seconds to complete each task. For Question 5 the subjects had 40 seconds to complete the task.

Results

The average score reported for amount of stress felt in the time pressure condition before the experiment was 2.7 on a scale ranging from 0 to 10. The average score of amount of stress felt in the time pressure condition after the experiment was 4.7. This difference is statistically significant ($F = 6.0$, $df = 1/72$, $p < 0.01$). Contrasting this, in the no-time-pressure condition the average score reported before was 2.7 and 2.8 after which is a nonsignificant difference. As for the questions that came after the experiment, all the means on these scales ("exposure too short," "had time to think," and "experienced time pressure") were significantly different for the time pressure and no-time-pressure groups except the last question about satisfaction. These conclusions were based on one way ANOVA analyses with $p < 0.01$.

The decision-problem data were coded in the following manner. There were two alternatives in each of the decision problems, A and B. The choice of Alternative A (always the certain alternative) was given a positive sign number. The choice of Alternative B (always the risky alternative) was given a negative number sign. Thus, if a student selected Alternative A and marked 3 on the rating scale (1= no attractiveness difference, 10= great attractiveness difference) the score would be 3.0. If a student selected Alternative B with the same degree of attractiveness difference, the score would be −3.0. The mean and standard deviations were computed across the subjects for each of the questions.

An analysis of variance ("positive framing–negative framing" × "time pressure–no time pressure") of the 19 subjects in each condition indicated that

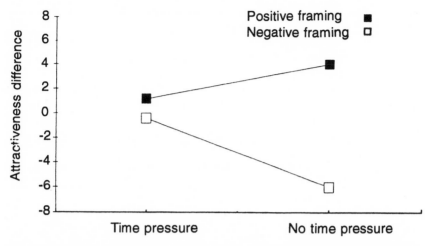

Figure 1. Attractiveness difference as a function of time limit in Experiment 1. The difference is positive if favoring the certain alternative (A) and negative for the uncertain alternative (B). In the time pressure condition, a decision had to be made in 40 seconds and in the no-time-pressure condition there was no time limit. Filled rectangles represent the positive framing, and open rectangles the negative framing condition.

none of the first four filler problems had a significant main effect. Therefore these problems will not be analyzed further.

In the AIDS question, however, there was a significant main effect for the framing factor. The mean attractiveness difference for positive framing was 2.51, whereas the mean for negative framing was −3.2 (two-way ANOVA, $F = 23.93$, $df = 1/72$, $p<.001$). There was no effect on mean attractiveness across positive and negative framing related to the time factor, but there was a significant interaction ($F = 12.69$, $df = 1/72$, $p<.001$). Thus, in the positive framing condition the certain alternative (A) was *more* preferred than the risky alternative (B) under no time pressure and in the negative framing condition the certain alternative was *less* preferred than the risky alternative (cf. Figure 1). In the time pressure condition there was no significant difference between framing conditions. In other words, time pressure *reduced* the framing effect. The mean for the time pressure negative framing condition was −0.42, and the mean for the no-time-pressure negative framing condition was −6.00 (in *post hoc* analysis $t = 3.44$, $df = 36$, p<.001). The mean for time pressure positive framing was 1.16, and the mean for no-time-pressure positive framing was 4.00 ($t = 1.68$, $df = 36$, $p<.05$).

These data support the hypothesis that framing effects are evolving over time. There is no evidence that they are immediate and analogous to perceptual

Table 1. Decision Problems Used in Experiment 2[a]

	Alternatives		Attractiveness difference (A–B)	
Problem type	A	B	No time pressure	Time pressure
1. *Easy–difficult* 570 tickets				
easy	8/10 to win SEK 48	2/10 sin SEK 192	1.40	−.15
difficult	456 tickets win SEK 48	114 tickets win SEK 192	−3.50	−.90
2. *Food poisoning* 120 kids or				
positive	30 kids saved	25% chance all saved 75% nobody saved	−1.95	3.10
negative	90 kids die	25% chance nobody dies 75% all die	−1.95	.35
3. *Breast cancer* 32 women lose one breast or				
positive	20 women save both breasts	62.5% all women save both breasts 37% nobody will save both breasts	4.35	1.15
negative	12 women lose one breast	62.5% nobody loses a breast 37% that all lose a breast	−3.65	−2.60

continued

or Level 1 decision processes (cf. Svenson, 1990) as suggested by Kahneman and Tversky (1984).

Experiment 2

This experiment was designed to test the robustness of the findings of Experiment 1 and whether they generalize to other types of framing problems. For example, Johnson, Payne, and Bettman (1988) suggested that changes to information displays can result in preference reversals. Consequently, a decision

Table 1. *continued*

Problem type	Alternatives A	Alternatives B	Attractiveness difference (A–B) No time pressure	Attractiveness difference (A–B) Time pressure
4. *Heart operation* 20 patients die or				
positive	6 patients cured	30% chance all cured 70% nobody cured	.65	1.95
negative	14 patients die	30% chance nobody dies 70% all die	−1.50	−.80
5. *Asian flu* 40 people die or				
positive	10 people saved	¹/₄ 40 people saved ³/₄ nobody saved	.85	−.85
negative	30 people die	¹/₄ nobody dies ³/₄ 40 people die	−1.75	−3.45
6. *AIDS* problem 600 people die or				
positive	200 people saved	¹/₃ 600 people saved ²/₃ nobody saved	4.15	1.50
negative	400 people die	¹/₃ nobody dies ²/₃ 600 people die	−3.80	−1.70

[a]The training example and one easy–difficult problem excluded. A choice of A is a certain choice in problems 2–6 and a B choice represents risk taking.

problem demanding relatively simple calculations in one version and relatively difficult calculations in the other was constructed (see Table 1 Problem 1). This problem was similar to the ones used by Johnson, Payne, and Bettman (1988). Here, framing refers to formally equal decision problems that are expressed in a simpler (including, e.g., a probability of 0.8) or a more complex form (including, e.g., a probability of 456/570). As the more complex form requires more elaborate processing, it is predicted that time pressure would reduce the effect of framing. Only if the framing effect is the result of a quicker process would framing effects stay the same under time pressure.

McNeil, Pauker, Sox, & Tversky (1982) also reported inconsistent preferences, this time in the domain of medicine. They studied how changes in framing, induced by variations in the way information is presented, can influence the choice of alternative therapies. The subject population consisted of three groups: patients, students (who had completed several statistics courses), and physicians. Their results demonstrated that all groups of subjects (even trained physicians) were influenced by framing. This result is alarming and therefore a problem similar to the one used by McNeil et al. (1982) was also included in this experiment. Here, the framings were positive and negative as in the original Asian flu problem. Based on the results from Experiment 1, weaker framing effects under time pressure are predicted than in conditions without time pressure.

Method

Subjects

Eighty senior high-school students served as voluntary participants. The students were randomly assigned into four treatment groups, each containing 20 students.

Material and Stimuli

Two introductory and six experimental decision problems were used. The latter included the Aids problem reported in Experiment 1 (cf. Table 1). The following exemplifies the exact wording of a problem schematically presented in Table 1 (no. 2).

Imagine an African village in which the children have been severely food poisoned. If nothing is done, 120 children are estimated to die. There are two alternative programs for curing the children: (a) This program will save 30 children ("leave 90 children to die" in negative version) and (b) This program provides a 25% chance that everybody is saved ("25% chance that nobody dies" in negative version) and 75% that nobody will be saved ("75% change that everybody dies").

The same questions about mood and time pressure were administered as in Experiment 1. The exposure time in the time pressure condition was determined in pretests and corresponded to approximately half the average time required for solving a problem under no time pressure. The exposure times were 30 seconds for problem No. 1 and 40 seconds for Problems Nos. 2–6 in Table 1.

Results

The data were coded as in the earlier experiment. First, the results from the mood and time pressure questions were all significant at the 5% level indicating that subjects experienced time pressure in the time pressure condition.

**Table 2. Proportions of Certain (A) Choices
in the Cancer, Heart Operation, Asian Flu,
and AIDS Problems**

Problem	No time pressure	Time pressure
Cancer		
Positive	.55	.68
Negative	.18	.09
Heart operation		
Positive	.59	.59
Negative	.45	.41
Asian flu		
Positive	.73	.64
Negative	.13	.27
AIDS		
Positive	.82	.64
Negative	.23	.27

The results from Experiment 1 were very clearly replicated in Experiment 2 in which the AIDS problem was No. 6 in Table 1. First, there was an overall effect of framing. The grand mean of positive framing was 2.82, and the mean for negative framing was -2.77. (Two-way ANOVA, $F = 27.16$, $df = 1/76$, $p < .001$.) As in Experiment 1, there was no main effect of time pressure, which instead interacted with framing leading to a significant interaction ($F = 4.78$, $df = 1/76$, $p < .05$). A plot of these data is very similar to those in Figure 1.

In the food poisoning problem (No. 2) the effect of the time variable was significant ($F = 7.78$, $df = 1/76$, $p < 0.01$), indicating a preference for the certain alternative under time pressure and for the uncertain alternative under no time pressure. There was no significant effect of framing, nor any interaction. In the cancer (No. 3), heart operation (No. 4), and Asian flu (No. 5) decision problems, there were significant effects of framing ($F = 23.89$, 4.83 and 5.23, respectively, $df = 1/76$, $p < 0.05$). There were no significant main effects of time pressure. The interactions were not significant except for the cancer problem in which marginal significance ($p < 0.08$) indicated a greater framing effect under no time pressure.

Problem 1 in Table 1 is different from the other problems and represents framing related to the easy–difficult manipulation. It demonstrated a significant effect of the easy–difficult factor ($F = 5.21$, $df = 1/76$, $p < 0.05$) and a marginally significant interaction (time $\times$ easy-difficult, $p < 0.09$). This indicates that there was less of a difference between the easy and difficult versions under time pressure.

Earlier studies of framing problems have reported proportions of choices instead of the more sensitive ratings analyzed in this chapter. Table 2 gives the corresponding choice proportions for the cancer (No. 3) heart operation (No. 4), Asian flu (No. 5), and AIDS (No. 6) problems as an illustrative comparison. It is clear that the proportions replicate the framing effects reported earlier. The table also indicates that the significant time pressure effect for judgments found in the AIDS problem is reflected in the choice proportions as well. Of the remaining three problems in the table, the effect of time pressure on the Asian flu problem shows the same tendency and the other two problems differ less between the time pressure–no-time-pressure conditions.

In conclusion, this experiment has shown that framing effects are not restricted to the Asian flu problem. The effect of time pressure was significant or near significant for three of the six problems, the food poisoning, the cancer, and the AIDS problems. Choice proportion data supported this result in the food poisoning and AIDS problems. Thus, the effects of time pressure were not as general as the framing effect. When there was an effect of time pressure, it was an interaction with framing; when time was short, there was less or no effect of framing, and when time was long, there was a stronger framing effect.

Discussion

The present study has demonstrated and extended the range of problems sensitive to framing. It has also demonstrated a very clear effect of time pressure on the AIDS problem that was an exact translation of the Asian disease problem. The Asian flu problem version used here had the number of lives reduced with a factor of 10 (e.g., 40 lives lost instead of 400). It also showed a significant framing effect.

When these problems were solved under time pressure only, the former with more lives at stake was clearly affected, with more time for processing the information producing a greater framing effect. Speculating about this, Differentiation and Consolidation Theory predicts that more important decisions lead to a greater degree of differentiation before a decision is made. If the number of lives at stake contributes to the importance of a decision, more differentiation should be predicted the more serious the problem. In general, a greater degree of differentiation is positively associated with longer processing time, and therefore time pressure would affect more important problems to a greater extent than less important decision problems. Wright (1974) and others (cf. Edland & Svenson, this volume) have reported that selective filtration of information under time pressure (Miller, 1960) often leads to overemphasizing the importance of negative information. However, as Edland and Svenson (this volume) point out, this is not always the case. Furthermore, because the number of lives at stake is confounded with the health problem factor, neither this nor the differentiation hypothesis can be tested in the present study but remains to be clarified by further research.

The AIDS problem's sensitivity to time pressure indicated that the processing could be seen as an elaboration process (cf. Maule, 1989) differentiating one alternative from the other rather than a quick perceptual process. Although significant framing effects were found among the remaining decision problems, the conclusion is not so clear concerning the effects of time pressure.

The result that different formulations of the same decision problem can lead to different preference orders remains a disturbing fact. Instructing decision makers to look at one and the same task from different perspectives, as suggested by Fischhoff (1983), may be needed to improve human decision making when framing is a critical issue. It is not self-evident that just giving people more time will help them get rid of framing biases. More time may instead make things worse.

ACKNOWLEDGMENT. This study was supported by grants from the Work Environment Fund, the Royal Swedish Academy of Science, and the Swedish Council for Research in the Humanities and Social Sciences. The authors want to thank Viveka Askeland von Gegerfelt, John Maule, Amparo Ortega, and Wivianne Runske for comments and assistance.

References

Fischhoff, B. (1983). Predicting frames. *Journal of Experimental Psychology: Learning, Memory and Cognition, 9,* 103–116.

Johnson, E., Payne, J., & Bettman, J. (1988). Information displays and preference reversals. *Organizational Behavior and Human Decision Process, 42,* 1–21.

Kahneman, D., & Tversky, A. (1979). Prospect Theory: An analysis of decisions under risk. *Econometrica, 47,* 263–291.

Keeney, R. L., & Raiffa, H. (1976). *Decisions with multiple objectives: Preferences and value tradeoffs.* New York: Wiley.

Maule, J. (1989). Positive and negative decision frames: A verbal protocol analysis of the Asian disease problem of A. Tversky and D. Kahneman. In Montgomery & O. Svenson (Eds.), *Process and structure in decision making* (pp. 163–180). Chichester: Wiley.

McNeil, B., Pauker, S., Sox, H., & Tversky, A. (1982). On the elicitation of preferences for alternative therapies. *The New England Journal of Medicine, 306,* 1259–1262.

Miller, J. G. (1960). Information input overload and psychopathology. *American Journal of Psychiatry, 116,* 695–704.

Svenson, O. (1992). Differentiation and Consolidation theory of human decision making: A frame of reference for the study of pre- and post-decision processes. *Acta Psychologica, 80,* 143–168.

Svenson, O. (1990). Some propositions for the classification of decisions. In K. Borcherding, O. Larichev, & D. M. Messick (Eds.), *Contemporary issues in decision making* (pp. 17–31). Amsterdam: Elsevier.

Svenson, O., & Edland, A. (1987). Change and preference under time pressure: Choices and judgments. *Scandinavian Journal of Psychology, 28,* 322–330.

Svenson, O., Edland, A., & Slovic, P. (1990). Choices and judgments of incompletely described
    decision alternatives under time pressure. *Acta Psychologica, 75,* 153–169.
Tversky, A., & Kahneman, D. (1981). The framing of decisions and the psychology of choice.
    Science, 211, 453–458.
Wright, P. (1974). The harassed decision maker: Time pressure, distraction and the use of evidence.
    Journal of Applied Psychology, 59, 555–561.

10

The Effects of Time Pressure on Choices and Judgments of Candidates to a University Program

Anne Edland

Introduction

An important characteristic of human decision making is that decisions in every-day life often have to be made under deadline conditions. These deadlines may engender feelings of time pressure. The purpose of the present study is to extend an earlier study by Svenson, Edland, and Slovic (1990) that examined time-pressure-induced changes in strategy when choosing between alternatives that were incompletely described. Svenson et al. (1990) found that time pressure resulted in a shift toward a strategy enhancing positive information. The present experiment attempts to supplement these results by determining whether similar changes in strategy occur when alternatives are described completely.

Much of research concerned with the effects of time pressure on decision making has drawn on ideas originally developed by Miller (1960) to explain how people adapt to information overload. Miller suggested seven different ways of coping, though decision researchers have tended to focus on just three of these—filtering, acceleration, and omission.

The *filtration mechanism,* refers to an increased selectivity of information processing, often associated with a greater emphasis on the most important

Anne Edland • Department of Psychology, Stockholm University, S-10691 Stockholm, Sweden.
Time Pressure and Stress in Human Judgment and Decision Making, edited by Ola Svenson and A. John Maule. Plenum Press, New York, 1993.

attribute. There has been considerable support for this mode of adapting from studies of decision making (e.g., Wright & Weitz, 1977; Ben Zur & Breznitz, 1981; Wallsten & Barton, 1982; Svenson & Edland, 1987; Payne, Bettman, & Johnson, 1988; Svenson, Edland, & Slovic, 1990) and judgment (e.g., Wright, 1974; Svenson, Edland, & Karlsson, 1985; Rothstein, 1986).

Initially studies of both judgment and decision making suggested that time pressure induced filtering involving an increased priority to negative information (Ben Zur & Breznitz, 1981; Wright, 1974). However, more recent research has provided contradictory findings. For instance, Svenson et al. (1990) reported increased use of positive information, whereas Maule and Mackie (1990) did not find any support for filtering in favor of either negative or positive information.

Acceleration, where subjects process the same information at a faster rate, has been demonstrated as a way of adapting to time pressure (Ben Zur & Breznitz, 1981; Maule & Mackie, 1990; Payne, Bettman, & Johnson, 1988). Finally, omission, where subjects completely ignore whole categories of information has also been found to occur under time pressure (Maule & Mackie, 1990).

The present study focuses on one of these modes of adapting, filtering, in the context of a recent study by Svenson et al. (1990). They reported that time pressure induced filtering in favor of positive information in a set of decision problems in which there was incomplete information about alternatives. The primary aim of the present study is to determine whether this mode of adapting continues to be important when each alternative is described fully.

The decision alternatives in the Svenson et al. study were students described by grades, ranging from 1 to 5, in Swedish, psychology, and natural science. The subjects' task was to choose which of two students in a pair would be more able to complete a university program for school psychologists. After each choice the subjects were instructed to judge the difference between the two students in a pair using an attractiveness-difference scale. These two measures were used to determine which decision rules subjects were using. A similar design is used in the present experiment, and a similar range of rules investigated. These are as follows:

1. *Maximum rule* (Max): Support for this rule occurs when subjects choose the alternative with the highest possible grade, that is Grade 5, on any of the three attributes.

2. *Minimum rule* (Min): Correspondingly, support for this rule occurs when subjects choose the alternative that *does not* have the lowest possible grade, that is Grade 1, on any of the three attributes.

3. *Majority of confirming dimensions* (MCD): Support for this rule occurs when subjects choose the alternative that is superior on two of the three attributes (cf. Russo & Dosher, 1983). In this study, MCD replaces the Common rule

considered by Svenson et al. (1990). In their study there was incomplete information such that there was only one attribute along which both alternatives were described. The MCD rule was called the "maximizing number of attributes with greater attractiveness" by Svenson (1979).

4. *Sum rule* (Sum): This rule assumes that subjects choose the alternative with the highest value when summing all the grades across the three attributes for that alternative. Differences in grades were fixed so that overall values of each pair never differed by more than one.

The results from Svenson, Edland, and Slovic (1990) study using incomplete information indicated that time pressure induced a shift toward a more frequent use of the Max rule. Because this rule is based on identifying the highest value on any attribute, it was assumed to reflect an increased priority for this kind of information and thereby taken as evidence for filtering in favor of positive information.

To further clarify these results, the present experiment uses the same kind of alternatives but with complete information on all attributes for both alternatives in a pair. This increases the amount of task-relevant information and thereby could be expected to increase the need to adapt under the time pressure condition. Based on this and on the results from the Svenson et al. study, it was predicted that time pressure would lead to an even greater shift toward the use of the Max rule.

Method

Subjects

Eighty students of psychology at the University of Stockholm served as subjects in the experiment. The ages of the subjects were between 20 and 40 years with approximately equal numbers of males and females. Subjects were allocated to one of two different conditions. Each group of 40 subjects was given either 8 seconds exposure time (time pressure) or 22 seconds exposure time (control). In a pretest, it was found that the two different exposure times were sufficient for each purpose. The exposure time of 8 seconds allowed subjects to make their choices and judgments and yet experience time pressure, whereas 22 seconds provided ample time and allowed the subjects to complete these activities without feelings of time pressure. Despite this pretest, five subjects in the time pressure condition had to be excluded from the experiment because they experienced the time as too short to make the decisions. Five new subjects took their place to maintain the group size at 40.

Task and Stimuli

Subjects were asked to decide which of the two students would be more able to follow a university program and graduate as a school psychologist. The information about each candidate was in terms of their high-school grades in Swedish, psychology, and natural science. This is, of course, far from complete information when making these kinds of decisions in the everyday world, but in the context of this experiment the information may be said to be complete in that there is a grade for each candidate on each attribute.

The twenty basic stimulus pairs were constructed as shown in Table 1. The table shows grades of candidates (A and B) on three attributes; Swedish (I), psychology (II), and natural science (III). They were constructed so that each choice would give some information about which of the four rules was likely to have been used. The stimuli in Table 1 are divided in five sections. Choices within a pair in the first three sections distinguish a preference for one rule over the other three. Sections four and five differentiate between pairs of decision rules. The Sum rule correlates so highly with the others that it cannot be isolated from the other three and tested alone. The allocation of attributes to these base stimuli was permutated according to the scheme outlined in Table 2. The order of the attributes in the 20 base stimuli shown in Table 1 were changed six times.

Table 1. The 20 Base Stimuli Used in the Experiment

Differentiating between decision rules	Attributes	Pairs and alternatives							
		A	B	A	B	A	B	A	B
(1) Min rule	I	3	1	1	3	4	1	1	4
versus	II	3	5	4	3	2	3	5	3
Sum-Max-MCD	III	2	3	5	3	2	5	4	2
(2) Max rule	I	4	5	5	4	5	3	3	5
versus	II	4	3	1	2	1	3	3	2
Sum-Min-MCD	III	2	1	2	3	3	4	3	1
(3) MCD rule	I	1	5	1	5	5	1	5	1
versus	II	4	2	4	3	2	3	2	4
Sum-Max-Min	III	3	2	4	3	3	4	3	4
(4) Max-MCD	I	1	4	4	1	1	4	4	1
versus	II	5	4	4	5	5	4	4	5
Min-Sum	III	3	2	2	3	4	3	3	4
(5) Max-Sum	I	5	2	5	2	2	5	2	5
versus	II	2	3	3	4	2	1	2	1
Min-MCD	III	1	2	1	2	4	3	3	2

Table 2. Distribution of Swedish (Sw),
Psychology (Ps) and Natural Science (Nat)
over Attributes and Labels

	Attribute		
Label	I	II	III
1	Sw	Ps	Nat
2	Sw	Nat	Ps
3	Nat	Ps	Sw
4	Nat	Sw	Ps
5	Ps	Nat	Sw
6	Ps	Sw	Nat

Thus, the six permutations across the 20 base stimuli provided a total of 120 different decision problems.

Pairs of possible candidates were presented on a computer screen, and subjects responded using a computer keyboard. The task required that subjects first choose Candidate A or B and then judge the difference between the two candidates in each pair on an attractiveness scale from 1 (almost no difference) to 10 (large difference).

Procedure

Each subject sat in front of the computer screen and started the session by reading the instructions to the experiment. This was followed by training in the use of the keyboard. Having completed these preliminary activities, subjects were asked to provide ratings of their present feelings of stress, calmness, restlessness, concentration, and tension. These mood and stress questions were presented on the computer screen as statements, for example, "I feel stressed," and subjects were asked to assess how much they agreed with each statement, on a scale from 0 (not at all) to 10 (very much).

Following this, a number of practice stimuli were given to the subjects; then the main experiment started. Each decision problem was presented on the screen for either 8 or 22 seconds, during which time subjects made a choice and an attractiveness-difference judgment. Having completed the 120 choice problems, subjects were again asked to provide ratings of their present mood and stress level. This was followed by another set of questions concerning how time pressured they felt during the experiment, if they were content with their decisions, and if they were able to think sufficiently about each decision problem. These questions were presented and answered in the same way as the mood and stress questions. Finally, subjects were asked to judge the importance of each subject (i.e., psychology, Swedish, and natural science) for making the decisions using a scale from 0 (not important at all) to 10 (very important).

Results

The results are reported in the following order. First, judgments of mood, stress, and subjects' assessments of other aspects of the experimental situation are presented. This is followed by the ratings of importance of the attributes, and finally, an analysis of the choice frequencies and attractiveness-difference judgments.

Judgments of Mood, Stress, and Related Aspects

The mood and stress assessments were made at the beginning and the end of the experimental session. Table 3 shows the group means of the assessments of stress at these two points for the two time conditions.

A comparison between ratings of the stress level at the beginning and the end of the experiment indicated a significant increase in stress for the 8-second group ($t = 2.21$, $df = 39$, $p<0.02$) and a significant decrease in stress for the 22-second group ($t = 5.15$, $df = 39$, $p<0.001$). Responses to the questions concerning calmness, concentration, restlessness, and tension did not differ before and after the session nor between the groups.

Table 3 also shows that the two groups differed in terms of the responses to other questions presented at the end of the experimental session. Subjects who experienced the short-deadline condition judged the time allowed to be "too short exposure time" ($t = 7.04$, $df = 78$, $p<0.001$), they experienced greater "feelings

**Table 3. Arithmetic Means of Responses to Questions
Given in the Experiment**

Question	Before session		During session	
	22	8	22	8
(1) I feel stressed	3.82	3.20	1.88	4.15
(2) The exposure time was too short	—	—	2.38	6.15
(3) I felt time pressure during the experiment	—	—	2.02	5.90
(4) I was able to think about each problem	—	—	7.25	3.95
(5) I am content with the decisions	—	—	5.90	4.12

of time pressure" ($t = 5.63$, $df = 78$, $p<0.001$), were less "able to think about each problem" ($t = 5.75$, $df = 78$, $p<0.001$), and were less "content with the decisions" ($t = 3.66$, $df = 78$, $p<0.001$).

Thus, the 8-second exposure time was successful in inducing feelings of time pressure and was judged to be too short as a exposure time for making the decisions and judgments. The group without a time limit did not report feeling pressured and were also more content with the decisions and more able to think about each problem.

Rated Importance of Attributes

Both groups judged psychology as the most important attribute for making the decisions (mean of 7.8 and 7.85 for the 8-second and 22-second conditions, respectively). Swedish was judged as the second most important attribute (5.38 and 6.22, respectively), and natural science the least important (4.62 and 4.58, respectively). The differences between the judged importance of psychology and Swedish were significant for the 8-second condition ($t = 3.87$, $df = 39$, $p<0.001$) and for the 22-second condition ($t = 3.23$, $df = 39$, $p<0.001$). There was no difference in judged importance of Swedish and natural science in the 8-second condition, but there was in the 22-second condition ($t = 3.1$, $df = 39$, $p<0.001$).

Analysis of Choice Behavior

Table 4 summarizes the choice behavior of subjects in the two time conditions in terms of the extent to which it supports the use of each of the four decision rules. There were a total of 24 cases (four pairs × six attribute orders) in each of the five groups. The final row of Table 4 reports the overall frequency that choice behavior was consistent with a particular rule, including those occasions when the choice was consistent with other rules as well (theoretical maximum is 120). The Min, Max, and MCD rules were each individually pitted against the other three rules in 24 cases. These comparisons are underlined in Table 4. The data show no strong support for the use of the Max rule in either condition. When the Max rule is individually pitted against the others, the imposition of time pressure increases the frequency from 0 to just 2 and from 46 to 47 when all the 120 cases are analyzed. These findings fail to support the prediction that time pressure increases the use of the Max rule. Furthermore, the Min and Sum rules seem to be the most used rules in both conditions. However, it is important to remember that the Sum rule only gets support in tests confounded by the other rules, which may give that rule a misleading appearance of

**Table 4. Frequencies of Choices Supporting Particular Rules
under the Two Time Conditions**

Groups of differentiating rules	Max 22	Max 8	Min 22	Min 8	Sum 22	Sum 8	MCD 22	MCD 8
(1) Min rule versus Sum-Max-MCD	15 (24)	15 (24)	9 (24)	9 (24)	15 (24)	15 (24)	15 (24)	15 (24)
(2) Max rule versus Sum-Min-MCD	0 (24)	2 (24)	24 (24)	22 (24)	24 (24)	22 (24)	24 (24)	22 (24)
(3) MCD rule versus Sum-Max-Min	18 (24)	13 (24)	18 (24)	13 (24)	18 (24)	13 (24)	6 (24)	10 (24)
(4) Max-MCD versus Min-Sum	4 (24)	8 (24)	20 (24)	16 (24)	20 (24)	16 (24)	4 (24)	8 (24)
(5) Max-Sum versus Min-MCD	9 (24)	9 (24)	15 (24)	15 (24)	9 (24)	9 (24)	15 (24)	15 (24)
Sum/theoretical maximum	46 (120)	47 (120)	86 (120)	75 (120)	86 (120)	75 (120)	64 (120)	70 (120)

aNote that the sum in group 3 in the 8-second condition is only 23 (13 + 10); this is because one of the arithmetic means in that condition was 0 indicating no support for any of the rules.

popularity. Taken together, these findings fail to reveal any evidence for a consistent change in strategy under time pressure.

A further analysis was undertaken in order to see if the use of the Max rule increases when looking only at the most important attribute. Psychology was established as the most important attribute for making the decisions under all conditions. An analysis of the choice behavior revealed that the time pressure group chose the alternatives with the highest grade on psychology (i.e., using a Max rule on the most important attribute) in 97 cases out of 120. In the group without any time pressure, the frequencies of these choices were 87 out of 120. The difference between the two groups was not significant, though it is in the predicted direction. However, this analysis suggests that much of the choice behavior in both conditions can be explained by assuming that subjects adopt a strategy based on choosing the alternative that is best on the most important attribute.

In conclusion, time pressure does not seem to affect choice behavior in terms of changing strategies in favor of positive information. Below, the effects of time pressure will be considered in terms of attractiveness difference judgments.

Attractiveness Difference Judgments

A second way of investigating possible changes in strategy is by considering the judgments of differences in attractiveness between the alternatives. The mean of these judgments was computed across the subjects in each group for each of the 120 pairs. The difference was coded as positive when Alternative A was chosen, and as negative when Alternative B was chosen. This allowed the data from the two different time conditions to be compared according to the direction of change brought about by the time constraint for each of the 120 choice problems. This change in mean rated attractiveness difference was registered as supportive or not of the different decision rules. The results of this analysis are presented in Table 5. The table shows the numbers of changes when comparing the two conditions of exposure times (22 and 8 seconds, respectively) toward each of the four rules in each group. There was a total of 24 cases in each of the five groups. When comparing the two exposure conditions across all 120 cases, the changes are as follows: In 59 cases the change supported the Max rule, thus, not more than can be expected by chance. The changes toward the Min and Sum rules were even less frequent, 39 and 19 cases, respectively. The changes supporting the MCD rule were 72 out of 120 cases.

Finally, the two conditions were compared in the 24 cases where each of the three rules, Max, Min, and MCD, were pitted against the others. A reduction in time from 22 to 8 seconds induced changes in attractiveness consistent with an increased use of the Max rule in 21 of the 24 cases. Similar analyses for Min and MCD revealed 16 and 22 cases out of 24, respectively. To conclude, it seems that the attractiveness-difference judgments are going toward an increased use of the Max and MCD rule when reducing the exposure time.

With the initial prediction that the Max rule will become stronger under time pressure, a further analysis to evaluate this prediction was undertaken. For each of the 120 stimuli, the difference between the two groups' (22 and 8 seconds) averages was computed. The differences were coded as positive if indicating increased support for the Max rule in the time pressure group (and as negative if it did not support Max). In this way, 120 differences were computed, the means of which were tested against the null hypothesis of zero indicating no effect of time pressure. A t-test showed a marginally or nonsignificant result ($t = 1.37$, $df = 119$, $p<0.08$) (cf. Glass & Stanley, 1970, p. 298). To refine the analysis further, this was repeated for the 24 stimuli that pitted the Max rule against the other rules. This showed a significant result ($t = 7.43$, $df = 23$, $p<0.001$). This partial analysis was repeated for the 24 cases in which Min was compared to the other rules. This test indicated a significant result ($t = -1.77$, $df = 23$, $p<0.05$). Correspondingly, the 24 MCD comparisons gave strong significance ($t = -5$, $df = 23$, $p<0.001$). Because the test was constructed to evaluate support for the Max rule, support for other rules generated t-values that were negative.

**Table 5. Number of Time Pressure Related Changes
of Attractiveness Difference Ratings Supporting Particular Rules**[a]

Groups of differentiating rules	Rule supported			
	Max	Min	Sum	MCD
(1) Min rule versus Sum-	8	16	8	8
Max-MCD	(24)	(24)	(24)	(24)
(2) Max rule versus Sum-	21	2	2	2
Min-MCD	(24)	(24)	(24)	(24)
(3) MCD rule versus	2	2	2	22
Sum-Max-Min	(24)	(24)	(24)	(24)
(4) Max-MCD versus	22	1	1	22
Min-Sum	(24)	(24)	(24)	(24)
(5) Max-Sum versus Min-	6	18	6	18
MCD	(24)	(24)	(24)	(24)
Sum/theoretical maximum	59	39	19	72
	(120)	(120)	(120)	(120)

[a]Note that the sum in group (2) and (5) is only 23 (21 + 2) and (22 + 1), respectively; this is because one of the arithmetic means of the difference ratings was equal in both conditions.

To conclude, when the Max rule was applied only on the most important attribute, this was the rule that explained the great majority of the choices in both conditions. However, comparing the two time conditions and looking at the attractiveness-difference judgments, there is a change *toward* an increased use of the Max rule and the MCD rule. This is valid when the rules are compared alone against the others. The changes toward the Min rule are less frequent, especially when comparing the two exposure conditions across *all* the 120 cases.

Concluding Remarks

The primary aim of the present study was to identify changes in the use of a choice rule as a way to adapt to time pressure. Two kinds of data were undertaken, the subjects' choices and their attractiveness-difference judgments. Though difference judgments do not directly measure choice behavior, they are appropriate for two reasons. First, they reflect preference order between decision alternatives. Second, they are based on a 10-point scale and thereby are likely to be a more sensitive measure than simple binary choices. The use of sensitive measures is particularly important in time pressure research where effects can often be quite small. Even when there are no significant effects on choice data, the attractiveness-difference judgments can provide information about changes in the decision process.

In the present experiment, the choice data are consistent with those reported by Svenson et al. (1990) in showing that the Min rule appeared to be the most important rule when the analysis took account of all attributes. However, one version of the Max rule, which considered only the most important attribute, explains the data better than the Min rule. The explanation for this is that in 56 of the 120 cases a choice of the alternative having the highest grade on the most important attribute also supports the Min rule. Still, eliminating these 56 cases, the frequencies of supporting choices are higher for the Max rule than for the Min rule.

The attractiveness-difference judgments showed a less strong shift in favor of the Max rule than reported by Svenson et al. in their study with incomplete information. It was argued earlier that in the present experiment with greater amounts of information, there may be a stronger need for finding a strategy or choice rule to cope with time pressure. Maybe the time was so short that a general application of Max was not possible, and a modified version of Max focusing just on the most important attribute was adopted. Results from this experiment were consistent with an extensive use of the Max psychology strategy.

One important finding in the present study is the shift away from the Min rule under time pressure. This means that previous research (e.g., Wright, 1974; Ben Zur & Breznitz, 1981), arguing that time pressure induces filtering in favoring of negative information has not been supported in this study. One explanation could be that the Min rule demands higher cognitive capacity. First, the alternative having the Min value must be detected. Second, the alternative not having the Min value must be chosen.

To conclude, the choice data indicated that filtration in terms of favoring the positive information on the most important attribute provides a good way of describing choice behavior in this experiment. The attractiveness-difference judgments indicate, with time pressure, a change toward a use of the Max and MCD rules that both are associated with positive information. In the present study, two things seem to become important under time pressure, the most important attribute and positive information. There is a need for further research to determine whether such findings extend to other choice situations.

ACKNOWLEDGMENT. This study was supported by funds to Ola Svenson from the Swedish Work Environment Fund and the Swedish Council for Research in the Humanities and Social Sciences. The author wishes to thank John Maule, Ola Svenson, and Nils Malmsten for valuable advice. The author also would like to thank The Swedish Institute for a scholarship related to the work presented in this chapter.

References

Ben Zur, H., & Breznitz, S. J. (1981). The effect of time pressure on risky choice behavior. *Acta Psychologica, 47,* 89–104.

Glass, G. V., & Stanley, J. C. (1970). *Statistical methods in education and psychology.* Englewood Cliffs, NJ: Prentice-Hall, Inc.

Maule, J., & Mackie, P. (1990). A componential investigation of the effects of deadlines on individual decision making. In K. Borchering, O. I. Larichev, & D. M. Messick (Eds.), *Contemporary issues in decision making* (pp. 449–461). Amsterdam: North-Holland.

Miller, J. G. (1960). Information input overload and psychopathology. *American Journal of Psychiatry, 116,* 695–704.

Payne, J. W., Bettman, J. R., and Johnson, E. J. (1988). Adaptive strategy selection in decision making. *Journal of Experimental Psychology: Learning, Memory, and Cognition, 14,*(3), 534–552.

Russo, J. W., & Dosher, B. A. (1983). Strategies for multiattribute binary choice. *Journal of Experimental Psychology: Learning, Memory, and Cognition, 9,* 676–696.

Rothstein, H. G. (1986). The effects of time pressure on judgment in multiple cue probability learning. *Organizational Behavior and Human Decision Processes, 37,* 83–92.

Svenson, O. (1979). Process description of decision making. *Organizational Behavior and Human Performance, 23,* 86–112.

Svenson, O., & Edland, A. (1987). Change of preferences under time pressure: Choices and Judgments. *Scandinavian Journal of Psychology, 29*(4), 322–330.

Svenson, O., Edland, A., & Karlsson, G. (1985). The effect of numerical and verbal information and time stress on judgments of the attractiveness of decision alternatives. In L. B. Methlie & R. Sprague (Eds.), *Knowledge representation for decision support systems* (pp. 133–144). Amsterdam: North-Holland.

Svenson, O., Edland, A., & Slovic, P. (1990). Choices between incompletely described alternatives under time stress. *Acta Psychologica, 75*(2), 153–169.

Wallsten, T. S., & Barton, C. N. (1982). Processing probabilistic multidimensional information for decisions. *Journal of Experimental Psychology; Learning, Memory, and Cognition, 8,* 361–384.

Wright, P. (1974). The harassed decision maker: Time pressure, distraction and the use of evidence. *Journal of Applied Psychology, 59,* 555–561.

Wright, P., & Weitz, B. (1977). Time horizon effects on product evaluation strategies. *Journal of Marketing Research, 14,* 429–443.

11

On Experimental Instructions and the Inducement of Time Pressure Behavior

Ola Svenson and Lehman Benson, III

Introduction

Deadlines seem to have different effects on human activities. For example, when located far in the distant future, they may slow down a decision or a problem-solving process because there is so much time available. When the deadline for the completion of a task is closer, it may speed up and make the solution process more efficient. However, when still closer, deadlines may alter decision or problem-solving processes resulting on some occasions in inferior outcomes; on other occasions improvements result as compared with situations when more time is available (cf. the review by Edland and Svenson, this volume; Payne et al., 1992).

 Although deadlines may be defined objectively, time pressure is experienced by the decision maker in response to the deadline. Time pressure is experienced when a discrepancy appears between what a person would like to do or feels he/she should do, and what he/she actually believes can be done before the deadline runs out. This means that both (a) the objective deadline and (b) the subjective appraisal of both task demands and the ability to meet these demands in terms of cognitive and energetic resources should affect cognitive processes

Ola Svenson • Department of Psychology, Stockholm University, S-10691 Stockholm, Sweden.   **Lehman Benson, III** • Department of Psychology, Lund University, S-22350 Lund, Sweden.
Time Pressure and Stress in Human Judgment and Decision Making, edited by Ola Svenson and A. John Maule. Plenum Press, New York, 1993.

under time pressure. Although earlier research has been focused on the effects of varying deadlines (a) (Edland & Svenson, this volume; Svenson & Edland, 1989; Svenson et al., 1990), this study will discuss the various aspects of (b) (Mac-Gregor, this volume).

The subjective appraisal of task demands on energetic resources (cf. Maule and Hockey, this volume) relies on experience gained from earlier, identical or similar problems, including the person's aspiration level concerning the quality of the output. In repeated tasks, the first few problems may be used in this appraisal process, in particular if the problem is of an unfamiliar type. At the same time as a problem is assessed with regard to the cognitive and energetic resources and the time required, the decision makers assess the availability of their own cognitive resources (competence) and the amount of time they perceive they can allocate to the task.

This process of appraisal involves a comparison between the resources needed (R_N) and those available (R_A) for solving a decision problem. The relative resource ratio

$$R_R = R_N/R_A \qquad (1)$$

describes the comparison. If $R_R > 1.0$, then the decision maker has to cope with the situation through changing the nominator or the denominator. Thus, one response to this could be to decrease R_N, which can be decreased through, for example, simplifying the decision strategy. A second response could be to increase R_A, for example, through mobilization of energetic resources (Maule & Hockey, this volume).

The appraisal of time needed is part of the demand component R_N, and the appraisal of time available is part of the resource component, R_A in equation (1). The instruction to a subject about, for example, time needed for making a decision affects the appraisal of R_N, and if the relative resource ratio R_R, tends to approach or exceed 1.0, this may trigger resource mobilization to cope with the situation. It may also lead to a change of strategy in solving problems as mentioned above.

It is well known that time pressure generated through decreasing the time available for solving a decision problem is associated with coping behavior in terms of changes in the use of decision rules (Edland & Svenson, this volume). This seems to correspond primarily to a manipulation of the R_A time resource component that is counteracted by a simplification of the decision process so that less resources R_N are needed.

The present study was performed to investigate the effects of variation of task instructions concerning the time needed to solve a decision problem. Objective time allowed for solving each problem was always constant and sufficient for making the decisions. The instruction, however, varied according to whether the time given was sufficient or not for a problem.

In one condition, the time available was said to be *longer* than usually allowed in experiments with the decision problems to be solved. In another condition, the time available was said to be *shorter* than that usually allowed.

This instruction may result in several different outcomes in relation to coping behavior under real time pressure, of which the following three are most interesting in this context. First, it may be ineffective not producing any significant change in relation to the changes we know occur under real time pressure.

Second, the instruction that time was shorter than usual may lead to the inducement of time-pressure-type coping behavior and changes in decision rules used. Correspondingly, the instruction that time was longer could produce the same behavior as under no-time-pressure conditions. In relation to equation (1), the instruction that time was short would induce feelings of insufficient resources available and lead to coping behaviors comparable to those that occur under "real" time pressure.

Third, the instruction that time was shorter than usual could lead to mobilization of energetic resources R_A to cope with the lack of time indicated in the instruction. Correspondingly, the instruction that time was longer than usual would lead to a relaxation of energetic resources R_A. As a result, when the experiment starts, the first group of subjects would find that the resources they have mobilized are more than sufficient to solve the problems, and consequently they perform as if they were not under time pressure. However, the group instructed that there was plenty of time would not have mobilized R_A to the degree actually needed in the experiment and may have to cope with this either through mobilization of resources to increase R_A or decreasing task demands R_N. If feelings of time pressure are induced in this situation, changes in decision process of the same type as in the real time pressure situation may be found. In particular, R_N can be decreased through more use of less resource-demanding decision rules, as regularly found in the time pressure literature (Edland & Svenson, this volume).

The present study was designed to investigate whether differences in behavior can be caused through information about time available without changing actual time allowed. A further issue addressed in this chapter is, if differences in behavior can be found, which of the second and third of the above hypothetical explanation apply.

Experiment

The present experiment used decision problems found earlier to be particularly sensitive to time pressure to create a sensitive test of time pressure effects (Svenson, Edland, & Slovic, 1990).

Subjects

A total of 64 subjects participated in the investigation. They were recruited from a high school in Malmöe, Sweden, and they were between 17 and 18 years of age.

Stimuli

Subjects were asked to select one of two simultaneously presented student candidates to a school psychologist university program. The candidates were described through their (Swedish) high-school grades in psychology, natural sciences, and Swedish. However, for each candidate in a pair, information for one of the three attributes was missing. As the missing information was never the same for both candidates, there was always one and only one attribute with information for both candidates. Table 1 provides an example of one of the choice pairs used in the experiment.

The stimuli were projected onto a screen in front of the subjects. A total of 12 seconds were given each choice task before the next one appeared on the screen. In all, there were 33 incomplete choice pairs, each exposed one time.

Procedure

There were two experimental conditions, one in which the instruction indicated that the 12-second deadline was "really too short if the choices should be correct and the judgment sensitive. We know this because we have had subjects

**Table 1. Examples of Choice Pairs
Used in the Experiment[a]**

Subjects	Choice alternative	
	A	B
Swedish	—	5
Psychology	4	—
Natural sciences	3	1

[a]Grades in the Swedish high schools range from 1 (extremely poor) to 5 (excellent).

in another context make the same judgments in 25 seconds. But now we want to see how one makes his/her decisions and judgments with less time available." In the other group, the 12 seconds were described as a time "which you may think sounds short, but which you will find is quite sufficient for the task after a little training. We know that it is enough time because we have had subjects in other contexts make these judgments in as short time intervals as 4 seconds. It was clear that after some training, they were able to make sensitive choices and judgments in spite of the fact that the time was so short. But now we want to see how one makes his/her decisions with more time available."

The first of these groups will be called "the too-short group," and the second "the sufficient group." The 64 subjects were randomly distributed with 32 participants in each condition. That is, every second form handed out in a group contained the instructions of one condition and in the others the other instruction. The procedure was as follows for both instructional groups: (1) The experimenter introduced the experiment, (2) subjects responded to mood questions, (3) subjects read the instruction for incomplete choice pairs, (4) four introductory cases were presented on the screen, (5) presentation of the experimental stimuli, (6) mood questions were responded to again, (7) questions about experimental conditions (time pressure, etc.) were answered, and (8) question about the subjects' expectations about problems and experience of problem difficulty in relation to these expectations. Between 6 and 7 another choice task not analyzed here was inserted.

The mood questions were responded to on a scale 0–10 (not at all–very) and were the following. The first question asked subjects to state degree of how "stressed" they felt at the moment. The other questions were, I feel (2) "calm," (3) "restless," (4) "concentrated," and (5) "tense." The questions about the experiment were given last and concerned (1) "how difficult the decisions were," (2) "how satisfied were you with your decisions taking what seemed reasonable to achieve into consideration?" (3) "was the time for each decision too short or too long?" and (4) "did you experience time pressure during the experiment?" The last and fifth question asked subjects if they considered the problems easier or more difficult to solve than they thought initially. All questions were responded to on 100-mm-long bipolar scales.

When a decision problem was projected on the screen, the subject should read the information, make a decision and mark which alternative he or she preferred (through circling A or B for left- and right-hand alternative). He or she also gave a judgment of the attractiveness difference between the two alternatives by circling one of the numbers 0 (no difference) through 10 (great difference). Throughout this study a choice of the left-hand alternative was denoted with a positive sign for the difference, and a choice of the right hand alternative was to give a negative sign.

Results

Mood Scales

There were no significant differences between the two groups. This may indicate that the instructions did not produce effects strong enough to affect mood and experience of arousal, differentiating the two groups or that the scales were not sensitive enough.

Ratings of Time Pressure and Task Characteristics

Group 1 with the "too-short" time instruction rated the available time shorter than the other group ($M_1 = 31$ and $M_2 = 4.56$, $t = 2.12$, $df = 31$, $p<0.07$). There were no significant differences between the groups concerning judged difficulty in relation to expectations and how satisfied the subjects were with their answers.

Decisions

Adaptation in terms of strategy change was studied in the following way. Based on the earlier study (Svenson, Edland, & Slovic, 1990), the following decision rules (cf. Svenson, 1979) for making the choices were investigated: choice of the alternative with the greater grade in psychology, (1) *Max P* (where missing information was regarded as zero), (2) *Max S*, with the higher grade in Swedish, (3) *Max N*, with the higher grade in natural science, (4) *Max*, the maximum grade in any class (there were no ties), (5) *Com*, the higher grade for the common attribute class, (6) *Min*, not having the lower grade in the pair across all classes, and (7) *Sum*, the greater sum of grades.

For each problem the choice predicted by each of the above rules was noted. After that, the mean across subjects was coded as following each rule or not. Each individual's choice was coded through giving an A choice in a pair a positive number and a B choice a negative number. The magnitude was the number circled. The mean across subjects was then obtained through summing the ratings for each choice across subjects and averaging. If the mean judged attractiveness rating was greater than zero, the mean choice was credited to the left-hand alternative (A) in the pair, and if it was less than zero, the choice was credited to the right-hand alternative (B). It was found that only three rules (1) *Max P*, (6) *Min*, and (7) *Sum* predicted the choices significantly better than chance. Table 2 gives the proportions of correct predictions for the two groups.

Table 2 indicates that the *Min* rule seems to be a very good predictor, but

Table 2. Proportions of Average Choices Predicted
by Each of Three Different Decision Rules[a]

Condition	Rule Max P	Rule Min	Rule Sum	N
Sufficient time	0.75**	0.78**	0.68*	33
Too short time	0.64**	0.94**	0.70*	33

[a]There were 33 different decision problems and the table exposes the rules
which were significantly more effective than chance predictions.
* = significance at the 0.05 level.
** = significance at the 0.01 level.

that both *Max P* and *Sum* are reasonably efficient as well. The *Min* rule explains most of the variance of the decisions in both conditions. Within the rules the *Min* rule explains more of the variance in the "too-short" condition, whereas the *Max P* rule gains in the "sufficient" condition. In the following, the more sensitive attractiveness-difference ratings will qualify these findings further.

Ratings

In order to relate the magnitude of the judged attractiveness differences across conditions, the following codings of the results and problems were performed.

As mentioned above, all attractiveness-difference scores for which alternative A was preferred were assigned positive values, and all choices in which B was preferred the difference were given negative values. The different decision rules were regarded as independent variables, and the predictions about which alternative to prefer were coded as follows. When a rule predicted choice of the A alternative for a particular case, this variable was given a value of 1 for this case. If a rule predicted choice of the B alternative, the variable was given the value of zero for an A choice. In this way a positive correlation between the independent variable and the dependent variable could be interpreted as support for a specific decision rule. The seven rules presented above were applied to the 33 decision problems, and a stepwise regression analysis was performed with mean attractiveness difference as the dependent variable for the "sufficient" and "too-long" groups respectively.

The result showed that only *Max P* and *Min* contributed significantly to the linear regression model for both groups, indicating that also the more sensitive scale values of attractiveness differences can be related to these two major rules. In the "sufficient" group, *Max P* was entered first, whereas *Min* was the first variable in the "too-short" group. The differences in regression weights for the same predictor variable across groups did not reach significance, however.

Change of Ratings across Conditions

The average direction of change from the "sufficient" to "too-short" condition was scored as positive or negative relative to each rule. Only two rules were significantly related to this variable, the *Min* and the *Sum* rules. In one problem there was no change, but for the 32 cases, 21 of the changes were predicted by the *Min* rule and 22 by the *Sum* rule that corresponds to *p* values of 0.06 and 0.03, respectively. In the 11 cases when these two rules gave opposite predictions, data for 7 problems supported the *Min* and 4 the *Sum* rule. Thus, simply scoring the direction of change did not differentiate significantly between the leading two rules.

The mean difference in ratings between conditions were related to the *Min* and *Sum* rules in the following procedure. If the change in mean-attractiveness-scale value from the "sufficient" to the "too-short" condition favored the choice alternative predicted by the *Min* (*Sum*) rule, this difference between the conditions was coded as a positive number. In other words, if the "too-short" group had results more in compliance with a given rule, that decision problem was given a positive average scale value. If the change was toward the other alternative, the difference was coded as negative (not supported by the rule). To repeat, a positive mean difference across the 33 decision problems indicates support of a rule, and a negative average nonsupport. The mean differences of support for the *Min* and *Sum* rules were 0.73 and 0.30, indicating statistical significance for the *Min* rule ($t = 2.96$, $p < 0.028$, $df = 32$), but no support for the *Sum* rule ($t = 1.09$, $p < 0.14$, $df = 32$). In Table 2, the *Min* rule was shown to be both the superior predictor of the choices and the rule most sensitive to the instruction parameter.

To conclude, the change in instruction from "sufficient" to the "too-short" condition causes a change in decision strategy. In the "sufficient" condition, the *Max P* rule was more applicable according to the regression analyses than the *Min* rule, and the *Sum* rule played only a minor role. In the "too-short" condition the *Min* rule became the most applicable rule according to both the regression analyses and the comparisons of the mean differences. Thus, the results indicate significance effects of the instruction on decision behavior. Furthermore, the results indicate that the effect was in the direction of creating more time-pressure-type behavior in the "sufficient time" instruction group.

Discussion

As mentioned above, the decision problems in this study were taken from an earlier study (Svenson et al., 1990). This earlier study indicated that subjects cope with time pressure by decreasing their use of the *Min* rule. This way of coping is functional (cf. Edland, this volume) because to implement this rule involves scanning all information, finding the minimum and choosing the *other* alternative. In contrast to this, the *Max* rule requires scanning of all information, finding the maximum, and selecting *that* alternative. Thus the *Max* rule does not require the *switch* to the other alternative and therefore needs one cognitive operation less, and thereby less cognitive resources, assuming that the rating procedure does not vary systematically between the two rules.

The present experiment has illustrated that genuine time pressure effects cannot be induced simply through an instruction that there is a scarcity of time. Instead, subjects, who were given this instruction and who were confronted with the same constant objective deadline condition, chose a process for solving the decision problems of the same type as when there was plenty of time. However, the instruction that time was sufficient did induce time pressure in subjects when confronted with the objective deadline condition. In summary, this study has pointed out the need for analyzing and controlling subjects' task appraisal and their relations to instructions of judgments and decision making under time pressure.

ACKNOWLEDGMENT. This study was supported by grants to Ola Svenson from the Swedish Work Environment Fund and the Swedish Research Council for Research in the Humanities and Social Sciences and a grant to Lehman Benson, III, from The Royal Swedish Academy of Sciences. The authors want to thank Viveka Askeland-von Gegerfelt, Anne Edland, John Maule, Amparo Ortega Rayo, and Wivianne Runske for their valuable contributions to this study.

References

Payne, J. W., Bettman, J. R., Johnson, E. J., & Coupey, E. (1992). A constructive process view of decision making: Multiple strategies in judgment and choice. *Acta Psychologica, 80,* 107–141.
Svenson, O. (1979). Process descriptions of decision making. *Organizational Behavior and Human Performance, 23,* 86–112.
Svenson, O., & Edland, A. (1989). Changes of preferences under time pressure: Choice and judgments. In H. Montgomery & O. Svenson (Eds.), *Process and structure in human decision making* (pp. 225–236). Chichester: Wiley.
Svenson, O., Edland, A., & Slovic, P. (1990). Choices and judgments of incompletely described decision alternatives under time pressure. *Acta Psychologica, 75,* 153–169.

12

Time Pressure and Payoff Effects on Multidimensional Probabilistic Inference

Thomas S. Wallsten

Introduction

Background

Beginning with Miller (1960), numerous authors (e.g., Ben Zur & Breznitz, 1981; Maule & Mackie, 1990; Payne, Bettman, & Johnson, 1988; Svenson & Edland, 1987) have distinguished the possible effects of time pressure on decision processes on the assumption that a given decision requires a sequence of mental steps prior to its execution. Most authors have considered four possible time pressure effects. One, termed *acceleration,* is that processing does not fundamentally change, but rather, each step is simply accelerated under a deadline. A second, termed *filtering,* is that the processing sequence is altered so that only the most important subset of the information is attended to or handled prior to the decision. Third, the decision maker may select strategies that are appropriate for the available time. Although not generally pointed out, these latter two alternatives are not mutually exclusive. That is, strategies under time pressure may focus on only the most important facets of the information whereas those in the absence of time pressure may utilize the available information more completely. The fourth possibility is that time pressure has no effect on the strategic aspects

Thomas S. Wallsten • Department of Psychology, University of North Carolina, Chapel Hill, North Carolina 27599-3270.
Time Pressure and Stress in Human Judgment and Decision Making, edited by Ola Svenson and A. John Maule. Plenum Press, New York, 1993.

of information processing. Rather, the person simply stops processing when the time is up and makes a decision.

An alternative, possibly orthogonal, approach to the study of time pressure has been suggested by Busemeyer (1985, this volume), who conceives of predecisional processing as consisting of sequential comparisons. According to this view, based on decision field theory (Busemeyer & Townsend, 1992), the decision maker sequentially considers features or elements of choice alternatives. Each feature results in a comparison value that moves preference from its current point toward one or the other of the choice alternatives. Preference moves in a random walk over time until it crosses the decision bound corresponding to a particular alternative, resulting in that alternative being selected. Busemeyer suggests that the placement of the decision bounds depends upon, among other factors, the available time. Rapid decisions result in decision bounds placed closer to the starting point than do more leisurely decisions. Consequently, decisions are generally made after sampling only a few features in the former case and after a more thorough search in the latter case. Busemeyer's proposal is not inconsistent with the filtering and acceleration hypotheses mentioned above because his theory is open with regard to the decision features searched and the way in which they result in comparison values. For example, nothing in his general formulation requires features to be searched in the same order, or more generally, according to the same probability distribution, regardless of time pressure.

Wallsten and Barton's (1982) Model

Busemeyer's model applies to choices under uncertainty. Wallsten and Barton (1982) proposed a very similar approach to probabilistic inference. The task here is to decide which of (usually two) possible states of the world is responsible for the available information rather than to decide which of (usually two) alternatives is preferable. When a payoff structure is imposed on the probabilistic inference task, as Wallsten and Barton did, then the problem is really one of risky (if the probability structure is specified) or uncertain (if the probability structure is not specified) choice. Wallsten and Barton proposed their model as representative of a class of theories of inference studied by investigators such as Einhorn, Kleinmuntz, and Kleinmuntz (1979); Nisbett and Ross (1980), and Wallsten (1977, 1980). Consistent with Busemeyer, this model suggests that an individual starts with a prior opinion that is then adjusted in a random walk fashion according to the sequential consideration of information until one or the other decision boundary is crossed. The two models are similar in assuming that the placement of decision boundaries depends on the cost and payoff structure as well as on the available time. Thus, all things being equal, the decision bounds are closer to the starting point when time is restricted (or observations are costly), or payoffs are less extreme. Finally, the two models also agree on the assumption of path independence that says that the impact of a feature depends on its value and on the preference state at the moment but not on the sequence of features that led up to that state.

The Wallsten and Barton model is more specific than Busemeyer's in two regards. First, it assumes that features of the information are processed sequentially in order from most to least salient. Second, it assumes that, equating for statistical diagnosticity, the expected impact of a feature is monotonically related to its salience. These two assumptions imply that the order in which the features are processed and their average impact on the decision are correlated and are determined by the features' perceptual salience.

The remainder of this chapter summarizes Experiment 2 from Wallsten and Barton, which tests the model just described by looking at the interactive effects of time pressure and payoff on multidimensional probabilistic inference. The results are then discussed with respect to sequential sampling models in general and are also considered in conjunction with the filtering and change of strategy hypotheses mentioned earlier.

The Experiment

Predictions

If the decision criteria are less extreme when subjects are under time pressure than when they are not and if information dimensions are attended to sequentially from most to least salient, then it follows that subjects under time pressure will use only a most salient subset of the dimensions used by subjects not under pressure. A payoff manipulation can be expected to interact with the time manipulation in that the former should have a large effect when subjects are under time pressure but should have little or no effect when subjects can respond leisurely. More specifically, we hypothesized that the payoff manipulation would have little effect on decision criteria in the absence of time pressure because regardless of the payoff there is sufficient time (and no cost) to attend to all the dimensions. However, under time pressure, subjects with an extreme payoff function will have set their decision criteria further apart than subjects with a moderate payoff function and therefore will attempt to process more dimensions. In addition to testing these hypotheses, we sought evidence with regard to the assumption of path independence.

Method

Subjects were run independently in a computer-controlled probabilistic task in which they had to decide whether a sample of information containing five binary dimensions more likely came from population A or population B. Each trail began by the subject observing a display on the computer screen such as that shown below the continuous horizontal line in Figure 1. Each of the five sets of two pairs of identical symbols constitutes a dimension. Thus there are bracket, brace, vertical line, parenthesis, and slash dimensions, referred to respectively as dimensions $D_1, \ldots, D_5$. Each dimension is binary with the two levels of long and short represented by the widths of the intervals between the pairs of symbols. The bracket dimension, for example, consists of a pair of brackets with a long interval between them and immediately below that, a pair with a short interval between them. With equal probabilities, the computer went into State A or State B and independently sampled the binary dimensions according to the sampling probabilities under that state. The sampled dimensions were then displayed at the top of the computer screen as shown in Figure 1. Upon being asked, "What is your decision?", the subject indicated whether the sample more likely came from Population A or B and also provided a confidence estimate of between 50 and 100 in his or her decision. A confidence of 50 indicated absolute uncertainty in the correctness of the binary decision; 100 indicated complete certainty and numbers in between indicated intermediate degrees of certainty.

We assumed that D_1, the bracket dimension, was most salient and that saliency decreased monotonically to D_5, the slash dimension. This assumption was based on three considerations: (1)Most people read from top to bottom. (2) The discrimination of the dimension values became successively more difficult from D_1 to D_5. (3) The sampled dimension values were written in sequential order on the computer screen with approximately .2-seconds intervening between successive lines. Note in Figure 1 that each dimension value has a likelihood ratio $L = P(D|A)/P(D|B)$ of either $.80/.20 = 4$ or $.20/.80 = 1/4$. Trials with these sampling probabilities and likelihood ratios are referred to as Type I trials. Type II trials used sampling probabilities of .60 and .40, leading to likelihood ratios of 1.5 and 1/1.5. Thus each dimension's statistical diagnostisity was independent of its perceptual salience.

Subjects won or lost money on each trial according to their confidence estimate and the correct answer. Payoffs were calculated according to a spherical scoring rule expressed as

$$S = x + yp/(1 - pq)^{1/2} \qquad (1)$$

where p equals the subjective probability (confidence/100) assigned to the correct answer and $q = 1 - p$.

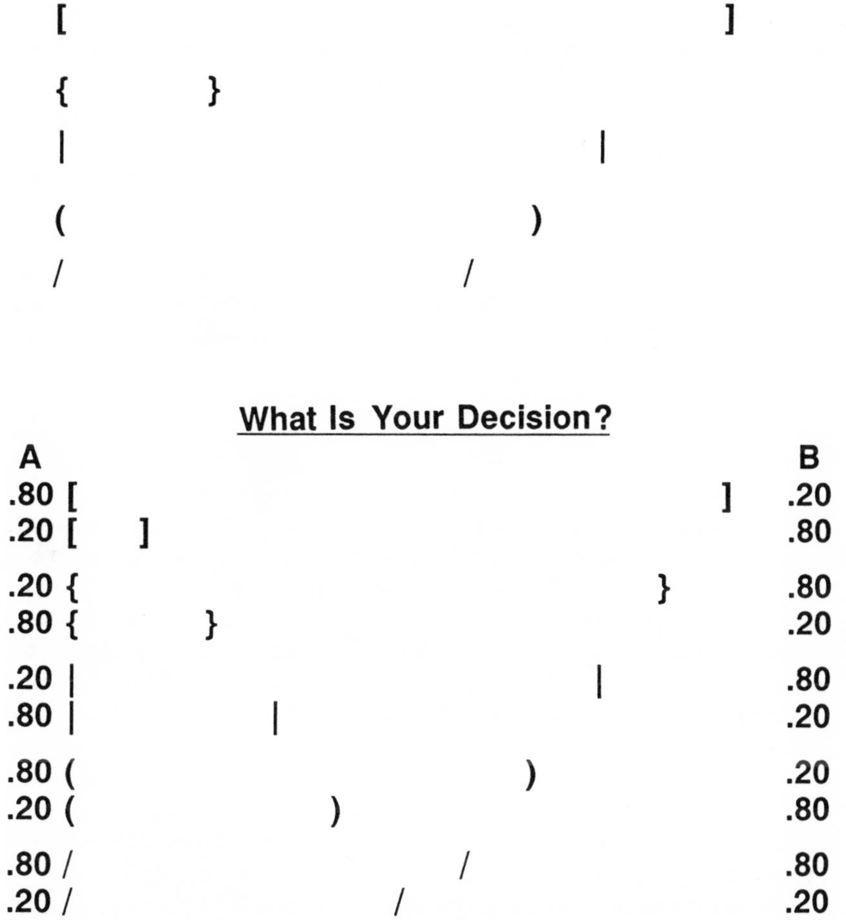

[   ]

{   }

| |

(   )

/   /

What Is Your Decision?

A				B
.80 [			]	.20
.20 [	]			.80
.20 {		}		.80
.80 {	}			.20
.20 |		|		.80
.80 |	|			.20
.80 (		)		.20
.20 (	)			.80
.80 /	/			.80
.20 /	/			.20

Figure 1. Display for one trial.

There were two between-subjects manipulations. Half of the subjects were required to respond within 9 seconds of the information display, whereas the remaining subjects were allowed 20 seconds. Pilot work had demonstrated that in the absence of a time limit, 9 seconds was approximately the median response time, and most responses took less than 20 seconds. Crossed with the time factor was a payoff manipulation. For half of the subjects, the constants x and y in Equation (1) were set as $x = -7.07$ and $y = 10.0$ to yield a moderate payoff function. The remaining subjects were under an extreme payoff function with $x = -154.8$ and $y = 200$. These latter constants were chosen so that payoffs were relatively extreme and were guaranteed to be negative unless a confidence of at least 55 was expressed for the correct hypothesis. At the end of the experiment, conversion from points into money was different for the two groups so that subjects in each averaged $3.00/hour.

Nine subjects were assigned to each of the four groups obtained by crossing two levels of time pressure with two levels of payoffs. They were paid strictly according to performance. Subjects were run for three sessions of approximately an hour and a half each separated by 2 or 3 days. The first session was devoted to instruction and practice. Data were collected in the remaining two sessions, which consisted of 384 trials each. Subjects worked at their own pace, received feedback after each trial, and were free to take breaks as they wished. Decision times were also recorded. See Wallsten and Barton for additional details.

Results

Confidence estimates were converted to a scale of 0 to 100 representing the degree to which the subject thought Population A was correct. Thus, for example, a response of 70% confidence in Population B was converted to 30% in A. Responses favoring A were not transformed. Then, the responses of each subject on a 0 to 100 scale were converted to dimension contrast scores, separately for the Type I and II problems. For each subject, the contrast for each dimension was calculated by subtracting that subject's mean response to all samples when the dimension favored B from his or her mean response to all samples when it favored A. The magnitude of the contrast for each dimension is a measure of its relative contribution to the subject's judgment. Thus, if a dimension were ignored, its contrast would be zero, and in general, the stronger a dimension's impact, the larger its contrast.

The mean contrasts are shown in Figure 2 separately for each of the four groups. The fact that the Type I contrasts are greater than the Type II contrasts indicates that subjects were sensitive to the likelihood ratios. Analyses were performed separately on the Type I contrasts, the Type II contrasts, and on the differences between them, using in each case the multivariate analysis of variance (MANOVA) approach to repeated measure (McCall & Appelbaum, 1973). The three MANOVA designs were each 2 × 2 (Time Pressure × Payoff Condition), and the multiple variables were the orthogonal polynomial contrasts across the five dimensions calculated for each of the three sets of repeated measure: Type I contrasts, Type II contrasts, and the difference between them

There were no significant effects on differences between the Type I and Type II contrasts, indicating that problem type did not interact with any of the variables. This lack of interaction is represented be the nearly parallel lines in each panel of Figure 2.

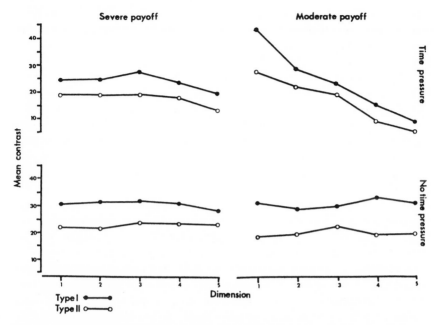

Figure 2. Mean contrasts as a function of subject group, probability type, and dimension number for Experiment 2. (From Wallsten & Barton, 1982).

The remaining MANOVAS are summarized in Table 1. The important results are the time by dimension double interactions, and the time by payoff by dimension triple interactions, which are precisely the ones predicted by the theory. They can be seen in Figure 2. The time by dimension double interaction reflects the fact that the five dimension contrasts were equal under the no-time-

Table 1. MANOVA Results on the Type I and Type II Contrasts

Effect	df	Type I		Type II	
		F	p <	F	p <
Dimensions (D)	4, 29	5.42	.002	12.17	10^{-5}
Time (T)	1, 32	12.23	.002	3.48	.08
Payoff (P)	1, 32	.04	.900	.78	.40
$T \times P$	1, 32	.00	1.000	.37	.60
$T \times D$	4, 29	5.90	.002	6.74	.001
$P \times D$	4, 29	1.80	.200	2.25	.09
$T \times P \times D$	4, 29	3.20	.030	2.46	.07

From Wallsten & Barton, 1982.

pressure condition but monotonically decreased from D_1 to D_5 under the high-time-pressure condition. The triple interaction reflects the fact that under high time pressure, the differences among the five dimension contrasts were smaller given the extreme payoff than given the moderate payoff.

To summarize these results, the subjects who could respond leisurely used all five dimensions equally under both payoff conditions. Subjects who were hurried, however, relied primarily on the earlier dimensions, with succeeding dimensions contributing successively less. However, in the latter case, subjects under the severe payoff rule used the five dimensions somewhat more equivalently than did the subjects under the moderate payoff rule.

The results just described show how *on average* subjects processed dimensions of decreasing salience. They are silent, however, with regard to possible sequential effects in the consideration of these dimensions. Assuming that dimensions are in fact considered from most to least salient, additional analysis asked whether there are primacy or recency effects in this processing. For primacy effects we asked, for example, whether the subjects attended to the *subsequent* dimensions when the *first n* dimensions favored the same population? For example, for $n = 4$, did subjects make use of D_5 when the first four dimensions all favored Population A (or Population B)? To answer this question, the mean confidence estimate or latency when D_1–D_4 all favored one population and D_5 favored the other was subtracted from the mean confidence estimate or latency when D_1–D_5 all favored the same population. If subjects ceased attending when D_1–D_4 were in agreement, then differences between both the mean confidence estimates and the mean latencies should be zero. If, however, the subjects did use D_5 in this case, then the differences should be nonzero—positive for confidence estimates and negative for latencies. Analogous contrasts were constructed for $n = 1, 2,$ and 3. The solid lines in Figure 3 display the mean response differences as a function of n, separately for the four groups, with confidence differences at the top of each panel and latency differences at the bottom. On the assumption that the dimensions are processed in the order D_1 to D_5, the differences may be considered to represent a kind of primacy effect.

On the same assumption, the dashed lines in the figure represent a recency effect. These curves show whether subjects made use of the *prior* dimensions when the *last n* dimensions agreed with each other. They were obtained by

Figure 3. Confidence and latency differences obtained by subtracting the mean response when the first *n* dimensions favored one population and the next dimension favored the other from the mean response when the first $n + 1$ dimensions were all in agreement (solid curves) or obtained by subtracting the mean response when the last *n* dimensions favored one population and the immediately preceding dimension favored the other from the mean response when the last $n + 1$ dimensions were all in agreement (dashed curves), as a function of *n* and subject group for Experiment 2. (HT = high time pressure; EP = extreme payoff; MP = moderate payoff; LT = low time pressure.) (From Wallsten & Barton, 1982).

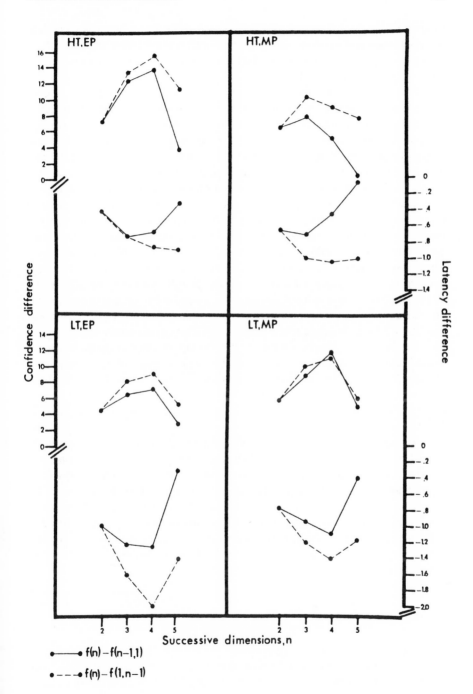

$\bullet\!\!-\!\!-\!\!-\!\!\bullet$ $f(n) - f(n-1,1)$

$\bullet\!-\!-\!-\!\bullet$ $f(n) - f(1,n-1)$

subtracting the mean response to patterns in which the last n dimensions favored one population and the immediately preceding dimension favored the other from the mean response to patterns in which the last $n + 1$ dimensions favored the same population, for $n = 1, \ldots, 4$.

For purposes of interpreting the results in Figure 3, note that the corresponding subtractions carried out on the optimal Bayesian posterior probabilities yields a monotonically decreasing function from .439 at $n = 1$ to .014 at $n = 4$. Temporarily restricting consideration to the three groups, excluding HT, MP (high time pressure, moderate payoff), note that for $n = 1, 2, 3$, the subjects not only attended to the dimension that immediately followed or preceded the initial or final agreeing n dimensions, but its contribution actually increased with n. This positive effect is somewhat greater in the recency component (dashed curves) than in the primacy (solid curves). However, when $n = 4$, that is, when the first or last four dimensions agreed with each other, the remaining dimension was attended to less strongly, as indicated by the curves bending toward zero. These results might be understood by assuming that whenever the initial or final 1, 2, or 3 dimensions agreed with each other, the following or preceding dimension, respectively, was utilized if it, too, was in agreement but that it was ignored otherwise. However, whenever four sequential dimensions were homogeneous, then the fifth was less frequently utilized regardless of its implication.

The results are similar for the HT, MP group except that the curves move toward zero at $n = 3$ instead of $n = 4$. In other words, these subjects consistently attended to only three successive dimensions. Indeed, when D_1–D_4 were in agreement, D_5 was ignored altogether, as evidenced by confidence and latency differences of zero. However, D_1 was not ignored entirely when D_2–D_5 were in agreement.

An additional analysis, not reproduced here, showed yet another form of sequential dependency. Specifically, Wallsten and Barton demonstrated that confidence estimates and latency were sensitive to the sequential order in which the dimensions favored the two populations. For example, if three dimensions favored Population A and two dimensions favored Population B, confidence was higher and latency was shorter if the three dimensions favoring A occurred in sequence than if they were interspersed with the dimensions favoring B. This type of sequential effect is impossible under any model assuming path independence of processing.

Discussion

On average, the results are precisely those predicted by a sequential sampling model that assumes (1) decision thresholds modulated by available time and payoff contingencies and (2) dimensions attended to in decreasing order of salience. When information could be considered at a leisurely pace, all the dimensions contributed equally to the judgment. Because there was no cost to sampling the information, the payoff manipulation did not effect the decision criteria. When information processing was hurried, however, decision boundaries were closer, and dimensions contributed to final judgment in decreasing order of salience. Moreover, under severe payoffs, the contributions of the dimensions in the decision criteria were more nearly equal than under the moderate payoffs, reflecting a difference in boundary placement.

The sequential effects, however, demonstrate that the sampling model is wrong with regard to its assumption of path independence. The subjective contribution of a dimension to final judgment depends upon the entire stimulus pattern. Indeed, no sequential sampling model of the form described could yield the recency effects found here, which imply that the interpretation of an early dimension depends upon the values of later dimensions.

Wallsten and Barton (1982) suggested in response to these results that final opinion may be formed in two stages. The first stage involves a qualitative partitioning of the dimensions according to the population each favors, yielding a tentative binary choice between the two populations. In the second processing stage, the dimensions are attended to individually for purposes of modifying quantitative opinion. They are processed configurally, rather than independently, in this stage, such that the impact of a dimension is positively related to the opinion held when the dimension is considered. Processing in this second stage is sequential and continues until one of the two decision thresholds is crossed. This two-stage and configural modification remains to be verified in subsequent research but has not been incorporated in any models to date.

Conclusions

In terms of the possible effects of time pressure mentioned at the beginning of this chapter, most experiments have concluded either that subjects select processing strategies according to the time available or that time pressure causes subjects to filter information so that they attend to only the most important subset. With regard to strategy selection, Zakay (1985) showed in a context of choice under uncertainty that subjects tended to use a noncompensatory process under time pressure and a compensatory process otherwise. Payne, Bettman, and Johnson (1988) in a risky choice situation involving information search showed that subjects changed their search strategy in response to time limitation. With regard to filtering information, both Wright (1974) and Svenson and Edland (1987) demonstrated in a riskless choice context that subjects under time pressure tended to focus on negative evidence more strongly than positive evidence. Indeed, Svenson and Edland's effect was so strong that preferences were reversed between high-and low-time-pressure situations. Similarly, Ben Zur and Bretnitz (1981) showed in a risky choice context that subjects under time pressure spent more time observing the negative than the positive dimensions. Payne et al. (1988) found that subjects not only shifted their strategy under time pressure but also selectively spent more time on certain attributes.

Thus, the Wallsten and Barton results are consistent with others in demonstrating that time pressure causes subjects to be relatively more influenced by some features than by others. Presumably, this occurs because the decision thresholds are sensitive to time pressure and payoffs, which affects the degree to which less salient dimensions are processed. The present results do not suggest that time pressure affects subjects' strategies in any other manner, but the experiment was not designed to demonstrate such changes if in fact they occur. A proper elucidation of time pressure effects requires both simultaneous consideration of the choice or judgment task and of the subjects' cognitive processing, as well as a precise specification of the model. For example, the sequential sampling model discussed here was developed specifically for a task of probabilistic inference based on multidimensional samples. Modification would be required to apply it to situations of risky, uncertain, or riskless choice. The various results in the literature are not necessarily in conflict with each other. However, only when decision tasks and decision-making requirements are considered jointly within well-specified models will we be able to sort out completely the effects of time pressure on decision making.

ACKNOWLEDGMENT. Table 1, Figure 2, and Figure 3 are copyright 1982 by the American Psychological Association and are reprinted by permission of the publisher. Preparation of this chapter was supported by NSF Grant BNS-8908554.

References

Ben Zur, H., & Breznitz, S. J. (1981). The effects of time pressure on risky choice behavior. *Acta Psychologica, 47,* 89–104.

Busemeyer, J. R. (1985). Decision making under uncertainty: A comparison of simple scalability, fixed sample, and sequential sampling models. *Journal of Experimental Psychology: Learning, Memory, & Cognition, 11,* 538–564.

Busemeyer, J. R., & Townsend, J. T. (1992). Fundamental derivations from decision field theory. *Mathematical Social Sciences, 23,* 255–282.

Einhorn, H. J., Kleinmuntz, D. N., & Kleinmuntz, B. (1979). Linear regression and process-tracing models of judgment. *Psychological Review, 86,* 465–485.

Maule, A. J., & Mackie, P. (1990). A componential investigation of the effects of deadlines on individual decision making. In K. Borcherding, O. I. Larichev, & D. M. Messick (Eds.), *Contemporary issues in decision making* (pp. 449–461). Amsterdam: Elsevier Science Publishers.

McCall, R. B., & Appelbaum, M. I. (1973). Bias in the analysis of repeated-measures designs: Some alternative approaches. *Child Development, 44,* 401–415.

Miller, J. G. (1960). Information input overload and psychopathology. *American Journal of Psychiatry, 116*, 695–704.

Nisbett, R. E., & Ross, L. (1980). *Human inference: Strategies and shortcomings of social judgment.* Englewood Cliffs, NJ: Prentice Hall.

Payne, J. W., Bettman, J. R., & Johnson, E. J. (1988). Adaptive strategy selection in decision making. *Journal of Experimental Psychology: Learning, Memory & Cognition, 14*, 534–552.

Svenson, O., & Edland, A. (1987). Change of preferences under time pressure: Choices and judgments. *Scandinavian Journal of Psychology, 28*, 322–330.

Wallsten, T. S. (1977). Processing information for decisions. In N. J. Castellan, D. B. Pisoni, & G. Potts (Eds.), *Cognitive theory* (Vol. 2, pp. 87–116). Hillsdale, NJ: Erlbaum.

Wallsten, T. S. (1980). Processes and models to describe choice and inference. In T. S. Wallsten (Ed.), *Cognitive process in choice and decision behavior* (pp. 215–238). Hillsdale, NJ: Erlbaum.

Wallsten, T. S., & Barton, C. (1982). Processing probabilistic multidimensional information for decisions. *Journal of Experimental Psychology: Learning, Memory, & Cognition, 8*, 361–384.

Wright, P. (1974). The harassed decision maker: Time pressures, distraction, and the use of evidence. *Journal of Applied Psychology, 59*, 555–561.

Zakay, D. (1985). Post-decisional confidence and conflict experienced in a choice process. *Acta Psychologica, 58*, 75–80.

13

Violations of the Speed–Accuracy Tradeoff Relation

Decreases in Decision Accuracy with Increases in Decision Time

Jerome R. Busemeyer

Introduction

Beginning with the seminal work by Simon (1955), decision making has been conceptualized in terms of information-processing systems that take anticipated future consequences as input, and after processing this information for some period of time, produce an action as output. Decision researches have considered two primary ways to measure the "performance" of a decision process. One way is in terms of the "accuracy" of the process—the probability that the process selects the "best" action, where *best* is defined by an accepted normative theory (e.g., Expected Utility Theory). The other way is in terms of effort—the average amount of time or number of mental operations required to reach a decision. The ideal decision process would be the one that maximizes accuracy and minimizes effort. Unfortunately, these two performance measures tend to be positively related—a decrease in effort usually produces a decrease in accuracy. Thus the decision maker has to tradeoff effort for accuracy. How this is done is the primary question addressed in this chapter.

Jerome R. Busemeyer • Department of Psychological Sciences, Purdue University, West Lafayette, Indiana 47807.

Time Pressure and Stress in Human Judgment and Decision Making, edited by Ola Svenson and A. John Maule. Plenum Press, New York, 1993.

Cost/Benefit Approach

One general view is called the cost/benefit approach (Beach & Mitchell, 1978; Johnson & Payne, 1985). According to this view, decision makers have a repertoire of qualitatively different decision strategies that vary along the dimensions of effort and accuracy. Strategy selection depends on the decision maker's willingness to trade accuracy for effort. Serious decisions are made using more accurate but more effortful strategies (e.g., the expected utility rule); less important decisions are made using less effortful but less accurate strategies (e.g., the lexicographic rule).

Although the precise details of strategy selection are not agreed upon, a few general principles provide the foundation for this approach (see Beach & Mitchell, 1978, for a more specific set of assumptions). If two strategies are equal in terms of accuracy, then the strategy producing the least effort is chosen. Similarly, if two strategies are equal in terms of effort, then the strategy producing the higher accuracy is chosen. Dominated strategies that involve greater effort and at the same time produce lower accuracy are rejected. Thus, if a strategy requires greater effort, then it must also yield greater accuracy before it will be selected. These principles are collectively called the cost/benefit tradeoff assumption.

The cost/benefit approach has also been used to explain the effects of deadline time limits (i.e., time limits that arise due to the imposition of a deadline) on decision performance. Payne, Bettman, and Johnson (1988) argued that under short deadline time limits, decision makers may be forced to resort to strategies that are less time consuming and less accurate; but with longer deadline time limits, decision makers would be free to use strategies that are more time consuming and more accurate. This line of reasoning led Payne et al. (1988) to predict that decision accuracy should be lower under high-time-pressure conditions (see Payne et al., 1988, p. 542).

Sequential Comparison Approach

Another approach to understanding accuracy–effort tradeoffs is called the sequential comparison approach (Aschenbrener, Albert & Schmalhofer, 1984; Busemeyer, 1985; Bockenholt, this volume; Edwards, 1965; Wallsten, this volume; Wallsten & Barton, 1982). According to this view, it is not necessary to assume that decision makers switch from compensatory to noncompensatory strategies to trade accuracy for effort. Instead, a single strategy is always used and effort–accuracy tradeoffs are achieved by adjustments of a continuous criterion parameter.

The sequential comparison process works as follows. At a particular moment in time, attention is focused on one of the many possible features that describe the consequences of each alternative. This results in a comparison value for each alternative—positive values indicate a relatively attractive value on the feature, and negative values indicate a relatively unattractive value. From moment to moment, attention switches from one feature to another producing a sequence of comparison values for each alternative. These comparisons are integrated over time producing a preference state at each moment for each alternative. The deliberation process continues until one preference state exceeds a criterion bound, and the first alternative to exceed the criterion is chosen.

Fast decisions are made by choosing a small criterion because this would permit a decision to be made after sampling very few features. Slow decisions are made by choosing a large criterion because this would require a large number of features to be sampled. Albert, Aschenbrenner, and Schmalhofer (1989) provide a review of experimental evidence from process-tracing studies of decision making that support the sequential comparison model. Myung and Busemeyer (1989) provide a detailed mathematical description of how the criterion is learned from experience with the outcomes of previous decisions.

The relation between speed and accuracy for the sequential comparison model depends on the initial state of preference that exists prior to sampling. (This initial state is similar to the prior log odds in Bayesian inference.) The initial preference state is very influential under short time limits when very little new information is sampled; but it loses its influence under long time limits when a great deal of new information is sampled.

If the decision maker begins with a neutral state of preference for each alternative, then the sequential comparison model predicts that decision accuracy is an increasing function of decision time. However, if the initial preference state is biased in favor of the "correct" alternative (due to past experience), then decision accuracy may decrease with decision time when it is very difficult to discriminate between the correct and the incorrect alternatives. In the latter case, the preference state will start out favoring the "correct" alternative but drift away from it as deliberation progresses. For example, a student's first reaction to an exam question may be correct but after mulling it over, he or she may become confused and ultimately choose the wrong answer.

Summary

The two approaches make different predictions regarding the effects of deadline time limits on accuracy. The cost/benefit approach generally predicts a speed–accuracy tradeoff relation, that is, decision accuracy is an increasing function of the deadline time limit. However, the sequential comparison approach predicts that the direction of this effect depends on (a) the initial preference state and (b) the discriminability of the difference between the correct and incorrect alternatives.

The purpose of this chapter is to (a) describe a set of experimental conditions under which a violation of the speed–accuracy tradeoff relation reliably occurs and (b) to provide a theoretical explanation for this violations in terms of the sequential sampling approach. In the next section of this chapter, an experiment by Busemeyer (1985) is reviewed which found systematic violations of the speed–accuracy tradeoff relation. In the third section, a new sequential comparison model, called Decision Field Theory, is used to account for these results. The final section explores some more general implications of the sequential comparison approach concerning the effects of time pressure on decision making.

Decision Making Under Deadline Time Pressure

Busemeyer (1985, Experiment 1) investigated the effects of deadline time limits on the accuracy of decisions made under uncertainty. The purpose of this section is to briefly summarize these earlier results, which provide the empirical basis for the new theoretical discussions in the third section. Additional details about this experiment can be obtained from the original article.

Design and Procedure

On each trial, subjects were given a choice between a certain alternative and an uncertain alternative. If the certain alternative was chosen, they would receive the displayed value for sure. If the uncertain alternative was chosen, they would receive a monetary payoff randomly sampled from a normal distribution.

Three different values of the certain alternative were employed in the experiment—+$.03, zero, and −$.03. Two different normal distributions were employed for the uncertain alternative—one with a mean of zero and a standard deviation (std) of $.05 (the small std condition) and the other with a mean of zero and a standard deviation of $.50 (the large std condition). Choices had to be made within a deadline time limit of 1, 2, or 3 seconds, and failure to meet the deadline cost $.25. These three factors were combined to form a $3 \times 2 \times 3$ factorial design, and each subject received all 18 conditions.

At the beginning of each choice trial, subjects were shown the deadline time limit. Then the two choice alternatives were presented—the value of the certain alternative was displayed on one side of a computer monitor, and a letter symbolizing the uncertain alternative was displayed on the other side (with a different letter for each std condition). Following each choice, subjects were shown the amount that would have been won or lost by choosing the uncertain alternative. This allowed them to learn the distribution of payoffs produced by the uncertain alternative from experience. Each subject received 15 sessions of training with 360 trials per session, but the results were based on the last 13 sessions. (There were no statistically significant effects of training after the first two sessions, and so it was concluded that learning had reached asymptote after the second session).

Following Payne et al. (1988), we define the correct alternative for this task as the alternative that produced the larger expected value. Recall that the mean of the uncertain alternative was always zero. Therefore, the uncertain alternative would be correct whenever the value of the certain alternative was negative, and the uncertain alternative would be incorrect whenever the value of the certain alternative was positive. There are four justifications for using the expected value to define the correct alternative. First, the amount of money won or lost on each trial was small (e.g., less than $1.00), and the utility function for money should be approximately linear within this small range. Second, subjects made hundreds of repeated decisions, and so the expected value provided a very close estimate of their average take-home pay. Third, the probability of choosing the uncertain alternative was very close to .5 when the certain value was zero. Fourth, the "correct" alternative was chosen more frequently than the "incorrect" alternative for every one of the 18 conditions, and so the word *correct* also can be interpreted as *more favorable*.

Results for Decision Time

Subjects rarely failed to beat the deadline time limit. The average response time systematically increased from .68 seconds to .88 seconds as the time limit increased from 1 second to 3 seconds, and the difference was statistically significant. There was no statistically significant interaction between the time limit and the std condition. Thus, subjects generally spent more time making decisions under the longer time limit.

Results for Decision Accuracy

Table 1 presents the proportion of correct decisions under the short deadline (first pair of columns), and the change in this proportion that resulted from increasing the deadline time limit (second pair of columns). The results are

Table 1. Effect of Deadline Time Pressure on Decision Accuracy

Subject	Proportion correct under short time limit		Change in proportion correct from short to long time limit		z statistic	
	Low Std	High Std	Low Std	High Std	Low Std	High Std
1	.88	.46	.07	−.16	2.86	−3.76
2	.87	.80	.03	−.08	1.07	−2.14
3	.96	.67	.01	−.26	.62	−5.95
4	.75	.60	.12	.03	3.49	.70
5	.95	.74	.03	−.06	1.86	−1.51
6	.90	.80	.07	.01	3.24	.29
Mean	.89	.68	.05	−.09	5.43	−5.03

Note. A correct decision was defined as the choice of the alternative producing the largest expected value. Positive changes indicate an increase in accuracy with an increase in deadline time limit. The proportions for each subject were based on approximately 260 observations. The z statistic is the z score for testing the difference between two proportions, and values greater than 1.96 exceed the cutoff for the .05 level of significance.

shown here for the first time separately for each subject and std condition (Busemeyer, 1985, only presented the results averaged across subjects). The z statistics for testing the differences between proportions are shown in the last pair of columns (the critical value for testing significance at the .05 level is 1.96). As can be seen in Table 1, accuracy increased for all six subjects under the low std condition, producing an average increase of +5% ($z = 5.44$, $p < .05$) but it decreased for four subjects under the high std condition producing an average decrease of −9% ($z = -5.02$, $p < .05$). This same pattern of results was replicated in a second experiment reported in Busemeyer (1985). Possible explanations for this crossover interaction effect are considered next.

Theoretical Explanations

Cost/Benefit Approach

According to this view, the increase in response time produced by the longer deadline time limit was due to subjects switching to a more time-consuming decision strategy. But according to the cost/benefit assumption, subjects would be willing to incur this cost in effort only if this change in strategy produced a benefit of increased accuracy. The latter conclusion is inconsistent with the results obtained from the high std condition. Consequently, the decrease in accuracy with increase in decision time obtained from the high std condition violates the speed–accuracy tradeoff relation assumed by the cost/benefit approach.

An alternative explanation is that subjects simply increased the speed of processing under short deadlines (i.e., the acceleration hypothesis of Ben Zur & Breznitz, 1981). On the one hand, the results obtained under the high std condition imply that increasing processing speed somehow increases accuracy; on the other hand, the results obtained under the low std condition imply just the opposite relation. In sum, this hypothesis also fails to give a coherent account of the entire pattern of results.

Sequential Comparison Approach

Decision Field Theory is a sequential comparison model that has been recently applied to a number of phenomena obtained in research on decision making under uncertainty including the Allais paradox (Busemeyer & Townsend, 1989) and preference reversals (Busemeyer & Goldstein, 1992). In this chapter, we will show how this theory also provides an explanation for violations of the speed–accuracy tradeoff relation reported by Busemeyer (1985). Only a brief description of the model is presented here, and further details can be obtained from Busemeyer and Townsend (1993).

The time index, t, represents the amount of time that has elapsed since the onset of the choice problem. At each point in time, the decision maker has a preference state, denoted $P(t)$. Positive values $(P(t) > 0)$ represent a preference state in favor of the uncertain alternative, negative values $(P(t) < 0)$ represent a preference state in favor of the certain alternative, and $P(t) = 0$ represents a neutral state of preference.

Immediately after the choice problem is first displayed, an initial preference state is retrieved from memory for the displayed choice problem. This initial state of preference is denoted $P(O) = z$, and it is biased by the value of the certain alternative: Subjects start out biased against the uncertain alternative when the certain value is positive $(z < 0)$, and they are initially biased in favor of the uncertain alternative when the certain value is negative $(z > 0)$. This initial preference state serves as the anchor point for the sequential adjustment process that follows.

During the ensuing deliberation process, the decision maker recalls the recently experienced payoffs produced by the uncertain alternative. At any given moment, the decision maker retrieves a particular payoff from memory for the uncertain alternative, and this retrieved uncertain value is compared with the value of the certain alternative. Each momentary comparison produces a valence at Time t, denoted $V(t)$, and these comparison values change from moment to moment as the retrieved value of the uncertain alternative fluctuates during deliberation. For this experiment, the valence, $V(t)$, is normally distributed. The mean of $V(t)$ (denoted by d) is equal to the difference in expected values between the uncertain and certain alternatives, and the variance of $V(t)$ (denoted by σ^2/h) is proportional to the variance of the uncertain alternative.

The valence at Time t, is integrated with the previous preference state at Time t, to form a new preference state at the next moment in time, $t + h$, where h symbolizes the time unit for each comparison. The new state preference is determined by the following sequential adjustment model:

$$P(t + h) = (1 - s \cdot h) \cdot P(t) + h \cdot V(t). \tag{1}$$

In other words, the new preference state is weighted average of the previous state and the valence, where $(1 - s \cdot h)$ is the weight applied to the previous state, and h is the weight applied to the input valence. The growth rate, s, controls the amount of adjustment of the previous preference state, $P(t)$, toward the new input valence, $V(t)$. For simplicity, s was set equal to $s = 1$, but the same pattern of predictions result from growth rates ranging from zero to 1.

Finally, the preference state continues to evolve during deliberation within a single choice trial until it exceeds a criterion bound, θ. The uncertain alternative is chosen as soon as $P(t) > \theta$ occurs, and the certain alternative is chosen as soon as $-P(t) > \theta$ occurs. The criterion bound is an increasing function of the deadline time limit.

The mathematical derivation of the equation for choice probability is presented in Busemeyer and Townsend (1992). The solution for the probability of choosing the uncertain alternative is given below (after allowing the time unit h to approach zero in the limit to produce a continuous time process):

$$\text{Prob [Choose uncertain]} = S(z)/S(\theta),$$

$$S(x) = \int_{-\theta}^{x} \exp[(s \cdot y^2 - 2 \cdot d \cdot y)/\sigma^2]dy. \tag{2}$$

Figure 1 shows the probability of making a correct choice calculated from the above equation. This probability is plotted as a function of the criterion bound, and recall that the criterion bound is an increasing function of the deadline time limit. The two vertical lines indicate the short and long deadline time-limit conditions. Note that for the small std condition, the probability of making a correct decision increases as the deadline time limit increases from short to long. But for the large std condition, the probability of making a correct decision decreases as the deadline time limit increases.

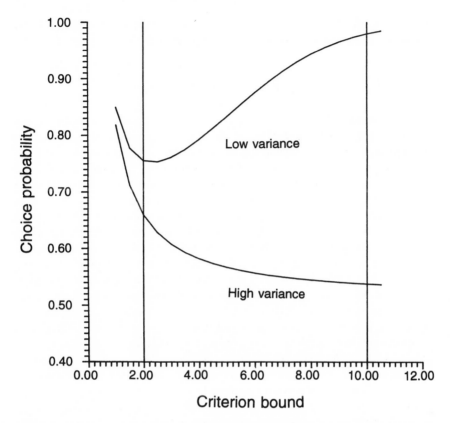

Figure 1. Probability of choosing the correct alternative predicted by the decision field choice model plotted as a function of the criterion magnitude, with a separate curve for the low and high std conditions.

Conclusions

Conditions That Lead to Violations of the Speed–Accuracy Relation

The theoretical analysis illustrated in Figure 1 indicates that the normal tradeoff relation between speed and accuracy will be violated when the following two conditions are present: (a) The preference state is initially biased in the direction of the correct alternative and (b) the discriminability between the correct and incorrect alternative is low. In this case, increasing the criterion bound will increase decision time and decrease accuracy. The preference state will start out favoring the correct alternative but later drift away from it.

Changes in Strategy versus Changes in Criteria

The sequential comparison approach provides a viable alternative to the cost/benefit approach for explaining the effects of time pressure on decision performance. There are several distinct advantages to be gained by using the sequential comparison approach. One is that it links decision research more closely to prior work on speed–accuracy tradeoffs in cognitive psychology (Link, 1978; Pachella, 1974), and the extensive amount of research in these related areas may provide new insights for decision researchers. The second is that sequential comparison models are capable of making precise quantitative predictions for both choice probability and the distribution of choice response times. The cost/benefit approach fails to describe exactly how strategies are selected (the tradeoff process is a mystery). Third, the sequential comparison model is more parsimonious—the same decision process is always employed.

Several years ago, Klayman (1983) warned decision researchers that changes in process measures (e.g., changes in variability of search or frequency of within-attribute search transitions) often fail to distinguish whether subjects change decision strategies versus change decision criteria. Yet this warning has gone unheeded. For example, Payne et al. (1988) concluded that the effects of time pressure on decision-making performance were due to changes in strategy. They overlooked the possibility that these effects were due to changes in the stopping criterion of a sequential comparison process.

One of the key properties of sequential comparison processes is the variability in the proportion of dimensions that are searched. Consider the simplest case—a binary choice task. As Schmalhofer, Albert, Aschenbrenner, and Gertzen (1986) point out, the proportion of dimensions searched will vary across choice pairs for the following reason: For some pairs, the criterion bound may be reached after sampling a small number of dimensions if the advantages on the sampled dimensions strongly favor one of the alternatives; but for other pairs, a larger number of dimensions may be sampled if the advantages and disadvantages tend to balance out.

Obviously, the mean proportion of dimensions searched is expected to be an increasing function of the criterion bound, and the latter is an increasing function of the deadline time limit. Perhaps it is less obvious that the variability in the proportion of dimensions searched is expected to follow an inverted U-shaped function of the deadline time limit. Consider once again the binary choice problem. Extremely short deadlines would force the decision process to terminate after sampling only a single dimension (probably the most important dimension), producing very low variability. Extremely long deadlines would permit a high criterion bound, and this would allow almost all of the dimensions to be searched, also producing low variability (assuming that the payoff magnitudes are sufficiently large to encourage extremely accurate decisions). Intermediate deadlines would produce the most variability because some choice pairs would require sampling only a few dimensions to reach the criterion, whereas others would require sampling a large number.

Dynamic Nature of Preference

According to the decision field model described in the third section, the preference state continuously evolves during deliberation. It can even change from positive to negative over time as new information is assimilated. This implies that the probability of choosing one alternative over another can change from below to above .5 simply by manipulating the deadline time limit. In fact, Svenson and Edland (1987) found that when subjects were asked to choose between a pair of fictitious apartments to rent, one apartment in a pair was chosen more frequently under a short-deadline time limit, but the other apartment in the same pair was chosen more frequently under a long-deadline time limit.

There are two situations that are expected to produce such drastic changes in choice probability as a function of deliberation time. One is where the decision maker is give a choice between one alternative that has an advantage on the most prominent dimension versus a second alternative that has advantages on all of the remaining dimensions. Under short deadlines, only the most prominent dimension tends to be processed, and the first alternative is chosen more frequently. Under long deadlines, many of the remaining dimensions beyond the primary dimension are also processed, and these consistently favor the second alternative, causing it to be chosen more frequently. This may explain the results found by Svenson and Edland (1987).

A different situation is where the decision maker is given a choice between a familiar status-quo alternative versus a new and unfamiliar alternative. Suppose that the new alternative is superior to the status quo, but its superiority can be revealed only by a careful assessment of a large number of features. Under short-deadline time limits, choice probability will be primarily determined by the initial preference state, which favors the status quo. Under long deadlines, the preference state will be driven away from the status quo by all of the advantages of the new alternative, causing the new alternative to be chosen more frequently.

These last two examples point out the potential influence that time pressure may have on moderating the direction of preference. They also underscore the need for dynamic models of preference. In conclusion, sequential comparison models (and Decision Field Theory in particular) provide a useful approach to

understanding the systematic but complex pattern of changes that occur in choice
probability as a function of manipulations of deadline time limits.

References

Albert, D., Aschenbrenner, K. M., & Schmalhofer, F. (1989). Cognitive choice processes and the
    attitude-behavior relation. In A. Upmeyer (Ed.), *Attitudes and behavioral decisions* (pp. 61–
    99). New York: Springer.
Aschenbrenner, K. M., Albert, D., & Schmalhofer, F. (1984). Stochastic choice heuristics. *Acta
    Psychologica, 56,* 153–166.
Beach, L. R., & Mitchell, T. R. (1978). A contingency model for the selection of decision strategies.
    Academy of Management Review, 3, 439–449.
Ben Zur, H., & Breznitz, S. J. (1981). The effects of time pressure on risky choice behavior. *Acta
    Psychologica, 47,* 89–104.
Busemeyer, J. R. (1985). Decision making under uncertainty: A comparison of simple scalability,
    fixed sample, and sequential sampling models. *Journal of Experimental Psychology: Learning,
    Memory, Cognition, 11,* 538–564.
Busemeyer, J. R., & Goldstein, W. M. (1992). Linking together different measures of preference: A
    dynamic model of matching derived from decision field theory. *Organizational Behavior and
    Human Decision Processes, 52,* 370–396.
Busemeyer, J. R., & Townsend, J. T. (1989). *Decision Field Theory: A dynamic-cognitive approach
    to decision making.* Purdue Mathematical Psychology Program Technical Report No. 89-7.
Busemeyer, J. R., & Townsend, J. T. (1992). Fundamental derivations from decision field theory.
    Mathematical Social Sciences, 23, 255–282.
Busemeyer, J. R., & Townsend, J. T. (1993). Decision Field Theory: A dynamic-cognitive approach
    to decision making in an uncertain environment. *Psychological Review, 100,* 432–459.
Edwards, W. (1965). Optimal strategies for seeking information: Models for statistics, choice reac-
    tion time, and human information processing. *Journal of Mathematical Psychology, 2,* 312–
    329.
Johnson, E. J., & Payne, J. W. (1985). Effort and accuracy in choice. *Management Science, 31,* 395–
    414.
Klayman, J. (1983). Analysis of predecisional information search patterns. In P. C. Humphreys, O.
    Svenson, & A. Vari (Eds.), *Analyzing and aiding decisions* (pp. 401–414). Amsterdam: North-
    Holland.
Link, S. W. (1978). The relative judgment theory analysis of response deadline experiments. In N. J.
    Castellan, Jr., & F. Restle (Eds.), *Cognitive theory, III* (pp. 117–138). Hillsdale, NJ: Erlbaum.
Myung, I. J., & Busemeyer, J. R. (1989). Criterion learning in a deferred decision-making task.
    American Journal of Psychology, 102, 1–16.
Pachella, R. G. (1974). The interpretation of reaction time in information processing research. In B.
    Kantowitz (Ed.), *Human information processing: Tutorials in performance and cognition.* (pp.
    41–82) Hillsdale, NJ: Erlbaum.
Payne, J. W., Bettman, J. R., & Johnson, E. J. (1988). Adaptive strategy selection in decision
    making. *Journal of Experimental Psychology: Learning, Memory & Cognition, 14,* 534–552.
Schmalhofer, F., Albert, D., Aschenbrenner, K. M., & Gertzen, H. (1986). Process traces of binary
    choices: Evidence for selective and adaptive decision heuristics. *The Quarterly Journal of
    Experimental Psychology, 38A,* 59–76.
Simon, H. A. (1955). A behavioral model of rational choice. *Quarterly Journal of Economics, 69,*
    99–118.

Svenson, O., & Edland, A. (1987). Change of preferences under time pressure: Choices and judgements. *Scandinavian Journal of Psychology, 28,* 322–330.
Swensson, R. G., & Thomas, R. E. (1974). Fixed and optimal stopping models for two choice discrimination times. *Journal of Mathematic Psychology, 11,* 213–236.
Wallsten, T. S., & Barton, C. (1982). Processing probabilistic multidimensional information for decisions. *Journal of Experimental Psychology: Learning, Memory, and Cognition, 8,* 361–384.

14

The Effect of Time Pressure in Multiattribute Binary Choice Tasks

Ulf Böckenholt and Keith Kroeger

Introduction

Constraints in resources such as time, money, and information have a strong and systematic influence on choice behavior. Although some of these constraints may occur as natural features of a choice situation, others may be self-imposed by the decision maker, to limit an agonizing deliberation process about a decision problem. It is surprising that despite their prevalent influence, the topic of resource constraints has received little attention in the decision-making literature. For example, only a few studies consider the impact of time pressure on the decision process, and even fewer studies examine the influence of self-imposed time constraints (Mano, 1989). However, the few systematic investigations examining subjects' judgment and decision-making behavior under time pressure demonstrate that time pressure may affect every stage in a decision process from the information selection, evaluation, and aggregation stages to the actual choice (Busemeyer, 1985; Payne, Bettman, & Johnson, 1988; Svenson & Edland, 1987; Wright, 1974). Effects of time pressure are also reflected by postdecisional variables such as confidence (Smith, Mitchell, & Beach, 1982; Zakay, 1985).

Ulf Böckenholt and Keith Kroeger • Department of Psychology, University of Illinois at Urbana–Champaign, Champaign, Illinois 61820.
Time Pressure and Stress in Human Judgment and Decision Making, edited by Ola Svenson and A. John Maule. Plenum Press, New York, 1993.

In this chapter we adopt the view that the manipulation of time pressure provides an important mechanism to investigate adaptive as well as constructive elements of a decision-making process. Thus, we assume that resource constraints such as time pressure motivate a decision maker not only to be adaptive by modifying his or her behavior to the requirements of the choice task but also to be constructive, for example, by developing new strategies and simplifying the decision problem (Payne, 1982; Russo & Dosher, 1983). We also posit that changes in a decision-making process as a result of time pressure are guided partially by a cost/benefit analysis of the decision maker (Beach & Mitchell, 1978; Payne, 1976). Thus, individuals examine the cost/benefit tradeoffs of choice strategies in an attempt to construct or select strategies that yield accurate choices but involve low costs of processing information in terms of both effort and time. In particular, the simulation studies and experimental results obtained by Payne, Bettman, and Johnson (1988) provide strong support for this viewpoint.

To examine these adaptive and constructive elements of a decision-making process in detail, we limit ourselves to binary choice situations with multiattribute alternatives. In previous research, it was shown that choice behavior in a binary decision task is well described by a class of criterion-dependent choice (CDC) models (Albert, Aschenbrenner, & Schmalhofer, 1989; Böckenholt, Albert, Aschenbrenner, & Schmalhofer, 1991). This class of models makes specific predictions about the various stages in a decision process related to the acquisition, evaluation, and aggregation of information. Moreover, this class includes many different choice strategies as special cases and is consistent with a cost/benefit approach.

The remainder of this chapter is structured as follows. We first review features of CDC models and summarize some recent experimental results that were obtained when testing the models' performances in describing binary choice behavior. Next, we derive predictions of the class of CDC models about subjects' behavior under time pressure and relate them to relevant findings in the literature. These predictions describe changes in the different subcomponents of a decision process and are tested in a process-tracing study.

The Class of Criterion-Dependent Choice Models

CDC models have proven useful to explain the information acquisition behavior of subjects when choosing between two multiattribute alternatives (Albert, Aschenbrenner, & Schmalhofer, 1989; Böckenholt, Albert, Aschenbrenner, & Schmalhofer, 1991). Similar versions of this class of models have also been presented by Busemeyer (1982, 1985) for one-dimensional risky choice situations and by Wallsten and Barton (1982) for probabilistic inference tasks. CDC models posit that decision makers process information about choice alternatives by comparing the alternatives with respect to the subjective evaluation of the features, one attribute at a time. Features of the alternatives are processed attributewise, and the results of the attributewise comparisons are accumulated over the processed attributes. When a person has accumulated enough evidence to be convinced that one alternative is better, the comparison process stops and an alternative is chosen.

More formally, let $v(x_i)$ and $v(y_i)$ denote the subjective evaluations of alternatives x and y, respectively, on attribute i. The difference of the subjective evaluations, $[v(x_i) - v(y_i)]$, are added over the selected attributes until the absolute sum of the aggregated differences is equal to or exceeds a critical value, k,

$$\left| \sum_i [v(x_i) - v(y_i)] \right| \geq k,$$

and a choice is made. Thus, it is assumed that subjects select, evaluate, and aggregate information sequentially. Although the aggregation process is compensatory, it allows for noncompensatory effects provided only a subset of the available information is considered. For example, if a particular set of feature differences is equal to or exceeds the critical value, k, a choice is made; however, a different set of feature differences or the additional selection of alternatives' features may possibly reverse the choice. As a result, inconsistencies in choice behavior are partially explained by the fact that subjects may select different attributes when comparing two alternatives repeatedly.

The scale level of the evaluation function of the alternatives' features, $v(\,\cdot\,)$, is left unspecified. Depending on the task characteristics, a decision maker may code a feature's attractiveness on a binary, ordinal, or interval scale level (Svenson, 1979). The critical value, k, is determined by the decision maker and assumed to be independent of a choice pair. A large k value implies that most or all of the attributes characterizing the alternatives have to be considered. In contrast, a small k value may lead to a choice after the consideration of only a few attributes. Consequently, both the size of the critical value as well as simplifications in the evaluative coding of the alternatives' features reflect the effort–quality tradeoff intended by the decision maker. Another important feature of the CDC model is that it includes many choice strategies as special cases. For example, the CDC model with a low critical value mimics the lexicographic decision rule (Tversky, 1969). In comparison, the CDC model with a very large criterion value becomes the additive rule (Svenson, 1979). Similarly, the majority of confirming dimensions (MCD) rule (Russo & Dosher, 1983) is a special variant of the CDC model if the subjective value differences are coded in a binary way, so that only the direction of the differences but not its size is taken into account (see also Aschenbrenner, Albert, & Schmalhofer, 1986).

Because of the general form of the class of CDC models, it is difficult to fit them to information acquisition and choice data. Only if simplifying assumptions are introduced or subjects make a large number of choices is it possible to estimate the parameters of a CDC model. For example, Böckenholt et al. (1991) assumed that the evaluation function $v(\cdot)$ is well approximated by subjects' independently elicited attractiveness ratings of the alternatives' features. Consequently, only one parameter, the critical value k, had to be estimated to predict, for example, the number of selected attributes before a choice was made. An alternative way to examine the appropriateness of the class of CDC models is to derive specific predictions that can be tested experimentally. This is the approach chosen in the following study.

Time Pressure Effects

Because time pressure may affect every stage of a decision process, we discuss the possible effects on the selection, evaluation, aggregation and post-decisional levels. This decomposition of a decision process is admittedly artificial but it facilitates a more precise formulation of time pressure effects. Our formulation of hypotheses is guided by predictions derived from the CDC models and studies investigating the effect of time pressure on judgment and decision making processes. In the following section we will use TP and NTP as abbreviation for time pressure and no time pressure, respectively.

Selection

Under TP it is expected that the critical value k is reduced. This implies that, overall, a subject will consider fewer pieces of information before making a choice. Although the CDC model is not explicit about the order in which information is selected, it is expected that the selection order is determined largely by the importance of the attributes (Aschenbrenner, Böckenholt, Albert & Schmalhofer, 1986). Clearly, the impact of the selection order on the choice outcome is stronger when less information is selected. Thus, it is hypothesized that under TP subjects have a higher probability of selecting more important attributes than under NTP, and a reversal of this relationship is predicted for less important attributes. This prediction is in agreement with several experimental findings in the literature. For example, Payne, Bettman, and Johnson (1988) found that when choosing among gambles under TP, subjects not only processed information faster but also focused selectively on a subset of the available information. Ben Zur and Breznitz (1981) also asked subjects to choose among gambles with various winning and losing amounts. These authors found that, under TP, subjects spend more time on the losing aspects than on the winning aspects of a gamble. In summary, we expect that subjects are more selective under TP, process less information and, as a result, focus more (in a relative sense) on the important attributes.

Evaluation and Aggregation

Instead of assuming that subjects may switch strategies under TP, it is posited that they use a CDC strategy that is modified to accommodate the requirements of the decision task. However, because the class of CDC models can mimic a variety of decisions rules, the observed information acquisition and choice behavior can be (erroneously) interpreted as a strategy switch. As a result, our prediction that subjects will lower their critical value and simplify the evaluation process of the alternatives is in general agreement with the finding that subjects tend to employ simple strategies of low analytical complexity under TP (Christensen-Szalanski, 1980; Wright, 1974).

The CDC models assume attributewise processing of the information in binary choices regardless of the severity of the TP constraint. Thus, although it is expected that subjects will process information faster under TP, the attributewise selection mechanism is not expected to be affected by the presence or absence of TP. This prediction is in contrast to Payne et al.'s (1988) finding that subjects show a stronger tendency of attributewise processing under TP. However, their result was obtained when subjects had to choose among multiple alternatives and may not hold for binary choice tasks. In summary, we expect that subjects accelerate their information processing under TP. We interpret this acceleration partially as an indication that subjects use simplified evaluation rules. However, we expect subjects to compare alternatives in an attributewise fashion under TP as well as under NTP.

Choice Prediction and Consistency

Consistency is defined as the agreement of choices in "identical" choice tasks. In a model-independent way, choice consistency serves as a reference point for a subject's performance under different choice conditions. It is important to distinguish choice consistency within the TP or the NTP condition (within-condition consistency) from choice consistency between both conditions (between-condition consistency). From discrimination and choice studies, it is well known that choice consistency is affected by the size of the attractiveness difference between two alternatives (Falmagne, 1985). Choices become more consistent the larger the difference between two alternatives. According to the CDC models, choices under TP should be as consistent as choices under the NTP condition. Thus, no change is expected in the within-condition consistency. In contrast, between-condition consistency is expected to be lower than within-condition consistency because subjects may simplify their evaluative coding of the features and put more weight on the important attributes under TP.

There is also some evidence indicating that, under TP, subjects seem to put more emphasis on the negative aspects of important attributes (Ben Zur & Breznitz, 1981; Svenson & Edlund, 1987; Wright, 1974). In particular, Svenson and Edlund (1987) observed that this behavior may lead to systematic preference reversals. Thus, choices between identical choice pairs may be different under TP and NTP not only because subjects may put more weight on the more important attributes but also because they may become more extreme in their evaluation of unattractive features under TP. These results imply that differences between within-condition and between-condition consistency may depend also on the attractiveness evaluation of the choice pair feature.

Predictions of choices are dependent on models that are (usually) based on assumptions about the choice process. According to the CDC models (and probabilistic choice models), the predictability of choices should improve as the size of the attractiveness difference increases. Because the evaluation process cannot be directly observed in a choice situation, some close substitute such as independently elicited attractiveness judgments of the choice alternatives has to be used to obtain a measure of the attractiveness difference. Similar to our choice consistency prediction, we expect that these attractiveness judgments provide a better prediction of choices obtained under a NTP condition. Predictions of choices under TP should be worse because subjects may evaluate alternatives differently under TP.

Postdecisional Variables

Postdecisional variables such as confidence in the quality of a decision may also reflect the influence of TP. For example, Smith, Mitchell, and Beach (1982) found that confidence in decisions decreased with TP. Because, in their studies, confidence was influenced by the complexity level of a selected strategy and TP, Smith et al. hypothesized that although a complex strategy may increase the confidence in decision quality, TP may handicap an adequate implementation of the strategy and thus reduce confidence. Moreover, Zakay (1985) emphasized that confidence may also be influenced by the conflict experienced when choosing among choice alternatives. Because in the following study we manipulate both the subjects' thoroughness in using a CDC strategy and choice conflict, we expect that confidence judgments are influenced by both factors. Thus, under TP, subjects are expected to lower their critical value and to select less information that should reduce their confidence in the choice. In addition, the conflict in choosing between two alternatives should also be affected by the size of the attractiveness difference of the choice alternatives. Thus, the larger the attractiveness difference the more confident a subject may feel about his/her choice.

A Process-Tracing Study

Our predictions may be summarized as follows. Under TP, subjects are more selective, process less information and, as a result, focus more (in a relative sense) on the important attributes. Subjects compare alternatives in an attributewise fashion under TP as well as under NTP, but under TP they accelerate their processing of information, and they may use simplified evaluation rules. Moreover, subjects may become more extreme in their evaluation of unattractive features. Because of these differences in selecting and processing of information, between-condition consistency is expected to be lower than within-condition consistency that is expected to stay the same under TP and NTP. Similar results are expected regarding the predictability of choices by attractiveness judgments of the choice alternatives. Finally, confidence should be reduced under TP and positively related to the attractiveness difference between two alternatives.

In a process-tracing study that did not involve time pressure, Böckenholt et al. (1991) found that subjects' selection behavior was not only influenced by the attractiveness difference between two alternatives but also by the overall attractiveness of each choice alternative. For the same attractiveness difference, the majority of the subjects selected more information for two unattractive than for two attractive alternatives. This finding demonstrated that subjects took into account more than just attractiveness differences. To account for this result, Böckenholt et al. (1991) introduced the "criterion shift hypothesis" by arguing that subjects adjust their critical value depending on the overall attractiveness of both alternatives. This adjustment reflects the goal of a decision maker to select the less poor of two unattractive alternatives. Thus, a decision maker may spend more effort when comparing two unattractive alternatives than when comparing two attractive alternatives because the costs associated with a poor choice between two unattractive alternatives may be higher than the costs associated with a poor choice between two attractive alternatives. This behavior is in accordance with an effort–quality tradeoff because in the latter case both alternatives are satisfactory. Of course, in other choice situations, decision makers may be predominantly interested in selecting the better of two attractive alternatives and care less about the unattractive options. For example, Russo and Rosen (1976) found in an eye fixation analysis that subjects spent more time comparing two attractive than two unattractive alternatives. An important prediction of the "criterion shift hypothesis " is that, independent of any adjustments due to the overall attractiveness of both alternatives, TP always reduces the critical value. This additional hypothesis was also tested in the following process-tracing study.

We constructed a set of multiattribute choice alternatives that differed in their overall attractiveness and paired them to obtain different attractiveness differences. Both the attractiveness difference between two alternatives and the attractiveness of an alternative were manipulated to examine the influence of both factors on the selection and choice behavior of subjects. To assess consistency, the same choice pairs were presented under a TP and a NTP condition, and some choice pairs were repeated within each condition.

Subjects

A total of 11 male and 24 female undergraduates at the University of Illinois participated as subjects to satisfy a course requirement. Ages ranged from 18 to 21 years. Each subject was tested individually.

Design and Procedure

Subjects were told that their goal was to select the person they preferred for a date in a computer dating task. The dates were described on eight attributes, (e.g., career goals, sociableness, attractiveness), and these eight attributes had five features each. For example, the attribute *career goals* had the five features, home maker, academic, managerial, professional, and skilled worker.

To reduce individual-difference effects in the choices as a result of differently valuing (features of) choice alternatives, choice alternatives were constructed such that they were identical in their rank values of the features for every subject. Thus, each choice alternative was defined by a feature rank pattern. For example, a date with a feature rank pattern {1 1 1 1 1 1 1 1} implies that for any selected attribute the feature is displayed that is most preferred by the subject. In contrast, a date with the feature rank pattern {5 5 5 5 5 5 5 5} implies that for any selected attribute the feature is displayed that is least preferred by the subject. Similarly, a choice alternative with the feature rank pattern {1 2 1 2 1 2 1 2} implies that on the first selected attribute, the subject would see his/her most preferred feature, on the second selected attribute, the subject would see her/his second most preferred feature, on the third selected attribute, she/he would see her/his most preferred feature on this attribute, and so forth. Because subjects may differ in their rank order of the features, the actual features of the choice alternatives may be different for every subject. To ensure that subjects arrived at a comparable overall evaluation of each alternative even when they differed regarding the number of inspected attributes, a choice alternative was described by a feature ranking pattern that repeated itself after the second attribute.

The experiment consisted of three parts. During the first part of the experiment, subjects were asked to provide a preference rank order of the five features for each of the eight attributes. In addition, subjects provided attractiveness ratings of the features. Next, the eight attributes were ranked and rated on an attractiveness scale. For the second part of the experiment, a computer program generated on-line for each subject the choice alternatives based on the subject's preference rankings. Subjects were asked to choose between pairs of 20 dates twice, under a time constraint of 15 seconds and under a NTP condition. In a pilot study, subjects took an average of about 50 seconds on a NTP trial. Time pressure was introduced with the cover story that people frequently develop their impression about another person at an early stage of the acquaintanceship. To simulate this situation the time available for a choice was limited. Subjects were given feedback on the elapsed time. After 15 seconds, subjects could not acquire additional information and were instructed to choose. Each trial began with a message indicating the TP or NTP conditions. The trials were presented in the same random order for every subject.

A 2 × 2 factorial combination of the *attractiveness-difference* and overall *attractiveness* factors was used to construct the alternatives. This design was similar to the design used in the Böckenholt et al. (1992) study. For each of the four cells, five pairs of alternatives were generated that yielded 20 pairs of alternatives. Four out of the five alternative pairs were unique; the fifth pair was a replication of one of the alternative pairs. The two levels of the *difference* factor were obtained by pairing alternatives such that the sum of their absolute rank feature differences of the first two attributes differed by at most one rank unit (small difference) or by more than one rank unit (large difference). The *attractiveness* of two alternatives was manipulated by pairing two attractive alternatives or by pairing two less-attractive alternatives. Attractive alternatives consisted of features that obtained the two highest rankings for the majority of the attributes, whereas the less attractive alternatives consisted of features that were ranked lowest and second lowest for the majority of the attributes.

On each trial, choice pairs were displayed on a video screen. Although the video screen always revealed the names of the attributes, an alternative's feature had to be separately uncovered by pressing a designated key. Subjects could select features from any of the eight attributes for either date. However, only one feature was displayed at a time. Before selecting a new feature, the displayed one had to be cleared. Subjects were told to look at as much information as they needed to make their choice. On each trial, the inspected features, their order, and the selection/inspection time of each attribute were recorded. After each choice, subjects gave a rating of preference for the selected date over the non-selected date, as well as a confidence rating for the choice made. In the last part of the experiment each date's entire profile on the eight attributes was presented and the subject judged the overall attractiveness of each date.

Results

The organization of the result section follows the section about time pressure effects. Thus, to investigate the adequacy of the class of CDC models, we tested specific predictions regarding the information selection and evaluation stages of the decision process. Some of the analyses involved fitting random effects regression models to the data. A detailed description of random effects regression models and possible generalizations can be found in Bock (1990) and Goldstein (1987). The random effects regression approach was chosen because it facilitates the simultaneous analysis of the data at the individual *and* group level.

Selection

We first examined if the number of processed attributes for a choice pair varied as a function of time pressure, attractiveness of each alternative, and the difference between the two alternatives. For every choice pair we computed the number of selected features as well as the mean and the difference of the overall attractiveness ratings of the corresponding choice alternatives.

Let $v_s(x)$ denote the overall attractiveness rating assigned to alternative x by subject s, $\#F_{xys}$ denote the number of selected features for the choice pair (x, y) by subject s, and T be an effect-coded variable denoting the absence or presence of the TP condition. A random regression model was specified to include the average attractiveness of both alternatives, their absolute attractiveness difference, the interactions of both variables, the time pressure variable, and higher-order interaction terms.

$$\#F_{xys} = \beta_{0s} + \beta_{1s} \left(\frac{v_s(x) + v_s(y)}{2} \right) + \beta_{2s} |v_s(x) - v_s(y)| + \beta_{3s} T$$

$$+ \beta_{4s} |v_s(x)^2 - v_s(y)^2| + \beta_{5s} T \left(\frac{v_s(x) + v_s(y)}{2} \right)$$

$$+ \beta_{6s} T |v_s(x) - v_s(y))| + \beta_{7s} T |v_s(x)^2 - v_s(y)^2| + \epsilon_{xys},$$

where $(\beta_{0s}, \beta_{1s}, \beta_{2s}, \beta_{3s}, \beta_{4s}, \beta_{5s}, \beta_{6s}, \beta_{7s})$ are unknown regression coefficients and ϵ_{xys} represents the random error term. In a random regression model, the variation in the individual regression parameters is described by

$$\beta_{ks} = \mu_k + \zeta_{ks},$$

for $k = 0, 1, \ldots, 7$ and ζ_{ks} is assumed to be normally distributed with mean zero. Because we are interested in the overall design effects, our interest lies in estimating the "mean" regression parameters, μ_k, and testing if they are significantly different from zero. Maximum likelihood methods are used for estimating the parameter, and large sample likelihood ratio χ^2-tests are applied to compare two nested models.

The estimated coefficients of the best-fitting random regression model, standard errors, t-tests, and corresponding p-values are displayed in Table 1. This model was found after successively eliminating nonsignificant higher-order terms in the regression equation. Significance tests were performed by comparing the increase in the likelihood ratio statistic to a χ^2-distribution with the number of degrees of freedom equal to the difference between the number of parameters of the two models with and without the higher-order terms.

On the group level, both the difference factor and the overall attractiveness factor are significant. However, both factors interact with the time pressure manipulation. Subjects selected a larger number of features when the attractiveness difference between two choice alternatives decreased and the average attractiveness of both alternatives increased. The same pattern is observed under TP. However, under the TP condition, the number of selected features is reduced by about a factor of 2 that diminished the effects due to the difference and attractiveness manipulations and produced the significant interactions of both factors with TP. Because the attractiveness judgments only approximate the perceived attractiveness of an alternative in a choice situation, we repeated the preceding analysis by computing the overall attractiveness of an alternative as an average of the attractiveness ratings of the inspected features for each choice trial. However, this analysis produced almost identical results.

To examine the relationship between initial importance ranking and the selected attributes under the TP and NTP conditions, we computed the relative frequency of the selected attributes for every subject separately for both condi-

Table 1. Random Effects Regression Results with Number of Selected Features as Dependent Variable

Parameter	$\hat{\mu}_k$	SE	T-statistic	p-value
Attractiveness difference	−1.651	.24	−6.96	.000
Average attractiveness	0.742	.24	3.12	.005
Time pressure	5.133	.78	6.59	.000
Time pressure by difference	−1.268	.22	−5.71	.000
Time pressure by attractiveness	0.524	.23	2.25	.035

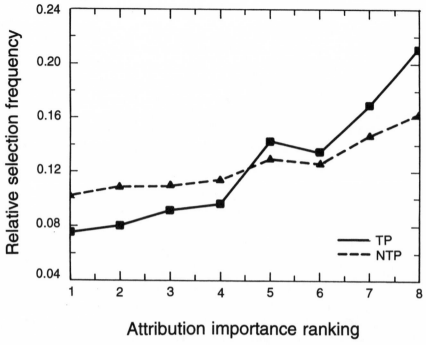

Attribution importance ranking

Figure 1. Relationship between correct choice prediction and absolute attractiveness difference. The dashed and continuous line is obtained under the NTP and the TP conditions, respectively. The third line (with dots and dashes) refers to the between-condition consistency.

tions. Figure 1 displays the group data. The continuous and dashed lines refer to the selection proportions under the TP and the NTP conditions, ordered by each subject's importance ranking of the attributes. As expected, in both conditions there is an almost perfect monotonic relationship between attribute importance and relative selection frequency. However, under TP subjects more frequently select important attributes. The interaction tests for differences in slopes indicated they are significantly different from each other ($F_{1,34} = 25.22, p < .001$).

Evaluation and Aggregation

The search pattern was described by Payne's (1976) index. This index compares the number of alternatives transitions (ALT) with the number of attributewise transitions (ATT) and is computed as ($ATT - ALT$)/($ALT + ATT$). Thus, a value of 1 indicates a perfect attributewise transition pattern, whereas a value of -1 indicates a perfect alternativewise transition pattern. This index was computed for each subject under the TP and NTP conditions. The mean values were .70 and .77 under the NTP and the TP conditions, respectively, and are not significantly different from each other ($F_{1,34} = 4.12$, $p > .05$). We also computed the average time for each inspected feature that were 1.10 and 0.71 seconds per feature under the NTP and TP conditions, respectively. The corresponding mean difference is highly significant ($F_{1,34} = 44.15$, $p < .001$).

Choice Predictability and Consistency

Choice predictability and consistency were examined in several ways. First, we investigated how well the overall attractiveness ratings predicted the subjects' choices. Next, we examined the subjects' consistency when choosing between the four identical choice pairs within the TP and NTP conditions, and, finally, we examined subjects' consistency in their choices between the two time pressure conditions.

Predictability of Choices by Attractiveness Ratings

35 subjects made 20 choices each under both the NTP and TP conditions. 81.0% and 76.8% of the 700 choices under the NTP condition and the TP condition, respectively, were predicted correctly by the differences between the attractiveness ratings. To examine the predictive performance of the attractiveness differences more closely, we grouped the data into six difference and three attractiveness categories both under the TP and NTP conditions and counted the number of correctly predicted choices for each of the 18 cells. These counts were submitted to a log-linear analysis to test for systematic effects of the design factors. Because the choice data are not independent in this and the following analyses, we only report the likelihood ratio χ^2-tests and the corresponding degrees of freedom. The log-linear analysis revealed that there is a significant difference effect ($\chi^2 = 125.1$, $df = 5$) and a significant TP effect ($\chi^2 = 6.0$, $df = 1$) but that the predictive ability of the ratings does not change under the different attractiveness levels ($\chi^2 = 4.01$, $df = 2$) or for difference by attractiveness combinations ($\chi^2 = 5.8$, $df = 10$). Thus, the probability of a correct prediction depends only on the size of the difference and is somewhat reduced under the TP condition. A plot of the relationship between the size of the attractiveness difference and the correct choice prediction is displayed in Figure 2. The dashed and the continuous lines refer to the NTP and TP conditions, respectively. Both lines are well separated and increase monotonically as a function of the difference between two alternatives.

Between-Condition Consistency

The third line (with dots and dashes) in Figure 2 refers to the between-condition consistency as a function of the size of the attractiveness difference.

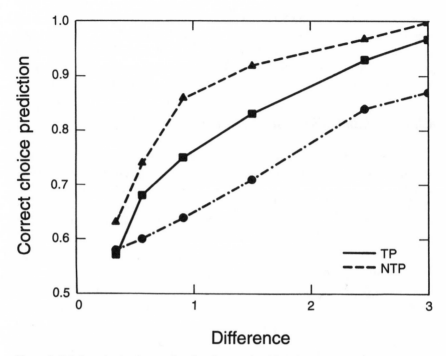

Figure 2. Relative selection frequencies of attributes ordered from least to most important under TP (continuous line) and NTP (dashed line).

Overall, 71% of the 700 choices from the NTP and the TP conditions were identical. Similar to the previous analysis, consistent choices were cross-classified according to attractiveness difference and overall attractiveness. A log-linear analysis of these data produced only a significant difference effect (χ^2 = 31.1, df = 5) and no-attractiveness effect (χ^2 = 5.8, df = 2).

Within Condition Consistency

Four choice pairs were replicated within the NTP and the TP conditions. Two choice pairs consisted of two attractive and two unattractive choice alternatives with a zero rank difference each. These alternative pairs are denoted by (++) and (− −) to represent their overall attractiveness. The two remaining choice pairs consisted of two alternatives of different attractiveness and a rank difference of two units. These two choice pairs are denoted by (+ −). Within the NTP and the TP conditions the choices were equally consistent for each of the four choice pairs with an overall within-condition consistency of 74%. Because

**Table 2. Within- and Between-Condition Consistency
for Four Choice Pairs**

	Consistent choices		Inconsistent choices	
Choice pairs	Between	Within	Between	Within
+ −	120	128	20	12
+ +	32	36	38	34
− −	36	42	34	28

no difference in consistency was found, the choices within each conditions were collapsed. Next, the numbers of consistent choices between both conditions were computed for the four choice pairs. The results of the within- and between-condition consistency are displayed in Table 2. Note that choices between alternatives with a zero rank difference are at chance levels. A log-linear analysis of this table revealed a weak difference between the within- and between-condition consistency ($\chi^2 = 3.30$, $df = 1$), a significant difference effect ($\chi^2 = 94.6$, $df = 1$), and no effect due to the overall attractiveness of the choice alternatives or higher order interactions ($\chi^2 = 1.91$, $df = 3$).

Confidence Ratings

After their choice, subjects were asked (on a scale from 0 to 100) how confident they felt about their choice. To examine the relationship between the design factors and subjects' confidence ratings a random effects regression model was used. This analysis proceeded in the same way as the analysis of the number of selected features. The estimated mean regression coefficients of the best-fitting model are presented in Table 3. Time pressure systematically reduced confidence in the choice, but no significant interactions of this factor with other factors were obtained. Subjects became more confident about their choices when

**Table 3. Random Effects Regression Results
with Confidence Rating as Dependent Variable**

Parameter	$\hat{\mu}_k$	SE	T-statistic	p-value
Attractiveness difference	13.421	1.65	8.15	.000
Average attractiveness	4.781	1.20	4.00	.001
Time pressure	8.944	1.02	8.74	.000
Attractiveness by difference	−3.167	.64	−4.97	.000

the attractiveness difference between the two choice alternatives increased. However, as indicated by the significant interaction effect, the change in confidence as a function of the attractiveness difference is smaller for attractive than for unattractive alternatives.

Discussion

Overall, the results are in agreement with the predictions derived from CDC models. The amount of information selected is determined by an additive combination of the two factors attractiveness difference and overall attractiveness. Subjects considered less information when the attractiveness difference between both alternatives is large and when both alternatives are unattractive. This occurred both under the TP and the NTP conditions. However, under TP, the effect of both factors was smaller than under the NTP condition. In addition, subjects focused (in a relative sense) more on the important attributes under TP. Their selection behavior was predominantly attributewise under both NTP and TP. Also, subjects accelerated their processing under TP, as indicated by the decreased time per selected feature. The hypothesis that subjects consistently employed a criterion-dependent strategy that is modified contingent on the task demands provides a good account of the data under *both* TP and NTP conditions.

Although the difference effect is expected under the CDC model, the attractiveness effect requires the additional assumption that subjects adjusted their critical value depending on the overall attractiveness level of both alternatives. Thus, subjects were more concerned about selecting the better of two attractive alternatives than the less poor of two unattractive alternatives. The finding that subjects considered more information when comparing attractive alternatives may also indicate that they were willing to spend more effort when comparing attractive alternatives. However, this interpretation assumes that effort is directly related to the number of selected features. In regard to our experiment, there is little doubt that subjects were curious about the potential dates in the computer dating task and, as a result, they may have compared two attractive dates, possibly more than "necessary" for making a choice, simply because they were interested in the comparison process. Thus, costs and effort associated with selecting and processing information may be attenuated by the interest in the choice task. For example, a car enthusiast who is in the process of buying a new car may compare two cars extensively (and much more than "necessary") if both cars are attractive because the comparison process itself is engaging.

Although it may be inappropriate to assume that the number of selected features is directly related to an underlying effort variable, we can investigate if there is a corresponding relationship between the amount of selected information and choice consistency. The hypothesized criterion adjustment implies that subjects' within-condition consistency should be different for attractive and unattractive alternatives. However, no systematic change was found in the within-condition choice consistency due to the alternatives' attractiveness. Although this result indicates that the additional selection of information did not affect choice consistency, it should be noted that there was little power in detecting an effect because only one attractive and one unattractive choice pair were repeated within the NTP and the TP conditions.

As expected, a strong and systematic relationship was found between attractiveness difference and choice consistency as well as choice predictability. Moreover, between-condition consistency was lower than within-condition consistency. Similarly, predictability of choices under NTP was significantly higher than under the TP condition. These findings are in agreement with our explanation that the selection and evaluation processes are different under both conditions. No effects due to the overall attractiveness of both alternatives were found. Choices between unattractive alternatives and attractive alternatives were equally well predicted. Similarly, the between-condition consistency did also not vary for different levels of the alternatives' attractiveness. Thus, even if the subjects were more extreme in their evaluation of unattractive features under TP, this did not lead to any systematic changes in the choice data.

The postdecisional variable confidence also reflects the systematic influence of the design variables. It was predicted that under TP, confidence is reduced because subjects simplify their decision process. Confidence was also expected to be influenced by the size of the attractiveness difference because this factor reduces the conflict in making a choice. Both hypotheses were supported by the data. However, the analyses also showed that the difference effect is moderated by the attractiveness of the choice alternatives. That is, the same attractiveness difference led to a smaller confidence difference for attractive than for unattractive alternatives. This interaction effect seems to indicate that subjects experienced more of a conflict when choosing between two attractive than when choosing between two unattractive alternatives with similar attractiveness differences. This interpretation is consistent with our explanation that subjects were more concerned about the quality of their choice when comparing two attractive than two unattractive alternatives.

In summary, most of the hypothesized effects were derived from the two predictions that under time pressure subjects lower their criterion value and change their evaluation of the choice alternatives. All of these hypothesized effects were supported by the experiment. This strongly supports our hypothesis that subjects used a criterion-dependent strategy in binary choices that they modified to accommodate the requirements of the choice tasks. Clearly, these results are in agreement with our initial assumption that subjects perform a cost/benefit tradeoffs when making choices. However, this study also demonstrated that subjects' understanding of the relationship between effort and choice quality may be limited. For example, neither consistency nor predictability changed for choices between attractive alternatives, despite the fact that subjects considered significantly more information for attractive alternatives. Similarly, our understanding of what constitutes costs and benefits from a subject's point of view may also be far from being perfect. Costs and benefits are multidimensional constructs and our focus, for example, on the number of selected features or choice consistency may not necessarily agree with the subject's interpretation of costs and benefits. We alluded already to the possibility that selecting information may not only have cost-related aspects and may thus not be a reliable indicator of an underlying cost dimension. Clearly, more work is needed that addresses the operationalization of *subjective* costs and benefits in choice experiments to better assess a subject's performance.

Finally, our finding that subjects may have used a general strategy that they modified to deal with the requirements of the choice situation may be related to the fact that binary choices are quite common in daily life. Consequently, the transfer of these skills to the experiment may have been straightforward for the subjects. However, it is clear that in order to select or modify an efficient strategy, subjects need to have a good understanding of a strategy's features and be able to assess its performance under different task conditions (Payne, Bettman, & Johnson, 1990). In complex task environments, subjects' understanding about the performance characteristics of strategies may be limited and, consequently, the effectiveness of their adaptive or constructive behavior may be reduced. In this case, time pressure may lead to overarousal that in turn may impact subjects' ability to compare strategies. As a result, subjects may apply ineffective strategies, with significant reductions in their performance (Janis & Mann, 1977). For example, Rouse (1979) showed that subjects' performance in a laboratory simulation of an electronic fault diagnosis task deteriorated significantly under time pressure. Subjects used a previously taught highly efficient strategy under the NTP condition but switched to a "brute force" strategy under time pressure that led to more diagnostic errors. Thus, though the subjects were trained extensively, they were not able to transfer and apply their knowledge in a time pressure situation. Our results suggest that strategy transfer under time pressure may only be successful if a strategy is used that can be simplified but still produces acceptable results. Unfortunately, there may be only few strategies that satisfy this requirement.

ACKNOWLEDGMENT. The authors appreciate helpful comments by Janet Sniezek, Elke Weber, Doug Wedell, and the reviewers. Reprint requests should be sent to Ulf Böckenholt or Keith Kroeger, University of Illinois at Urbana–Champaign, Department of Psychology, 603 East Daniel Street, Champaign, Illinois 61820.

References

Albert, D, Aschenbrenner, K. M., & Schmalhofer, F. (1989). Cognitive choice processes and the attitude-behavior relation. In A. Upmeyer (Ed.), *Attitudes and behavioral decisions* (pp. 61–99). New York: Springer Verlag.

Aschenbrenner, K. M., Albert, D., & Schmalhofer, F. (1986). Stochastic choice heuristics. *Acta Psychologica, 56*, 153–166.

Aschenbrenner, K. M., Böckenholt, U., Albert, D., & Schmalhofer, F. (1986). The selection of dimensions when choosing between multiattribute alternatives. In R. W. Scholz (Ed.), *Current issues in West German decision research* (pp. 63–78). Frankfurt: Lang Publisher.

Beach, L. R., & Mitchell, T.R. (1978). A contingency model for the selection of decision strategies. *Academy of Management Review, 3*, 439–449.

Ben Zur, H., & Breznitz, S. J. (1981). The effects of time pressure on risky choice behavior. *Acta Psychologica, 47*, 89–104.

Bock, R. D. (1990). *Multilevel analysis of educational data*. San Diego: Academic Press.

Böckenholt, U., Albert, D., Aschenbrenner, K. M., & Schmalhofer, F. (1991). The effect of attractiveness, dominance, and attribute differences on information acquisition in multi-attribute binary choice. *Organizational Behavior and Human Decision Processes, 49*, 258–281.

Busemeyer, J. R. (1982). Choice behavior in a sequential decision making task. *Organizational Behavioral and Human Performance, 29*, 175–207.

Busemeyer, J. R. (1985). Decision making under uncertainty: A comparison of simple scalability, fixed-sample, and sequential-sampling models. *Journal of Experimental Psychology: Learning, Memory, and Cognition, 11*, 538–564.

Christensen-Szalanski, J. J. J. (1980). A further examination of the selection of problem-solving strategies: The effects of deadlines and analytic aptitudes. *Organizational Behavior and Human Performance, 25*, 107–122.

Falmagne, J. (1985). *Elements of psychophysical theory*. Oxford: Oxford University Press.

Goldstein, H. (1987). *Multilevel models in educational and social research*. London: Griffin.

Janis, I. L., & Mann, L. (1977). *Decision making: A psychological analysis of conflict, choice, and commitment*. New York: Free Press.

Mano, H. (1989). Anticipated deadline penalties: Effects on goal levels and task performance. In R. M. Hogarth (Ed.), *Insights in decision making* (pp. 154–172) Chicago: The University of Chicago Press.

Payne, J. W. (1976). Task complexity and contingent processing in decision making: An information search and protocol analysis. *Organizational Behavior and Human Performance, 16*, 366–387.

Payne, J. W. (1982). Contingent decision behavior. *Psychological Bulletin, 92*, 382–402.

Payne, J. W., Bettman, J. R., & Johnson, E. J. (1988). Adaptive strategy selection in decision making. *Journal of Experimental Psychology: Learning, Memory, and Cognition, 14*, 534–552.

Payne, J. W., Bettman, J. R., & Johnson, E. J. (1990). The adaptive decision maker: Effort and accuracy in choice. In R. M. Hogarth (Ed.), *Insights in decision making* (pp. 129–153) Chicago: The University of Chicago Press.

Rouse, W. B. (1979). Problem-solving performance of maintenance trainees in a fault diagnosis task. *Human Factors, 21*, 195–203.

Russo, J. E., & Dosher, B. A. (1983). Strategies for multiattribute binary choice. *Journal of Experimental Psychology: Learning, Memory, and Cognition, 9*, 676–696.

Russo, J. E., & Rosen, L. D. (1976). An eye fixation analysis of multialternative choice. *Memory & Cognition, 3*, 267–276.

Smith, J. F., Mitchell, T. R., and Beach, L. R. (1982). A cost-benefit mechanism for selecting problem-solving strategies: Some extensions and empirical tests. *Organizational Behavior and Human Performance, 29,* 370–396.

Svenson, O. (1979). Process descriptions of decision making. *Organizational Behavior and Human Performance, 23,* 86–112.

Svenson, O., & Edland, A. (1987). Change of preferences under time pressure: Choices and judgments. *Scandinavian Journal of Psychology, 28,* 322–330.

Tversky, A. (1969). The intransitivity of preferences. *Psychological Review, 76,* 31–48.

Wallsten, T. S., & Barton, C. (1982). Processing probabilistic multidimentional information for decisions. *Journal of Experimental Psychology: Learning, Memory, and Cognition, 8,* 361–384.

Wright, P. (1974). The harassed decision maker: Time pressures, distractions, and the use of evidence. *Journal of Applied Psychology, 59,* 555–561.

Zakay, D. (1985). Post-decisional confidence and conflict experienced in a choice process. *Acta Psychologica, 58,* 75–80.

IV

Individual Differences

This part is devoted to studies of differences between individuals in terms of how they react to and manage time restrictions and how this affects their judgment and decision processes. The contributors identify three main dimensions along which individuals vary, namely Time Urgency, Action–State Orientation, and Need for Structure. Although these constructs emerge from different research traditions, there are similarities between them in the way they consider time pressure effects.

In Chapter 15, Rastegary and Landy present a Time Urgency construct reflecting differences between people in the degree to which they take on activities within a specific amount of available time. Subjects high on the Time Urgency scale take on a relatively large number of activities and manage this by, for example, accelerating their rate of information processing. The scale developed by Landy and colleagues to measure Time Urgency identifies nine basic dimensions related to (1) how to deal with too many activities in a limited time frame, (2) the impact of insufficient time on ordinary activities, and (3) a general awareness of the passage of time. High rating on Time Urgency is identified as one component in Type A behavior, thus linking this concept to the stress research tradition discussed by Lundberg in Chapter 3. Time is conceptualized in Chapter 15 as a stressor along with uncertainty. People differ in their tolerance of ambiguity or uncertainty, and it would be interesting to find out about the relationship between that construct and Time Urgency. Chapter 17 explores the possibly related construct of Need for Structure.

The major thrust of Chapter 15 is a review of research in the field of time urgency, including a generic model of how the factors identified within the review affect decision-making processes. In addition to a consideration of the ways individuals cope with time pressure, issues are discussed in the broader context of organizations thereby providing links to Chapter 8 by Carnevale, O'Connor, and McCusker.

Steinsmeier-Pelster and Schurmann, in Chapter 16, consider time pressure in the context of the Theory of Action Control. The theory asserts that success or failure in implementing decisions and intentions depends on how effectively action control is implemented. The construct Action versus State Orientation is used to distinguish between individuals in terms of action control and is determined by the extent to which they pay attention to their (1) present state, (2) intended future state, (3) discrepancy between present and future states, and (4) at least one action to reduce this discrepancy. As one or more of these four elements are lacking, so the person is more state orientated. The authors predict, and subsequently demonstrate in three experiments, that there are different ways of coping with time pressure for state- and action-orientated people. State-orientated individuals tend to accelerate their rate of information processing, whereas action-orientated individuals filter the available information. It is interesting to compare this with the assertion in Chapter 13 that time-urgent individuals may tend to accelerate, whereas non-time-urgent individuals may use filtration when coping with time pressure.

A third dimension, The Need for Structure construct, is considered in the context of time pressure by Kaplan, Wanshula, and Zanna in chapter 17. This is a motivational construct reflecting an individual's desire for structure and clarity of information during knowledge acquisition. The authors suggest that Need for Structure can be treated both as a situationally induced state as well as a dispositional trait. In the context of social judgment situations, one way of creating structure is to depend on stereotypes. It is assumed that this dependency on stereotypes would occur to different degrees under time pressure depending on a person's position on the Need for Structure dimension. This hypothesis was tested experimentally, with time pressure manipulated by asking subjects either to hurry or to take their time. The findings supported the hypothesis by showing no differences when there was no time pressure, but differences under time pressure, with subjects high in Need for Structure responding less positively to positive traits and less negatively to negative traits than subjects low in Need for Structure. This indicates that subjects high in Need for Structure use their initial stereotypes to a greater extent.

In summary, this part identifies a number of interesting and important differences in the way individuals cope with time pressure. A number of theoretical perspectives have been applied, providing a foundation from which it will be possible to develop a common framework for the study of individual differences and time pressure.

15

The Interactions among Time Urgency, Uncertainty, and Time Pressure

Haleh Rastegary and Frank J. Landy

Introduction

Since the beginning of the Industrial Revolution, the tempo of life has continually accelerated (McGrath & Kelly, 1986). At the close of the twentieth century, life revolves ever more around the clock, especially in Western cultures. Rifkil, in his book *Time Wars* (1987), proposes that computers are contributing to an exponentially accelerating time orientation. Computer hardware operations can be carried out as fast as billionths of a second, and this capability has set new temporal standards of organizational effectiveness and efficiency. This accelerated time orientation affects every aspect of a work organization. Perhaps the most substantial challenge facing employees as a result of this time orientation is trying to choose between alternative courses of action while under this time pressure. It is likely that time pressure does not affect everyone in the same way. It may prove challenging to one individual and debilitating to another. In fact, temporal orientation has been recognized as one of the fundamental parameters of individual differences (Bluedorn & Denhardt, 1988).

The inward sense of urgency characteristic of time-urgent individuals affects both the perception and the usage of time, as well as reaction to increased

Haleh Rastegary and Frank J. Landy • Center for Applied Behavioral Sciences, Pennsylvania State University, University Park, Pennsylvania 16802.
Time Pressure and Stress in Human Judgment and Decision Making, edited by Ola Svenson and A. John Maule. Plenum Press, New York, 1993.

time pressure. Thus, time urgency is an important factor to consider when studying how individuals make decisions under pressure. Note that we will make a distinction between *time pressure*, or *externally* imposed time constraints that vary between situations, on one hand, and *time urgency*, or *internally* imposed time constraints that vary between individuals, on the other. Thus, the position that we will take in this chapter is that the manifest differences that can be observed in time-relevant behavior represent an interaction between situational characteristics and individual attributes.

Because we will be dealing with the topic of stress extensively, some linguistic conventions might be useful. We will refer to antecedent variables in the environment as *stressors*. We will refer to the experience of the individuals exposed to those stressors as *strain*. The broad research area will be considered under the general rubric of *stress* (Landy, 1990).

Overview

Decision making is central to all aspects of an individual's professional and personal life. Researchers and practitioners alike are interested in the process of decision making, as well as the manner by which various factors affect the quality and efficiency of the decision-making process. The relationship between decision making and stress has been a popular research topic. In research on decision making and stress, the emphasis has generally been on the dysfunctional effect of stressors. It is abundantly clear that the stressor/strain equation has many components (For reviews of stress literature, see Sauter, Hurrell, & Cooper, 1989; Landy, 1990; Kahn & Byosiere, 1992). But two of these—time pressure and uncertainty—seem to be of particular relevance when considering the decision-making process.

Not every one responds to the same stressors in the same way (Eysenk, 1983). The importance of individual difference parameters as moderating influences between stressors and experienced strain, as well as experienced strain and health is generally recognized. This moderating effect has also been considered in the study of the interplay between stress and *performance*. Type A behavior is one of the most widely discussed personal characteristics contributing to the stress/health-performance paradigm (For review, see McMichael, 1978; Payne, 1988 & Ganster, Sime, & Mayes, 1989). What has *not* received much attention, however, is the manner by which individual differences might moderate the relationship between stressors (e.g., time pressure and uncertainty) and the decision-making process. Research discussing the moderating effect of Type A behavior on the relationship between stress and the decision-making process is especially scarce.

We believe that perception of time pressure and uncertainty is largely determined by the chronic level of time urgency experienced by an individual. In
other words, we propose that an individual's sense of time urgency will moderate
the individual's response to time pressure and uncertainty. Thus, we would
expect a high-time-urgent individual in a high-time-pressure environment to
reduce uncertainty by adding substantial structure to the situation through the
imposition of schedules, goals, deadlines, and the like.

As a construct, time urgency emerged from the consideration of Type A
behavior pattern and the relationship of that pattern to heart disease (Friedman &
Rosenman, 1974). In some respects, this was unfortunate because it provided a
limited focus for the consideration of time urgency. In effect, time urgency was
examined as a potential "pathogen." From this perspective, time urgency is seen
as entirely dysfunctional. A similar perspective has been carried over to the study
of time urgency and performance. This view needs to be balanced. It is plausible
that there are situations in which time urgency can be a facilitating, rather than
debilitating, attribute of an individual. This may be particularly true in the
domain of decision making. The decision-making domain provides an excellent
environment for a consideration of time urgency for several reasons. First, it can
help to clarify the overall nature of time-urgent behavior. In addition, it can add
depth to our consideration of the interaction of stressors (e.g., time pressure and
uncertainty). Finally, the examination of time urgency as an individual attribute
can help to illuminate the decision-making process.

Time Urgency

Background

The notion of time urgency was originally advanced by Friedman and
Rosenman (1959) as a core component of the Tupe A behavior pattern. In this
conceptualization, the state of time urgency was characterized by an accelerated
pace of activities that resulted from striving to accomplish more and more in a
shorter and shorter amount of time. Friedman and Rosenman (1974) further
explained that this accelerated pace will set the stage for the development of
other characteristics of the Type A behavior pattern including aggressiveness,
hostility, and competitiveness. This collection of behaviors has been identified as
a risk factor in coronary heart disease (CHD). Numerous studies have been
designed to examine the relationship between Type A behavior and development
of CHD (e.g., Rosenman, Friedman, Straus, Wurm, Jenkins, & Messinger,
1966; Haynes, Feinleib, & Kannel, 1980; French-Belgian Collaborative Group,
1982).

This link between Type A behavior and CHD is perhaps partly responsible for the popularity of the Type A concept among researchers in the psychological, medical, and organizational fields. Despite its popularity, however, very few studies have explored the relationship *among* various components of the Type A pattern. Furthermore, there has not been much research on the relationship between time urgency—what Friedman and Rosenman called the most central element of Type A behavior—and incidence of CHD. In fact, recent research has developed a narrower focus by concentrating on the anger and the aggression components as the main dysfunctional elements of the Type A behavior pattern (e.g., Mathews 1982; Booth-Kewley & Friedman, 1987; Mathews, 1988; Friedman & Booth-Kewley, 1988; Dembroski & Williams, 1989).

Recently, however, a parallel line of research has emerged pointing to the psychometric weaknesses of Type A measures (Edwards, Baglioni, & Cooper 1990). Reexamination of Type A measures has shown that they represent not a single unified set of responses, as originally assumed, but instead a constellation of interrelated but unique behaviors (e.g., Zyzanski & Jenkins, 1970; Edwards et al. 1990). Furthermore, each component itself appears to be multidimensional (Dembroski & Czajkowski, 1989; Landy, Rastegary, Thayer, & Colvin, 1991). For example, in earlier research (Landy et al., 1991), we have argued that the time urgency concept is multidimensional and demonstrated this by developing an instrument to identify these independent dimensions. Furthermore, we showed, using a factor analysis of combined items of time urgency from the most commonly used surveys of Type A behavior (i.e., Bortner, Framingham, Jenkins, and Thurstone), that, at least as far as these four measures are concerned, there are four distinct dimensions: "speech," "eating," "general hurry," and "task-related hurry." This reexamination of the measures of Type A behavior has led to a renewal of interest in the time urgency concept.

Characteristics of Time Urgency

In virtually all of the early research, time-urgent individuals were identified using the Hurry scale of the Jenkins Activity Survey. From that research, it would appear that time-urgent individuals schedule too many activities in their available time (Friedman and Rosenman, 1974; Wright, 1988). In doing so, they ignore obstacles that may require additional time (Price, 1982). Continually scheduling too many activities in a limited time frame leads to the chronic feeling of inadequate available time. Similarly, trying to achieve too many goals in too little time drives one to become extremely efficient. Strategies that help an individual obtain higher efficiency are thus developed and improved. Price (1982) suggests that setting deadlines, accelerating ordinary activities, and quick and stereotyped responses are methods by which individuals cope with a (albeit often self-imposed) hectic schedule.

When too many activities are scheduled, deadlines are used as heuristics to prioritize tasks. Indeed, time-urgent individuals appear to be preoccupied with setting deadlines (Glass, Snyder, & Hollis, 1974; Gastorf, 1980). It would appear that a deadline-driven schedule is the primary way to maintain order when an individual is overloaded with activities and commitments. Time-urgent individuals often report that this exposure to constant deadlines enables them to perform well under time pressure.

In order to be able to deliver all the commitments scheduled, time-urgent individuals adopt an accelerated pace (Burnam, Pennebaker, & Glass, 1975). To save time, they also accelerate *ordinary* activities such as walking, eating, and talking. Time can also be "saved" by rushing the activities of other people. As examples of these behaviors, Yarnold and his colleagues demonstrated that time-urgent[1] individuals completed tasks at a faster rate (Yarnold & Grimm, 1982; Yarnold & Meuser, 1984; Yarnold, Mueser, & Lyons, 1987) and Gastorf (1980) reported that time-urgent individuals arrived earlier for the scheduled experiment than less urgent subjects.

Another method to save time is to engage in multiphasic activities, that is, doing or thinking about more than two things simultaneously (Wright, 1988). Price (1982) believes that engaging in multiphasic activities can by dysfunctional in some respects. Thinking about something else while "listening" to a spouse, friend, or a coworker may create interpersonal conflict when it becomes obvious that the "listener's" mind is elsewhere. Similarly, thinking about something else when engaging in a task that requires substantial attention may result in accidents. Thus, Evans, Palsane, and Carrere (1987) found that Type A bus drivers had more accidents than their type B counterparts.

The manner by which individuals attempt to solve problems is also affected by a sense that available time is inadequate. Perceived rigid time constraints do not allow for careful evaluation of problems and challenges and would seem to encourage impulsive behavior. Typically, time-urgent persons act and think in ways that have previously met with success (Price, 1982). In situations that do demand a familiar approach, the stereotyped way of thinking appears to work well (Price, 1982). Experience in a particular situation increases effectiveness and efficiency in new, yet-familiar situations. However, relying on "what worked best before" may prove ineffective or even disastrous in a novel situation. These novel situations seem to represent particular challenges for time-urgent individuals because they hurry through a task, missing the nuances of the situation, not

---

[1]A point must be clarified. We used the term *Type A behavior* as well as time urgency when we are reporting empirical research. The term *Type A behavior pattern* is used when reporting studies that used the global Type A/B behavior pattern. On the other hand, we used the term *time urgency* when we are reporting studies that explicitly focused on the time-urgency component of Type A behavior.

recognizing that the situation is novel in some important respect. A Piagetian might label this a "failure of accommodation" or the "error of assimilation."

It is axiomatic to propose that time-urgent individuals react impatiently to situations that slow them down. Interruptions are not tolerated because they crowd the already inadequate available time. Furthermore, periods of inactivity or irrelevant activity are irritating for similar reasons. Glass et al. (1974) and Burnam et al. (1975) have demonstrated that time-urgent individuals have more difficulty in slowing down and show considerably greater tension than their less time-urgent counterparts.

The characteristics of time urgency presented are reflected in the behaviorally anchored time-urgency scales that we have developed (Landy et al., 1991). Seven dimensions comprise these scales. The dimensions are "deadline control," "scheduling," "list making," "eating behavior," "speech pattern," "nervous energy," and "time awareness." The first three dimensions seem to represent approaches used to deal with too many activities in a limited time frame. The next three dimensions appear to represent the impact of insufficient time on ordinary activities. Finally, the generalized time-awareness dimension is also implicated in the theoretical account of time urgency. This representation is reassuring because the structure was induced from the carefully elicited judgments of subjects considering the concept of time urgency, thus confirming earlier representations of the construct.

As noted, time urgency has been studied as one component of Type A behavior. This has contributed to the widespread use of global measures of Type A behavior in studies of time urgency. The Jenkins (Jenkins, Zyzanzki, & Rosenman, 1979) scale is commonly used in these survey studies (e.g., Glass, et al., 1974; Yarnold & Mueser, 1984; Bingham & Hailey, 1989). An early factor analysis of the items included in this scale purported to reveal three dimensions: job involvement, speed-impatient, and hard driving (Zyzanski & Jenkins, 1970). It is now abundantly clear (Edwards et al., 1990; Landy et al., 1991) that this unidimensional view of time urgency was misleading. As a result, much of the research based on this earlier view of the time-urgency construct must be reconsidered.

A theoretical framework to support the independent characteristics of time-urgent behavior is needed. Only a handful of articles have appeared in the literature that may be relevant to the social/psychological and motivational foundations of time urgency. One of the earliest motivational explanations of overachievement—a characteristic of a time-urgent individual—is the need to exert control over uncontrollable situations (Glass, 1977). Strube (1987; Strube & Boland, 1987) has argued that control is important *not* in and of itself, but because it solves the uncertainty about one's ability. Shalon and Strube (1988) argue that a childhood experience of high expectations and a lack of clear evaluation of a child's progress creates the need for ever-increasing achievement.

In response to the uncertainty about their abilities, Type A individuals develop this achievement orientation to generate the information necessary for a clearer and more concrete appraisal of abilities. Similarly, Price (1982) argues that Type A individuals ascertain their self-worth by accomplishing a larger number of tasks than others would seem capable of. It is clear that much more effort must go into the development of a theoretical superstructure to account for the development of time urgency in some individuals.

Uncertainty and Time Pressure as Stressors in Decision Making

Uncertainty as a Stressor

Uncertainty has been recognized as a major stressor that will affect health and performance and has a well-defined meaning in decision theories. In fact, recently, investigators have proposed that uncertainty be classified as major component of stress with its own large range of subtopics (Landy, 1990). Uncertainty, by its very nature, must be discussed in terms of decision making. Without a decision to be made, there is nothing to be uncertain about (Achrol, 1988). Therefore, uncertainty plays a significant role in most decision-theoretic approaches.

The definition of uncertainty has varied among researchers. (cf. from a management perspective Gifford, Bobbitt, & Slocum, 1979; Jauch & Kraft, 1986). But these definitions, as Gifford et al. (1979) have pointed out, can be classified into two interdependent categories: (1) the variability of a given situation and (2) the character of information regarding that situation. In other words, an approach that falls in the first category would speak of uncertainty in terms of the rate of change of a situation and the predictability of the possible outcomes of that situation, whereas an approach falling into the second category would tend to emphasize the completeness (or lack thereof) of the information a decision maker possesses regarding a given situation. In any case, predicting an outcome and obtaining information are made more difficult in complex and/or novel situations so there would seem to be a natural association between complexity and novelty on one hand and uncertainty on the other.

Uncertainty can occur at various levels—the environment, the organization, the unit, the group, and the individual level of analysis (Schuler & Jackson, 1986). Clearly uncertainty at one level influences the nature and degree of uncertainty at another level. The level of uncertainty is determined not only by sources of uncertainty unique to any one level but also by the contribution of sources from other levels as well. For example, the uncertainty facing an individual army officer deciding whether or not to follow orders in the recent failed coup in the Soviet Union may have been compounded by a perceived uncertainty in the coup leadership's commitment to carrying through their plans (exhibited by their apparent lack of decisiveness).

Furthermore, at each level there are a number of different sources of uncertainty. For example, *both* the degree of the complexity and the novelty of a given task will contribute to its level of uncertainty.

The response to these sources of uncertainty is further complicated by variations in characteristics of individuals. (We will term the effect of individual differences on uncertainty to be *perceived uncertainty*). These variations, which in turn affect perceptions, are for the most part related to cognitive ability, personality, and other individual characteristics of individuals. A person with a experience in a given situation would suffer much less uncertainty than one with no experience. A large amount of experience furnishes an individual with an ability to transfer information across similar situations reducing the perceived uncertainty, whereas a lack of ability to be able to transfer information across situations enhances the perceived uncertainty (e.g., Taylor, 1975; MacCrimmon & Taylor, 1976). In addition, the differential capacity to process information affects an individual's perception of uncertainty (MacCrimmon & Taylor, 1976). Those individuals who are able to process information at a higher rate as well as seek more information, perceive less uncertainty, whereas those individuals who reach a saturated state at a relatively low level of information perceive a higher level of uncertainty (MacCrimmon & Taylor, 1976).

Furthermore, those who are more tolerant of ambiguity seek out uncertainty, or, at the very least, they adapt to it more readily than those with a low tolerance for ambiguity (Budner, 1962). Research has also shown that those who feel in control of their environment perceive uncertainty as a challenge rather than as a threat and therefore respond to it using problem-solving strategies (Schuler & Jackson, 1986).

As with any stressor, the individual's perception of uncertainty determines his/her response to an uncertain situation. This begs the question of whether time-urgent individuals perceive uncertainty differently than non-time-urgent individuals. Do time urgent individuals actively seek out uncertainty? Do they adapt to uncertainty by developing effective strategies to deal with ambiguity? Are they intolerant of ambiguity? Ganster, Schaubroeck, Sime, and Mayes (1991) found a tentative positive relationship between time urgency and tolerance of ambiguity. They recognized also, however, that the relationship between proclivity for ambiguous situations and tolerance of ambiguity was a sort of "chicken-and-egg" question. Do the time-urgent individuals, motivated by their inherent tolerance for ambiguity, seek out these ambiguous situations, or is their tolerance for ambiguity enhanced by a constant exposure to those situations.

It is also plausible that scheduling too many activities is a reflection of a need for a "stable" or "familiar" environment, a strategy that might be adopted by those with a low tolerance of ambiguity. Thus, the situation can be made more comprehensible and predictable by tying it to a schedule of some sort, even if one is not exactly sure what the appropriate response might be at the appointed time. Researchers studying uncertainty have suggested that planning and synchronization are activities that function as coping approaches for dealing with this uncertainty (McGrath & Rotchford, 1983). Consistent with this view, then, a time-urgent person's approaches to work can be interpreted as coping techniques that are used to deal with excessive uncertainty. Note that this approach contradicts the assertion that a time-urgent person's tolerance of ambiguity will increase with exposure to uncertainty. Instead, we are proposing that a time-urgent person's *lack* of such tolerance would compel him or her to try to lower the ambiguity of the situation by controlling it (e.g., scheduling too many activities), even though the corresponding increase in efficiency in the face of uncertainty would easily be attributed to an increased tolerance of ambiguity.

In addition, the involvement of time-urgent individuals in many tasks may indicate their ability to process information at a higher rate. If this is true, this ability allows them to seek more information in order to reduce their perceived uncertainty. It follows that dealing with many activities provides them with a rich pool from which they can transfer information to other similar situations. It must be emphasized that these assertions merit empirical investigation.

Furthermore, we suggest that time-urgent individuals may tend to use an inhibitory approach to deal with the uncertainty that arises from novelty. As mentioned, more time-urgent individuals tend to use a "what-worked-best-before" strategy to save time. In facing unfamiliar situations, a time-urgent individual may transfer experience from a familiar situation to an unfamiliar one. This "functional fixedness," as MacCrimmon and Taylor (1976) put it, may prevent an "original" response. Time-urgent individuals may also avoid novel and unfamiliar situations because such situations demand more of their precious time.

Time Pressure

A concept closely related to uncertainty is time pressure. It is defined as the difference between the amount of available time and the amount of time required to resolve a decision task. Time pressure intensifies as the required time increasingly exceeds the available time. To the extent that a time limitation restricts a decision maker in collecting needed information, time pressure contributes to uncertainty. However, time pressure produces unique effects as well. For example, when a shorter time interval is available to resolve a decision problem, a decision maker who has to deal with this lack of time can cope by accelerating activities. This, in turn, results in information overload that has also been recognized as an element of stress (e.g., Landy, 1990; Kahn & Byosiere, 1992).

Perception plays a central role in defining time pressure. Time pressure arises when the available time is *perceived* to be insufficient. A necessary condition to feel pressure is that a person must recognize that the imposition of a time limit is obligatory and the violation of that limit will lead to sanctions (Bronner, 1982).

It is likely that time pressure is not constant across time. Learning and adaptation to a problem situation shift the experience of time pressure (Congelosi & Dill 1965/1966). Time pressure is intensified when learning a new task. For example, Landy, Rastegary, and Motowidlo (1987) proposed the existence of transitional stress experienced by clerical workers during the introduction of microelectronics to the workplace.

Time pressure is one of the most frequently cited problems in organizations (Hall & Lawler, 1970). Modern work organizations view time as a scarce and valuable resource that must be managed effectively. This view of time relates effective use of time to productivity and efficiency in organizations. Doob (1971) explains that "time is one of the three factors involved in appraising productivity . . . the other two are the work or goal achieved and the energy expended. . . . An operation is efficient when it is accomplished with smallest expenditure of energy and time" (p. 349). Accordingly, the basis of evaluation is not the completion of a task, but rather it is the amount of time it takes to arrive at an effective solution to a problem. The goal of higher efficiency is reflected in faster pace of work, heavier workload, and higher time pressure. In the pursuit of their goals, organizations schedule events, synchronize activities, and allocate the total amount of available time among activities (McGrath & Rotchford, 1983; McGrath & Kelly, 1986). Furthermore, organizations set deadlines to coordinate both their activities with other organizations and the activities among separate units within the organization. Therefore, organizations develop a time orientation that suits their needs and circumstances but may be at odds with the needs of individuals within that organization. Groups within an organization also often have dissimilar time perspectives. For example, the time orientation of an engineering-design group in an organization differs from that of a product-marketing group within the same organization. This difference reflects the time span of their goals. The goals of the former group are to be realized over a much longer time span than the latter group. Schriber (1985; Schriber & Gutek, 1987) provided empirical support for this differential time perspective among groups. She developed a questionnaire to measure the temporal perspective of various work groups. A factor analysis, based on data collected from 525 respondents from 51 workgroups in 23 organizations, revealed that the time perspective is composed of 12 dimensions: (1) schedules and deadlines, (2) punctuality, (3) future orientation and quality versus speed, (4) allocation of time, (5) time boundaries between work and nonwork, (6) awareness of time use, (7) work pace, (8) autonomy of time use, (9) synchronization and coordination of work with others through time, (10) routine versus variety, (11) intraorganizational time boundaries, and (12) time buffer in workday. In an exploratory analysis, she found major differences between workgroups within the same organization on many of these dimensions including schedules and deadlines, work pace, and autonomy of time use. Although 12 dimensions emerged from the preliminary analyses, it is still too early to tell if they will emerge from replications. Nevertheless, one might reasonably conclude that the first four or five dimensions will replicate.

Time pressure can, in fact, *increase* performance and efficiency. This effect is explained in terms of the motivational effect of goal setting. Locke and Latham (1984) explain that setting specific deadlines means setting goals. These deadlines, in turn, provide directions for people and increase motivational forces to achieve goals. Both laboratory and field research has provided support for this motivational explanation of deadlines. Averdson (1974) found that compared to a non/deadline situation, the rate of task completion was higher in situations when deadlines were present. He also found that the pace of work increased as the length of time allotted for a task decreased (more time pressure). Field studies have similarly demonstrated that logging crews (Latham & Locke, 1975) and clerical workers (Bassett, 1979) worked faster as the allotted time decreased. Kelly and McGrath (1985) showed that while time pressure increased the pace of work, it did not enhance the quality of it.

It is generally agreed, however, that the relationship between time pressure and performance is not linear. Instead, a curvilinear model is used in which the optimal level of performance is obtained at an intermediate level of time pressure. In this framework, "too little" and "too much" pressure are both detrimental to performance level. Andrews and Farris (1972) found that productivity of NASA scientists and engineers increased as time pressure increased, but only up to a point. Performance declined as time pressure became even more intense than at the peak performance level.

In addition to the effect of time pressure on performance, researchers have been concerned about the psychological impact of time pressure on the members of organizations. Indeed, time pressure has been recognized as a major source of stress (McGrath, 1976). Frankhauser and Gardell (1976) pointed out that jobs differ in degree of time pressure and that stress is prevalent in jobs that are high in time pressure. Ivancevich, Matteson, and Preston (1982) compared operating room environments and medical/surgical environments on six stressors. The medical/surgical environments were characterized by significantly higher levels of quantitative overload and time pressure. As was the case in considering the relationship between time pressure and performance, the relationship between time pressure and strain also follows the function of an "inverted u." As previously stated, time pressure is assumed to produce positively psychophysiological consequences within a specified range. Extremely high time pressure produces stress but too little time pressure leads to boredom (Freedman & Edwards, 1988).

Experimental studies have generally operationalized time pressure in terms of a set duration of clock time to complete a task. As stated, however, it has been suggested that time pressure is not only a matter of clock time but also a function of characteristics of both the individuals involved and the complexity of the task at hand (Holsti, 1971). Therefore, a subjective measure of time pressure is also informative. This subjective measure of time pressure should include workload (frequency, intensity, and duration of efforts and energy expenditure), work pace (speed demand of work), and deadline (starting and stopping point of activity).

Time Pressure and Time Urgency

People differ in their experience of time and their reaction to that experience of time. Because time passes more rapidly if filled, it is likely that the overloaded schedule of time-urgent individuals affects their perception of passage of time. This is consistent with the research finding that indicates that time-urgent individuals overestimate the passage of time but less time-urgent persons underestimate it. Burnam et al. (1975) asked the participants of their experiment to signal when they thought that 1 minute had passed. On average, time-urgent individuals indicated a passage of one minute at 52.6 seconds but less time-urgent individuals signaled it at 75 seconds. Yarnold and Grimm (1982) replicated this experiment. They found that time-urgent individuals indicated the passage of 1 minute at 61.4 seconds and less time-urgent individuals at 77.2 seconds. Note the consistency of the level of underestimation of less time-urgent individuals in the two experiments. It should also be noted, however, that the perception of time-urgent individuals was closer to the *objective* time than that of less time-urgent individuals. Researchers, however, have tended to focus on the implications of the overestimation of the passage of time.

It is important to study the implications of both types of time perception biases under various degrees of time pressure. In circumstances where tight deadlines are the norm, underestimation of the passage of time may prove costly to the organization. Underestimating the passage of time may lead to missing important deadlines, or it may mean a need to intensify the pace close to a deadline in order to make up lost time. In addition, in recent years, the concept of "just in time" manufacturing has appeared on the factory floor. This has led to an even greater level of time pressure.

For the time-urgent individual in the Yarnold and Grimm's study (1982), the perception of a minute in 61.4 seconds indicates the noteworthy degree of their accuracy (Baker, Dearborn, Hastings, & Hamberger, 1984) or awareness of time. In contrast, the time-urgent subjects in the Burnam et al. (1975) experiment overestimate the passage of time by almost 8 seconds. Freedman and Edwards (1988) proposed that such an overestimation of the passage of time creates an additional pressure for the time-urgent subject. This additional pressure, combined with time pressure from the workplace and an overloaded schedule, leads to a triple-pressure phenomenon.

In explaining reaction to time-urgent individuals to time pressure, Freedman and Edwards (1988) hypothesized that their internal time pressure pushes them to reach their optimal pressure faster. Therefore, they perform better in low and intermediate time pressure as compared to less time-urgent individuals who perform optimally under high time pressure. But Freedman and Edwards did not find support for this proposal. Contrary to their hypothesis, time-urgent individuals performed better than less time-urgent individuals in all three conditions of time pressure. The discrepancy between the hypothesis of Freedman and Edwards and their experimental findings may be explained by considering the "inverted U" output versus time pressure curve. It is clear that Freeman and Edwards assumed that the shape of the curve, that is, its width, slope, and the line would be the same for both time-urgent and non-time-urgent individuals. What *would* change is the position of the curve along the time pressure axis. This shift results from the fact that time-urgent individuals tend to be self-monitoring, thus need less time pressure than their non-time-urgent counterparts to reach their optimum work output. It is clear from the experimental results, however, that the output/time pressure curves are in fact shaped very differently, in such a way that time-urgent individuals can be said to have time-pressure-independent behavior. This is in contrast to non-time-urgent types who respond very strongly to time pressure. These trends are depicted graphically in Figure 1. What factors might be responsible for this time-pressure-independent behavior? It seems plausible that experience would tend to broaden an individual's output versus time pressure curve, making him/her sensitive to time pressure. This broadening should be further accelerated and exacerbated in time-urgent individuals because they tend to seek out more tasks and may tend to gain experience faster than non-time-urgent individuals. It might also be argued that time-urgent individuals, given their self-monitoring tendencies, are inherently less influenced by time pressure to begin with.

Time Pressure and Time Urgency as Influences on Decision Making

Both time pressure and uncertainty have been suggested to induce changes in cognitive strategies and to influence both the process of decision making and the quality of choices. Several approaches have been developed to explain the

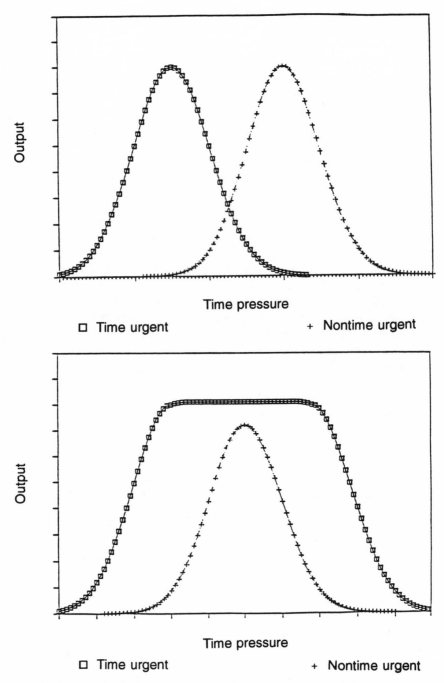

Figure 1. Optimal performance as a function of time pressure for time-urgent and non-time-urgent individuals. (a) Trends as hypothesized by Freedman and Edwards (1988). (b) Trends as found by Freedman and Edwards (1988).

process of decision making and the resolution of decision situations. Most models can be classified into one of three categories. The first category includes models of decision-making situations in which all possible information on the situation is available (complete certainty) and costs and benefits resulting from the implementation of available courses of actions can be measured in quantitative modes (Radford, 1989). Such decisions under uncertainty in this category include many routine operational and administrative processes.

The second category includes an array of models that all resemble gambling decision making (for review, see Slovic, Fichhoff, & Lichtenstein, 1977; Pitz & Sachs, 1984; Stevenson, Busemeyer, & Naylor, 1990; Yates, 1990). These models define a decision in terms of a choice between possible courses of actions that have each been assigned a probability of attaining a given goal. Quantitative outcomes or preferences for outcomes are considered. Because these models define uncertainty as the probability of an event's occurrence, they include only action and the outcome parts of a decision process. Not considering uncertainty regarding the initial problem severely limits this approach. Most important, these models assume situations that are so orderly and that contain certain choices that are so rational that they represent only the simplest decision-making situations. Thus this "gambling" approach can never deal with the complex decision situations (situations that may be characterized as "disorderly," "messy", or "discontinuous") that define everyday life.

The third category represents models of complex decisions situations. These are generally solution-centered decision problems (Cohen, March, & Olson, 1972; Nutt, 1984) and recognize intuition to be an important mode of operation when making a complex decision (Agor, 1986). Such models allow for uncertainty in all three parts of the decision-making process: uncertainty in the initial problem, in the available courses of actions, and in the consequences of each of these courses of action.

Certain decisions are made in environments that are inherently more uncertain than others. For example, uncertainty is extremely high in a situation where each of the available courses of action poses a sever social or material loss, and where the consequences of each alternative are highly unpredictable. Janis and Mann (1977) maintain that this kind of situation presents a state of psychological strain for decision makers. The more intense the level of uncertainty the more severe the resulting distress. Severe unpredictability of outcomes provokes anxiety, which results in reactive symptoms of sleeplessness, loss of appetite, agitation, and changes in physiological activities such as heart rate. The process of searching and selecting a proper course of action is affected by the degree of uncertainty that is present in a given decision situation. Janis (1982) explains that in the severe cases of uncertainty, a decision maker will apply a maladaptive hypervigilant way of coping to end this painful ambivalent state. This coping mechanism causes a decision maker to undertake a hasty, disorganized search, to rely on incomplete information, and to disregard the full range of consequences of each alternative course of action. Rushing through the decision process leads to faulty decisions and post/decisional regrets (Janis, 1982). Reaching a premature decision might be due to an attempt at reducing the intolerance for ambiguity under high stress (Smock, 1955). It might also be the result of the need to obtain immediate relief from the dilemma of selecting equally risky alternatives (Keinan, 1987).

It is unlikely that all individuals respond in this maladaptive way. Time-urgent individuals may respond differently than their non-time urgent counterparts. It has been demonstrated that learning reduces the degree of intolerance for ambiguity (Smock, 1955). The desire of time-urgent individuals to accomplish more provides them with more learning opportunities, which enable them to deal with uncertain decision situations. Therefore, their response to uncertainty is not necessarily a hypervigilant one, even though they are able to accelerate the decision-making process. On the other hand, in a novel decision situation, their intolerance for ambiguity may push them to view the situation in more familiar terms, which may be ineffective, or may lead them to a hasty decision.

It is also important to point out that uncertainty does not necessarily always produce strain. Neither does the same level of uncertainty at different stages of the decision-making process necessarily produce the same level of strain. It is likely that a type of uncertainty that might induce strain for time-urgent individuals may not induce strain for non-time-urgent individuals. Furthermore, uncertainty may not affect the stages of a decision process for time-urgent individuals in the same way that it affects the stages of the decision process for non-time-urgent types.

Both time-urgent and non-time-urgent individuals may differ in the techniques they use to deal with time pressure. Encountering time pressure, time-urgent individuals may use acceleration of activities to deal with lack of time, whereas non-time-urgent types may prefer filtration. In fact, time-urgent individuals may prefer the acceleration of an activity coping mechanism exactly because they have learned to master the accelerated pace. It is also likely that time-urgent individuals avoid decisions in a novel situation, whereas non-time-urgent individuals avoid decisions under intense time pressure.

It is important to understand how time-urgent individuals may use different coping approaches to alter consequences of time pressure and uncertainty. Although implicitly stated (Edwards, 1988), no systematic research has even been conducted to establish the coping repertoire of people in the context of the Type A/B behavior patterns. Furthermore, with the exception of Howard, Rechnitzer, and Cunningham (1975), the effectiveness of coping approaches used by Type A and Type B individuals has largely been neglected. Howard et al. (1975) reported that Type A individuals as compared to Type B individuals, use less effective coping approaches.

Summary and Concluding Remarks

In this chapter, we have asserted the importance of time urgency in studying decision making under stress. We have argued that time urgency can be related to all facets of decision making under time pressure and in the presence of other stressors. Time-urgent and non-time-urgent individuals differ in their perception of stress, their response to that perceived stress, and the strategies they use to make decisions. We discussed our argument of these variations in terms of two relevant stressors in decision making: uncertainty and time pressure. We have made a distinction between these two stressors and have argued how they affect time-urgent and non-time-urgent individuals differently.

Considering time urgency in decision-making studies is not only beneficial to our understanding of decision making, but it also allows us to broaden our definition of time urgency beyond epidemiological concerns. We have argued that the implication of the differential perception of time between time-urgent and non-time-urgent individuals must both be considered. Recognizing the importance of overestimation of the passage of time among time-urgent individuals, we have pointed out the implication of the underestimation of less time-urgent individuals in the context of the decision-making process. This underestimation of the passage of time may delay action and may even result in missing important deadlines. However, the conclusions of the previous studies regarding this biased perception of time should be validated because most of these studies are based on questionable measures of global Type A behavior. Replicating these studies using more specific measures of time urgency like the one we have developed is essential.

These differential perceptions of time, which are related to a preference for certain work patterns, affect both uncertainty and time pressure. We have argued that time-urgent individuals perceive less time pressure and withstand a higher level of time pressure than less time-urgent individuals. We have emphasized that time-urgent individuals' experience with working under time pressure, as a result of self-inflicted pressure, increases their threshold for pressure. Furthermore, we have argued that although time-urgent individuals are intolerant of ambiguity, their experience may facilitate their responses to uncertainty. Research should be designed to investigate the differential perception of time urgency regarding both uncertainty and time pressure for time-urgent and non-time-urgent individuals.

We have not only argued that their perceptions of stressors vary, but also that time-urgent and non-time-urgent individuals respond differently to both uncertainty and time pressure and in turn use different strategies to make a decision. For example, time-urgent individuals may use acceleration of activities to deal with time pressure, and non-time-urgent individuals are more likely to avoid a time pressure situation. Avoidance may also be used by time-urgent individuals but in response to a novel and unfamiliar situation. It is likely that a

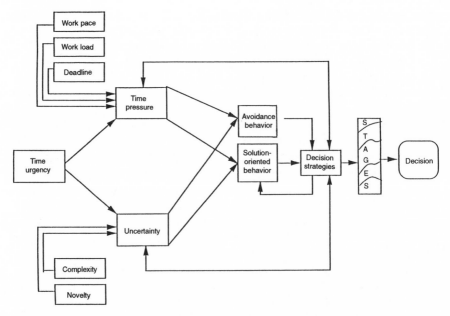

Figure 2. Relationship between time urgency, stress, and the decision-making process.

combination of techniques is generally used. For example, a time-urgent individual making a decision under pressure may use acceleration of mental activity, filtration, and delegation of responsibility. On the other hand, he or she may use different set of techniques if both time pressure and uncertainty exist. A fruitful area for investigation is a comparison of repertoires that time-urgent and non-time-urgent individuals use in various decision-making situations.

It has furthermore been proposed that the decision-making process is affected by stress differently at each stage of the process, and that this level of stress is in turn determined how time urgent a given individual is. Broadbent (1971) has suggested that stress has a larger effect at earlier stages of the decision-making process, such as problem definition and alternative generation. Different patterns of the stress/decision-making relationship may be a function of experience in previous similar decision situations. In such cases, a single index of stress at various stages of the decision-making process may be inappropriate. This differential pattern suggests two process studies. The first would consist of following individuals through a process of making a given decision, with the emphasis on the stages of the process used in making that decision. The second study would follow individuals over the course of many decisions and would emphasize the effect of experience or learning on how stress affects the decision-making process. In both studies, one can investigate the structure of stress across time by using "reference learning curves" or components according to such methods as one described by Tucker (1966). The resulting reference curves can then be studies in relation to the time urgency of the decision maker.

Throughout this chapter we have emphasized how the interaction between individual characteristics and the characteristics of the decision-making situation affects the perception of stress and an individual's response to it. This resulting response in turn affects each individual's decision-making strategies. A graphical representation of these complex relationships is given in Figure 2.

It is clear that decision making is influenced by many variables. Many of these variables have been identified but many have not. We consider time urgency to be one of those undiscovered variables. It is an individual attribute that would appear to have substance. It can be measured. It has been reliably associated with other behaviors. Progress along this line of research has been hampered by a simple-minded view of the time-urgency construct. We suggest that a good deal of basic work needs to be done in understanding the parameters of time urgency, its impact on various behaviors (including but not limited to decision making, its physiological concomitants, and the extent to which it might be modified). Additionally, more must be discovered about how this attribute interacts with environmental conditions (e.g., time pressure) to yield the full continuum of behavior. We cannot, with any confidence, suggest how large a role the time-urgency attribute might play in explaining or understanding decision-making behavior, but we can say with some confidence that it is a research avenue worthy of pursuit.

References

Achrol, R. S. (1988). Measuring uncertainty in organizational analysis. *Social Science Research, 17,* 66–91.

Agor, W. H. (1986). The logic of intuition: How top executives make important decisions. *Organizational Dynamics, 14*(3), 5–18.

Andrews, F. M., & Farris, G. F. (1972). Time pressure and performance of scientists and engineers: A five-year panel study. *Organizational Behavior and Human Performance, 8,* 185–200.

Averdson, L. A. (1974). *Deadlines and organizational behavior: A laboratory investigation of the effect of deadlines on individual task performance.* Unpublished doctoral dissertation. Stanford University.

Baker, L. J., Dearborn, M., Hastings, J. E., & Hamberger, K. (1984). Type A behavior in women: A review. *Health Psychology, 3*(5), 477–497.

Bassett, G. A. (1979). A study of the effects of task goal and schedule choice on work performance. *Organizational Behavior and Human Performance, 24,* 202–227.

Bingham, D., & Hailey, B. J. (1989). The time urgency component of the Type A behavior pattern: Time pressure and performance. *Journal of Applied Social Psychology, 19*(5), 425–432.

Bluedorn, A. C., & Denhardt, R. B. (1988). Time and organizations. *Journal of Management, 14*(2), 299–320.

Booth-Kewley, S., & Friedman, H. S. (1987). Psychological predictions of heart disease: A quantitative review. *Psychological Bulletin, 101*(3), 343–362.

Broadbent, D. E. (1971). *Decision and stress.* London: Academic Press.

Bronner, R. (1982). *Decision making under time pressure.* Lexington: Lexington Books.

Budner, S. (1962). Intolerance of ambiguity as a personality variable. *Journal of Personality, 30,* 29–50.

Burnam, M. A., Pennebaker, J. W., & Glass, D. C. (1975). Time consciousness, achievement striving, and the Type A coronary-prone behavior pattern. *Journal of Abnormal Psychology, 84*(1), 76–79.

Cohen, M., March, J. G., & Olson, J. P. (1972). A garbage can model of organizational choice. *Administrative Science Quarterly, 17,* 1–25.

Congelosi, V. E., & Dill, W. R. (1965/1966). Organizational learning: Observations toward a theory. *Administrative Science Quarterly, 10,* 175–203.

Dembroski, T. M., & Czajkowski, S. M. (1989). Historical and current developments in coronary-prone behavior. In A. W. Siegman & T. M. Dembroski (Ed.), *In search of coronary-prone behavior: Beyond Type A* (pp. 21–39). Hillsdale, NJ: Lawrence Erlbaum Associates.

Dembroski, T. M., & Williams, R. B. (1989). Definition and assessment of coronary-prone behavior. In N. Schneiderman, R. Kaufmann, & S. M. Weis (Eds.), *Handbook of research methods in cardiovascular behavioral medicine* (pp. 553–569). New York: Plenum Press.

Doob, L. W. (1971). *Patterning of time.* New Haven: Yale University Press.

Edwards, J. R. (1988) The determinants and consequences of coping with stress. In C. L. Cooper & R. Payne (Eds.), *Causes, coping, and consequences of stress at work* (pp. 233–263). Chichester: John Wiley & Sons.

Edwards, J. R., Baglioni, A. J., Jr., & Cooper, C. L. (1990). Examining relationships among self-report measures of the Type A behavior patterns: The effects of dimensionality, measurement error, and differences in underlying constructs. *Journal of Applied Psychology, 75*(4), 440–454.

Evans, G., Palsane, M. N., & Carrere, S. (1987). Type A behavior and occupational stress: A cross-cultural study of blue-collar workers. *Journal of Personality and Social Psychology, 52*(5), 1002–1007.

Eysenk, M. W. (1983). Anxiety and individual differences. In G.R.J. Hockey (Ed.), *Stress and fatigue in human performance.* (pp. 273-298). Chichester: John Wiley & Sons.

Frankenhauser, M., & Gardell, B. (1976). Underload and overload in working life: Outline of a multidisciplinary approach. *Journal of Human Stress, 2,* 35–46.

Freedman, J. L., & Edwards, D. R. (1988). Time pressure, task performance, and enjoyment. In J. E. McGrath (Ed.), *The social psychology of time* (pp. 113–133). Newburry Park, CA: Sage Publications.

French-Belgian Collaborative Group. (1982). Ischemic heart disease and psychological patterns. *Advances in cardiology, 29,* 25–31.

Friedman, H. S., & Booth-Kewley, S. (1988). Validity of Type A construct: A reprise. *Psychological Bulletin, 91,* 293–323.

Friedman, M., & Rosenman, R. H. (1959). Association of specific overt behavior pattern with increases in blood cholesterol, blood clotting time, incidence of arcus senilis and clinical coronary artery disease. *JAMA: The Journal of the American Medical Association, 169,* 1286–1296.

Friedman, M., & Rosenman, R. H. (1974). *Type A Behavior and your heart.* New York: Knopf.

Ganster, D. C., Sime, W. E., & Mayes, B. T. (1989). Type A behavior in the work setting: A review and some new data. In A. W. Siegman & T. M. Dembroski (Eds.), *In search of coronary-prone behavior: Beyond Type A* (pp. 169–194). Hillsdale, NJ: Lawrence Erlbaum Associates.

Ganster, D. C., Schaubroeck, J., Sime, & W. E., Mayes, B. T. (1991). The nomological validity of the Type A personality among employed adults. *Journal of Applied Psychology, 76*(1), 143–168.

Gastorf, J. W. (1980). Time urgency of the Type A behavior pattern. *Journal of Consulting and Clinical Psychology, 48*(2), 299.

Gifford, W. E., Bobbitt, H. R., & Slocum, J. W., Jr. (1979). Message characteristics and perceptions of uncertainty by organizational decision makers. *Academy of Management Journal, 22*(3), 458–481.

Glass, D. C. (1977). *Behavior patterns, stress, and coronary disease.* Hillsdale, NJ: Lawrence Erlbaum & Associates.

Glass, D. C., Snyder, M. L., & Hollis, J. F. (1974). Time urgency and the Type A coronary-prone behavior pattern. *Journal of Applied Social Psychology, 4*(2), 125–140.

Hall, D. T., & Lawler, E. E. (1970). Job characteristics and pressures and the organizational integration of professionals. *Administrative Science Quarterly, 15,* 271–281.

Haynes, S. G., Feinleib, M., & Kannel, W. B. (1980). The relationship of psychosocial factors to coronary heart disease in the Framingham study: III. Eight-year incidence of coronary heart disease. *American Journal of Epidemiology, 3,* 37–58.

Holsti, O. R. (1971). Crisis, stress, and decision making. *International Social Science Journal, 23,* 53–67.

Howard, J. H., Rechnitzer, P. A., & Cunningham, D. A. (1975). Coping with job tension-effective and ineffective methods. *Public Personnel Management, 4,* 317–326.

Ivancevich, J. M., Matteson, M. T., & Preston, C. (1982). Occupational stress, Type A behavior, and physical well being. *Academy of Management Journal, 25,* 373–391.

Janis, I. L. (1982). *Stress, attitudes, and decisions.* New York: Praeger.

Janis, I. L., & Mann, L. (1977). *Decision making: A psychological analysis of conflict, choice, and commitment.* New York: The Free Press.

Jauch, L. R., & Kraft, K. L. (1986). Strategic management of uncertainty. *Academy of Management Journal, 11*(4), 777–790.

Jenkins, D. C., Zyzanski, S. J., & Rosenman, R. H. (1979). *Jenkins activity survey manual (Form C).* New York: The Psychological Corp.

Kahn, R. L., & Byosiere. (1992). Stress in organizations. In M. Dunnette & L. Hough (Eds.), *Handbook of industrial and organizational psychology* (2nd ed., Vol. 3, pp. 571–650). Palo Alto, CA: Consulting Psychologists. Press, Inc.

Kelly, J. R., & McGrath, J. E. (1985). Effects of time limits and task types on task performance and interaction of four person groups. *Journal of Personality and Social Psychology, 49,* 395–407.

Keinan, G. (1987). Decision making under stress: Scanning of alternatives under controllable and uncontrollable threats. *Journal of Personality and Social Psychology, 52*(3), 639–644.

Landy, F. J. (1990, March). *Work design and stress.* Paper presented at APA/NIOSH Conference, Washington, DC.

Landy, F. J., Rastegary, H., & Motowidlo, S. (1987). Human-computer interactions in the work place: Psychosocial aspects of VDT use. In M. Frese, E. Ulich, & W. Dzida (Eds.), *Psychological issues of human-computer interaction in the workplace,* (pp. 3–22). New York: North-Holland.

Landy, F. J., Rastegary, H., Thayer, J., & Colvin, C. (1991). Time urgency: The construct and its measurement. *Journal for Applied Psychology, 76,* 644–657.

Latham, G. P., & Locke, E. A. (1975). Increasing productivity with decreasing time limits: A field replication of Parkinson's Law. *Journal of Applied Psychology, 60,* 524–526.

Locke, E. A., & Latham, G. P. (1984). *Goal setting for individuals, groups, and organizations.* Chicago: Science Research Associates.

MacCrimmon, K. R., & Taylor, R. N. (1976). Decision making and problem solving. In M. D. Dunnette (Ed.), *Handbook of industrial and organizational psychology* (pp. 1397–1453). Chicago: Rand McNally College Publishing Company.

Mathews, K. A. (1982). Psychological perspectives on the Type A behavior pattern. *Psychological Bulletin, 91,* 293–323.

Mathews, K. A. (1988). Coronary heart disease and Type A behavior: Update on and alternative to the Booth-Kewley and Friedman (1987) quantitative review. *Psychological Bulletin, 104,* 373–380.

McGrath, A. J. (1976). Stress and behavior in organizations. In M. D. Dunnette (Ed.), *Handbook of industrial and organizational psychology.* (pp. 1351–1395). Chicago: Rand McNally College Publishing Company.

McGrath, J. E., & Rotchford, N. L. (1983). Time and behavior in organizations. In L. L. Cummings & B. M. Staw (Eds.), *Research in organizational behavior* (vol. 5, pp. 57–101). Greenwich, CT: JAI Press Inc.

McGrath, J. E., & Kelly, J. R. (1986). *Time and human interaction: Toward a social psychology of time.* New York: The Guilford Press.

McMichael, A. J. (1978). Personality, behavioral, and situational modifiers of work stressors. In C. L. Cooper & R. Payne (Eds.), *Stress at work,* (pp. 127–147). Chichester: John Wiley & Sons.

Nutt, P. (1984). Types of organizational decision processes. *Administrative Science Quarterly, 29,* 414–450.

Payne, R. (1988). Individual differences in the study of occupational stress. In C. L. Cooper & R. Payne (Eds.), *Causes, coping and consequences of stress at work* (pp. 209–232). Chichester: John Wiley & Sons.

Pitz, G. F., & Sachs, N. J. (1984). Judgment and decision: Theory and application. *Annual Review of Psychology, 35,* 139–163.

Price, V.A. (1982). *Type A behavior pattern: A model for research and practice.* New York: Academic Press.

Radford, K. J. (1989) *Individual and small group decisions.* Springer-Verlag, NY: Captus University Publications.

Rifkil, J. (1987). *Time wars: The primary conflict in human history.* New York: Henry Holt.

Rosenman, R. H., Friedman, M., Straus, R., Wurm, M., Jenkins, C. D., & Messinger, H. B. (1966). Coronary heart disease in the Western Collaborative group study: A follow-up experience of two years. *Journal of the American Medical Association, 195,* 130–136.

Sauter, S., Hurrell, J. J., & Cooper, C. L. (1989). *Job control and worker health.* New York: Wiley.

Schriber, J. B. (1985). *An exploratory study of the temporal dimensions of work organizations.* Unpublished doctoral dissertation: The Claremont Graduate School, Claremont, CA.

Schriber, J. B., & Gutek, B. A. (1987). Some time dimensions of work: Measurement of an underlying aspect of organization culture. *Journal of Applied Psychology, 72*(4), 642–650.

Schuler, R. S., & Jackson, S. E. (1986). Managing stress through PHRM practices: An uncertainty interpretation. *Research in Personnel and Human Resource Management, 4,* 183–224.

Shalon, M., & Strube, M. J. (1988). Type A behavior and emotional responses to uncertainty: A test of the self-appraisal model. *Motivation & Emotion, 12*(4), 385–398.

Slovic, P., Fischhoff, B., & Lichtenstein, S. (1977). Behavioral decision theory. *Annual Review of Psychology, 28,* 1–39.

Smock, C. D. (1955). The influence of psychological stress on the "intolerance of ambiguity." *Journal of Abnormal and Social Psychology, 50,* 177–182.

Stevenson, M. K., Busemeyer, J. R., & Naylor, J. C. (1990). Judgment and decision-making theory. In M. D. Dunnette & L. M. Hough (Eds.), *Handbook of industrial and organizational psychology* (2nd ed., vol. 1, pp. 283–374). Palo Alto, CA: Consulting Psychologists Press, Inc.

Strube, M. J. (1987). A self-appraisal model of the Type A behavior pattern. In R. Hogan & W. H. Jones (Eds.), *Perspectives in Personality* (vol. 2, pp. 201–250). Greenwich, CT: JAI Press Inc.

Strube, M. J., & Boland, S. M. (1987). Type A behavior pattern and the self-evaluation of abilities: Empirical tests of the self-appraisal model. *Journal of Personality and Social Psychology, 52*(5), 956–974.

Taylor, R. N. (1975). Age and experience as determinants of managerial information processing and decision making performance. *Academy of Management Journal, 18,* 74–81.

Tucker, L. R. (1966). Learning theory and multivariate experiment: Illustration by determination of generalized learning curves. In R. B. Cattell (Ed.), *Handbook of multivariate experimental psychology* (pp. 476–501). Chicago: Rand McNally & Company.

Wright, P. (1974). The harassed decision maker: Time pressures, distractions, and the use of evidence. *Journal of Applied Psychology, 59*(5), 555–561.

Wright, L. (1988). The Type A behavior pattern and coronary artery disease: Quest for the active ingredients and the elusive mechanism. *American Psychologist, 43*(1), 2–14.

Yarnold, P. R., & Grimm, L. G. (1982). Time urgency among coronary-prone individuals. *Journal of Abnormal Psychology, 91*(3), 175–177.

Yarnold, P. R., & Mueser, K. T. (1984). Time urgency of Type A individuals: Two replications. *Perceptual and Motor Skills, 59*, 334.

Yarnold, P. R., Mueser, K. I., & Lyons, J. S. (1988). Type A behavior, accountability, and work rate in small groups. *Journal of Research in Personality, 22*(3), 353–360.

Yates, J. F. (1990). *Judgment and decision making.* Englewood Cliffs, NJ: Prentice Hall.

Zakay, D., & Wooler, S. (1984). Time pressure, training and decision effectiveness. *Ergonomics, 27*(3), 273–284.

Zyzanski, S. J., & Jenkins, C. D. (1970). Basic dimensions within the coronary-prone behavior pattern. *Journal of Chronic Diseases, 22*, 781–795.

16

Information Processing in Decision Making under Time Pressure
The Influence of Action Versus State Orientation

Joachim Stiensmeier-Pelster and Martin Schürmann

Introduction

Over the past two decades, research on decision making has shown that individuals use a variety of decision-making strategies and that the strategies selected are contingent upon both the characteristics that are inherent in the decision problem itself, such as reversibility, complexity, ambiguity, or unfamiliarity, and the characteristics that describe the decision environment, such as importance and time pressure or time constraints (Beach & Mitchell, 1978; Einhorn & Hogarth, 1981; Ford, Schmitt, Schechtman, Hults, & Doherty, 1989; Payne, 1982. In the study by McAllister, Mitchell, and Beach (1979), for example, people preferred more complex and more accurate strategies when making decisions for which they were accountable and decisions that were irreversible than when making decisions for which they were not accountable and decisions that could be reversed. In the studies by Christensen-Azalanski (1978, 1980), to give another example, subjects used strategies that were more complex, required more infor-

Joachim Stiensmeier-Pelster and Martin Schürmann • Universität Bielefed, Abteilung für Psychologie, Postfach D-4800, Bielefeld 10013, Germany.
Time Pressure and Stress in Human Judgment and Decision Making, edited by Ola Svenson and A. John Maule. Plenum Press, New York, 1993.

mation processing, and were more accurate with important decisions than with unimportant decisions.

Several studies have analyzed the influence of time pressure and time constraints on decision-making behavior. These studies have identified different strategies to cope with time pressure and deadlines. Although retaining their decision-making strategy, people may respond to time pressure by reducing the amount of information processed or by accelerating information processing. Ben Zur and Breznitz (1981) and Wright (1974) have shown that people try to filtrate the information necessary to arrive at a decision by focusing on important information and neglecting relatively unimportant information. Furthermore, Ben Zur and Breznitz (1981) have found that people spend less time looking at individual items of information when deciding under time pressure.

However, sometimes people even change their decision-making strategy when confronted with time pressure. In a study by Payne, Bettman, and Johnson (1988 Experiment 2), people had to decide on various sets of risky options given no, moderate, or high time pressure. The results of this study led to the conclusion that people confronted with time pressure may initially retain their strategy and try to accelerate information processing. If acceleration is not sufficient to cope with time pressure, they may try to filtrate information. Finally, when time pressure becomes extreme, they may change their strategy.

Although a substantial amount of research has shown a high degree of adaptivity in human decision-making behavior, we maintain that people often fail to adapt. Many of us will recall situations requiring a quick decision in which we were indecisive or unable to make up our minds. Sometimes the induction of time pressure even increases our indecisiveness, as the following example will show. Consider someone looking for a second-hand car who has found a car that shows most of the aspects he/she desires. The decision has crystallized, and only a last kick is needed to reach the final decision. The salesman now mentions that he has a second prospective customer and that the car is only available if one makes an immediate decision. The salesman' induction of time pressure may revitalize our indecisiveness, and we back away from a decision.

In our view, the degree to which people can adapt to different tasks or environmental demands is related to the effectiveness with which action control can be implemented. We have derived our assumptions from Kuhl's theory of action control (Kuhl, 1984, 1985; Kuhl & Beckmann, 1993). Thus, before discussing several studies testing this assumption, we shall sketch the theory of action control. First, we will focus on a person characteristic called action versus state orientation. Second, we will discuss the influence of action versus state orientation on decision making with and without time pressure, and then we will present data from three experiments testing our assumptions. Studies dealing with action versus state orientation and decision making under other conditions than time pressure are discussed elsewhere (Stiensmeier-Pelster, 1993).

The Theory of Action Control

From the 1950s to the early 1980s , motivational research was guided by the implicit assumption that people realize their intentions once they are sufficiently able and motivated. However, Kuhl (1984, 1985) has reminded us that this assumption is not universally valid. For example, it may happen that a person with a strong intention to play tennis over the weekend may not find him/herself on the tennis court but rather in front of his/her television watching a baseball game. Furthermore, recent learned-helplessness research has demonstrated that people may display marked performance deficits despite high motivation and the capacity to achieve success (Kuhl, 1981; Stiensmeier-Pelster & Schürmann, 1990).

According to Kuhl's (1985) theory of action control, success or failure in implementing one's intentions depends on how effectively action control is implemented. Action control comprises volitional processes such as active attentional selectivity (restricting one's attention to the information relevant to optimal execution of one's intentions), parsimony of information processing (reducing information processing to an indispensible amount), motivation control (focusing on the positive and neglecting the negative aspects of one's goals), affect control (favoring action-promoting affects and avoiding action-detrimental affects), and environmental control (e.g., making social commitments).

We assume that the effectiveness with which people adapt to time pressure is particularly influenced by three volitional processes: active attentional selectivity, parsimony of information processing, and affect control. Active attentional selectivity means that people prefer intention-supporting information and at the same time actively avoid information that is inconsistent with their intention. The spreading-apart effect, well known from research on cognitive dissonance, can be regarded as a consequence of active attentional selectivity. After tentatively deciding in favor of one alternative, people show a preference for decision-supporting information. This secures their ability to decide and act. It helps them to transform their intention (e.g., to play tennis) into the appropriate behavior (see Beckmann & Kuhl, 1984, for a more detailed discussion of this point). Parsimony of information processing relates to the definition of stop rules for information processing. Whenever an actor believes that further information processing reveals information that undermines the motivational power of his/her current intentions, this process brings information processing to a halt. People unable to employ parsimonious information processing will often be found to ponder on alternatives, even when a preferred course of action has crystallized. Affect control is defined as a volitional process that controls emotional states in order to facilitate the enactment of current intentions, that is, producing hope, confidence, and so forth and avoiding doubt, fear, uncertainty, and the like.

The effectiveness with which action-control processes can be implemented again depends on two action-control modes: action and state orientation. An individual is called action-oriented, when he/she focuses on a fully developed action structure, that is, when he/she simultaneously or successively pays attention to (a) his/her present state, (b his/her intended future state, (c) the discrepancy between present and future states, and (d) at least one action alternative that can reduce the discrepancy. If one or more of these elements are lacking, a person is said to be state-oriented. Examples of extreme state orientation are ruminating about past failure or wishful thinking and fantasizing about an aspired future state. According to the theory of action control, a high degree of action orientation promotes an effective operation of action-control processes and thereby facilitates the enactment of one's current intentions. On the other hand, state orientation, because of its dysfunctional, persevering cognitions on some fixed aspects of a present, past, or future state, impairs efficient action control.

Kuhl maintains that an individual's degree of action versus state orientation depends on both situational and dispositional parameters. Thus, despite situational demands, some people will be especially prone to ruminate about some aspects of the present, past, or future state (i.e., state-oriented), whereas others characteristically focus on the change-promoting aspects of a situation (i.e., action-oriented).

To assess these individual differences, Kuhl (1984, 1985) has developed the Action Control Scale (ACS). The ACS contains subscales with forced-choice items addressing three types of action versus state orientation: (1) failure-related action versus state orientation (i.e., making plans to reverse past or to prevent new failures versus ruminating about past failures), (2) performance-related action versus state orientation (focusing on the activity versus on the goal while performing an action), and (3) decision-related action versus state orientation (decisiveness versus indecisiveness). Decision-related action versus state orientation, for example, is assessed by such items as:

If I had to work at home:
———I would often have problems getting started (state-oriented).
———I would usually start immediately (action-oriented).
When I want to see someone again:
———I try to set a date for the visit right away (action-oriented).
———I plan to do it some day (state-oriented).

Studies analyzing the influence of action versus state orientation on the effectiveness with which action-control processes are implemented have shown that action-oriented individuals employ action control more efficiently than state-oriented individuals. Stiensmeier-Pelster and Schürmann (1993), for example, have reported various studies showing that action-oriented individuals (a) restrict their attention to the information necessary to realize their intentions, (b) process information parsimoniously, and (c) promote action-furthering affects and inhibit action-detrimental emotions more than state-oriented persons. Furthermore, Stiensmeier-Pelster and Schürmann (1993) have shown that action- compared to state-oriented individuals are more flexible and self-determined in their behavior and are more able to adapt to changes in their lives.

Action versus State Orientation and Decision Making With and Without Time Pressure

Several studies have analyzed the influence of action versus state orientation on decision-making behavior. Results of these studies have supported the assumption that action orientation is associated with more parsimonious processing of decision-related information than state orientation (Kuhl & Beckmann, 1983; Niederberger, Engemann, & Radtke, 1987; Stiensmeier & Schnier, 1988). Unfortunately, none of these studies has analyzed the influence of action versus state orientation as a function of tasks or environmental parameters. However, action versus state orientation should promote different responses to at least one environmental parameter, namely time pressure.

According to Payne et al. (1988), people may show different responses to time pressure. They may (a) accelerate information processing or (b) filtrate information. If acceleration and filtration are not sufficient, they may (c) even change their decision-making heuristic or strategy. These responses obviously differ in the amount of action control they require. Acceleration of information processing, that is, doing the same thing faster, is not a new response to the changing environment. It is a very rigid and mostly an inappropriate response to time pressure. Therefore, it does not require a substantial amount of action control. Filtration, on the other hand, indicates a substantial change in information processing. The important components of the available information are processed preferentially and the less important are ignored. Thus, filtration demands the implementation of the action-control processes of active attentional selectivity and parsimony of information processing.

Furthermore, because parts of the available information are ignored, filtration may cause decision-detrimental emotions, such as fear of being inaccurate. Affect control serves to avoid such detrimental emotions.

The greatest degree of action control is presumably required by the third response: changing the decision-making strategy. It requires an individual who is highly flexible in her or his behavior and highly adaptive to changes in life. As discussed above, the state-oriented are less able to employ action control, are less flexible in their behavior, and less adaptive to changes in life than the action-oriented. Thus, the state-oriented should respond with an acceleration of information processing, whereas the action-oriented should respond with filtration and, if the situation demands it, with a change in their decision-making strategy.

To test these assumptions, we have completed three experiments using different experimental procedures. Because of space restrictions, we focus on the most important methodological details and results. However, all experiments are described at length elsewhere (see references), and all reported differences are supported by appropriate statistical analyses.

Study 1

Using an experimental procedure introduced by Kuhl and Beckmann (1983), students had to decide which of 36 dice games they wished to play (Stiensmeier-Pelster, John, Stulik & Schürman, 1989, Experiment 1). Subjects were given 36 sheets of paper, with each sheet indicating the possible reward (ranging from 17 to 83 Pfennigs) and the probability of winning (p between .17 and .83) in one game. Subjects were informed that they had to stake 15 Pfennigs on each chosen game and that they could attain the reward if they succeeded in throwing the expected number on the dice. Furthermore, they were told that the selected games had to be played after they had reported their choices on all 36 games. Half the subjects decided under time constraint (all 36 choices had to be made within 3 minutes) and the other half without time constraint. A pilot study had shown that the deadline allowed subjects to decide on all 36 games on the basis of expectancy-value calculations if they applied total concentration and speed to their calculations.

All subjects were given the decision-related subscale of the ACS. On the basis of their action versus state orientation scores, subjects were assigned to action- (8 points or less, $N = 24$) and state-oriented groups (12 points or more, $N = 16$; upper and lower 30; see Figure 1).

To test the effects of time pressure and action versus state orientation on decision making, we applied the method of logical statement analysis (Kuhl, 1982) to determine whether subjects' choices could be predicted better by a simple expectancy rule (i.e., choice or rejection of a game depends on the probability information only) or by a combined expectancy-value rule (i.e., choice or rejection depends on probability (expectancy) $\times$ reward (value) calculations). That is, we determined which of the 36 games would be chosen by the simple expectancy rule and which by the combined expectancy-value rule. Subsequently, the predicted choices were compared with subjects' choices.

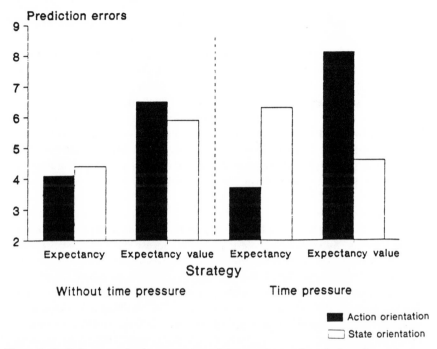

Figure 1. Prediction errors for the expectancy and the expectancy-value rule for action- and state-oriented subjects as a function of time pressure (from Stiensmeier-Pelster et al., 1989).

Figure 1 shows the frequency of false predictions of the above-mentioned rules for action- and state-oriented individuals as a function of time pressure. As the figure shows, there were no differences between action- and state-oriented subjects in the absence of time pressure but marked differences in the presence of time pressure. Whereas the choices of the action-oriented were better predicted by the simple expectancy-based rule, the choices of the state-oriented were better predicted by the combined expectancy-value rule. Furthermore, time pressure prompted action-oriented subjects to resort to the simple expectancy-based rule, that is, to a more parsimonious information processing, whereas state-oriented subjects became even more attached to the more complex expectancy-value rule requiring the processing of more information. However, all action- and all state-oriented subjects completed their decisions within the time limit.

The results are in line with our theoretical considerations. Action- and state-oriented individuals respond to time pressure in different ways. Whereas the action-oriented show an increased tendency to filtrate under time pressure, that is, focus on probability information, the state-oriented increase the amount of information processing.

Study 2

The most important problem for Experiment 1 was that decision-making behavior, that is, whether an expectancy- or an expectancy-value based rule was implemented to choose the games, could only be deduced from subjects' choices and not assessed directly. Thus, the conclusions about differing responses to time pressure in action- and state-oriented individuals could easily be criticized. Therefore, we tried to replicate our findings using a procedure adopted from Christensen-Szalanski (1978, 1980) that enables a more direct assessment of the information processed and the time required (for a detailed description of this experiment, see Stiensmeier-Pelster, Schürmann, John, & Stulik, 1991, Experiment 1).

Twenty-one students of economics had to imagine that they were stock exchange brokers who were interested in estimating their expected stock exchange profits. Subjects were told that they could use one out of six available packages of information ranging from *no information at all* (1) to *all the information necessary to make the correct estimation* (6) to prepare their estimations. The information consisted of probabilities that the dollar would rise in value (e.g., a rise of 5 Pfennigs with a probability of 45%, 10 Pfennigs with a probability of 33%, 15 Pfennigs with a probability of 15% and more than 15 Pfennigs with a probability of 7%), and its influence on stocks (e.g., if the dollar increased 5 Pfennigs the stock value would increase with a probability of 71% to DM 2,500, with a probability of 23% to DM 1,500 and with a probability of 6% to DM 500). Furthermore, they were told to report their estimation by indicating a range to which the profit could be assigned. Ignoring part or all of the available information enabled subjects to save time but inevitably led to diffuse ranges, that is, inaccurate estimations. However, the information attainable was such that the possible gain in estimation accuracy from every new item of information decreased as a function of items already processed. This allowed subjects to respond to time pressure by acceleration as well as filtration (i.e., stopping information processing when the possible gain in estimation accuracy fell behind the costs associated with the processing of this item).

Time pressure was manipulated by informing subjects either that payment would depend exclusively on the accuracy of their estimations, that is, payment increases with a decreasing range (no time pressure), or that payment would depend on both the accuracy of their estimations and the amount of time required, that is, payment increases with a decreasing range and amount of time required (time pressure). Again subjects were assigned to action- and state-oriented groups on the basis of their decision-related ACS scores (extreme group allocation, upper and lower 40%).

Figure 2 shows (a) the mean extent of information requested and (b) the amount of time required by action- and state-oriented subjects as a function of

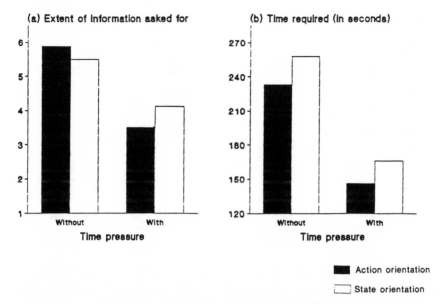

Figure 2. Extent of information asked for (a) and time required (b) for action- and state-oriented subjects as a function of time pressure (from Stiensmeier-Pelster et al., 1991).

time pressure. Decision making differed markedly as a function of time pressure. Given high time pressure, subjects asked for less information and required less time to arrive at their estimations. Furthermore, the data revealed the expected interaction effects between person and situation regarding information requested but no interaction regarding time required. These results confirmed both the results and conclusion of Study 1. Action- and state-oriented individuals adapted their decision-making behavior to time pressure in different ways. Whereas the action-oriented coped with time pressure particularly by decreasing the amount of information processed, the state-oriented responded particularly with an acceleration of information processing, that is, they processed the same amount of information at a faster rate.

There may be one counterargument to our conclusions. It can be argued that we only recorded which information package was chosen but not whether all the information it contained was actually used. Thus, one may argue that the state-oriented chose packages containing much information but only used some of it.

Study 3

To deal with the problem of acceleration and filtration and to analyze the decision-making process of action- and state-oriented individuals in more detail,

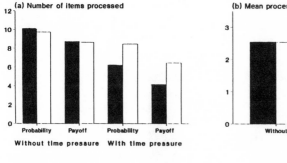
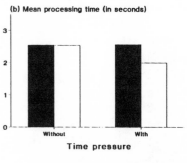

Figure 3. Number of probability and payoff items processed (a) and mean processing time (b) for action- and state-oriented subjects as a function of time pressure (from Schürmann & Stiensmeier-Pelster, 1991).

we conducted an experiment using a procedure adopted from Payne, Bettman, and Johnson (1988). A detailed description of this experiment is given by Schürmann and Stiensmeier-Pelster (1991).

Thirty-five subjects had to work on six sets of four risky options (gambles). Each gamble in a set offered a possible outcome (payoff ranging from 10 to 90 Pfennigs) and a probability for the outcome (p between .10 and .90). The probabilities did not sum to 1. The gambles in a set differed in that one gamble in two sets was particularly distinguished from all others by its high payoff, by its high probability, or by its high average expected value. The six sets of gambles were presented under two time conditions. One involved no time pressure at all, that is, subjects could take as much time as they wanted. The other condition involved a 20-second time constraint.

The experiment was run on an IBM-equivalent personal computer. A 2 (probability and payoff) by 4 (number of gambles) matrix was presented on the display with the available information hidden behind the boxes. Subjects had the choice of opening whichever box they wanted, and the box remained open until the subject made her/his choice. Subjects were told that they could play the six gambles they had chosen at the end of the experiment and that they would be allowed to retain the money won.

As can be seen from Figure 3a, time pressure caused a marked decrease in the extent to which information on the probabilities and the payoffs was processed. As expected, this decrease was more pronounced in the action- than in the state-oriented subjects. Furthermore, under both conditions, both groups processed more information on probabilities than on payoffs.

To analyze whether time pressure led to an acceleration of information processing, we calculated the time spent on each item of information. Therefore we divided the total time for the selection of each game by the number of items of information processed to select the game. As can be seen from Figure 3b, there were no time pressure differences in the action-oriented, but an acceleration of information processing in the state-oriented. In sum, the data of our third experiment showed once more that action-oriented individuals coped with time pressure by filtering the available information, whereas the state-oriented responded with an acceleration of information processing.

Concluding Remarks

Although they use markedly different procedures, the reported experiments show similar results. In each of the experiments, the action-oriented adapt to time pressure particularly by filtrating the available information. In contrast, the state-oriented especially accelerate their information processing. That is, when confronted with time pressure, they do the same thing, but faster. This pattern of results is completely in line with our theoretical considerations derived from Kuhl's theory of action control. According to this theory, action, compared to state orientation, promotes a more efficient employment of volitional (action-control) processes, such as active attentional selectivity, parsimony of information processing, and affect control. As discussed, filtration requires a more efficient implementation of these processes than acceleration.

Our results have important implications, and they raise some further questions. Regarding an economic investment of cognitive resources, filtration seems to be more advantageous than acceleration. Processing the same amount of information in a shorter time period requires an intensification of cognitive effort. Therefore acceleration makes decision making more straining than filtration, especially if one has to solve a great number of decision tasks. It also involves the risk of losing concentration and becoming inaccurate. Thus, due to their different adaptations to time pressure, the state-oriented should experience decision making as more of a strain than the action-oriented. Furthermore, state- compared to action-oriented run more of a risk of being inaccurate when preparing their decisions and thus producing suboptimal decisions.

According to Payne et al. (1988), people confronted with time pressure may first attempt to accelerate their processing. If acceleration is not sufficient, they may respond with filtration. In line with our results, it may be assumed that, when confronted with time pressure, both the action- and the state-oriented first try to accelerate information processing. However, if acceleration turns out to be insufficient, the action-oriented are able to change from acceleration to filtration, whereas the state-oriented persevere in their response, and they may attempt to increase acceleration. Unfortunately, our experiments did not vary the amount of time pressure, and so we could not test these assumptions.

Finally, past research on decision making has focused on the influence of task and context variables, whereas the decision maker him/herself has mostly been neglected. However, our experiments clearly demonstrated that decision-making behavior is contingent not only on task and/or context variables but also on personal characteristics, such as action versus state orientation. Furthermore, persons adapt differently to changes in task and/or context. Thus, we maintain that future research on decision making should consider individual differences more carefully.

ACKNOWLEDGMENT. Preparation of this chapter was supported by the Benningsen-Foerder-Preis to Joachim Stiensmeier-Pelster.

References

Beach, L. R., & Mitchell, T. R. (1978). A contingency model for the selection of decision strategies. *Academy of Management Review, 3,* 439–449.

Beckmann, J., & Kuhl, J. (1984). Altering information to gain action-control: Functional aspects of human information processing in decision-making. *Journal of Research in Personality, 18,* 224–237.

Ben Zur, H., & Breznitz, S. J. (1981). The effect of time pressure on risky choice behavior. *Acta Psychologica, 47,* 89–104.

Christensen-Szalanski, J. J. J. (1978). Problem solving strategies: A selection mechanism, some implications, and some data. *Organizational Behavior and Human Performance, 22,*307–323.

Christensen-Szalanski, J. J. J. (1980). A further examination of the selection of problem-solving strategies: The effects of deadlines and analytic aptitudes. *Organizational Behavior and Human Performance, 25,* 107–122.

Einhorn, H. J., & Hogarth, R. M. (1981). Behavioral decision theory: Processes of judgment and choice. *Annual Review of Psychology, 32,* 53–88.

Ford, J. K., Schmitt, N., Schechtman, S. L. Hults, B. M., & Doherty, M. L. (1989). Process tracing methods: Contributions, problems, and neglected research questions. *Organizational Behavior and Human Decision Processes, 43,* 75–117.

Kuhl, J. (1981). Motivational and functional helplessness: The moderating effect of state versus action orientation. *Journal of Personality and Social Psychology, 40,* 155–170.

Kuhl, J. (1982). The expectancy-value approach in the theory of social motivation: Elaborations, extensions, critique. In N. T. Feather (Ed.), *Expectations and actions: Expectancy-value models in psychology (pp. 125–162).* Hillsdale, NJ: Erlbaum, 1982.

Kuhl, J. (1984). Volitional aspects of achievement motivation and learned helplessness: Toward a comprehensive theory of action control. In B. A. Maher (Ed.), *Progress in experimental personality research* (Vol. 13. pp. 99–171). New York: Academic Press.

Kuhl, J. (1985). Volitional mediators of cognition-behavior consistency: Self-regulatory processes and action versus state orientation. In J. Kuhl & J. Beckmann (Eds.), *Action Control: From cognition to behavior (pp. 101–128).* Berlin: Springer.

Kuhl, J., & Beckmann, J. (1983). Handlungskontrolle und Umfang der Informationsverarbeitung: Wahl einer einfachen (nicht optimalen) Entscheidungsregel zugunsten rascher Handlungsbereitschaft. [Action control and quantity of information processing: Choice of a simple, nonoptimal decision rule facilitating a state of action.] *Zeitschrift für Sozialpsychologie, 14,* 241–250.

Kuhl, J., & Beckmann, J. (1993). *Volition and personality: Action- and state-oriented modes of control.* Göttingen: Hogrefe.

McAllister, D. W., Mitchell, T. R., & Beach, L. R. (1979). The contingency model for the selection of decision strategies: An empirical test of the effects of significance, accountability, and reversibility. *Organizational Behavior and Human Performance, 24,* 228–244.

Niederberger, U., Engemann, A., & Radtke, M. (1987). Umfang der Informationsverarbeitung bei Entscheidungen: Der Einfluß von Gedächtnisbelastung und Handlungsorientierung. [Amount of information processing in decision-making: The influence of memory strain and action orientation.] *Zeitschrift für experimentelle und angewandte Psychologie, 34,* 80–100.

Payne, J. W. (1982). Contingent decision behavior. *Psychological Bulletin, 92,* 382–402.

Payne, J. W., Bettman, J. R., & Johnson, E. J. (1988). Adaptive strategy selection in decision making. *Journal of Experimental Psychology: Learning, Memory, and Cognition, 14,* 534–552.

Schürmann, M., & Stiensmeier-Pelster, J. (1991). *Der Einfluß von Handlungs- und Lageorientierung auf den Entscheidungs- prozeß mit und ohne Zeitdruck* [The influence of action and state orientation in decision-making with and without time pressure]. Arbeiten aus der arbeitseinheit Allgemeine Psychologie II (No. 3). Bielefeld: Universität Bielefeld.

Stiensmeier, J., & Schnier, R. (1988). Auswhla und Verwirklichung von Absichten bei lage- und handlungsorientierten Senioren [Selection and implementation of intentions in state- and action-oriented elderly persons.] *Zeitschrift für Entwicklungspsychologie und Pädagogische Psychologie, 20,* 134–145.

Stiensmeier-Pelster, J. (1993). Choice of decision-making strategies and action versus state orientation. In J. Kuhl and & J. Beckmann (Eds.), *Volition and personality: Action- and state-oriented modes of control.* Göttingen: Hogrefe.

Stiensmeier-Pelster, J., John, M., Stulik., A., & Schürmann, M. (1989). Die Wahl von Entscheidungsstrategien: Der Einfluß von Handlungs- und Lageorientierung und die Bedeutung psychologischer Kosten. [The selection of decision-making strategies: The influence of action and state orientation and the significance of psychological costs.] *Zeitschrift für experimentelle und angewandte Psychologie, 36,* 292–310.

Stiensmeier-Pelster, J., & Schürmann, M. (1990). Performance deficits following failure: Integrating motivational and functional aspects of learned helplessness. *Anxiety Research, 2,* 211–222.

Stiensmeier-Pelster, J., & Schürmann, M. (1993). Antecedents and consequences of action versus state orientation: Theoretical and empirical remarks. In J. Kuhl & J. Beckmann (Eds.), *Volition and personality: Action- and state-oriented modes of control.* Göttingen: Hogrefe.

Stiensmeier-Pelster, J., Schürmann, M., John, M., & Stulik, A. (1991). Umfang der Informationsverarbeitung bei Entscheidungen: Der Einfluß von Handlungsorientierung bei unterschiedlich dringlichen und wichtigen Entscheidungen [Amount of information processing in decision-making: The influence of action and state orientation on decisions of varying time pressure and importance]. *Zeitschrift für experimentelle und angewandte Psychologie, 38,* 94–112.

Wright, P. (1974). The harassed decision maker: Time pressures, distractions, and the use of evidence. *Journal of Applied Psychology, 59,* 555–561.

17

Time Pressure and Information Integration in Social Judgment
The Effect of Need for Structure

Martin F. Kaplan, L. Tatiana Wanshula, and Mark P. Zanna

Introduction

Contributions to this volume report accumulated knowledge and theory with respect to the effects of time pressure on judgment. This chapter deals particularly with *social judgments,* that is, our judgments and evaluations of other people. We also introduce an individual difference variable in the study of time pressure, and embed the effects of pressure in a general framework of social judgment formation.

Time Pressure and Judgment

Conditions that constrict or interfere with information processing promote the use of simpler strategies in forming judgments (Christensen-Szalanski, 1980; Svenson & Edland, 1987). In addition to restricted time to consider and process

Martin F. Kaplan and L. Tatiana Wanshula • Department of Psychology, Northern Illinois University, De Kalb, Illinois 60115.   Mark P. Zanna • Department of Psychology, University of Waterloo, Waterloo, Ontario N2L 3G1, Canada.
Time Pressure and Stress in Human Judgment and Decision Making, edited by Ola Svenson and A. John Maule. Plenum Press, New York, 1993.

information, such conditions include distraction, task complexity, emotional arousal, and information overload (e.g., Bodenhausen, 1990). When such conditions exist, judges are less likely to consider individual details and their complex interrelations, and instead will use judgmental heuristics to simplify the cognitive task. Heuristics are necessary when a quick, less effortful response is necessary. A common heuristic is one's stereotype, which is useful if one does not have sufficient ability or time to engage in effortful thought (Bodenhausen, 1990).

It is clear that time pressure is one means of limiting effortful thought. If one does not have the time to think about individuating information and complex relationships, one must fall back on simpler, general knowledge. Svenson and Edland (1987) suggest that it is not lack of time alone that interferes with processing. Severe time stress acts as any other stressor to produce emotional arousal, which reduces the range of cue usage and leads to a focus on one stimulus element. Similarly, Bodenhausen and Kramer (1990) suggest that *any* emotional state produces distraction, which increases reliance on simpler strategies and stereotypes. Thus, in addition to not allowing time for complex, effortful thought, time pressure may produce distracting emotion.

In the remainder of this chapter, we address three questions. What are the effects of time pressure on social judgments, that is, judgments of other people? How may these effects be conceptualized as part of a general model of social judgment formation? And finally, are there individual differences in susceptibility to the simplifying effects of time pressure?

Time Pressure and Social Judgment

Though most did not directly manipulate time pressure, a series of studies by Tesser and his colleagues are instructive. In these studies, subjects were given information about several target persons, and asked to form judgments under either distracting or nondistracting conditions. Distraction was created by having subjects engage in competing tasks. Responses were more extreme when conditions were not distracting, that is, when they permitted thought (Tesser, 1976). In other words, judgments were more positive in response to positive stimulus information, and more negative in response to negative information given sufficient thought. The polarizing effect of thought, then, refers to the observation that judgments will be more extreme when subjects are able to give sufficient thought to polar information. As further examples, the polarizing effect of thought was more evident when four items of information were presented compared to eight (Tesser & Cowen, 1975), and when information about the target was ambiguous and internally inconsistent (Tesser & Cowen, 1977). These results were interpreted as showing that thought allows the addition of inferential information to smaller sets (thoughtful subjects had *relatively* more information than distracted subjects when given smaller sets than when given larger sets), and reinterpretation and resolution of differences in inconsistent sets. In the only study in which time was varied, a set-size polarization effect was found; when more time was allowed for judgment, more polarization was found with added information (Tesser & Conlee, 1975). That is, responses to sets of negative information were more negative, and responses to sets of positive information were more positive, given increases in amount of information in the respective valenced sets, and more so when more time was allowed. However, it is not clear why adding inferences, resolving inconsistencies, or even considering more given and implied information should lead to greater polarization. To relate the polarizing effect of thought in social judgments to the general literature on time pressure and use of heuristics, a judgmental model of the relationship between preexisting biases and information value is needed.

Information Integration Theory (Anderson, 1981) provides a general model of how judgments are formed from multiple sources of information. Each piece of information is assigned a subjective *scale value* reflecting its position on the judgment dimension. For example, information that a target is *crude* possesses a fairly negative value on the dimension "like very much . . . dislike very much," whereas the descriptor *honest* has a positive value. In integrating several such pieces of information into a unitary judgment of likableness, one combines the relevant scale values by means of an algebraic rule, most commonly averaging (Anderson, 1981). In this average, each value will have a *weight* as well, reflecting its subjective importance to that judgment. For example, information about a target's social characteristics may have more weight than information about her intellect for judgments of likableness (while the opposite may be true for judgments of respect).

Another component of this cognitive algebra is critical to our analysis. Along with the weighted values of the target information, judges also integrate a value corresponding to an initial impression, or preexisting disposition toward *all* targets (Kaplan, 1976). Judgments are based not only on the information we are given, but also on our dispositional biases toward the class of targets, for example, people in general. Some of us may be pessimistic in our disposition toward judging others and possess a negative initial impression. Consequently, a negative value is averaged with the scale values that correspond to the individual target information. Others may feel positively toward the human race, and accordingly average a positive value into the cognitive equation (see Kaplan, 1975, 1976, for a full discussion).

In an unselected group of judges, these individual differences in predisposing initial impressions tend to balance out, so that the mean initial impression can be expected to be fairly moderate or neutral with respect to likableness value (see Kaplan, 1976, for normative evidence). Thus, if target information is predominantly univalent (i.e., positive or negative), the initial impression will be more moderate in value than the target information. If more information of a non-neutral nature is given, or more weight is given to that information, the person's judgment will more closely approach the value of the information than the value of the initial impression. In other words, *if more nonneutral information is taken into account, judgments will become more polar because the initial impression is contributing less to judgment.* This result has been called the *set-size effect.* The effect of time pressure, then, is to reduce usage of target information in favor of the preexisting element—the initial impression. Where the latter is more moderate in value than target information, time pressure, which restricts processing of information should lead to more moderate (or less polarized) judgments, as indeed is suggested by the Tesser studies.

This analysis accords with the notion that time pressure shifts the focus from target information to preexisting stereotypes. We suggest that the more general case is that stereotypes may include a generalized impression of others that in many circumstances is more neutral than target information. To the degree that one is prevented from processing information, one will revert to the generalized impression and produce a more moderate judgment. Kaplan found in a series of studies (summarized in Kaplan, 1975, 1976) that the effect of initial impression increased if information was presented as unreliable or potentially invalid. To the extent that information unreliability/invalidity prevents its processing, these data support the conclusion that initial impressions are invoked more when processing is constrained.

Individual Differences in Reaction to Time Pressure

In an early indication that people may differ in their reaction to time pressure in forming social judgments, Sieber and Lanzetta (1966) found that people differ in the length of time taken to reach decisions. The time needed was a function of differences in encoding, associative processes, and cognitive differentiation. People who need more time to process information for social decisions should be more disadvantaged by pressure, and should therefore need to resort more to stereotypes and other heuristics. More recently, Bodenhausen (1990) reported that correspondence of time of day with judges' circadian rhythm affected the ability to process information. Judgments at nonoptimal times of the day reflected stereotypes more. Thus, cognitive and motivational characteristics can modify the extent to which time pressure affects stereotyping in social judgment.

The need for structure construct (Jamieson & Zanna, 1989; Kruglanski, 1980) is conceptually harmonious with current views of time pressure and judgment and is therefore a promising means of studying individual differences in time pressure effects. Need for structure is a motivation governing the process of knowledge acquisition. Specifically, it is a desire for clear, certain, and unambiguous knowledge (Kruglanski, 1980). It has been proposed that pressure, because task demands will now exceed cognitive capacity, activates the need for structure, which in turn produces a retreat to overlearned orientations, including prior stereotypes (Jamieson & Zanna, 1989). Stereotypes serve as heuristics in pressure situations, causing one to judge objects along lines that specify their basic desirability. Pressure, then, leads to evaluative simplicity and use of stereotypes as heuristics. For example, racial (Kruglanski & Freund, 1983) and gender (Bechtold, Naccarato, & Zanna, 1986) stereotypes about targets affect judgments more under time pressure. This reversion to heuristics is not limited to *time* as a source of pressure. When persons are given diverting tasks to increase their cognitive busyness, they are more likely to apply an activated racial stereotype to judgment (Gilbert & Hixon, 1991).

The need for structure construct invokes an internal motivation to account for the effects of time pressure. Posing this intervening internal state does not in itself appear to add to the explanatory power of previously mentioned cognitive interpretations that center on stress- or time-based restrictions in processing (e.g., Bodenhausen, 1990; Christensen-Szalanski, 1980; Svenson & Edland, 1987). However, invoking an intervening need state raises the possibility of individual differences in the need for structure, and consequently, in the tendency to retreat to overlearned orientations under pressure. That is, need for structure may be treated as both a situationally induced state (e.g., Kruglanski & Freund, 1983) and a dispositional trait, with the potential for individual differences (Jamieson & Zanna, 1989).

Thompson, Naccarato, and Parker (1989) devised the Need for Structure Scale to assess chronic tendencies that would be the dispositional parallel to acute or situational states of the need. Individuals high in the need for structure

> prefer structure and clarity in most situations, with ambiguity and "grey areas" proving troublesome and annoying. Characterized by decisiveness and confidence in their judgments, such people should experience discomfort if they perceive structure and clarity to be missing from situations (Thompson et al., 1989, pp. 5–6).

> High scorers on the scale endorse such items as: "It upsets me to go into a situation without knowing what I can expect from it," "I hate to be with people that are unpredictable," and "I like to have a place for everything and everything in its place." Low scorers endorse such items as: "I like being spontaneous," "I'm not bothered by things that upset my daily routine," and "I enjoy the exhilaration of being put in unpredictable situations."[1]

---

[1]Factor analysis of the final 12-item version of the scale yielded a one factor solution, with factor loadings between .54 and .70, accounting for 37.8% of the variance in the scores. Reliability analysis of the scale yielded a Cronbach alpha of .84, with item-total correlations ranging from .42 to .58.

Given the availability of the means of identifying differences in the need for structure, there are three possible ways in which such differences might interact with time pressure. First, dispositional need may exert a constant effect, so that persons high in need for structure (*HNS*) rely on stereotypes in judgment more than persons who are low in need for structure (*LNS*) whether under time pressure or not. Second, HNS judges may use stereotypes regardless of time pressure condition, whereas LNS judges may revert to stereotypes only when pressured. Third, need for structure may be a latent disposition, aroused only under pressure, so that HNS will revert to stereotypes more than LNS but only under time pressure. Systematically varying prior need for structure permits a test of the interactive effects of disposition and time pressure.

An Empirical Test of Individual Differences and Time Pressure

Overview and Predictions

Each subject judged the likableness of a number of target persons each described by a set of two, four, or six traits. Each set was composed of traits that were uniformly positive or negative, resulting in six types of targets, defined by number and valence of descriptive traits. Subjects preselected to be either high or low in need for structure made all their judgments either under time pressure or not.

Drawing upon prior research on time pressure and judgment, and on an information integration analysis, several predictions were made:

1. Under time pressure, judgments of nonneutral target information should be less extreme than without pressure. This is because pressured judges are less able to process the positive or negative information, and should thus rely more on their more neutral initial impressions.
2. With larger set-sizes, judgments should be more extreme, but this *set-size polarization effect* should be smaller under time pressure. Increasing the amount of univalent information offsets the neutral initial impression, producing increasingly extreme judgments. Under time pressure, however, there is less opportunity for considering and integrating added information, and therefore less countervalence to the initial impression.
3. Under time pressure, HNS should revert more to their preexisting initial impressions, and thus should be more moderate in their judgments and less sensitive to the set-size polarization effect than LNS. It was predicted that pressure activates chronic need for structure, so that only (or

primarily) under time pressure, HNS should make *greater* use of the initial impression (compared to LNS), and thereby be affected *less* by increasing amounts of information.

Subjects and Targets

Approximately 300 students enrolled in the introductory psychology course at Northern Illinois University were administered the Personal Need for Structure Scale (Thompson et al., 1989). Students voluntarily participate in experiments to earn extra credit in the course. Students whose scores fell into the upper or lower thirds of the scale range (-23 to $+41$) were respectively identified as high or low in need for structure, and were invited to participate further in the experiment. Thirty-two students of each type served in the experiment, 16 in each experimental condition (time pressure vs. no pressure controls). Subjects were equally divided among the sexes within each pressure by need-level condition.

The main task was to judge the likableness of 40 target persons, each described by two to six traits. Judgments were given on a scale ranging from "Dislike extremely" (1) to "Like extremely" (10). The trait sets were identical to those used in Kaplan (1972), and were constructed as follows. The first four sets (targets) were practice sets, each composed of two, three, four, or five moderately likable traits. Likability was determined by reference to norms reported in Anderson (1968). The experimental targets were described by 24 sets, half of which contained positive traits (mean normative likableness ratings across all traits $= 5.27$ on a scale of 0 to 6), and half of which contained negative traits (mean normative ratings $= .75$). Within each likableness level, there were four replications of set-size 2, four of set-size 4, and four of set-size 6, giving a total of 12 positively described and 12 negatively described targets. Twelve additional sets were filler targets, given so that subjects would not fall into a pattern of using the extreme points of the response scale. Half of the fillers were composed of moderately positive, and half of moderately negative traits, two sets each of sizes 2, 4, or 6. Responses to filler sets were not analyzed for purposes of testing the hypotheses.

Within normative levels of likableness, traits were chosen randomly from the normatively scaled pool of traits (Anderson, 1968), with replacement. Some traits were exchanged between sets so that (a) normative ratings were equated between all sets within likableness levels, that is, all sets of size 2, 4, or 6, and replications 1 through 4 had similar mean normative values; (b) redundancy within sets was minimized; and (c) four traits appeared at least once at each set-size so that trait content and set-size would not be confounded. The four positive traits were *kind, considerate, sincere, honest,* and the four negative traits were *insincere, malicious, thoughtless, narrowminded.*

Traits were randomly ordered within sets, and save for the practice sets, experimental and filler targets were randomly ordered for presentation, with the exception that one negative set of size 6 was always presented last in order to provide a common stimulus for a subsequent memory test.

Procedure

General instructions and the pressure/no-pressure manipulation were introduced to individually run subjects via a consent form as follows:

> Sometimes we have to form judgments of other people rapidly, that is, we are often forced to form "snap" judgments of others. In this experiment, we are trying to simulate the "real world" of impression formation by putting some people under time pressure. People serving in this experiment will be assigned to one of two groups. The Experimental Group will be given a very brief time to view the information about other people and will have to reach a quick decision about each person. The Control Group will be allowed to take all the time they need, that is, they will be able to think about their judgments without time pressure.

Instructions went on to tell the subject that he or she had been randomly assigned to the pressure or the control condition and reminded the subject of the requisite for that condition. Although the experimenter was aware of the subject's experimental condition, she was, of course, unaware of the subject's personality type.

Stimulus sets were presented sequentially via a slide projector, one set to a slide. Subjects controlled the duration of each slide's projection by advancing the slide. A blank slide was inserted between each set so that subjects could record their impression of the target after advancing past the target slide. Though all subjects were told to take enough time to read the trait descriptions and to reach a decision, *no-pressure controls* were regularly reminded to take all the time they needed to carefully consider the information, whereas *pressured subjects* were regularly told to hurry and to record their decision as soon as it was reached.

Pressuring subjects (or not) while allowing them to select their own presentation and decision times had the desired effect. Subjects in the pressure condition projected the slides for less time prior to response ($M = 1.76$ seconds) than controls ($M = 4.86$ seconds). Moreover, pressured subjects reported more pressure than controls in response to the question, "how much pressure did you feel in making a timely response to the items?" ($Ms = 6.88$ and 2.81, respectively, on a scale of 1 [absolutely no pressure] to 10 [extreme pressure]). Time and subjective pressure differences between treatment groups were consistent across positive and negative targets, and set-sizes 2, 4, and 6.

Results

Three predictions were made regarding the main variable of interest, the impression ratings of the targets. To test these, the mean impression ratings, collapsed across the four replications (see Table 1) were subjected to an analysis of variance for the between-subjects variables of Pressure (pressure vs. control) and Personal Need for Structure (high vs. low), and the within-subject variables of Target Traits (positive or negative) and Trait Set-Size (2, 4, or 6).

The first prediction was that judgments made under pressure would be more moderate than under no pressure. Table 1 confirms this prediction; under pressure, responses to positively described targets were less positive ($Ms = 8.09$ vs. 8.75 for pressure and control conditions, respectively), and responses to negative targets were less negative ($Ms = 2.24$ vs. 1.92). This observation is supported by the significant interaction between Pressure and Traits, $F(1,60) = 12.77, p < .01$.

The second prediction was that responses to larger set-sizes would be more extreme, but that this *set-size effect* would be attenuated by pressure. The set-size effect was confirmed by a significant interaction between Set-Size and Traits, $F(2,120) = 66.29, p < .01$, whereby positive sets were rated more positively, and negative sets more negatively, as Set-Size grew larger. Though the interaction between Set-Size, Traits, and Pressure was not significant, $F(2,120) = 2.32$, separate analyses of each pressure condition showed a stronger Set-Size by Traits

Table 1. Impression Ratings by Pressured and Nonpressured Subjects of Targets Described by Positive or Negative Traits

	Condition			
	Control		Pressure	
Set-size	*HNS*	*LNS*	*HNS*	*LNS*
Positive Traits				
2	8.52	8.25	7.67	8.11
4	8.61	8.52	7.39	8.28
6	9.33	9.25	7.88	9.20
Negative Traits				
2	2.17	2.36	2.45	2.44
4	1.92	1.95	2.28	2.31
6	1.47	1.66	2.14	1.83

Note. Ratings were made on the scale 1 ("Dislike extremely") to 10 ("Like extremely"). HNS refers to high-need-for-structure subjects; LNS refers to low-need-for-structure subjects. Each pressure condition by personal need cell contains 16 subjects.

interaction in the control condition, $F(2,60) = 52.17$, $p < .01$, than in the pressure condition, $F(2,60) = 21.28$, $p < .01$.

The third prediction concerned the effects of personal need for structure. Two patterns were expected in the data. First, persons with a high need for structure, compared to those with a low need, should judge targets more moderately under pressure but not in the control condition. Note in Table 1 that the two need groups did not differ when not under pressure (Columns 1 vs. 2), but that under pressure, HNS responses to positive trait sets were less positive, and to negative sets were less negative, than were LNS responses (Columns 3 vs. 4). The corresponding Pressure by Traits by Need interaction reflects this pattern, $F(1,60) = 5.36$, $p < .05$. Moreover, separate analyses for each pressure condition found a significant Traits by Need interaction under pressure, $F(1,30) = 8.08$, $p < .01$, but not in the control condition, $F(1,30) = .44$, ns.

The second expected pattern involving personal need was that the tendency for larger set-sizes to produce more extreme responses should be attenuated for HNS under pressure. Support for this expectation was reasonably strong, though not unequivocal. Although the set-size effect was greater for LNS (Traits by Set-Size by Need, $F(2,120) = 3.85$, $p < .05$), the expected four-way interaction with Pressure did not reach a conventional level of significance, $F(2,120) = 2.51$, $p < .10$. Nevertheless, in separate analyses for pressure conditions, HNS were less affected than LNS by set-size when under pressure (compare the difference between two and six positive traits (.21) and two and six negative traits (.31) for HNS in Column 3 against the corresponding differences in Column 4 for LNS (1.09 and .61, respectively), Traits by Set-Size by Need interaction for the pressure condition, $F(2,60) = 5.12$, $p < .01$), whereas the need groups did not differ in the extent of the set-size effect under no pressure (compare the difference between two and six positive traits (.81) and two and six negative traits (.70) for HNS in Column 1 against the corresponding differences in Column 2 for LNS (1.00 and .70, respectively), Traits by Set-Size by Need for the no-pressure condition, $F(2,60) = .52$, ns). The separate analyses support the expectation.

The only other effect reaching significance in the overall analysis was obvious; positive trait sets elicited more positive impressions than did negative sets, $F(1,60) = 2150.03$, $p < .01$.

In addition to the target impressions and the single rating of pressure, some subjects were also given a recall test. Immediately after the last impression was recorded, half the HNS and half the LNS subjects in the pressure condition were given a surprise recall test. They were asked to write as many traits as they could recall from the last slide (which consisted of six negative traits). To have a basis of comparison, 16 additional subjects were run (half of each sex) under the same conditions as the no-pressure controls. These were subjects who had scored in the middle range of the Personal Need for Structure Scale. With regard to both time taken to respond and target impression ratings, they did not differ significantly from the no-pressure controls, and thus they were comparable to the HNS and LNS no-pressure controls (which, as the reader will recall, did not differ).

The number of traits correctly recalled from the last-presented set (maximum = 6) did not significantly differ for pressured ($M = 1.88$) and nonpressured ($M = 2.63$) subjects, $F(2,29) = 2.07$, ns). And within the pressured group, HNS ($M = 2.00$) and LNS ($M = 1.75$) did not differ in traits correctly recalled, $F(1,14) = .31$, ns. Thus, neither pressure nor personal need for structure appeared to influence recall of information.

Conclusions

The data described here are consistent with the notion that time pressure leads judges to revert to existing stereotypes. It is not startling that this phenomenon is demonstrable in social as well as other judgments. It is useful, however, to embed the stereotype effect in a model of information integration in which judgment is an averaged function of the value of information and a preexisting neutral initial impression. By incorporating time pressure into the integration model, we can generate clear predictions regarding the response-moderating effect of pressure and can account for the fact that conditions that constrict information processing result in less extreme judgments by invoking the greater role of the initial impression in the cognitive equation. Note that unlike earlier studies of stereotype usage under pressure, we found pressure effects on the use of a *generalized* stereotype toward person judgment. It would be interesting to extend the methodology of our study to subject populations with *different* preexisting initial impressions, that is, judges with positive or negative generalized dispositions toward others (see Kaplan, 1975, 1976). It would be expected that differences in judgments between judges who have different dispositions would be enhanced as they resort more to their dispositions under pressure.

The second main point of the study is that there are individual differences in the extent to which stereotypes will be used as heuristics under time pressure. These differences correspond to the extent to which one has a need for certainty in ambiguous situations. This study strengthens the growing evidence that persons with a high need for structure revert to their biases when under pressure more than persons low in this need (Jamieson & Zanna, 1989). The presence of individual differences helps account for the single instance where time pressure made no difference in social judgments (Simpson & Ostrom, 1975). In their study, Simpson and Ostrom had unselected subjects write narrative paragraphs about target persons either as "snap" or "thoughtful" judgments. It may be that the presence of low need for structure subjects watered down the effect of pressure. Moreover, the task of writing a narrative may permit thought about the judgment, and thus may not produce the necessary constriction on processing, even under instructions to reach a snap decision.

The two main points should have general implications. The present analysis and results suggest that it would be interesting to determine the sorts of initial impressions or biases (or default options) that individuals bring to various decision-making contexts. For example, in the reward allocation context, persons are asked to partition rewards to two or more targets who have jointly engaged in a task. Information is usually provided about the needs and/or inputs (i.e., effort, work accomplished, contribution to the project) of the participants. In allocating rewards, one may consider the information regarding participants' relative merit, but may also incorporate an initial bias toward equal sharing based on the reasonable assumption of equal input in the absence of merit information (Kaplan & Yehl, 1984). According to our analysis, pressure (especially for HNS) ought to result in more equal allocations (that is, less use of the differential merit information).

The fact that neither personal need nor pressure conditions affected the amount of information correctly recalled suggests that the pressure effect was due to processing and integration, and not to encoding and recall of information. That is, pressured and nonpressured subjects appeared to *possess* the same amount of nonneutral information, but personal and situational factors determined the extent to which this information was *incorporated* into judgment. Because these data are preliminary, it will be important to test the distinction between acquisition and integration of information as loci of time pressure effects in this and other judgment domains.

References

Anderson, N. H. (1968). Likableness ratings of 555 personality trait words. *Journal of Personality and Social Psychology, 9,* 272–279.
Anderson, N. H. (1981). *Foundations of information integration theory.* New York: Academic Press.
Bechtold, A., Naccarato, M. E., & Zanna, M. P. (1986, June). *Need for structure and the prejudice-discrimination link.* Paper presented at the annual meeting of the Canadian Psychological Association, Toronto.
Bodenhausen, G. V. (1990). Stereotypes as judgmental heuristics: Evidence of circadian variations in discrimination. *Psychological Science, 1,* 319–322.
Bodenhausen, G. V., & Kramer, G. P. (1990, June). *Affective states trigger stereotypic judgments.* Paper presented at the annual meeting of the American Psychological Society, Washington DC.
Christensen-Szalanski, J. (1980). A further examination of the selection of problem solving strategies: The effects of deadlines and analytic aptitudes. *Organizational Behavior and Human Performance, 25,* 107–122.
Gilbert, D. T., & Hixon, J. G. (1991). The trouble of thinking: Activation and application of stereotypic beliefs. *Journal of Personality and Social Psychology, 60,* 509–517.

Jamieson, D. W., & Zanna, M. P. (1989). Need for structure in attitude formation and expression. In A. R. Pratkanis, S. J. Breckler, & A. G. Greenwald (Eds.), *Attitude structure and function* (pp. 383–406). Hillsdale, NJ: L. Erlbaum.

Kaplan, M. F. (1972). The modifying effect of stimulus information on the consistency of individual differences in impression formation. *Journal of Experimental Research in Personality, 5,* 213–219.

Kaplan, M. F. (1975). Information integration in social judgment: Interaction of judge and informational components. In M. F. Kaplan & S. Schwartz (Eds.), *Human judgment and decision processes* (pp. 139–171). New York: Academic Press.

Kaplan, M. F. (1976). Measurement and generality of response dispositions in person perception. *Journal of Personality, 44,* 179–194.

Kaplan, M. F., & Yehl, H. M. (1984, May). *Deservingness and equality in children's reward allocations: Developmental trends.* Paper presented at the annual meeting of the Midwestern Psychological Association, Chicago.

Kruglanski, A. W. (1980). Lay epistemologic process and contents: Another look at attribution theory. *Psychological Review, 87,* 70–87.

Kruglanski, A. W., & Freund, T. (1983). The freezing and unfreezing of lay-inference: Effects on impressional primacy, ethnic stereotyping, and numerical anchoring. *Journal of Experimental Social Psychology, 19,* 448–468.

Sieber, J. E., & Lanzetta, J. T. (1966). Some determinants of individual differences in predecision information-processing behavior. *Journal of Personality and Social Psychology, 4,* 561–571.

Simpson, D. D., & Ostrom, T. M. (1975). Effect of snap and thoughtful judgments on person impressions. *European Journal of Social Psychology, 5,* 197–208.

Svenson, O., & Edland, A. (1987). Change of preferences under time pressure: Choices and judgments. *Scandinavian Journal of Psychology, 28,* 322–330.

Tesser, A. (1976). Attitude polarization as a function of thought and reality constraints. *Journal of Research in Personality, 10,* 183–194.

Tesser, A, & Conlee, M. C. (1975). Some effects of time and thought on attitude polarization. *Journal of Personality and Social Psychology, 31,* 262–270.

Tesser, A., & Cowen, C. L. (1975). Thought and number of cognitions as determinants of attitude change. *Social Behavior and Personality, 3,* 165–173.

Tesser, A., & Cowen, C. L. (1977). Some attitudinal and cognitive consequences of thought. *Journal of Research in Personality, 11,* 216–226.

Thompson, M. M., Naccarato, M. E., & Parker, K. H. (1989, June). *Measuring cognitive needs: The development of the personal need for structure (PNS) and personal fear of invalidity (PFI) scales.* Paper presented at the annual meeting of the Canadian Psychological Association, Halifax.

V

Time Pressure and Stress in Applied Settings

In real life, the time pressure variable is not as well behaved as in the laboratory. Instead of varying independently, it is often coupled with other stressors, some of which can be internally generated and related to the mobilization of energetic resources to cope with a situation. This part is devoted to studies of time pressure in applied settings.

In the chapter by Wickens and coworkers and in Lusk's contribution, the approach chosen is to accept that time pressure often appears with other stressors affecting individuals interacting with or predicting dynamic systems, giving ecological validity at the cost of a loss of experimental control. In the middle chapter of this Part, Shanteau and Dino have studied more complex cognitive processes under stressors that can be associated with time pressure in applied settings.

Using a componential approach, Wickens and coworkers studied pilots flying a simulator under different time and other stress conditions. Specifically cognitive processes related to (a) spatial processing, (b) working memory processing, and (c) knowledge retrieval and processing were analyzed in detail. The results revealed interesting changes in, for example, spatial processing under different levels of stress.

Shanteau and Dino used a chamber with a group of people in which variables such as crowding, sleep loss, and temperature served as stressors. Using a wide variety of tasks, they found that subjects were able to cope relatively well with the cognitive tasks but that some more demanding problems caused problems under stress.

Finally, Lusk studied meteorologists, making complex forecasts under varying time pressure conditions mainly depending on weather situations. In a componential analysis, she used regression analyses to study the effect of different sources of variance, including, for example, outcome events and forecast bias. Generally speaking, the weather forecasters demonstrated high-quality coping behavior and maintained the efficiency in their work also under time pressure.

In conclusion, this section demonstrates problems of studying applied time pressure and stress situations, how these problems can be handled, and some of the fascinating and important findings that may result from such studies.

18

The Effects of Stress on Pilot Judgment in a MIDIS Simulator

Christopher D. Wickens, Alan Stokes, Barbara Barnett, and Fred Hyman

Introduction

Faulty pilot judgment has been identified as a contributing cause in a majority of aircraft accidents attributed to pilot error (Jensen, 1981; Diehl, 1991; Orasanu, 1993). Furthermore, given that such errors often occur in bad weather following instrument or system failure and in time-pressured circumstances, it is reasonable to assume that the resulting stress from these anxiety-provoking situations may exert an important degrading influence on the quality of decision making. Indeed, there is an ample abundance of anecdotal reports and post-hoc accident and failure analyses that attributes faulty decision making, in part, to the degrading influence of stress (e.g., Connolly, Blackwell, & Lester, 1987; Lubner & Lester, 1987; Simmel, Cerkovnik, & McCarthy, 1987; Simmel & Shelton, 1987).

Post-hoc analysis has an important role to play (for example, in National

We would like to dedicate this chapter to the memory of Dr. Fred Hyman, who tragically lost his battle with cancer in 1993. Fred's love of flying, love of research, and love of people are fondly remembered by all of us.

Christopher D. Wickens and Alan Stokes • Aviation Research Laboratory, University of Illinois at Urbana–Champaign, Willard Airport, Savoy, Illinois 61874.   **Barbara Barnett** • McDonnell-Douglas Aircraft Co., P.O. Box 516, St. Louis, Missouri 63166-0516.   **Fred Hyman** • National Transportation Safety Board, Washington, DC 20008.

Time Pressure and Stress in Human Judgment and Decision Making, edited by Ola Svenson and A. John Maule. Plenum Press, New York, 1993.

Transportation Safety Board accident investigation), but as a research method, this approach is less than fully satisfactory for two reasons. In the first place, post-hoc analyses are always subject to the 20–20 vision of hindsight, and risk loading the dice toward interpretations of events that reinforce, or at least are consistent with, preconceptions, assumptions, and expectations. Second, although post-hoc analysis can plausibly posit that stress affected the performance of a particular crewmember in a particular situation, this provides little basis for generalization and prediction.

Given these difficulties, experimental research structured within a coherent model of stress and decision making is a necessary complement to post-hoc analysis. Such a model should permit the formulation of experimental manipulations that would allow the performance effects of stress to be studied in a controlled environment. This approach is facilitated by the existence of a relatively rich database on the effects of stress on performance, stemming, in large part, from experiments carried out in the 1950s and 1960s (see Broadbent, 1971; Hamilton & Warburton, 1979; Hockey, 1984, 1986; for good reviews). On the other hand, most of these studies were designed to examine performance on relatively simple perceptual–motor and cognitive tasks, rather than on "realistic" decision-making tasks in a complex dynamic environment. Nevertheless, a considerable amount of useful predictive information may be derived from such studies. For example, stress has been shown to selectively influence different information-processing skills. Anxiety, for example, has been linked to a reduction in working memory capacity and selective attention (Hockey, 1986). To the extent that decision making can be analyzed into such skills or components, it should be possible to predict which type of operational decision tasks will be influenced most by stress.

Figure 1 presents a simplified information-processing model of decision making, derived from Wickens and Flach (1988) and Stokes, Barnett, and Wickens (1987). According to the model, multiple cues are selectively sampled to formulate a hypothesis or establish situation awareness in working memory. Then, after comparing risks, certain actions are selected on the basis of some decision criterion. The repertoire of both possible hypotheses and actions are stored in long-term memory. The important characteristics of the model from the standpoint of the current analysis are the specific effects attributable to stress that are also highlighted by Hockey's (1986) analysis. Three effects are identified:

1. *Cue sampling.* Many decision problems require the integration of information from a number of sources. Decision performance will be expected to suffer to the extent that the number of these sources is restricted by stress, and the more informative cues, rather than the irrelevant cues, are filtered.
2. *Working memory capacity.* The topmost box in Figure 1 contains the processing activities in decision making that depend upon the fragile,

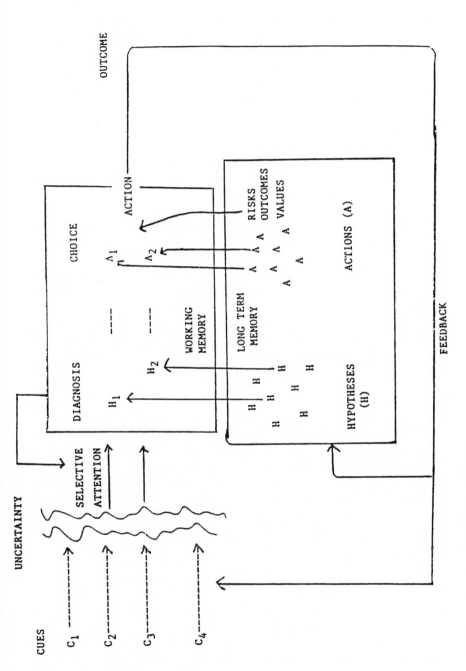

Figure 1. A model of stress and decision making.

resource-limited characteristics of working memory. These include such processes as considering hypotheses or evaluating and comparing the expected utilities of difficult choices of action. Also included are the spatial transformations and representations necessary to bring spatial awareness to bear on a decision problem (Baddeley, 1986). Stress variables that decrease the capacity of the working memory system will be expected to have degrading effects on decision-making performance.

3. The two stages in the model related to situation assessment and choice are both subject to a speed–accuracy tradeoff. For both processes, the quality of the output (i.e., the extent to which all information is considered and all alternatives are carefully weighed) will vary with the time available for the decision process.

The previous analysis suggests that the quality of decision making will inevitably degrade under the influence of a stressor that affects cue sampling or working memory. However, such a conclusion fails to consider that many aspects of decision making may depend less on these "fragile" attention and memory components, than upon direct retrieval of information from long-term memory represented in the box at the bottom of Figure 1 (Klein, 1989; Stokes et al., 1987). For example, the skilled pilot may immediately recognize a pattern of instrument readings as attributable to an underlying failure mode without going through a (time-consuming) logical reasoning process (Stone, Babcock, & Edmunds, 1985). Because the direct retrieval of familiar information from long-term memory may be relatively immune to the effects of stress (Stokes, Belger, & Zhand, 1990), it is conceivable that some aspects of decision making may not suffer stress effects.

Although the model of stress effects presented in Figure 1 appears to be intuitively plausible and can be justified on logical grounds, it remains to be validated. In particular, there appear to be no decision studies that have operationally manipulated stress in a way that corresponds directly to risk/anxiety. However, using time stress and task loading, four investigations of probabilistic decision making have supported the validity of the model. Wright (1974) examined the effects of time stress and the distracting effect of irrelevant noise (a radio program) on the integration of attributes in a car-purchasing decision. He found that both stressors reduced the optimality of information integration—cue sampling—in such a way that subjects gave more weighting to negative cues (what was wrong with a car) than on positive ones. Bronner (1982) manipulated time stress for subjects engaged in a business decision-making simulation and observed a general loss in the quality of performance.

Barnett and Wickens (1986) examined the influence of time stress and dual task loading on an information integration task involving an abstract aviation decision-making task. Subjects integrated probabilistic information from a number of cues regarding the advisability of continuing or aborting a flight mission (e.g., weather information, engine temperature). Cues varied in their diag-nosticity and in their physical location on the display. Barnett and Wickens found that time stress produced a slight tendency to focus processing on more salient (top left) display locations, replicating an effect reported in a more abstract paradigm by Wallsten and Barton (1982). Barnett and Wickens also found that workload "stress" caused by diverting cognitive resources to a concurrent task produced an overall loss in decision quality. The latter effect appeared to be related to the accuracy with which the mental integration of the cues was carried out. That is, diverting cognitive resources appeared to reveal a working-memory limitation similar to that associated with anxiety (Hockey, 1986).

Finally, on the basis of post-hoc incident analysis with large sample size, McKinney (1993) observed degraded diagnostic performance of non-routine mal-functions. Since these malfunctions occurred in actual flight, often with single-pilot aircraft, the joint effects of both time-pressure and stress can be assumed.

It should be noted that both tasks used by Wright and by Barnett and Wickens were "computationally intensive," and neither one required decision making in which an extensive knowledge base had to be consulted to yield direct retrieval of solutions from long-term memory (i.e., the putatively stress-resistant component at the bottom of Figure 1).

A study by Wickens, Stokes, Barnett, and Davis (1987)—which forms the basis of the study reported in this chapter—used a microcomputer-based simula-tion of pilot decision tasks known as MIDIS (Stokes, 1989; Stokes, Wickens, & Davis, 1986). Subjects viewed a computer display that contained an operating instrument panel and a text window. The text window was used to display a description of various decision "problems" as they unfolded in the course of a realistic flight scenario. Each problem was characterized by a set of *cognitive attributes* e.g., its demand for cue integration, working memory capacity, or the accurate utilization of risk information). Correspondingly, each of the 38 instrument-rated pilots (20 novices, 18 experts) who participated in the experi-ment were also characterized by a set of 11 cognitive attributes, assessed on a battery of standardized tests. These attributes are defined in Table 1.

The analysis of decision performance in this study resulted in a number of interesting conclusions. First, expert pilots did not make better decisions than novices, although experts were significantly more confident in their choices. Second, the cognitive variables that predicted performance for "dynamic" prob-lems (i.e., those requiring real-time integration of information off a changing instrument panel) were different from those that predicted performance for "stat-ic" problems (presented via text above a static panel). Third, the variables that predicted performance for experts were different from those that predicted perfor-mance for novices. In particular, although performance on dynamic problems was predicted for both groups by tests of working-memory capacity, substantial differences between the groups were found on static problems. Variance in the performance of novices was related to declarative knowledge. But most variance

**Table 1. Scenario Demands
of Cognitive Attributes**

 1. Flexibility of closure
 2. Simultaneous mental integrative processes
 3. Simultaneous visual integrative processes
 4. Sequential memory span
 5. Arithmetic load
 6. Logical reasoning
 7. Visualization of position
 8. Risk assessment and risk utilization
 9. Confirmation bias
10. Impulsivity–reflectivity
11. Declarative knowledge

in the performance of the experts was simply unrelated to any of the cognitive tests employed in the battery. These included tests of memory, attention, and cognitive ability as well as tests of declarative knowledge stored in long-term memory (i.e., facts about instrument flight assessed through FAA test questions). We concluded that expertise in pilot judgment may be more heavily related to *procedural knowledge* or to direct memory-retrieval processes (Klein, 1989) than to the computationally intensive processes tapped by our tests of logical reasoning, memory, and attentional capacity. If in fact this is the case, then in accordance with the decision model in Figure 1, it may well be that certain aspects of pilot judgment are indeed relatively immune to stress effects, particularly for the expert pilot.

The objective of the current experiment then was to validate the use of the model in predicting stress effects on pilot decision performance. A MIDIS flight, similar to the one employed in the previous study by Wickens et al. (1987) was used for this second study. The stress condition was defined according to a cognitive-appraisal model in which perception of task demand, cognitive resources, uncertainty, and the importance of succeeding were manipulated via the imposition of four variables simultaneously: (1) Financial risk imposed by ensuring that a steep loss in monetary reward ensued if flight time exceeded a time deadline and by penalizing suboptimal responding during the flight. (2) Increased workload imposed by requiring performance of a concurrent Sternberg memory search task. This workload was rendered difficult to shed by virtue of the financial penalty. (3) Distracting noise imposed as an irritating sequence of tones at a sound pressure of 74 to 77 dB spl at each incorrect Sternberg response. Uncertainty was also increased by the presentation of the tones at random intervals (ostensibly as a warning that overall performance was becoming marginal). (4) Time stress imposed by requiring the flight to be completed in one hour. This was a most stringent requirement, because the 1-hour criterion was derived from the mean time taken by unstressed subjects, that is, subjects whose performance was untrammeled by distractions, workload, and so forth.

Our purpose in combining the four manipulations in this way was to operate from the basis of a coherent and defensible model of operational stress (see, for example, Stokes, Barnett, & Wickens, 1987), and thus to permit important stress variables to act synergistically in influencing performance. It was not our purpose to attempt to assign variance in performance parameters to individual components of the stress condition—this would, of course be a different experiment. Rather, our focus was upon closely simulating the high-workload time-pressured cockpit in order to examine stress effects within the framework of our information-processing decision model. Having stated this, it should be borne in mind that all four stress manipulations are individually predicted to impose specific loads on the "fragile" components of the model. The competition between pilots, enhanced by the financial rewards and penalties, was expected to induce performance anxiety, and noise, albeit at higher sound pressures, has been found to mimic the performance effects of anxiety. Hence, these manipulations could be expected to work in concert to shift the speed–accuracy tradeoff and to reduce the breadth of cue sampling. Furthermore, these two should also combine with concurrent task loading to deplete working-memory capacity, and, importantly, with time stress to exaggerate the restriction of cue sampling. Hence, our prediction is that the four stress variables will operate in concert upon those decision problems that heavily demand these fragile computation-intensive processes. Equally important, we would expect them to leave relatively unaffected those problems that depend more on pattern matching through long-term memory retrieval.

Methods

Subjects

The subjects were 20 instrument-rated pilots with a mean level of 306 hours of total flight time and a range of 155 to 520. All subjects were recruited from the sample that had served in the previous MIDIS experiment (Wickens et al., 1987). Subjects were selected to fall in the midrange of flight experience of the original sample and were chosen with the constraint that each subject could be "paired" with another who had roughly equivalent flight hours and optimality score on the previous MIDIS flight. A subsequent examination also revealed that the two groups did not differ significantly from each other on the cognitive abilities, assessed prior to the previous experiment. In this way, a set of matched pairs was constructed, allowing greater comparability between the stress and nonstress group.

The MIDIS Task

MIDIS has a full, high-fidelity instrument panel based on a Beech Sport 180 aircraft, the type of aircraft used for training at the University of Illinois Institute of Aviation. This display, implemented via the HALO graphics package and 16 color enhanced Graphics adapter, represents a full IFR "blind flying" panel with operating attitude, navigational and engine instruments. The MIDIS software allows the readings on the instrument panel to change throughout the course of the "flight" in synchrony with the prevailing scenario. These changes may occur either discretely or continuously. MIDIS does not attempt to simulate the flight dynamics of an aircraft from control inputs. Rather it imposes judgment requirements by presenting a series of time slices or "scenarios" in the course of a coherent unfolding flight. At some decision points, the subject's choice of action can affect the nature of the flight, and therefore the content of future scenarios. Figure 2 presents a screen print of a typical MIDIS display.

A scenario can be defined by either the instrument panel together with a text description of particular circumstances or by the particular normal or abnormal configuration of the instrument panel alone. These two representations are know as *static* and *dynamic* scenarios, respectively. In the static scenarios, examples of which are shown in the Appendix, the instruments are stable—showing no rate of change. In the dynamic scenarios when there is no text, the instruments can show a rate of change. This allows us to study an important class of decisions, those involving the detection of changes and the integration of decision cues in real time. The dynamic scenario may represent a problem, or it may not. A problem scenario is one in which the circumstances have clear and present implications for the efficiency or safety of the flight, requiring diagnostic and corrective action to be taken. For example, it may involve a loss of oil pressure or a rate of climb that is too slow for the given power setting.

After viewing the static display describing the scenario, subjects press the return key to request the options. After viewing these, subjects select one option by a keypress and then select a second numerical keypress to indicate confidence on a scale ranging from 1 to 5. This response automatically steps the program forward to the next flight scenario (which may or may not be contingent upon the nature of the response option just selected). When a dynamic scenario is viewed, subjects are allowed to press a special key to indicate whether they believe that an abnormality has occurred. After the dynamic scenario is played out (usually 1–3 minutes), assuming that a failure actually had occurred, the list of possible options is presented, and the subject proceeds as in the static scenarios.

Altogether 38 scenarios were presented in the flight, 17 of which were dynamic. In addition to those dynamic scenarios that involved a problem, the flight consisted of a number of episodes of nonproblem flight, preserving some of the natural dynamic characteristics of normal flight.

INITIAL RADIO CONTACT WITH BOSTON CENTER

While climbing to 7000 feet, initial contact is made with Boston Center. They advise "radar contact, advise reaching 7000." As you climb through a broken layer you experience light turbulence. Once on top you see widely scattered cumulus with tops you estimate to be between 10000 and 15000.

Press YELLOW bar for options

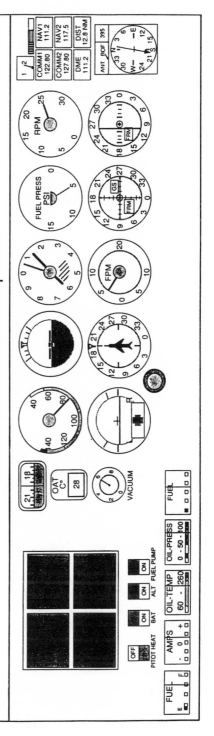

Figure 2. A representative MIDIS display panel.

Seven performance variables were monitored, most of them unobtrusively. Four of these relate to response selection: decision choice, optimality, decision time (latency), and decision confidence. Each subject's mean reading speed was unobtrusively calculated in syllables per second during the reading of the program-run instructions. Because scenarios and options were analyzed for word and syllable counts, as described above, individual differences in reading speed could then be factored out of the data.

Attribute and Option Coding

After creating each MIDIS scenario, the flight instructor on the design team proceeded to generate two kinds of codes, which were applied to, and characterized, the scenario in question. First, each option in a decision scenario was assigned an *optimality rating*, on a scale from 5–1, in which the correct (best) option was assigned a value of 5, and the less-optimal options were assigned values ranging from 1–4, depending upon how close they were to being plausible alternatives. Second, the correct option in each scenario was assigned an *attribute value code* for each of the 11 critical cognitive attributes listed in Table 1. These attributes were selected based upon our content analysis of the flight scenarios in MIDIS, guided by our expert analysis of pilot judgment. A value of zero indicated that the attribute was not relevant to the decision. Values from 1–3 indicated how critical it was for the subject to possess strength in the attribute in question, in order to choose the correct option. In this way, each scenario can be characterized by a profile of demand levels that allow prediction of how it should be affected by stress. The optimality ratings were cross-checked by a second pilot on the experimental design team, and any differences were resolved through discussion.

Concurrent Task/Stress Manipulations

The secondary task consisted of a Sternberg memory search task (Sternberg, 1975). Prior to the beginning of the MIDIS flight, subjects were presented with a four-letter memory set that they were to memorize. Subsequently during the flight, probe stimuli (single letters) would appear in the blank panel on the left side of the instrument panel as shown in Figure 2. These stimuli would occur at semirandom intervals from 2 to 7 seconds following a response, and subjects were instructed to indicate with a keypress response whether the letter was or was not a member of the memory set. Target members were presented on 50% of the trials. Letters were displayed in relatively large format (1.5 cm square). When subjects were seated a standard distance of $\frac{2}{3}$ meter from the display, the letters could be perceived in peripheral vision even when fixation was on the far corner of the display. Presentation of the noise, an annoying computer-generated warbling sound of 74–77 dB spl, was governed by two independent procedures: (1) There was contingent noise, which would only be presented if the subject failed to respond correctly to the Sternberg task within 4 seconds after stimulus presentation. This noise remained on for a duration of 12 seconds, unless the subject subsequently made a correct response. When a correct response was made, the noise terminated after a fixed duration of 2 seconds, and the next stimulus letter was presented. (2) Bursts of noise at random times of 15 seconds' duration that would appear independently of the subjects' action. Thus, by appropriately dealing with the secondary task, subjects could eliminate half of the distracting noise.

Procedure

Subjects participated for one session of approximately 1 $\frac{1}{2}$-hours' duration. Subjects were first reacquainted with the details of the MIDIS system (recall that subjects had served in a previous MIDIS experiment). They were then introduced to the specifics of the flight from Saranac, New York, to Boston's Logan Airport and were allowed up to half an hour for preflight planning, during which time they were given maps of the relevant airspace and meteorological information. Subjects in the stress condition were then given instructions regarding payoffs and concurrent task requirements. They were instructed that the consequences of ignoring the concurrent task would be twofold: (1) the initiation of distracting noise and (2) and depletion of a pool of financial resources—$8.00 that was reserved for them contingent upon completing the flight, while meeting the various performance criteria. The pool was depleted at a rate of 10 cents for every Sternberg task stimulus that was missed or responded to correctly after the deadline. In addition, this pool was depleted by $1.00 for every 5 minutes that the flight extended beyond 1 hour. This contingency was included in order to impose an overall level of time stress on the flight task. The 1-hour baseline estimate was derived on the basis of the mean performance of the nonstressed group, all of whose data had been collected prior to running subjects in the stressed condition.

All subjects in both groups were paid a base rate of $7.50 for the session. In addition, subjects in both groups were in competition for a first prize of $10.00 for the top scorer in the flight, and two second prizes of $5.00. Scores were based upon a combination of optimality and latency, and the competition was implemented in order to insure a high motivation to meet the criteria of safety and efficiency.

Results

The data were analyzed from two perspectives with increasing levels of specificity regarding the effects of the stress manipulations. The first analysis was intended to determine if the manipulations had any overall effect on performance; the second analysis assessed the specific pattern of those effects on problems that differ in the types of demands. In the analyses, each subject was paired with his or her "matched" associate on the basis of experience and prior MIDIS score.

At the first level of analysis, there was a clear reduction in performance for the stressed group. This reduction was evident in decision optimality [$F(1,9) = 6.41; p = 0.032$] and in the lower level of confidence [$F(1,9) = 5.18; p = 0.05$] but not in terms of an increase in decision latency ($F < 1$). The absence of an effect on latency was anticipated because a major component of the stress manipulation *was* indeed the imposition of time pressure—the incentive to respond more rapidly.

To accomplish the second level of analysis detailing the more specific effects of our manipulations, it was necessary first to define subsets of problems that were rated high, medium, or low on three different cognitive attributes. The factor analysis of cognitive abilities from the earlier MIDIS study (Wickens et al., 1987) had revealed three important attribute clusters, which were related to spatial demands, working-memory demands, and knowledge demands. To assess spatial demands, the coded value of attributes related to flexibility of closure and visualization of position (see Table 1) were summed for each scenario, and the scenarios were then assigned to one of three categories of spatial demand. This categorization scheme assigned roughly 13 scenarios each to the low-, medium-, and high-spatial-demand categories. A similar procedure was employed to categorize problems into three levels of working-memory demand, and three levels of dependency on long-term memory. In the former case, coded values were summed across the attributes of simultaneous mental integrative processes, sequential memory span, and logical reasoning, all of which impose intense demands on working memory. The resulting scheme assigned approximately equal numbers of scenarios to the low-, medium-, and high-memory-demand conditions. To categorize problems on the basis of stored knowledge, the coded values were summed across the two attributes of declarative knowledge and risk utilization. Here 3, 18, and 17 problems belonged to the low, medium, and high categories respectively. (The small number of problems in the "low" category reflects the fact that most decision scenarios that were created required a substantial degree of declarative knowledge in this context-specific domain.) Examples of the static decision problems that were coded low and high, respectively, on each of the three "macroattributes" are shown in the Appendix.

Figures 3a, 3b, and 3c present the mean optimality scores across the three

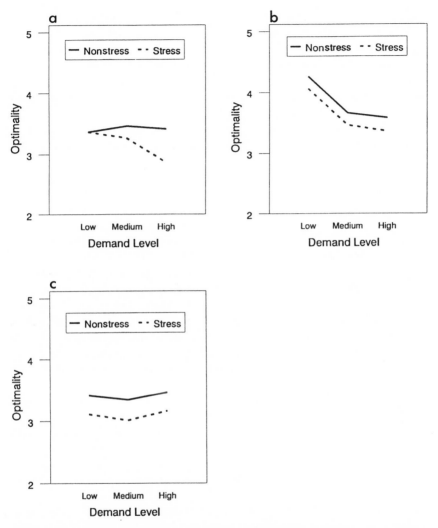

Figure 3. Effect of three kinds of demand level on decision optimality for subjects in stressed (dashed line) and control (solid line) group. (a) Spatial demand. (b) Knowledge demand. (c) Working memory demand.

demand levels, when these levels were coded by spatial demand, knowledge demand, and memory demand, respectively. The two curves in each figure represent ratings of the control (solid line) and stressed (dashed line) groups. Examining first the spatial-demand analysis, three features are evident. First as shown also in the overall analysis, the stressed group shows a reduced level of optimality. Second, there was a main effect for spatial demand on optimality (F = 9.78; p = 0.002). Problems coded higher on the spatial demand attributes generally yielded less optimal decision choices. Third, this effect seems to be primarily confined to the stress group, and the interaction between these two variables approached statistical significance [$F(2,18)$ = 2.99; p = 0.075]. (When the analysis is repeated with only the two extreme levels, this interaction is significant; $F(1,9)$ = 5.64; p = 0.042—in spite of the reduced number of degrees of freedom.) Therefore, the data in Figure 3a suggest that problems with high spatial demand are particularly sensitive to the degrading influence of our experimental stress manipulations.

The data in Figure 3b also show a clear dependence of problem optimality on problem demand. Those scenarios that called for greater utilization of declarative knowledge and risk assessment yielded significantly less optimal choices [$F(2,18)$ = 24.4; p < 0.001]. However, this effect is identical for the two groups, thereby suggesting that the influence of increasing knowledge demand is immune to the effects of stress (F interaction < 1). Here again one of the proposed hypotheses is supported: Problems that are more dependent upon direct retrieval of stored knowledge information are not more affected by stress.

The data in Figure 3c depicting optimality as a function of verbal working-memory demand, present a less intepretable pattern. There is once again a main effect of stress (this is the same as that viewed in Figure 3a because the total set of problems is identical). However, beyond this, there are no significant effects. Problems coded high on working-memory demand are no more sensitive to the degrading effects of stress than the problems that are coded low.

As noted above, confidence ratings were lower for the stressed group than for the nonstressed group. However, across the problems coded by working-memory demand and spatial demand, the effect of problem demand on conficence, although significant, was nonmonotonic.[1] Only for problems categorized by knowledge demand was the effect of demand significant and montonically related to demand level. Ironically the effect of knowledge demand was *reversed* from the effect on optimality. Problems that required higher knowledge (which had received less optimal responses) were responded to with *greater* confidence than the problems that required less knowledge demand.

As noted above, latency was not affected by stress manipulation, nor did this manipulation interact with problem demand for any of the three coding schemes. Latency was affected in a nonmonotonic fashion by spatial demand

---

[1]The finding of a nonmonotonic relation of performance across the demand level of one attribute is not surprising. This is because our scenario development did not insure that equal levels of all other attributes were preserved across all three levels of a given attribute. There was, in short, the potential for correlation between attribute coding across scenarios. Hence, it is always possible, for example, that the middle level of demand on Attribute A may contain a substantial number of problems that were coded high on Attribute B.

[$F(2,18) = 16.8$; $p < 0.001$] and was *reduced* for problems with increasing knowledge demand [$F(2,18) = 7.60$; $p < 0.01$], a trend that is consistent with that observed for confidence.

The previous analyses have considered both static and dynamic scenarios together. The differential effect of the stress manipulations was also examined for static and dynamic scenarios separately. This analysis revealed that the effects of the stress manipulations on optimality were primarily confined to the dynamic scenarios. During the static (text-based) scenarios, stress did produce a loss in decision confidence but brought about no significant reduction in decision optimality.

Concurrent task performance of the stress group was also analyzed and revealed a mean response latency of 2.9 seconds. Although single Sternberg task performance was not measured in the current study, the value of 2.9 seconds is well above the value that would be expected from single task performance in other laboratory studies (around 500 msec). Subjects were also generally quite accurate in performing the secondary task, with a mean error rate of 6.6%. This is consistent with our objective of ensuring that subjects would have to attend to the workload-increasing task, rather than merely dropping it to the focus all resources upon decision making.

Discussion

In our experimental examination of the influence of stress on pilot judgment, it was first important to demonstrate that the manipulations had indeed imposed a cost on decision-making quality. The performance data in Figure 3 suggest that such an effect was in fact obtained. This result in itself is significant and important, for in spite of the many anecdotal reports of stress effects on pilot judgment, there are very few experiments in the literature that have actually manipulated stress and systematically induced a performance decrement on domain-specific decision behavior. Subsequent to the research reported here, a second study using MIDIS also revealed a corresponding stress-induced decrement on MIDIS performance (Stokes, Belger, & Zhang, 1990). Here also, effects were primarily observed with dynamic scenarios. It is, then, an important initial finding (and a sine qua non for our subsequent analyses) that performance on a realistically complex operational decision task can be significantly degraded by our laboratory-based stress simulation. Given this result, it is appropriate to go on to review the qualitative manner in which performance was affected by stress: degraded for problems with high spatial demands but not for those with high demands on verbal working memory or long-term memory.

Two cognitive attributes, rated by our flight instructor, were employed in conjunction to define problems of high spatial demand. These were flexibility of closure and visualization of position. Flexibility of closure defines the ability to locate visual information in a complex perceptual field. Visualization of position defines the spatial awareness necessary to locate one's aircraft in space, relative to ground landmarks, weather patterns, and other traffic, and to mentally translate and rotate the aircraft representation as needed. Both of these abilities clearly demand some degree of spatial working memory (Baddeley, 1986; Logie, 1989; Wickens & Weingartner, 1985), and the working-memory system is predicted to be susceptible to stress manipulations like those used in the present study. Indeed, Stokes et al. (1990) confirmed the vulnerability of performance measures on component tests of spatial abilities, and the results in Figure 3 showed that decision performance did degrade to the extent that problems were coded high on this attribute of spatial demand.

Whether one or more of the four experimental manipulations contributed disproportionately to the degrading effect (and whether it would do so out of the context of the other manipulations) cannot of course be determined from the current data because we purposely manipulated all four together. One possibility is that the total effect was due simply to the visual scan time imposed by the concurrent task stimulus. In this case, the effect could not really be labeled one of stress at all, but simply one resulting from the delay in attaining the necessary information. We have some reason, however, to doubt that this was the sole source (or even the primary source) of the effect. Our argument is based on the fact that the time required to encode the single-letter stimuli, whether processed in foveal or peripheral vision can be estimated to be in the order of one-fourth second. With Sternberg task stimuli arriving at a frequency of roughly 1 every 7 seconds, this would indicate that only one-twenty-eighth of the total time was required for visual attention to be directed away from the MIDIS display; this was not really enough to produce the magnitude of performance decrement observed here. Hence, it is presumed more likely that the effects were the result of degraded perceptual/cognitive processes, and not simply receptor-level effects.

The present data also indicate that our manipulations did not simply produce equivalent effects across all decision problems, as revealed by the *absence* of stress effects when the spatial load was small (Figure 3a). Correspondingly a conclusion that *any* manipulation of problem demand might enhance the degrading influence of stress is countered by the analysis of problems categorized by the second macroattribute—knowledge demand. Here we had combined two cognitive attributes—declarative knowledge and risk utilization—that were suggested in our previous study (Wickens et al., 1987) to cluster together both in terms of cognitive abilities and in the prediction of decision performance. Problems with high demand for this direct retrieval of information from long-term memory, although performed less optimally, were no more disrupted by the stress manipulation than problems without such demand. Within the framework of the model, this direct retrieval process is not one that engages heavy reliance on the "fragile" information-processing components of attention and working memory and hence was not predicted to suffer a degrading effect of this sort. Here also, the study by Stokes et al. (1990) was supportive by indicating that answering FAA questions of declarative knowledge was not affected by the same stress manipulations used here. The study by Stokes et al. (1990) was also consistent in another way with the current results. They observed that for dynamic scenarios, the decision performance of expert pilots (who might be more expected to use direct memory retrieval) was not affected by stress manipulation, whereas the performance of novices (expected to rely more on spatial working memory) was significantly affected.

A second interesting characteristic that emerged from our analysis of the coding of problems by knowledge demand concerned the tradeoff between decision optimality, on the one hand, and latency and confidence, on the other. As problems required greater dependence upon declarative knowledge, the decisions were less optimal but were made more rapidly with greater confidence. This tradeoff illustrates a phenomenon that Fischoff (1977) and Fischoff and Mac-Gregor (1981) have examined in other domains of decision making and forecasting, and labeled *cognitive conceit*. It describes the tendency of people to become overconfident regarding the extent of their own knowledge of the world. The current data indicate that this tendency is manifest in our pilot subjects as well.

The influences of working memory were less well predicted than those of memory retrieval and spatial demand. Problems of greater coded demand on working memory were not responded to less optimally, nor were those problems more influenced by the stress manipulation.There are three possible interpretations to these negative results. These are offered, given the premise that working-memory capacity *is* resource limited and therefore *should* be sensitive both to the diversion of resources allocated to the concurrent task and to the anxiety-producing stress effects that were shown to have robust effects on other aspects of processing (Hockey, 1986). This sensitivity was demonstrated on working memory tests by Stokes et al. (1990).

The first possibility is that the decision model, captured in Figure 1, is incorrect and that most decision problems do not involve the "workbench" of working memory. Although this possibility is acknowledged, it contradicts both an intuitive analysis of decision making, as well as previous work that has found effects of secondary task loading on computational-intensive decision performance (Barnett & Wickens, 1986). Thus, a second possibility is that our coding of working-memory demands may have been inaccurate. This would explain jointly the lack of effect of problem demand on optimality and absence of interaction of memory demand with stress level. The potential for such inaccuracy exists because only one set of independent attribute codings was used— those assigned by a single flight instructor. Yet a third possibility relates to the lack of independence of attribute levels across problems. That is, low, medium, and high levels of one attribute were not equally represented across the three levels of other attributes. Thus, it is possible that performance on those problems that were coded low on working-memory demands was dominated by particularly high problem demands on a different resource-sensitive attribute. This possibility is the subject of future analysis.

In conclusion, the results of the current analysis have shown a substantial degree of internal consistency between three sets of variable: model predictions, difficulty demand, and stress effects. Where the model predicts stress effects and performance indicates that a demand effect was obtained (spatial demand), a stress effect was found. Where the model predicts no stress effect (increasing knowledge demand), none was found, in spite of the observed effect of demand. Finally, when no difficulty effect was observed (working-memory demand), then no stress effect was found. The only surprise here is why no effect of working-memory demand was found in the first place.

The results highlight the emerging distinction between what Klein (1989) has referred to as *recognition-primed decisions* (direct long-term memory retrieval) and the more algorithmic form of decision making that is conventionally studied in the laboratory. To the extent that distinct and different stress effects are found between these two types, as suggested by the data reported here, then care must be taken in overgeneralizing conclusions regarding the influence of stress on decision making.

ACKNOWLEDGMENT. This research was supported by a subcontract DOE EGG C87-101376-2 by the Idaho National Electronics Laboratory. Source funding for the work was provided by the Air Force Aeromedical Research Laboratory Human Engineering Division at Wright Patterson AFB, Ohio. Gary Reid was the technical monitor. The authors wish to acknowledge the contributions of Tom Davis for developing the MIDIS concept and Rob Rosenblum and Tak Ming Lo for the software development.

Appendix

Examples of Low- and High-Attribute-Coded Problems

1. Low Spatial
   After performing a preflight, including your weather briefing, and avionics checks you check the weight and balance. Using the weights provided during your preflight, you determine that the aircraft is 28 lb over maximum allowable gross takeoff weight and within CG limits. You proceed as follows.

(a) You are not concerned about the 28 lb as you will burn this off before takeoff.

(b) You are not concerned, as the weights of passengers and baggage are not that accurate to begin with.

(c) You know the density altitude is high today and you will drain an additional 5 gallons of fuel.

2. High Spatial

You are climbing and are in an out of altocumulus clouds; you are looking for the traffic but have negative contact with the advised traffic. You are aware that you will need to level off while entering the hold and maintain hold air speed. ATC advises VFR traffic 11 o'clock 2 miles westbound intersecting course, altitude fluctuating, indicating 9,000 at present unverified.

(a) You acknowledge the advisory with "negative contact" and continue climbing and looking for traffic. You recognize that your wind correction the traffic is more like your 10 o'clock position.

(b) You acknowledge the advisory with "negative contact" and request vectors around the traffic.

(c) You commence an immediate right turn using a bank of about 45 degrees and advise ATC of your turn that you would like to continue in a "360" until traffic is no longer a factor.

(d) You commence an immediate left turn using a bank of about 45 degrees and advise ATC of your turn and that you would like to continue in a "360" until traffic is no longer a factor.

3. Low Memory

While climbing to 7,000 feet, initial contact is made with Boston Center. They advise "radar contact, advise reaching 7000." As you climb through a broken layer you experience light turbulence. One on top you see widely scattered cumulus with tops you estimate to be between 10000 and 15000.

(a) Your mode C is probably not working; you will confirm this with Boston Center.

(b) Convective activity is unlikely to present a problem as you should be able to circumnavigate this activity.

(c) Mode C is probably "OK"; ATC simply needs to verify their readout.

(d) Convective activity is probably going to present a major problem on this flight.

4. High Memory

As you approach GRISY intersection, you wish to retune your navigation radios to identify GRISY. You make the following changes.

(a) You set the #1 nav to 115.1 (CTR) with the OBS set to 016 and the DME to 110.6 (GDM).

(b) Tune the #1 nav to 110.6 (GDM) with OBS set to 118, the DME to 110.6 (GDM), and leave the #2 nav on 117.8 (ALB).

    (c) Tune the #1 nave to 110.6 (GDM) with the OBS set to 118, #2 nav to 115.1 (CTR) with the OBS set to 016, and the DME set to 110.6 (GDM).
5. Low Knowledge

You are just about to your clearance limit and are about to call Boston Center when they call you. "Sundowner 9365S hold northwest of Keene on the 339 radial maintain 7,000, expect further clearance, as requested, at 1815Z, time now is 1754Z.

    (a) You need to slow the airplane up, and you should have called ATC sooner.

    (b) ATC expects that you will intercept the 339 radial prior to the fix and have reduced your air speed to 80 knots.

    (c) You are required to read back the clearance report when you are established in the hold. ATC should have given you the hold on the 350 radial.

    (d) You will slow the aircraft up and make a direct entry to the holding pattern. You should have contacted ATC sooner.

6. High Knowledge

Boston Center informs you to maintain your original course and that they will have a turn for you in approximately 5 minutes. The turbulence has not abated. You ask if there is conflicting traffic at your altitude and are informed that ATC needs the time to process a new route for you.

    (a) You inform ATC that you are proceeding from your present position direct to Cambridge VOR and request clearance from Cambridge via 169 radial to GRAVE, V2 GDM, V431 BOS as you understand that course is south of the convective activity.

    (b) You request of ATC to remain out of the area of cumulus buildups, informing them that you either need to proceed south or west to insure this. You also request clearance to Cambridge, Cambridge 169 radial to GRAVE, V2 GDM, V431 BOS.

    (c) You WILCO ATC's instructions and request a clearance from your present position direct to Cambridge VOR and request clearance from Cambridge via 169 radial to GRAVE, V2 GDM, V431 BOS as you understand that course is south of the convective activity.

References

Baddeley, A. (1986). *Working memory*. Oxford: Claredon Press.

Barnett, B., & Wickens, C. D. (1986). *Non-optimality in the diagnosis of dynamic system states* (Technical Report CPL-86-8). Champaign, IL: University of Illinois, Cognitive Psychophysiology Laboratory, Department of Psychology.

Broadbent, D. (1971). *Decision and stress*. New York: Academic Press.

Bronner, R. (1982). *Decision making under time pressure*. Lexington, MA: D.C. Heath.

Connolly, T. J., Blackwell, B. B., & Lester, L. F. (1987). A simulator-based approach to training in aeronautical decision making. *Proceedings of the Fourth International Symposium on Aviation Psychology.*

Diehl, A. (1991). The effectiveness of training programs for preventing aircrew "error." In R. Jensen (Ed.), *Proceedings Sixth International Symposium on Aviation Psychology* (pp. 97–106). Columbus: Ohio State University.

Fischoff, B. (1977). Perceived informativeness of facts. *Journal of Experimental Psychology: Human Perception and Performance, 3,* 349–358.

Fischoff, B., & MacGregor, D. (1981). *Subjective confidence in forecasts* (Technical Report PTR-1092-81-12). Woodland Hills, CA: Perceptronics.

Hamilton, P., & Warburton, D. (Eds). (1979). *Human stress and cognition,* Chichester: John Wiley & Sons.

Hockey, G. J. R. (1984). Varieties of attentional state: The effect of environment. In R. S. Parasuraman & D. R. Davies (Eds.), *Varieties of attention* (pp. 449–484) Orlando: Academic Press.

Hockey, G. J. R. (1986). Changes in operator efficiency. In K. Boff, L. Kaufman, & J. Thomas (Eds.), *Handbook of perception and performance* (Vol. II pp. 44-1–44-49). New York: John Wiley & Sons.

Jensen, R. J. (1981). Prediction and quickening in prospective flight displays for curved landing and approaches. *Human Factors, 23,* 333–364.

Klein, G. A. (1989). Recognition-primed decisions. In W. Rouse (Ed.), *Advances in man-machine systems research, 5,* 47–92. Greenwich, CT: JAI Press, Inc.

Logie, R. M. (1989). Characteristics of visual short-term memory. *European Journal of Cognitive Psychology, 1,* 275–284.

Lubner, M. E., & Lester, L. F. (1987). A program to identify and treat "pilot error," particularly, poor pilot judgment. *Proceedings of the Fourth International Symposium on Aviation Psychology.*

McKinney, E., Jr. (1993). Flight leads and crisis decision-making. *Aviation, Space, & Environmental Medicine, 64*(5), 359–362.

Orasanu, J. M. (1993). Decision making in the cockpit. In R. Helmreich, B. Kankie, & E. Wiener (Eds.) *Cockpit Resource Management* (pp. 137–172). Orlando, Fl: Academic Press.

Simmel, E. C., & Shelton, R. (1987). The assessment of nonroutine situations by pilots: A two-part process. *Aviation, Space, and Environmental Medicine,* 1119–1121.

Simmel, E. C., Cerkovnik, M., & McGarthy, J. E. (1987). Sources of stress affecting pilot judgment. *Proceedings of the Fourth International Symposium on Aviation Psychology.*

Sternberg, S. (1975). Memory scanning: New findings and current controversies. *Quarterly Journal of Experimental Psychology, 27,* 1–32.

Stokes, A. F. (1989). MIDIS—A microcomputer Flight Decision Simulator for Research and Training. *Proceedings of the Western European Association of Aviation Psychology XVIII Annual Conference.* University of Sussex, Brighton, UK (September).

Stokes, A. F., Wickens, C. D., & Davis, T. (1986). *MIDIS—A Microcomputer-based Flight Decision Training System.* Association for the Development of Computer-based Instructional Systems (ADCIS), 28th International Conference, Crystal City, Arlington, VA, November 10–13. (Abstract in *Proceedings,* p. 380).

Stokes, A. F., Barnett, B. J., & Wickens, C. D. (1987). Modeling stress and bias in pilot decision-making. *Proceedings of 20th Annual Conference of the Human Factors Association of Canada* (pp. 45–48). Montreal, Canada.

Stokes, A., Belger, A., & Zhang, K. (1990). *Investigation of factors comprising a model of pilot decision making: Part II. Anxiety and cognitive strategies in expert and novice aviators* (Technical Report ARL-90-8/SCEEE-90-2). Savoy, IL: University of Illinois, Aviation Research Laboratory, Institute of Aviation.

Stone, R. B., Babcock, G. L., & Edmunds, W. W. (1985). Pilot judgment: An operational view-point. *Aviation, Space, and Environmental Medicine, 56,* 149–152.

Wallsten, T. S., & Barton, C. (1982). Processing probabilistic multidimensional information for decision. *Journal of Experimental Psychology: Learning, Memory, and Cognition, 8*(5), 361–383.

Wickens, C. D., & Flach, J. (1988). Human information processing. In E. Wiener & D. Nagel (Eds.), *Human factors in aviation* (pp. 111–155). New York: Academic Press.

Wickens, C. D., Stokes, A., Barnett, B., & Davis, T., Jr. (1987). *Componential analysis of pilot decision making* (Final Technical Report ARL-87-4/SCEEE-87-1). Savoy, IL: University of Illinois, Aviation Research Laboratory, Institute of Aviation.

Wickens, C. D., & Weingartner, A. (1985). Process control monitoring: the effects of spatial and verbal ability and current task demand. In R. Eberts & C. Eberts (Eds.), *Trends in ergonomics and human factors* (pp. 25–42). North Holland Pub. Co.

Wright, P. (1974). The harassed decision maker: Time pressures, distractions and the use of evidence. *Journal of Applied Psychology, 59,* 555–561.

19

Environmental Stressor Effects on Creativity and Decision Making

James Shanteau and Geri Anne Dino

Introduction

Higher thinking processes require a variety of cognitive processing abilities, such as problem solving, creativity, memory, and decision making (Hogarth, 1987). Both psychological theory and common sense maintain that thinking ability may be impaired under highly stressful conditions. For instance, it has been hypothesized that individuals under stress will exhibit a narrowing of focus and stereotyped responding (Mandler, 1979, 1984). Such shifts would be incompatible with the cognitive processes necessary for effective high-level thinking (Halpern, 1989).

Early research on attention (Callaway & Dembo, 1958) and cue utilization (Easterbrook, 1959) suggests that one reaction to stress involves a narrowing of attention. Later research has focused on exploring the effects of time stress on various basic cognitive processes, such as attention and vigilance (e.g., Hockey, 1979). There has been little research, however, on the effect of environmental stressors on complex cognitive functioning.

The purpose of this research project is to evaluate the effects of environmental stressors on higher cognitive processing. Initially, subjects were given a series

James Shanteau • Department of Psychology, Kansas State University, Manhattan, Kansas 66506.   **Geri Anne Dino** • Department of Psychology, Frostburg State University, Frostburg, Maryland 21532.
Time Pressure and Stress in Human Judgment and Decision Making, edited by Ola Svenson and A. John Maule. Plenum Press, New York, 1993.

of simple and complex tasks to complete in a comfortable, nonstressful situation. They were then placed in a climate-controlled chamber characterized by noisy, uncomfortable, and crowded conditions. During their stay, subjects completed the same series of tasks to evaluate their cognitive ability. Comparisons can be made between the two conditions.

In addition, there was a control group that completed the tasks in a non-stressful environment. Thus, stress effects can be evaluated by comparing experimental subjects to control subjects.

The research was guided by two central questions. First, do environmental stressors effect cognitive performance? It is possible that such external factors have little impact on cognitive functioning. Second, if there are stressor effects, are they greater in more complex tasks, such as decision making and creativity, than in simpler tasks? That is, are higher-level processes more disrupted by stress effects than low-level processes?

The present study examined stressor effects in three ways. First, subjects' performance in each task was evaluated at successive time intervals—stressor effects should appear as a deterioration in behavior. Second, the results for tasks varying in complexity can be compared to determine if environmental stressors influence some behaviors more than others. Third, the performance of experimental subjects can be compared to nonstressed control subjects.

Method

Four groups of eight experimental subjects were placed in a small, crowded, uncomfortable chamber for 1 or 2 days. Nurses were present to monitor the subjects and to administer the research instruments. Subjects were given a series of cognitive tasks to perform at various times during their stay. Control subjects were treated similarly, except they were in a normal experimental room.

Environmental Chamber

A special chamber was constructed in the Institute for Environmental Research at Kansas State University. The chamber measured 12' by 9.6' and contained two bunk beds, a toilet, a storage cabinet, an exercise bicycle, and a research table. There was about 10 square feet of open area per person. The chamber was climate controlled, with two levels of temperature (72 ° F/22 °C, 86 ° F/30 °C), two humidity levels (50% Rh, 86% Rh), and two duration levels (24 hr, 48 hr).[1]

[1]Originally, the plan was to have eight groups of subjects in a $2 \times 2 \times 2$, temperature $\times$ humidity $\times$ duration, design. However, the study was terminated after only four groups were run because of

The conditions in the chamber were characterized by (1) complete confinement during the duration of the study. (2) Normal sleep patterns were disrupted with a series of 4-hour alternating work/rest schedules.[2] (3) During the awake periods, subjects were kept busy with a series of cognitive tasks involving memory, problem solving, attention, and decision making. (4) Participants were also required to ride a special exercise bicycle (which ran a ventilation fan) for two 15-minute periods during each 24-hour period. (5) Normal eating habits, as well as personal hygiene patterns, were disrupted by the constraints of the chamber environment. According to subjects' postexperimental reports and the nurse–experimenters' observations, these conditions did create a very uncomfortable and stressful environment.

Subjects

Stress Group

The 16 women and 16 men in the stress group were obtained by distributing fliers to a variety of police, fire, and medical agencies in Riley County, Kansas.[3] Each participant was given an initial physical examination by a registered nurse and required to fill out a detailed medical history. These results were reviewed by a physician; only those individuals the physician felt could handle the stress of the environmental chambers could take part. The participants worked as police officers, nurses, and firefighters. Subjects in the 24-hour tests were paid $200 for their participation; those in the 48-hour group were paid $350.

Two participants could not complete the experiment. One male in a 24-hour group reported feeling too claustrophobic and asked to leave. One female in a 48-hour group could not tolerate the heat and lack of sleep; she was removed from the chamber by the nurse–researchers. The data from these subjects were not used.

Control Group

The 16 men and 16 women in the control group were obtained from a newspaper advertisement. Twenty-one of the participants were students, with the

---

changes in funding priority by the project sponsor. Separate analyses were conducted for each group. There were no consistent differences between the groups for any of the instruments reported here. Therefore, the results have been combined across the four groups.

[2] Only four bunk beds were available for sleeping. Therefore, separate work/rest schedules were constructed for the eight subjects. Half of them rested while the other half worked.

[3] One of the goals of the Federal Emergency Management Agency that supported this project was to study how emergency personnel functioned in a highly confined envrionment. Therefore, it was necessary for the project to use subjects whose occupation and experience exposed them to environmental stressors.

remainder from the local community. The control subjects were paid $20 for their time. These subjects wre somewhat younger than the experimental subjects.

One male and one female had scores on the creativity test lower than the tabled norms. Therefore, control-group results are reported on the data for 15 women and 15 men.

Experimenters

Two registered nurses were responsible for initial physical examinations of the stress group. They also administered the research instruments and monitored the subjects well-being while in the chamber. One nurse was present in the chamber at all times; they alternated 12-hour shifts. They were paid for their time.

Two students connected with the project were the experimenters for the control groups. They ran the control subjects in a manner parallel to the experimental session. They were paid for their time.

Procedure

A common procedure was used for all tasks. Before entering the chamber, subjects went through the first version of the instruments under nonstressful conditions. Once in the chamber, they then completed at least one and as many as three more versions of all instruments. The number of presentations of each task depended on the availability of alternative forms and total time in the chamber (24 or 48 hours). The different forms were randomly assigned for presentation at various times. The results reported here make clear how often each task was presented.

Control subjects completed the task under similar timing conditions. However, they were run in comfortable surroundings with normal sleep, eating, hygiene, and the like patterns.

Instruments

Ten cognitive tasks were used, ranging from attention and memory to problem solving and decision making. Six of the tasks are reported here; the results for the remainder were not different in any substantial way from these six. In addition, subjects performance on the exercise bicycle was monitored; those results are not relevant here.

Memory Recall

As a measure of memory performance, immediate and delayed recall tasks were used (Lindsay & Norman, 1977). Subjects heard a list of 18 words. Immediately after the presentation, they were asked to recall as many words as possible. Following an intervening task lasting 20 minutes, they were asked again to recall as many words as they could.

Various lists were used. One was presented before the experiment began, and others were presented at varying times during subjects' stay in the chamber.

Anagram Solution

As a measure of verbal ability, subjects were asked to solve a set of anagrams (Feather, 1982). For example, they had to determine which word(s) could be made from a reordering of the letters in "ONEASS" (The answer is given at the end of the section). The anagrams were chosen to be of about equal difficulty, with roughly 50% solution rates (Feather, 1965).

Various sets of anagrams were presented, the first in the prechamber session and the remainder during different times in the chamber. Subjects were given 30 seconds to solve each of seven anagrams in a set. (The answer to the anagram is "SEASON.")

IQ Measure

Despite the controversy over their uses (and misuses), IQ tests provide a highly reliable measure of individual differences (Morris, 1988). However, IQ scores can be subject to various short-term and long-term environmental factors (Sternberg, 1986). To measure IQ, subjects were given several versions of a standardized test developed by Eysenck (1962).

Subjects had 30 minutes to complete booklets (labeled *puzzle solving*) contained 40 questions each. An example of one of the questions is: "Insert the missing number: 4 9 17 35 — 139" (the answer is given below). Other question types involved odd-man-out identifications, relationship between figures, missing words, and anagrams. Various versions were administered before and during the time in the chamber. IQ scores were estimated using norms developed by Eysenck (1962) for adults. (The answer is "69.")

Creativity

The ability to generate novel solutions to problems is vital to effective thinking (Adams, 1986). Creativity was measured using the AC Test of Creative Ability (Industrial Relations Center, 1953, 1954). Two forms were administered, one in the prechamber session and one in the final part of the subjects' stay in the chamber. The test was designed to measure the quantity and quality of ideas people generate in work situations; this is better suited to the subjects' background than more academically oriented tests.

There were three sections in the instrument: In the first 20-minute section, subjects were to list as many possible consequences of a work situation as they could, for example, "In a final assembly department employing 16 women inspectors, only 7 come to work on a given day." Subjects were then to list all the consequences they could think of.

The second 10-minute section required subjects to produce reasons why a particular work situation might be true, for example, "April is the month when the fewest accidents of any kind occur in the United States." They were to list all the reasons that it might be true.

In a third 15-minute part on originality, subjects generated as many uses for five common objects (e.g., "a red brick") as they could. This is similar to the Unusual Uses test (Torrance, 1966).

Calibration

The ability to assess accurately the state of one's uncertainty can be measured by calibration. For a well-calibrated decision maker, the stated probabilities should match the observed proportion of events. Under stress, it might be expected that subjects' ability to assess probabilities would become less accurate. To determine calibration, subjects gave probability assessments for general knowledge questions; this task has been widely used in risk assessment research (e.g., Fischhoff, Slovic, & Lichtenstein, 1977).

Two versions of the calibration instruments were given to subjects, one in the prechamber session and one at the end of the stay in the chamber. These two versions have been established as equivalent in previous analyses (Slovic, personal communication, 1983). Each version had 50 two-alternative questions such as, "Which magazine had the largest circulation in 1970, *Playboy* or *Time?*" Subjects then gave probability assessments of being correct.

Impression Formation

One of the most frequently used tasks in social judgment research is impression formation. Subjects are asked to form an impression of a person described by several personality or character traits (e.g., Anderson, 1962). In the task used here, subjects evaluated job applicants described on realistic personnel forms; the task was developed by Nagy (1981) and Gaeth (1984).

Subjects assessed 32 hypothetical applicants for the job of computer programmer. Each applicant was described by two job-relevant cues (years of relevant experience and recommendation of past employer) and three job-irrelevant cues (age, gender, and physical attractiveness).[4] Other items, such as phone, address, and so on were included as fillers to make the application form more realistic. The 32 cases were generated from a $2 \times 2 \times 2 \times 2 \times 2$, experience $\times$ recommendations $\times$ age $\times$ gender $\times$ attractiveness, factorial design. Subjects (unknowingly) judged all cases twice to estimate an error term for the analysis of variance. The subjects went through the task in the prechamber and in the chamber session.

Results and Discussion

The findings for the various tasks were analyzed in two ways. First, the results for each task were compared across the different test administrations; this led to either a prechamber–chamber or prechamber–earlychamber–latechamber, within-group analysis. Second, the experimental (chamber) subjects were compared to the control (nonchamber) subjects; this led to a between-group analysis. The general strategy will be illustrated in detail for the memory recall task.

Memory Recall

As expected, experimental subjects remembered more words in the immediate recall condition (Mean = 10.6) than in the delayed recall condition (M = 3.0). Immediate recall was somewhat better in the prechamber session (M = 11.4) than in the chamber sessions (M = 10.3). Delayed recall also was better in the prechamber (M = 4.3) than in the chamber (M = 2.5).

Recall results for control subjects were comparable. For instance, immediate recall (M = 10.2) was superior to delayed recall (M = 3.2). Surprisingly, control subjects (like their experimental group counterparts) had higher recall scores in the first session (M = 4.0) than in the last three sessions (3.0.)

Analyses of group $\times$ session interactions were significant for both immediate, $F(3,180)$ = 4.31, and delayed recall, $F(3,180)$ = 2.80.[5] For immediate recall, experimental subjects showed a decline across sessions, with some improvement in the last session; control subjects showed a gradual increase across all four sessions. For delayed recall, experimental subjects had a steady decline across the first three sessions with an improvement in the last session; control subjects had a similar but less pronounced pattern.

In all, recall scores were worse with exposure to environmental stressors. However, there are two factors to consider before drawing any conclusions.

[4]Hiring laws in the United States and Kansas prohibit discrimination in employment on the basis of age or gender.
[5]All significant effects reported at the .05 level.

First, there is no consistent evidence that increased time in the chamber had an effect. Second, performance of control subjects shows the same pattern as the experimental subjects. Taken together, these findings provide mixed evidence of environmental effects on recall.

Anagram Solution

The analyses showed no significant differences in any of the tests. In the prechamber session, for instance, the mean number of correctly solved anagrams was 4.5 for experimental subjects. In the chamber, the overall mean was not significantly different at 3.9. Moreover, the first and second chamber sessions were nearly identical ($M = 3.8$ and $M = 4.0$). Thus the anagram task was not sensitive to environmental effects.

IQ Measure

As shown in Figure 1, there were sizable differences in mean IQ measures for experimental subjects across sessions, $F(3,177) = 48.12$. The prechamber results were lowest, with the middle session in the chamber yielding the highest values. The plot shows an inverted-U shape.

Control subjects revealed a similar pattern except for the last session. There was a significant groups $\times$ sessions interaction, $F(3,177) = 3.11$. Further analyses revealed the interaction was concentrated in the last session; with it removed, the interaction drops out, $F(2,118) < 1$. There was no apparent reason for the differences in the last session.

Although there were significant results, the pattern is not that expected from stressor effects for three reasons. First, performance improved from prechamber to experimental sessions; this may reflect learning but is not indicative of stress. Second, the trend peaks during the middle session, not at the beginning or the end; this does not show the monotonic relationship expected from continued exposure to stressors. Finally, except for the final session, there is a constant difference between experimental and control subjects. Thus, the IQ measure does not show sensitivity to stressor effects.

Creativity

The mean creativity scores for experimental and control groups on the prechamber and chamber administrations of the creativity test appear in Figure 2.

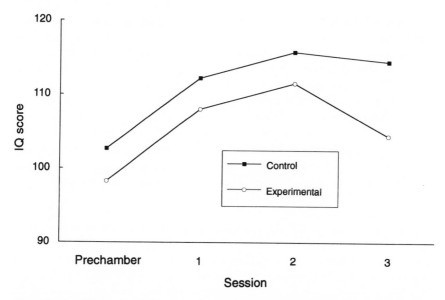

Figure 1. Mean IQ (puzzle solving) scores for experimental and control groups over four sessions.

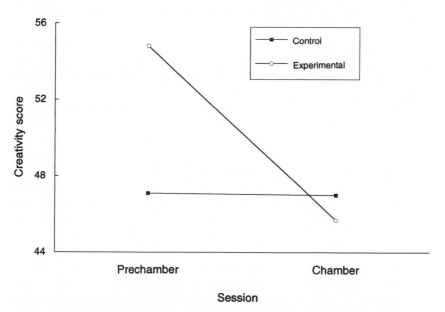

Figure 2. Mean creativity scores for experimental and control groups over two sessions.

302   James Shanteau and Geri Anne Dino

The experimental subjects show a sizable decline, whereas the control subjects are unchanged.

Statistical tests revealed in significant groups × session interaction, $F(1,58)$ = 19.94. The decrease in experimental scores is significant, $t(58)$ = 6.51, whereas the control scores are not significantly different. Three other analyses were conducted to determine the consistency of the results. First, the decline was examined for the four separate groups of experimental subjects. A 4 × 2, groups × session, analysis of variance revealed a significant session main effect, $F(1,26)$ = 32.20, but no groups main effect or interaction. Thus, similar effects were observed in all experimental groups.

Second, separate t-tests were conducted to examine the three parts of the creativity test. All parts showed significant decrements with stress, $t(29)$ = 5.11, 3.82, and 3.32 respectively.

Third, changes for individual subjects were examined. For the experimental group, 24 of 30 subjects had a decrease in creativity, 4 increased, and 2 were unchanged. For the control group, 14 subjects decreased, 15 increased, and 1 was unchanged. The difference is significant, $\chi^2(2)$ = 9.33.

The reliability of the creativity measure was examined by correlating the scores on the two forms of the test; the order of these forms was counterbalanced across sessions. The reliability coefficients for the parallel forms were $r(28)$ = .73 and .77 for the experimental and control groups. These values are similar to that reported in the test manual (r = .75) for parallel forms. In addition, reliability was checked by having the tests scored by two independent raters; the intercorrelation was quite high, $r(58)$ = .99.

The pattern of creativity scores reveals a clear stressor effect both in the prechamber–chamber decline and in the difference between experimental and control subjects. Interesting, the experimental subjects started with higher scores than control subjects; in the second session, the two groups are nearly alike. Thus, the performance of the experimental group falls to the level of the control group.

Calibration

The calibration scores for probability assessments were comparable to results obtained in prior studies (e.g., see Lichtenstein, Fischhoff, & Phillips, 1982). That is, subjects were overconfident in their estimates for items of moderate and high difficulty. There was no difference, however, between the prechamber and chamber conditions in the calibration scores for experimental subjects. Furthermore, the experimental and control subjects were not significantly different. Thus the overconfidence in the calibration scores was not effected by stressors.

Impression Formation

The pattern of job-applicant evaluations was comparable to the results reported by Gaeth (1984) and Nagy (1981; also see Shanteau & Nagy, 1984). That is, subjects relied primarily on the job-relevant attributes of experience and past recommendations in making judgments. Less emphasis was placed on job-irrelevant attributes of age and gender. There was no evidence the pattern of results changed as a function of stress.

Comparisons between experimental and control subjects revealed minor differences not related to stress. For instance, controls placed more emphasis on the age attribute than experimental subjects. This may be due to the relative inexperience of control subjects in job-hiring situations. Although the implications of this effect are worth exploring for personnel hiring practices, there was no evidence of change as a function of environmental stressors. Thus, impression formation strategies were not influenced by stress.

General Discussion

The study produced two interesting results. The first involves the psychological effects that environmental stressors produced on creativity. The second involves the absence of stressor effects on other cognitive processes, particularly judgment and decision making. Each of these results will be discussed followed by some comments on the generality of the present findings.

Stress and Creativity

The present results clearly show that creativity is reduced in a stressful environmental. Mean performance on the AC Test of Creativity revealed a significant decline for the experimental subjects, whereas the performance for control subjects was unchanged. Follow-up analyses confirmed the reliability of this trend. That is, similar decrements were observed in all three parts of the creativity instrument. Moreover, individual analyses showed that 80% of the experimental subjects had declining creativity scores, whereas the controls were evenly split between showing gains and declines. Thus, environmental stressors produced a consistent decrement in creativity scores.

One surprising result was that performance did not differ across the four experimental groups. It was expected that longer exposure to stressors (48 vs. 24 hr), higher humidity (86% Rh vs. 50% Rh), and greater heat (86 °F/30 °C vs. 72° F/22 °C) would enhance stress effects. Although there were some trends in that direction, the results did not reach significance. More research is needed to determine if there is a temporal or climatic component to the observed effect.

The finding has both specific and broad implications for how people cope with stressful environments. Specifically, in emergency enclosures, such as storm shelters, responsible individuals could find their well-being dependent on creative responses to unexpected problems. Moreover, it seems likely that stress in an actual shelter might be greater than in this study. If creativity is reduced under stress, then adaptive behaviors may be impaired.

It is important to consider the development of appropriate techniques for coping with these effects. It may be helpful, for instance, to warn individuals about the negative effects of environmentally induced stress on creativity. Alternatively, people might "prethink" solutions to difficult problems instead of relying on spontaneous answers; expert decisions makers were observed by Shanteau (1992b) using prethinking as a strategy to deal with difficult problems. In any case, the observed decrement in creativity has important implications for emergency behavior.

In a broader sense, the present results have implications for a variety of stressful environments. Although researchers have speculated about effects of environmental stressors such as noise, fatigue, and crowding on workplace behaviors (Ivancevich & Matson, 1980; Sharit & Salvendy, 1982), the effects on creativity remains unexplored. Yet, many jobs may call for creative responses in stressful situations.

Although the environmental research chamber used here may seem artificial, there are a variety of real-world settings that involve similar circumstances. Many workplaces are characterized by crowded, uncomfortable surroundings and workshifts that disrupt normal day–night sleep cycles. Indeed, the experimental subjects (police, nurses, and fire fighters) often work in such settings. It is notable, therefore, that stress effects were observed for these experienced subjects. Presumably less experienced subjects would be even more susceptible.

Other Psychological Processes

The behaviors analyzed in this study, excluding creativity, can be separated into two categories. The first involves verbal behavior in the memory recall, anagram, and written IQ tests. The second involves the decision-making processes of probability calibration and impression formation. Despite the many differences between these two categories, minimal stressor effects were observed for both.

The failure to find stressor effects in verbal behaviors might be explained by the overlearning and highly repetitive practice associated with language. Any skill rehearsed as much as word usage may be more or less resistant to environmental influence. This is supported by the anecdotal observation of the nurse–experimenters that subjects maintained their conversational styles in the chamber. Although often terse and showing signs of irritation, subjects could carry on normal discussions and express themselves even at the end of the session. This suggests that well-practiced skills may be unaffected by environmental stressors.

The finding that decision-making performance was not influenced by environmental factors was more surprising. Judgment and decision making, along with creativity and problem solving, are usually classified as "higher cognitive processes" (Solso, 1991). These processes are the most complex and involve the highest levels of human thought. Given the depth of cognitive analysis necessary, it seems reasonable that stressors might interfere with these processes.

Nonetheless, the present results show little impact of the stressors on the probability calibration and impression formation tasks. Both involve thought and analysis and take some time to complete. Like creativity, these decision-making tasks call for multilevel cognitive processing. Then why did stressor effects appear for creativity and not for these tasks?

One possible answer is that both calibration and impression formation are repetitive tasks. Although the stimuli change from trial to trial, the response requirements are unchanged. Thus, once a subject adopts a decision strategy, it may be possible to keep applying that same strategy under stress. Indeed, the initial task presentation in the prechamber session may allow subjects to develop such a consistent strategy. This strategy can then be followed when the subject is faced with environmental stressors.

In contrast, the creativity instrument was the only task used here that is not repetitive. Not only are the various sections of the measure different, but the type of questions preclude developing a common strategy. This suggests that other nonrepetitive tasks, including some decision problems, may be subject to stressor effects.

Generality

Consideration of the generality of present findings can be addressed at three levels; tasks, subjects, and stressors. Each of these deserves discussion.

Task Generality

The choice of specific tasks to represent cognitive domains is crucial (Shanteau, 1992a). It is possible that different tasks could have produced different results. For instance, recognition memory might have shown a greater decrement under stress than recall. And there are a variety of other decision tasks that might have been used, such as gambling choices.

There were seven criteria used to select the tasks used here. First, each task had to be representative of the domain. Second, there had to be multiple versions available. Third, the results must be easy to score. Fourth, subjects' performance had to be measurable in quantitative terms. Fifth, the task should be understandable by the experimental subjects (who were older, less educated, but more experienced than college students). Sixth, the tasks as a set had to contain a balanced assortment of problem types. Lastly, there had to be a reasonable chance that stressor effects would emerge.

Given these constraints, many tasks were considered and rejected. Most were eliminated for failure to meet several of the criteria above. Others were eliminated because they needed special equipment that could not be maintained in the experimental chamber, such as computers.

Obviously, there is no way to know whether the observed results will generalize to other tasks. We do believe, however, the tasks are representative of various domains and tap into processes and strategies common to each domain. Therefore, we are comfortable that the tasks chosen have as good a chance as any to produce generalizable results.

Subject Generality

The sample of experimental subjects was selected from an unusual population. Police, fire fighters, and nurses are atypical subjects. They work in high-stress occupations with relatively low pay and professional status. Except for nurses, they were not college educated and, as the IQ scores show, they have average intelligence. They also are older than the typical research subject, more likely to be married with children, and tend to live in less affluent areas of town. In short, they are better described as "blue collar" than "white collar."

We would argue that these subjects are closer to the larger population than the typical college students. More important, the experimental subjects were the most relevant for the research project. They are likely to have experience and to be involved in environmental stressor situations. And given the nature of their occupations, other people depend on them to cope effectively with stress. Thus, their results are important for this project.

From another view, these subjects because of their background should be better able to handle environmental stressors. Using a "toughest-case" logic, if these subjects show stress effects, then similar effects will probably be found for others. Thus, it is likely that less experienced subjects would show even larger effects.

Perhaps it reflects the subjects' experience that few of the tasks showed any stress effects. Most of their performance was more or less unchanged by continued environmental stressors. The subjects' general ability to perform at a consistent level makes the stress effects that did occur notable.

Stressor Generality

There is another question of generality: Will the results here generalize to other types of stressors? In the present study, there were a variety of stress factors. These included the physical stressors of crowding and noise. There also were personal-state stressors of irritability and sleeplessness. Lastly, there were task-related stressors of time pressure (in most tasks) and performance anxiety.

Because many studies of stress use only one or two stressors, it is difficult to compare our results to other studies. Given the variety of stressors used here, it is not possible to say which stressor or combination of stressors had the greatest impact. It is also impossible to determine whether our specific findings will generalize to other situations. Clearly, more research is needed on the generality of effects observed with different stressors.

ACKNOWLEDGMENTS. This research was supported, in part, by a contract from the Federal Emergency Management Agency (Contract No. EMW-C-0589). We wish to acknowledge the important contributions of our co-investigators on the project, Leon Rappoport, Frederick H. Rholes, and Stephan A. Konz. We also want to thank Paul Slovic and Kenneth R. Hammond for their help and advice in consulting on this research project. We gratefully recognize the efforts of Michele Binkley and Angela Spenser in analyzing various phases of the research. The efforts of the two nurse–experimenters, Marlys Gardner and Bonnie Hamilton, deserve particular mention.

Requests for further information on the research can be sent either to James Shanteau, Department of Psychology, Bluemont Hall, Kansas State University, Manhattan, KS 66506-5302, or to Geri Anne Dino, Department of Psychology, Frostburg State University, Frostburg, MD 21532.

References

Adams, J. L. (1986). *Conceptual blockbusting: A guide to better ideas* (3rd ed.). Reading, MA: Addison-Wesley Publishing Company.

Anderson, N. H. (1962). Application of an additive model to impression formation. *Science, 138,* 817–818.

Callaway, E., & Dembo, D. (1958). Narrowed attention: A psychological phenomenon that accompanies a certain physiological change. *AMA Archives of Neurology and Psychiatry, 79,* 74–90.

Easterbrook, J. A. (1959). The effect of emotion on cue utilization and the organization of behavior. *Psychological Review, 66,* 183–201.

Eysenck, H. J. (1962). *Know your own I.Q.* Harmondsworth, England : Penguin Books.

Feather, N. T. (1965). Performance at a difficult task in relation to initial expectation of success, test anxiety, and need achievement. *Journal of Personality, 33,* 200–217.

Feather, N. T. (Ed.). (1982). *Expectations and actions: Expectancy-value models in psychology.* Hillsdale, NJ: Lawrence Erlbaum Associates.

Fischhoff, B., Slovic, P., & Lichtenstein, S. (1977). Knowing with certainty: The appropriateness of extreme confidence. *Journal of Experimental Psychology: Human Perception and Performance, 3,* 552–564.

Gaeth, G. J. (1984). *The influence of irrelevant information in judgment processes; Assessment, reduction, and a model.* Unpublished doctoral dissertation, Kansas State University.

Halpern, D. F. (1989). *Thought and knowledge: An introduction to critical thinking* (2nd ed.). Hillsdale, NJ: Erlbaum.

Hockey, R. (1979). Stress and the cognitive components of skilled performance. In V. Hamilton & D. M. Warburton (Eds.), *Human stress and cognition* (pp. 141–177). Chichester, UK: John Wiley & Sons.

Hogarth, R. (1987). *Judgment and choice* (2nd ed.). Chichester, UK: John Wiley & Sons.

Industrial Relations Center, University of. Chicago. (1953). *AC test of creative ability (Revised short form A).* Chicago: Author.

Industrial Relations Center, University of. Chicago. (1954). *AC test of creative ability (Revised short form B).* Chicago: Author.

Ivancevich, J. M., & Matteson, M. T. (1980). *Stress and work.* Glenview, IL: Scott Foresman.

Lichtenstein, S., Fischhoff, B., & Phillips, L. D. (1982). Calibration of probabilities: The state of the art to 1980. In D. Kahneman, P. Slovic, & A. Tversky (Eds.), *Judgment under uncertainty: Heuristics and biases* (pp. 306–334). Cambridge: Cambridge University Press.

Lindsay, P. H., & Norman, D. A. (1977). *Human information processing* (2nd ed.). New York: Academic Press.

Mandler, G. (1979). Thought processes, consciousness and stress. In V. Hamilton & D. M. Warburton (Eds.), *Human stress and cognition* (pp. 180–202). Chichester, UK: John Wiley & Sons.

Mandler, G. (1984). *Mind and body: Psychology of emotion and stress.* New York: W. W. Norton & Company.

Morris, C. G. (1988). *Psychology: An introduction* (6th ed.). Englewood Cliffs, NJ: Prentice Hall.

Nagy, G. F. (1981). *How are personnel selection decisions made? An analysis of decision strategies in a simulated personnel selection task.* Unpublished doctoral dissertation, Kansas State University.

Shanteau, J. (1992a). Competence of experts: The role of task characteristics. *Organizational Behavior and Human Decision Processes, 53,* 252–266.

Shanteau, J. (1992b). The psychology of experts: An alternative view. In G. Wright & F. Bolger (Eds.), *Expertise and decision support* (pp. 11–23). New York: Plenum Press.

Shanteau, J., & Nagy, G. F. (1984). Information integration in person perception. In M. Cook (Eds.), *Issues in person perception* (pp. 48–86). London: Methuen.

Sharit, J., & Salvendy, G. (1982). Occupational stress: Review and appraisal. *Human Factors, 24,* 129–162.

Solso, R. L. (1991). *Cognitive psychology* (3rd ed.). Boston: Allyn & Bacon.

Sternberg, R. J. (1986). *Intelligence applied: Understanding and increasing your intellectual skills.* San Diego: Harcourt Brace Jovanovich.

Torrance, E. P. (1966). *Directions manual and scoring guide (Verbal test A).* Lexington, MA: Personnel Press.

20

Assessing Components of Judgments in an Operational Setting
The Effects of Time Pressure on Aviation Weather Forecasting

Cynthia M. Lusk

Introduction

Aviation weather forecasting provides an excellent opportunity to study judgment and decision making under time pressure. Because the weather information
supplied to air traffic controllers often determines traffic patterns, the timeliness
of advisories can become critical. Significant weather activity increases demand
on forecasters for rapid assimilation of information and rapid judgments. In
addition, aviation forecasting represents an operational setting in which the only
data available for analysis may be forecasts and outcomes. That is, in this
setting, forecasters are working in "real time," generating forecasts on the basis
of dynamic information. In such a setting, it is inappropriate for researchers to
intervene in order to introduce some type of experimental control. Yet it is just
such situations that are the most representative and important regarding the
effects of time pressure on judgment and decision making. Consequently, in such

Cynthia M. Lusk • Center for Research on Judgment and Policy, University of Colorado, Boulder,
Colorado 80309-0344.
Time Pressure and Stress in Human Judgment and Decision Making, edited by Ola Svenson and A.
John Maule. Plenum Press, New York, 1993.

situations, statistical decomposition of judgment and outcome data may be the best means of gaining insight into characteristics of performance affected by time pressure.

What follows first is a brief description of the aviation forecasting study from which the data analyzed are drawn, and a description of some results of previous analyses of those data. Following that is a brief description of decomposition analyses suggested by Yates (1982; Yates & Curley, 1985). Analyses of data from the aviation forecasting study is then presented to demonstrate how such analyses might delineate some effects of time pressure on judgment and decision making. The results are then discussed in the context of previous literature on the effects of time pressure, further hypotheses to be tested in more controlled situations, and issues regarding other characteristics that may be associated with time pressure in this and other operational settings.

Aviation Forecasting Study

Mueller, Wilson, and Heckman (1988) report the results of an aviation forecasting study in which a team of two to three forecasters made forecasts of convection (thunderstorm activity) for Stapleton International Airport and its Kiowa gateway. Specifically, forecasters predicted the probability that the radar reflectivity (measured in dBZs) would reach particular levels in storms. Higher reflectivity levels indicate denser clouds with the potential to produce lightning, hail, microbursts, and high winds, all of which could be catastrophic to aircraft, particularly when landing or taking off. For the purposes of demonstrating the utility of the analyses described below, only a small subset of the Mueller et al. (1988) data are considered. However, a full description of the forecasting situation is presented here.

During the study, two to three forecasters made consensus probability forecasts each hour between noon and 7 P.M. for 37 days. At each forecast time, they made several forecasts for two different levels of thunderstorm severity for four different time periods following the forecast time for both the Stapleton and Kiowa locations. Thus, at each forecast time 16 forecasts were made: two levels of storm severity (30 and 50 dBZ) × two locations (Stapleton and Kiowa) × four forecast periods (0–15, 15–30, 30–45, and 45–60 minutes after the forecast time). Because there were 7 forecast times each day, 112 forecasts per day are available. The operationalization of time pressure incorporates all 112 forecast times, but the decomposition analyses reported below only include the following subset of forecasts: the 30 dBZ forecasts for the 30- to 45-minute period following the hour for both locations (Stapleton and Kiowa).

Time pressure is experienced while forecasting aviation weather when the environment becomes active, according to one of the participating forecasters asked about time pressure. Therefore, the activity level present on each day was identified to operationalize time pressure. This is discussed in more detail below.

Previous Analyses

Harvey, Hammond, Lusk, and Mross (1992) analyzed data from the aviation forecasting study, utilizing a Signal Detection Theory (SDT) framework. SDT assumes a forecaster combines information to arrive at a value representing the strength of the evidence for the occurrence of an event. This value is compared with one or more internal decision criteria. If the evidence is greater than a particular decision criterion, the forecast is made. When a forecaster uses N different response probabilities, $N-1$ different decision criterion values may be identified. Harvey et al. compared the decision criteria for the same forecast probabilities under low-time-pressure conditions to those under high-time-pressure conditions. Their comparison indicated a general shift to lower values under high-time-pressure relative to low-time-pressure conditions. This implies that for these forecasters it took less evidence to forecast the same probability level under high- versus low-time-pressure conditions.

Decomposition of the Mean Probability Score

The present analysis was undertaken to further determine the effect of time pressure on aviation weather probability judgments. Yates (1982; Yates & Curley, 1985) presents a procedure for decomposing the external correspondence between forecasts and outcomes into components representing various aspects of the outcome and of forecasting behavior.

The mean probability score (MPS) is a measure of the external correspondence between the forecast and the observed event (e.g., an outcome index with 0 indicating the storm did not reach the 30-dBZ severity level and a 1 indicating the storm did reach 30 dBZ). It is, simply, the mean squared difference between the forecast and the outcome index. When external correspondence is perfect, the MPS is zero. Yates decomposes the MPS into several components, representing (1) variance of the outcome event, (2) conditional minimum variance in the forecasts, (3) the excess variance in the forecasts, (4) the bias in the forecasts, and (5) the covariance between the forecasts and outcomes. The first four components contributes positively to the MPS, whereas the fifth component contributes negatively to the MPS. That being the case, in order to minimize the MPS the forecaster should attempt to minimize each of the first four components while maximizing the covariance.

The variance of the outcome component is not under the forecaster's control but is an important reference point when interpreting performance, particularly when comparing performance across samples as will be indicated below. The covariance component is described by Yates as "the heart of forecasting skill" (1982, p. 140). It reflects the forecaster's ability to make distinctions among the outcomes, that is, the forecaster's sensitivity to cues indicative of thunderstorms forming and becoming severe. However, the covariance can be further decomposed into the outcome variance and slope components. Removing the outcome variance from the covariance yields the slope as a measure of the covariation that is truly under the control of the forecaster. The slope is the difference between the conditional forecast means when the event does and does not occur. In the present situation, it is the difference between the mean forecast when the thunderstorm did reach the criterion level of severity and the mean forecast when it did not. Because it is the slope that is under control of the forecaster, it is the slope the forecaster should seek to maximize. While maximizing the difference between the conditional means, the forecaster should minimize the variability around each conditional mean. Yates identifies the conditional minimum forecast variance given the covariance and compares this to the actual variance of the forecasts to determine the excess variability in the forecasts, or "scatter." Yates suggests that the scatter component may reflect the forecaster's responsiveness to cues not related to the outcome occurrence or inconsistency in judgments. Finally, the bias component is simply the squared difference between the forecast mean and the outcome mean. It represents calibration performance and reflects the ability of the forecaster to match the mean forecast to the outcome relative frequencies; in this case the match is between the average probability forecast and the base rate of thunderstorm activity. Judgments are biased if the mean judgment is too low or too high, relative to the outcome mean (the base rate). This component may indicate forecasters' knowledge about the base rate and/or may reflect a response bias.

Decomposition Analyses of the Aviation Forecasting Study

Operationalizing Time Pressure

Time pressure is experienced while forecasting aviation weather when the environment becomes active. That is, when forecasters must cope with a lot of environmental activity, they feel pressured to attend to more potential storms in more locations and therefore have less time to attend to any given storm. Therefore, the activity level for each day was identified to operationalize time pressure. Specifically, for each forecast day, the total number of occurrences (i.e., the outcome index) over the 112 forecasts was summed. For 15 days, that sum was 0 indicating absolutely no weather activity occurred on these days. These days were excluded from further analyses because on these days there is nothing happening to forecast. In addition, when there are no events, the full complement of decomposition components, in particular the slope, can not be computed. Exclusion of these days left 22 days in the sample.

Sample and Analysis Strategy

As indicated above, only a subset of the Mueller et al. data were analyzed. The 30- to 45-minute forecast period was selected for two reasons: (1) these forecasts are removed enough in time from the forecast time so that they are forecasts rather than nowcasts and (2) this time period had slightly fewer more occurrences of the event being predicted than did other time periods, thus allowing more cases for computing the slope and more power when conducting statistical tests.

The unit of analysis used in the following is day. For each day, up to 14 forecasts were available (7 forecast times × 2 locations). Some days had slightly fewer forecasts due to missing data. The decomposition statistics were computed for each day separately. Note that for two low-time-pressure days, the slope could not be computed because there were no event occurrences in the sample for that day. In addition to the decomposition measures, the base rate was also computed. Then correlations were computed between the decomposition measures and the time pressure measure. In order to indicate the relative magnitude of the decomposition measure under low and high time pressure, the sample was separated into low- and high-time-pressure days on the basis of a median split of the time pressure measure. Then descriptive statistics were computed for the low- and high-time-pressure days. In addition, tests were run to determine if the difference between the low- and high-time-pressure days was significant. Because the sampling distributions of the decomposition measures are unknown, nonparametric statistical tests were conducted.

Results

The correlations in Table 1 indicate that most of the decomposition measures, as well as the base rate are positively associated with time pressure, except for the bias that is negatively associated with time pressure. Most of these relationships are statistically significant, except for bias, which is marginally significant, and the slope, which is nonsignificant. The descriptive statistics in Table 2 indicate a similar conclusion.

It is not surprising that higher time pressure is associated with a higher outcome mean because time pressure was operationalized as activity level of the environment. The lower MPSs for lower time pressure indicate better perfor-

**Table 1. Spearman Correlations with
Time Pressure ($n = 22$, except as noted)**

Outcome mean	.73**
Outcome variance	.73**
MPS	.43**
Covariance	.67**
Slope ($n = 20$)	.24
Scatter	.41**
Bias	−.35*

*$p = .055$
**$p < .05$

mance, in terms of external correspondence, for low-time-pressure relative to high-time-pressure days. On the other hand, the covariance indicates the opposite result; higher covariances are associated with higher time pressure, indicating better performance under high time pressure. Recall, however, that the covariance confounds outcome variance with the slope, the latter being a truer measure of discriminative ability. The outcome variance is highly correlated with time pressure, whereas slope is also associated with time pressure, but not reliably.

Another informative measure that separates components of external correspondence that are and are not under the control of the forecast is the "controllable accuracy" (Yates, McDaniel, & Brown, 1991). Controllable accuracy is that part of the MPS left after the variance of the outcome (The uncontrollable portion of the MPS) is removed. Controllable accuracy was also computed for each day, and it is negatively correlated with time pressure ($r = -.51$, $p < .05$). This indicates that as time pressure increases, controllable accuracy decreases.

Taken together, a comparison of the values in Table 1 for the MPS, the outcome variance, and the covariance demonstrate one reason why it is difficult to compare the MPS across samples. The MPS and covariance values indicate different conclusions regarding performance, and the difference is due in large part to the difference in the variance of the outcome. Although the outcome variance indicates that forecasts should be more variable under higher time pressure, the scatter measure indicates forecasts were more variable than necessary, and more so under high time pressure. Finally, bias was negatively associated with time pressure, indicating lower bias as time pressure increases. However, it is important to note from Table 2 that the absolute values of the bias measures were very similar, but the direction of the bias was different. That is, the magnitude of the bias was similar, but the direction of bias was not. Under low time pressure, forecasters produced higher values than they should, whereas under high time pressure, forecasters produced lower values than they should. In

Table 2. Descriptive Statistics:
Low versus High Time Pressure

	Low		
	Mean	*sd*	Median
Outcome mean***	.067	.039	.071
Outcome variance***	.066	.037	.071
MPS***	.059	.043	.044
Covariance***	.016	.019	.018
Slope	.262	.281	.254
Scatter**	.020	.015	.017
Bias*	.030	.041	.025

	High		
	Mean	*sd*	Median
Outcome mean***	.191	.118	.143
Outcome variance***	.153	.066	.132
MPS***	.103	.050	.099
Covariance***	.057	.033	.051
Slope	.386	.204	.379
Scatter**	.035	.024	.030
Bias*	−.035	.100	−.022

*$p = .12$.
**$p = .06$.
***$p < .05$.

sum, the higher MPS in the high- relative to low-time-pressure condition is due not to decreased discriminative ability, as indicated by the slope. Instead, the performance decrement is due to increased outcome variance and scatter in high- versus low-time-pressure conditions.

Discussion

In sum, these findings suggest the following about aviation weather forecasting in high- relative to low-time-pressure conditions:

- Better performance, in terms of external correspondence, is associated with lower time pressure.
- Better discriminative ability, in terms of slope (though not reliably so), under high-time-pressure conditions.
- The occurrence of storms reaching the criterion level of severity is more variable under high time pressure.

- There is less "controllable accuracy" under high time pressure.
- Forecasters produced more variable forecasts than necessary in both time pressure conditions, but more so under high-time-pressure conditions.
- The average forecast was lower than the base rate of storms reaching the criterion level of severity under high-time-pressure conditions, and the average forecast was higher than the base rate of storms under low-time-pressure conditions.

These results suggest different, but related kinds of hypotheses regarding the effects of time pressure in such an operational setting. The first class of hypotheses concerns how the forecasters' cognitive processes might be different under low and high time pressure. The second class of hypotheses concerns the task environment in which the forecasters are working. In addition, Yates and Curley (1985) have considered the incentives imposed on the forecaster as another source of variation in the decompositions measures. Each will be discussed below.

Forecaster Incentives

Yates and Curley (1985) report a positive bias in precipitation forecasts. That is, forecasters tended to overforecast by providing values larger than those that occurred. They speculated that this was due to the relative costs of missing a rain event ("misses") versus "false alarms" (predicting an event, e.g., rain, that does not occur). It is not terribly costly to carry an umbrella if it does not rain, whereas it is more costly to be caught in rain without an umbrella. In the aviation weather situation, the forecasts were for a potentially more costly event, and therefore one might expect even more bias toward overforecasting. However, the cost of a false alarm in aviation weather is much greater than that in precipitation forecasts. Whereas carrying an umbrella may not be too costly, rerouting and delaying air traffic may be quite costly, particularly at an airport as busy as Stapleton. Therefore, it is likely that forecasters were motivated to avoid both misses and false alarms, which would lead them on low-activity days to overforecast in order to avoid misses and conversely on high-activity days to underforecast in order to avoid false alarms. This was exactly the pattern of results found in the data analyzed.

Cognitive Processes

In a review of the literature on the effects of time stress on cognitive processes, Edland and Svenson (this volume, Chapter 2) summarized three responses to time stress: (1) acceleration of cognitive processing, (2) filtration of information, and (3) changing strategies. Acceleration of cognitive processing could be manifested in the aviation forecasting situation by inconsistency in the judgments. Yates (1990) has argued that inconsistency in judgments is reflected in the scatter. The above results indicate that higher time pressure is associated with increased scatter. Because these forecasts were consensus forecasts, it is likely that forecasters had time for discussion under low time pressure and through such discussion could increase consistency and thereby reduce the scatter. Under high time pressure, however, it is unlikely they would have time for much discussion, and inconsistency might increase.

An alternative source of increased scatter discussed by Yates (1990) is sensitivity to nonpredictive cues. In the aviation weather study, it is less likely that this could be the explanation for scatter increasing with time pressure because forecasters' discriminative ability as measured by the slope was not adversely affected by time pressure. If forecasters were utilizing nonpredictive cues under high time pressure, one would expect their discriminative ability to degenerate. In addition, support for the filtration hypothesis in the aviation weather situation (discussed below) indicates that forecasters are using fewer, more important cues under high relative to low time pressure.

Previous research regarding the effects of time pressure indicates that time pressure leads to a filtration of information such that the most important information is more likely to be processed (Ben Zur & Breznitz, 1981). Further, in simulation studies, Payne, Bettman, and Johnson (1988) found that under time pressure, elimination-by-aspects and lexicographic heuristics produced better performance. That increased performance may be due to the most important attributes being more likely to be processed under high time pressure. Previous analyses of the aviation weather data (Harvey et al., 1992) found that less evidence was necessary to produce the same probability forecast value under high time pressure, which suggests that forecasters may attend to less information. This finding lends some support to the filtration hypothesis. What may at first be surprising, however, is that such filtration does not lead to a decrement in discriminative ability (the slope) and may lead to a better ability to discriminate between events and nonevents. If filtration leads to consideration of the most important information first, it leaves forecasters with no time to consider other information, that may in fact be of little diagnostic help. Because these forecasters were interested in the scientific models underlying their forecasts (i.e., their conceptual models of the physical dynamics underlying convection), it is possible that under low time pressure they had time to consider a wider range of information sources, some of which may be nondiagnostic and could have, in fact, led them astray.

Within the perspective of Social Judgment Theory (SJT; Brehmer & Joyce, 1988; Hammond, Stewart, Brehmer, & Steinmann, 1975) the filtration hypothesis would lead to the prediction of different forecasting regression models under the two time pressure conditions. If filtration is occurring, one would predict that different regression models would emerge under the two conditions. Cues receiving the largest relative weights under the low-time-pressure conditions should have even larger weights under high-time-pressure conditions, whereas cues with the smallest relative weights under low time pressure should receive no weight under high-time-pressure conditions (cf. Svenson & Edland, 1987). The larger scatter values under high pressure may be due to such overweighting under the high-time-pressure conditions.

Because only the outcomes and forecasts were available in this operational study, the above hypotheses regarding inconsistency and filtration due to time pressure cannot be directly investigated. To investigate such hypotheses, one would have to know the cue values in order to determine the weight placed on cues, as well as collect repeated judgments from the same forecaster judging the same information. This would, of course, require a laboratory rather than operational setting. These hypotheses and findings from the aviation weather study also suggest that much more can be learned about forecasting performance in laboratory settings than simply external correspondence.

The final cognitive response to time pressure that has received some support in the literature is a change in cognitive strategy. As indicated above, Payne et al. have suggested that under time pressure one may switch to a simpler cognitive strategy. Hammond (1988; Hammond, Hamm, Grassia, & Pearson, 1987) has suggested that the time period to complete a task is one task characteristic that induces an intuitive cognitive strategy, whereas a long time period to complete a task induces an analytic strategy. In his Cognitive Continuum Theory (CCT), Hammond has outlined not only the task properties that induce intuitive versus analytic cognition, but he has also outlined the performance properties of the different modes of cognition. Of these performance properties, only one can perhaps be addressed with the present data, and that is the distribution of errors. Hammond has hypothesized that when one uses an intuitive strategy, the errors will be normally distributed. Analysis, on the other hand, leads to few but large errors. The MPS, as a measure of error, indicates that there were more errors under high time pressure. The distribution of errors was such that most of the low-time-pressure days had MPSs below .05, with the largest MPS at about .14. For the high-time-pressure days, most of the errors were between .05 and .15, with the highest at about .19. This lends mixed support to CCT. The MPSs were more normally distributed under high time pressure, indicative of an intuitive strategy, consistent with CCT. However, the more extreme errors were also found under high time pressure, which is indicative of analysis. It is important to keep in mind, as discussed above regarding bias, that forecasters may be seeking to avoid extreme errors. Any conclusions regarding CCT from these data are probably not warranted. The issue is raised here to suggest that another avenue for future research is to address the relationship between different cognitive strategies and a variety of performance properties.

Task Environment

Hammond's CCT also highlights the importance of task characteristics as a determinant of judgment behavior, and the relationship between time pressure and other task characteristics is another fruitful direction for future research. For example, in the aviation forecasting study, higher time pressure was associated with higher base rates, higher variance in the outcome, and less controllable accuracy. Yates (1990) has argued that (1) the closer the base rate is to .5, the harder it is to predict the outcome and (2) predictability of an event is indexed by the outcome variance; the larger the variance the more difficult it is to predict the event. Thus, the base rate, the variance in the outcome, and the controllable accuracy results all indicate that the prediction task itself, independent of time pressure, may be more difficult to predict under high time pressure, as time pressure has been defined in this study. Clearly much more work needs to be directed at considering how time pressure interacts with other task characteristics to produce different aspects of performance. Hammond's CCT may be an excellent point of departure for such research.

It is beyond the scope of this chapter to fully consider the ramifications of CCT for the study of the effects of time pressure on judgment and decision making. However, consider for a moment how two of the task characteristics outlined by Hammond, number of cues and redundancy in the cues, might be associated with time pressure in operational settings. Hammond hypothesizes that tasks with a large number of highly redundant cues induce intuitive cognitive processes. In aviation weather forecasting, the cue structure (i.e., number of cues and their intercorrelation) is presently unknown, and any difference in the cue structure under low- and high-time-pressure conditions is also unknown. However, it is easy to imagine operational settings in which the number of cues present may in fact be a task characteristic that induces time pressure. Increasing information load leads to less information that can be processed for each unit of time, thereby increasing time pressure. It is also likely that in some environments, more activity may lead to more redundancy among the cues. Under high time pressure with redundant cues, one might not expect a decrement in discriminative ability. Consider the effect of filtration when cues are highly correlated. With such redundancy, if one can process at least one cue that is predictive of the outcome, then any negative effects of filtration on discriminative ability should be circumvented.

CCT raises a number of interesting issues regarding the task characteristics relevant to research on the effects of time pressure on judgment and decision making that have not been addressed in the literature thus far. There is another issue regarding the task characteristics associated with time pressure that should be addressed. It is not clear where, on a time pressure continuum, the two time pressure conditions represented in the aviation forecasting study reside. This echoes a general concern regarding the operationalization of stress in other research settings. In this aviation forecasting experiment, there was clearly more time pressure in the high conditions than in the low, but how much more is unclear. It could be that the high-time-pressure condition actually represents the optimal arousal condition for the forecasters: just enough activity so the forecasters were not bored, but not more activity than they could handle.

Conclusion

One goal of this chapter was to demonstrate how decomposition analysis of data that include only forecasts and outcome information yields useful information regarding the effects of time pressure on judgment and decision making. The results are consistent with previous research regarding the effects of time pressure on cognitive processing. It has been demonstrated that Yates' decomposition analyses may be informative regarding the effects of time pressure on different performance characteristics. Further, it has been argued that to further understand the effects of time pressure on judgment and decision making, the interaction between task characteristics, cognitive processes, and performance properties must be considered.

ACKNOWLEDGMENT. This work was supported by the Office of Basic Research, Army Research Institute, Contract MDA903-86-C-0142. The view, opinions, and findings contained in this report are those of the author and should not be construed as an official Department of the Army position, policy, or decision, unless so designated by other official documentation.
The author wishes to thank J. Frank Yates and William Moninger for comments on earlier drafts of this chapter. In addition, this chapter could not have been completed without the assistance of Cynthia Mueller, Mary Luhring, Deborah Smith, and Doreen Petersen. Special thanks are due to Kenneth Hammond.

References

Ben Zur, M., & Breznitz, S. J. (1981). The effects of time pressure on risky choice behavior. *Acta Psychologica, 47,* 89–104.
Brehmer, B., & Joyce, C. R. B. (1988). *Human judgment: The SJT view.* Amsterdam: North Holland.

Hammond, K. R. (1988). Judgment and decision making in dynamic task. *Information and Decision Technologies, 14*, 3–14.

Hammond, K. R., Hamm, R. M., Grassia, J., & Pearson, T. (1987). *IEEE Transaction on systems, man, and cybernetics, SMS-17*, 753–770.

Hammond, K. R., Stewart, T. R., Brehmer, B. & Steinmann, D. (1975). Social judgment theory. In M. F. Kaplan & Schwartz (Eds.), *Human judgment and decision processes* (pp. 271–312). New York: Academic Press.

Harvey, L. O., Jr., Hammond, K. R., Lusk, C. M. & Mross, E. F. (1992). The application of signal detection theory to weather forecasting behavior. *Monthly Weather Review, 120* (5), 863–883.

Mueller, C. K., Wilson, J. W., & Heckman, B. (1988). Evaluation of the TDWR aviation nowcasting experiment. In *Preprints of the 3rd International Conference on the Aviation Weather System* (pp. 212–216). Boston: American Meteorological Society.

Payne, J. W., Bettman, J. R., & Johnson, J. J. (1988). Adaptive strategy selection in decision making. *Journal of Experimental Psychology: Learning, Memory, and Cognition, 14*, 534–552.

Svenson, O., & Edland, A. (1987). Changes of preferences under time pressure: Choices and judgments. *Scandinavian Journal of Psychology, 28*, 322–330.

Yates, J. F. (1982). External correspondence: Decompositions of the mean probability score. *Organizational Behavior and Human Performance, 30*, 132–156.

Yates, J. F. (1990). *Judgment and decision making*. Englewood Cliffs, NJ: Prentice Hall.

Yates, J. F., & Curley, S. P. (1985). Conditional distribution analyses of probabilistic forecasts. *Journal of Forecasting, 4*, 61–73.

Yates, J. F., McDaniel, L., & Brown, E. (1991). Probabilistic forecasts of stock prices and earnings: The hazards of nascent expertise. *Organizational Behavior and Human Decision Processes, 49*, 60–79.

Concluding Remarks

A. John Maule and Ola Svenson

Introduction

Given that psychological processes take time to execute, time is necessarily an important factor in human judgment and decision making. This volume has focused, primarily, on one aspect of this factor, considering the ways in which people make judgments and decisions when time is in short supply. Considering the diversity of approaches used to study judgment and decision making, it would be presumptuous to attempt to formulate one unifying theory to explain either the importance of time in general or how people adapt when time is in short supply. Instead, these concluding remarks first briefly classify the contributions to this volume into a number of general approaches. Following this we discuss a way of characterizing similarities and differences in these approaches based on a view of time pressure conceptualized as a restriction on a resource necessary for making a judgment or a decision. Finally, some research themes for the future will be outlined.

A. John Maule • School of Business and Economic Studies, University of Leeds, Leeds LS2 9JT England.   **Ola Svenson** • Department of Psychology, Stockholm University, S-10691 Stockholm, Sweden.
Time Pressure and Stress in Human Judgment and Decision Making, edited by Ola Svenson and A. John Maule. Plenum Press, New York, 1993.

Approaches to the Study of Time Pressure

Though the contributions to this volume are very diverse, they may be classified into a smaller number of more general approaches. The first of these is the decision-theoretic approach in which the effects of time restrictions are considered in terms of the theories and concepts associated with behavioral decision theory. For instance, Svenson and Benson in Chapter 9 discuss time pressure in terms of its effects on framing, a concept drawn from Prospect Theory, whereas Johnson and coauthors in Chapter 7 consider time pressure in the context of cost/benefit determination of decision strategies. The second approach draws on stress theory with time pressure treated as stressor and conceptualized in the same way as other stressors. Its effects on behavior are explained in terms of the demands it makes on the allocation of energetic and other resources. The contributions by Lundberg (Chapter 3) and Maule and Hockey (Chapter 6) illustrate this approach.

A third approach to understanding time constraints focuses on individual differences. Three chapters in Part IV of the volume show that people demonstrate systematic differences in their sensitivity to time constraints and the way they cope with time pressure. Previous decision research has tended to neglect individual differences, though the contributions to the present volume reinforce the view that it is an interesting theme worth developing in the future. A fourth approach extends consideration of time pressure to situations involving more than one individual. For example, Carnevale, O'Connor, and McCusker in Chapter 8 discuss time pressure in the context of negotiation and mediation. The final approach, concerned with dynamic decisions for controlling complex systems, is illustrated by Wickens and coauthors in Chapter 18. This perspective emphasizes the importance of learning to make decisions in the context of a dynamic environment and includes time as a defining parameter of the environment. This approach brings several methodological issues into focus. Of these, the problems of experimental control pose serious limitations that have to be counterbalanced by high relevance and ecological validity.

This diversity of approaches makes it difficult to develop a unifying theory of the effects of time pressure in decision making. However, all the approaches conceptualize, explicitly or implicitly, time as a necessary resource for judgment and decision making, and this view can provide a way of linking these different approaches as illustrated in the next section.

Time and Coping with Time Pressure as Conceived in Time Pressure Studies

The different approaches outlined above generally conceptualize time pressure as a restriction on a resource necessary for making judgments and decisions. The decision maker must cope with or adapt to this restriction that in turn, may lead to changes in judgment and decision processes. The approaches differ in terms of how time and time pressure are reflected when studying and explaining how people cope with time restrictions. The discussion that follows identifies some prototype characterizations of how people cope or adapt to a restriction in time. These characterizations are not mutually exclusive. Rather, they outline a space in which different studies of time pressure may be described.

Time as a Determinant of Resource Allocation

Time is identified as one of the factors that determine the allocation of energetic and other psychological resources (which may be compared to "energy" in physics) necessary to make judgments and decisions. As time to complete a task changes, so this may affect the allocation of these resources. Within reasonable limits, time pressure can be compensated for by allocating more resources per unit time (which may be compared to "effect" in physics), such that the output of judgment and decision processes remain largely unaffected. This is, perhaps, the most fundamental characterization that builds on concepts parallel to those in physics and underlies most studies of time pressure.

Time-Induced Changes in Affect

A shortage of time is assumed to induce affective changes through a generally increasing arousal level, which in turn may interact with the activities associated with time as a determinant of resource allocation, described above, to change judgment and decision-making processes. Changes in arousal up to a certain level may be compensated for such that the output of judgment and decision processes remain largely unaffected. Beyond this, changes may occur.

This represents a more elaborate characterization than the previous one, relating time pressure to perspectives from stress research and one that emphasizes the importance of "hot" processes. It is a generic approach that often has problems in predicting the details of judgment and decision behavior. Chapter 3 by Lundberg and Chapter 6 by Maule and Hockey illustrate this characterization.

Monitoring of Time

The awareness of a time constraint necessitates the monitoring of time, an activity assumed to make demands on central processing resources. This reduces the resources available for judgment and decision processes that in turn, may lead to changes in the nature of these processes. In Chapter 4, Zakay elaborates this characterization, and it also appears as a feature of action control discussed by Steinsmeier-Pelster and Schürmann in Chapter 16. This characterization is related to the two presented above and together they emphasize the complexity of resource issues underpinning time pressure effects.

Time as a Task Variable

Time available can be characterized as one among a number of task variables that determine how decision makers adapt their use of decision rules. For example, a cost/benefit approach is assumed to mediate this adaptation, with the efficiency of each (sequence of) decision rule(s) assessed and weighed against the processing effort and time for implementation.

This characterization is in contrast to the "hot" view presented earlier. This characterization is more focused than earlier ones and is sometimes associated with more distinct predictions of decision behavior. In Chapter 7, Johnson, Payne, and Bettman provide an illustration of this approach, but almost all chapters use this characterization of time and the effects of time pressure as a bottom line.

Time as an Interactive Situational Resource Variable

Time available is considered as a situational resource variable and is assessed in conjunction with the decision problem and the decision maker's available resources. This characterization makes a distinction between the time needed for a decision task, which is a task variable as described earlier and time available, which is a situational variable. From this standpoint, variations in time have their effects at a more strategic level in terms of the activation of goals, strategies, and decision rules for later implementation in the decision process. This characterization further extends the view of time as a task variable, and is related to the characterizations based on changes in affect and monitoring of time, as presented earlier. Svenson and Benson in Chapter 11 provide an illustration of this dimension, though it also is a feature of the discussions presented by Zakay in Chapter 4 and Carnevale, O'Connor and McCusker in Chapter 8.

Time as an Independent Situational Resource Variable

This characterization takes a more limited view of time as a situational variable than described in the previous section and is developed in the context of binary choice situations. The time available is assessed as a means of determining the attractiveness criterion to be met before one alternative is chosen over the other. Time pressure lowers this criterion, and through this, reduces the amount of information that is processed. This may alter the decision outcome. All other aspects of the decision process remain unaffected, a view that contrasts with many of the other characterizations suggesting a greater degree of change under time pressure. The concept of time as an independent situational resource variable is developed in Chapter 12 by Wallsten, Chapter 13 by Busemeyer, and in Chapter 14 by Böckenholt and Kroeger.

Componential Time Effects

This characterization reflects contemporary cognitive theory in assuming that decision processes can be conceptualized in terms of a sequence of separate cognitive components. A shortage of time may affect cognitive components differentially. The ways in which components are affected may be described in terms of the other characterizations, for example, the monitoring of time or time as a task variable. One of the key issues is the level at which components are to be described. In Chapter 7, Johnson, Payne, and Bettman use the term *component* to describe cognitive elements that undertake one simple mental operation like retrieve an item of information or evaluate the subjective value of an attribute. These components are defined in relation to the specific requirements for decision making. In contrast, Wickens and coauthors in Chapter 18 describe components in a different way, assuming that each one is responsible for many different kinds of cognitive operations, for example, working memory. In this case, the components are defined in the context of more general cognitive theory designed to explain a broad range of cognitive activity. As yet, it is not possible to describe the relation between components described at different levels, nor is it clear whether one is likely to be better than another as a means for understanding time pressure effects.

The characterizations described in this section provide some of the different ways in which the contributors to this volume have conceptualized how decision makers cope with or adapt to restrictions in time. Together they demonstrate that there are a variety of different perspectives on time pressure and how these can be used in understanding different approaches to studying time pressure.

Some Themes for Future Research

The research presented in this volume demonstrates the importance of including the time variable into models and theories of judgment and decision making. In Chapter 1, Maule and Svenson provide a brief review of contemporary decision research and demonstrate that only a minority of theories and approaches integrate time into their conceptual framework. If future research is to redress this, it is necessary for the development of decision research to become more process orientated. This will involve empirical research in which time is studied both as an independent variable (e.g., time pressure) and as a dependent variable (e.g., latency of a decision process).

An important benefit accruing from the development of a more general consideration of the time dimension in decision making is that it will provide a theoretical and empirical framework for the more specific issue of understanding time pressure. As indicated in both Chapters 5 and 6, there have been many different ways of operationalizing time pressure, and a broader theoretical framework is needed to evaluate and interpret these different views. A first step toward this more general aim would be to create a classification of procedures used to induce time pressure. A second and related step would be to develop a more comprehensive definition of time pressure that includes guidelines for determining when this state occurs. Indeed, several different states are possible (i.e., time pressure and time stress) as the time is reduced.

Further developments in our understanding of time and decision making are likely to depend on process-oriented research, particularly componential approaches of the kind illustrated in Chapters 7, 18, and 19. These models describe the effects of time pressure in terms of a dynamic process that adapts to task and situational variables, including scarcity of time, by initiating a range of coping responses. Research efforts following this line need to make stronger links to similar developments in the fields of perception and cognitive psychology, where existing research may provide important insights into why some cognitive components underlying decision making are more vulnerable to time pressure and others are more resilient to this manipulation.

A second important consideration from a componential standpoint is the recognition that there may be different kinds or levels of decisions, each involving different components. In Chapter 1, examples of these different levels were discussed. For example, if a decision is repeated many times, it becomes more perceptual in character, quicker, and more automatic, as it moves from one level to another. Given that cognitive components may be differentially sensitive to the effects of time pressure, so different kinds or levels of decision making may also be associated with different modes of adapting. Future research needs to address these differences.

Many of the contributions to this volume have drawn on general stress theory in highlighting the importance of an appraisal mechanism in determining how people adapt to time pressure. Individuals are assumed to appraise the demands of the decision problem, the time needed, and the resources available to solve the problem, including time. This view gives rise to two lines of research.

First, individuals may appraise the same situation in different ways, suggesting the importance of individual differences as an area of future research. This has not been a popular theme among decision researchers, though the present volume has included three chapters (Chapters 15, 16, and 17) that demonstrate the importance of this theme for decision research, in general, and for an understanding of time pressure, in particular. Second, the links with general stress theory suggest other ways of conceptualizing and investigating time pressure. For instance, general stress theories highlight the importance of the resources available to individuals and how these may alleviate demands placed on them. Conceptualizing time pressure in this way provides a strong body of existing theory to draw on to understand time pressure effects and a framework in which to develop research questions about the nature of time pressure. Linking this area with decision research may also provide some new insights into the nature of decision making in general.

Index

Acceleration, 28, 33, 34, 37, 86, 88, 94, 110, 145, 146, 167, 187, 199, 242, 245, 246, 248–251
Accuracy, 34–36, 91, 106, 181, 185, 274, 277
Acquisition, 196
Action, 21, 244, 251
  control, 242–246, 251
  control scale, 244, 246, 248
  orientation, 242, 244–246, 252
Activation, 90, 91, 97
Adaptation, 20, 34, 89, 103, 110, 146, 162, 196, 242
Additive rule, 105, 197
Adoption decision, 18
Adrenaline, 42
Adrenal medulla, 42
Affect, 83, 84, 86, 89, 91, 97
Affect control, 243, 245, 251
Aggregation, 195–197
AIDS, 133
Aircraft accident, 271
Alternative-based processing, 5, 16
Anchoring, 29
Anxiety, 84, 97, 272, 275, 277, 287
Appraisal, 2, 90, 97, 98, 157, 158, 165
Arousal, 2, 28, 90, 162
Aspiration, 32
Assembly line work, 47
Attention, 3, 90, 275, 287
  capacity, 276
  model, 62, 63, 65, 66

Attention (*Cont.*)
  narrowing, 90
  resources, 63, 65, 69
  selectivity, 243, 245, 251, 272
Attractiveness difference, 9, 20, 135–137, 146, 149, 150, 152–155, 161, 163, 200
Attribute-based processing, 5, 16, 34, 197, 199
Automatic processes, 4, 20
Averaging rule, 6
Aviation, 274
Avoidance, 17, 33, 38
Axioms, 10, 11

Bargaining, 13
Benefits, 17
Biases, 143, 257, 266
Binary choice, 9, 16, 196, 199
Bolstering, 17

Calibration, 302, 304
Choice, 3–5, 7, 30–33, 142, 146, 147, 150, 151, 154, 195, 197, 274
  models, 9
  probability, 188
  rules, 9, 155
  strategies, 196
Cognitive adjustment, 87
Cognitive algebra, 257
Cognitive appraisal, 276
Cognitive capacity, 155